BEQUIA

The best fun
in Bequia

P.O. Box 16, Bequia,
St. Vincent & the Grenadines.
E-mail:bobsax@caribsurf.com

web: www.dive-bequia.com

Tel:784-458-3504
Fax:784-458-3886
VHF:16/68

Bob works in close association with dive
shops in St. Vincent and the Grenadines,
so you can buy a dive package good
throughout the area, or start a full certification course in Bequia and finish it as
you sail through the islands
Sounds Good? then Call:
    DIVE BEQUIA

SAILORS GUIDE TO THE

Chris Doyle	Text, charts, design
Sally Erdle	Illustrations
Sally Erdle	Photos
John Douglas	
Jeff Fisher	
Chris Doyle	

DISTRIBUTION

USA AND WORLDWIDE
Cruising Guide Publications
P.O. Box 1017
Dunedin, Florida 34697-1017
Tel: 727-733-5322
Fax: 727-734-8179
E-Mail: cgp@earthlink.net

ST. VINCENT AND THE
GRENADINES
Frances Punnett, Box 17
St. Vincent, W. I.
Tel: 784-458-4246
Fax: 784-456-2620

ST. LUCIA
Cecil Baptiste, Box 1457
Castries, St. Lucia, W.I.
Tel: 758-452-0823
Fax: 758-452-8702

GRENADA
Jeff Fisher,
Tikal, Box 51, Young St.
St. George's, Grenada
Tel: 473-440-2556
E-Mail: Fisher@caribsurf.com

Cover photo, Bequia Regatta
P16: Upper Concord Falls, Carriacou house, Tyrrel Bay mangrove lagoon, Bequia boat
P17: St. George's, Grenada Garden.
P32: Rodney Bay Marina, Martinique yole, fishing boats in Petite Anse D'Arlet, financial center in St. Pierre, Flamboyant flower.
P33: Petit Bacaye, Grenada

AUTHOR'S NOTES

In the text we give a very rough price guide to the restaurants. This is an estimate of what you might spend to eat out and have a drink:

$A is $50 U.S. or over
$B is $25 to $50 U.S.
$C is $12 to $25 U.S.
$D is under $12 U.S.

We are happy to include advertising. It gives extra information and keeps the price of the book reasonable. If you wish to help us keep it that way, tell all the restaurateurs and shopkeepers "I read about it in the Sailors Guide." It helps us no end.
If you like, tell us about your experiences, good or bad. We will consider your comments when writing the next edition.

Chris Doyle
c/o Cruising Guide Publications
P. O. Box 1017, Dunedin,
FL34697-1017
Fax: 813-734-8179
E-Mail: redstart@sover.net

Printed in Italy by
Studio Deer Paris / Medi-Graf

ACKNOWLEDGEMENTS

To everyone who helped: from those who sit me down in their bars and shops to explain what they are trying to achieve, to those who tap me on the shoulder and say "Hey you know what you should put in your guide?" and also to those who have written in with suggestions - a big thank you to all of you. The book would not be the same without your input. Chris Doyle

WINDWARD ISLANDS

PUBLISHED BY
CHRIS DOYLE PUBLISHING
in association with
CRUISING GUIDE
PUBLICATIONS

ISBN 0-944428-46-0

First edition published 1980
Second edition published 1982
Third edition published 1984
Third edition revised   1985
Third edition revised   1986
Fourth edition published 1988
Fifth edition published 1990
Sixth edition published 1992
Seventh edition published 1994
Eighth edition published 1996
Ninth edition published 1998

SKETCH CHART INFORMATION

Our sketch charts are interpretive and
designed for yachts drawing about 6.5 feet.
Deeper yachts should refer to the depths
on their charts.

LAND   HILLS   ROADS PATHS

LAND HEIGHTS ARE IN FEET AND APPROXIMATE

WATER TOO SHALLOW FOR NAVIGATION OR DANGEROUS IN SOME CONDITIONS

SURFACE REEF   ROCKS DEEPER REEF

NAVIGABLE WATER   60 9 DEPTHS IN FEET AND ARE APPROXIMATE

1.5 KNOTS CURRENT   CHURCH

MANGROVES   ANCHORAGE

WRECKS   DAY STOP ANCHORAGE

GREEN BEACON
GREEN BUOYS (PORT)

RED BEACON
RED BUOYS (STARBOARD)   N W ⊕ E S

ISOLATED BEACONS AND BUOYS   IALA B MARKS SHOWING DIRECTION OF DANGER (BUOYS & BEACONS)

YELLOW BUOYS

RED & BLACK BUOYS   MOORING OR OTHER BUOY

SECTOR   LIGHTS
WHITE (W)   FL = FLASHING, F = FIXED, L = LONG, Q = QUICK, M= MILES
GREEN (G)   LIGHT EXPLANATION
YELLOW (Y)   FL (2) 4S, 6M
RED (R)   LIGHT GROUP FLASHING 2 EVERY FOUR SECONDS, VISIBLE 6 MILES

NOTICE

Salt Whistle Bay

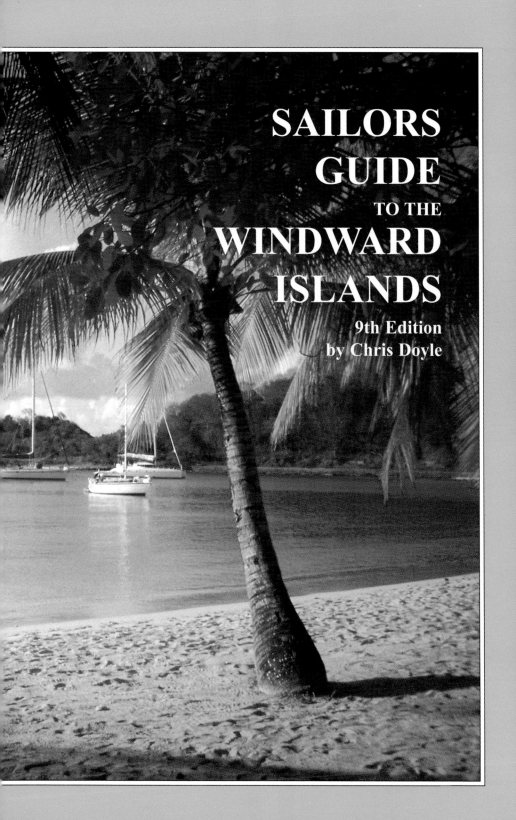

SAILORS GUIDE
TO THE
WINDWARD
ISLANDS

9th Edition
by Chris Doyle

	Page
STAR CHARTS	10
INTRODUCTION	12
ALL ABOUT THE ISLANDS	16
LOCAL LORE	18
BUGS, BEASTS AND PLANTS	20
PEOPLE	25
PHOTOGRAPHY	29
FISHING	29
MEDICAL CARE	30
ENTERTAINMENT AND SPECIAL EVENTS	30
CRUISING INFORMATION	32
WEATHER	34
LOCAL RADIO	35
NAVIGATION	36
GPS TABLE	39
CUSTOMS AND IMMIGRATION	40
PROTECTING THE ENVIRONMENT	40
MILEAGE TABLE	41
SCUBA DIVING	44
MARTINIQUE	48
ST. PIERRE	54
CASE PILOTE	58
FORT DE FRANCE	59
RIVIÈRE SALÉE	71
COHE DE LAMENTIN	72
TROIS ILETS	72
TROU ETIENNE	74
ANSE MITAN	74
ANSE A L'ANE	81
ANSE NOIR	82
GRAND ANSE D'ARLET	83
PETITE ANSE D'ARLET	85
THE SOUTH COAST OF MARTINIQUE	85
ST. ANNE	85
MARIN	88
EAST COAST OF MARTINIQUE	97
BAIE DES ANGLAIS	98

TABLE OF CONTENTS

	Page
PASSAGES BETWEEN MARTINIQUE AND ST. LUCIA	99
ST. LUCIA	100
RODNEY BAY	106
CASTRIES AND VIGIE	126
MARIGOT BAY	132
ANSE COCHON	137
SOUFRIERE AND THE PITONS	138
NAVIGATION, SOUTH COAST, PITONS TO VIEUX FORT	148
VIEUX FORT	148
PASSAGES BETWEEN ST. VINCENT AND ST. LUCIA	151
ST. VINCENT AND THE GRENADINES	152
ST. VINCENT	155
CHATEAUBELAIR	158
TROUMAKA BAY	160
CUMBERLAND BAY	160
WALLILABOU	162
BARROUALLIE	163
PETIT BYAHAUT	164
OTTLEY HALL	166
KINGSTOWN	166
SOUTH COAST OF ST. VINCENT	170
YOUNG ISLAND CUT	171
BLUE LAGOON	179
NORTHERN GRENADINE PASSAGES	180
BEQUIA	185
ADMIRALTY BAY	188
MOONHOLE TO FRIENDSHIP BAY	211
FRIENDSHIP BAY AND PETIT NEVIS	212
MUSTIQUE	215
CANOUAN	221
SOUTHERN GRENADINE PASSAGES	225

	Page
DIVING IN THE SOUTHERN GRENADINES	228
MAYREAU	231
SALT WHISTLE BAY	231
SALINE BAY	232
THE TOBAGO CAYS	237
PALM ISLAND	240
UNION ISLAND	241
OTHER UNION ANCHORAGES	246
PSV AND PETITE MARTINIQUE	248
PSV	248
PETITE MARTINIQUE	250
GRENADA AND CARRIACOU	254
CARRIACOU	257
HILLSBOROUGH	259
SANDY ISLAND AND L'ESTERRE BAY	263
TYRREL BAY	265
PASSAGES BETWEEN CARRIACOU AND GRENADA	272
GRENADA	273
GRENADA'S WEST COAST	278
ST. GEORGE'S	280
GRAND ANSE	292
PT. SALINE TO PRICKLY BAY	300
TRUE BLUE	301
PRICKLY BAY	302
THE SOUTH COAST BEYOND PRICKLY BAY	311
MOUNT HARTMAN BAY	311
HOG ISLAND	314
CLARKES COURT BAY	316
EAST OF CALIVIGNY ISLAND	317
PORT EGMONT	317
CALIVIGNY HARBOUR	318
WESTERHALL POINT	318
PETIT BACAYE	318
ST. DAVID'S HARBOUR	318

	PAGE
CHARTERING	320
EXOTIC TROPICAL FOOD	322
EATING OUT	322
ISLAND FOODS	324
TROPICAL VEGETABLES AND STAPLES	324
TROPICAL FRUITS	326
SEAFOOD	328
MEAT	330
GENERAL INDEX	332
ADVERTISERS INDEX	334

DIRECTORY   A separate booklet is attached to the first printing of this edition

View through ruin, Hillsborough, Carriacou

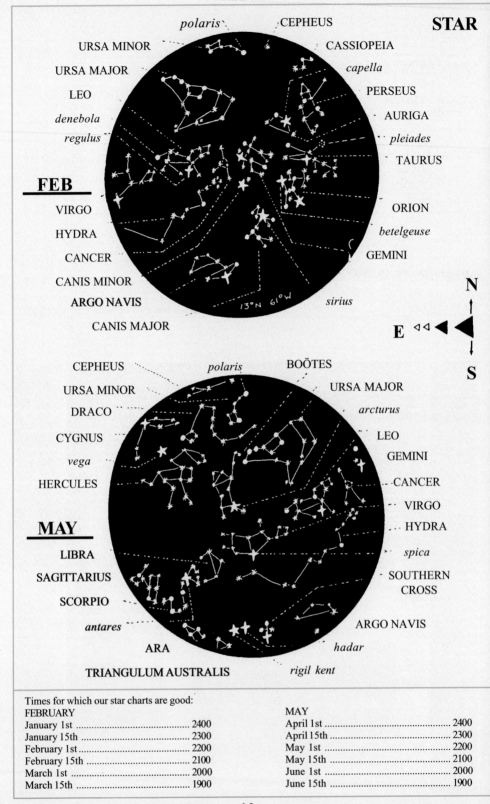

STAR

FEB

polaris · CEPHEUS · CASSIOPEIA
URSA MINOR · capella
URSA MAJOR · PERSEUS
LEO · AURIGA
denebola · pleiades
regulus · TAURUS

VIRGO · ORION
HYDRA · betelgeuse
CANCER · GEMINI
CANIS MINOR
ARGO NAVIS
CANIS MAJOR · 13°N 61°W · sirius

N
E ◁◁ ◀ ◀
S

MAY

CEPHEUS · polaris · BOÖTES
URSA MINOR · URSA MAJOR
DRACO · arcturus
CYGNUS · LEO
vega · GEMINI
HERCULES · CANCER
· VIRGO
LIBRA · HYDRA
SAGITTARIUS · spica
SCORPIO · SOUTHERN CROSS
antares · ARGO NAVIS
ARA · hadar
TRIANGULUM AUSTRALIS · rigil kent

Times for which our star charts are good:

FEBRUARY		MAY	
January 1st	2400	April 1st	2400
January 15th	2300	April 15th	2300
February 1st	2200	May 1st	2200
February 15th	2100	May 15th	2100
March 1st	2000	June 1st	2000
March 15th	1900	June 15th	1900

CHARTS

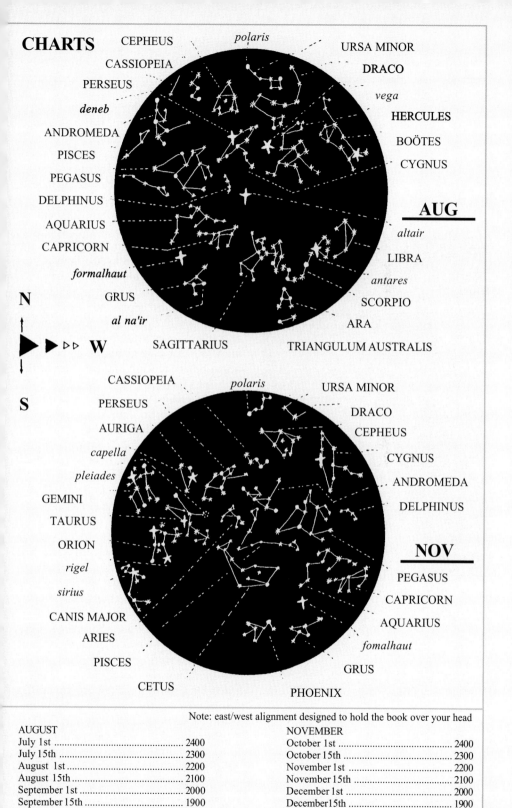

AUG

NOV

N · W · S

Note: east/west alignment designed to hold the book over your head

AUGUST		NOVEMBER	
July 1st	2400	October 1st	2400
July 15th	2300	October 15th	2300
August 1st	2200	November 1st	2200
August 15th	2100	November 15th	2100
September 1st	2000	December 1st	2000
September 15th	1900	December 15th	1900

Palm Island

The islands of the Caribbean sweep southwards in a huge arc, making a bridge of giant sized stepping stones from Florida to Venezuela. On the eastern or windward side the Atlantic Ocean pounds the shore. On the leeward side the calmer Caribbean Sea lies tranquil, sparkling in the sun.

The Windward Islands are at the southern end of this chain, the last links before Trinidad and South America. They were called the Windwards by the British, because to get there from many of their other possessions you had to beat to windward.

They lie almost across the easterly trade winds which makes for easy passages north or south. They are just far enough apart to allow for some wild romps in the open ocean before tucking into the calm of the next lee shore.

The four main Windward Islands – Martinique, St. Lucia, St. Vincent and Grenada – are lush and richly tropical, with high mountains that trap the clouds and produce dense green vegetation. Here you can find excellent examples of tropical rain forest, easily accessible to those who like to hike.

Between St. Vincent and Grenada lie the Grenadines – a host of smaller islands, some with hills of a thousand feet, others no more than a reef-enclosed sand cay sprouting a few palms. Drier than the large islands, they all have perfect white beaches, crystal clear waters and colorful reefs.

Over 2000 years ago the islands were colonized by Arawaks, oriental looking people who were great navigators, artists and sportsmen. However, they were overtaken by a more warlike tribe called the Caribs who were in residence in the Windwards by the time Columbus sailed in. The Caribs resisted the Europeans and refused to be slaves. In Grenada the northern town of Sauteurs marks the spot where the last of the Grenada Caribs leapt to their deaths rather than be taken captive. They held out

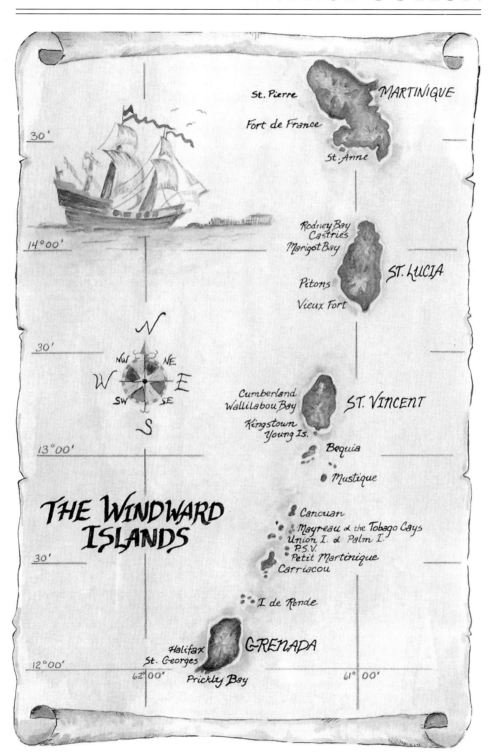

St. Pierre

MARTINIQUE

Fort de France

St. Anne

30'

14°00'

Rodney Bay
Castries
Marigot Bay

Pitons

ST. LUCIA

Vieux Fort

30'

N

NW NE

W E

SW SE

S

Cumberland
Wallilabou Bay

ST. VINCENT

Kingstown
Young Is.

13°00'

Bequia

Mustique

THE WINDWARD
ISLANDS

Canouan

Mayreau & the Tobago Cays
Union I. & Palm I.
P.S.V.
Petit Martinique
Carriacou

30'

I de Ronde

12°00'

Halifax
St. Georges

GRENADA

62°00'

Prickly Bay

61°00'

the longest in St. Vincent where the steep terrain made colonization harder. Even here they were eventually driven out by the European colonists. Today just a handful remain in the Windwards, on the north end of St. Vincent in a village called Fancy.

Years of colonization followed and the Windward Islands were fought over by the British and French. Plantation owners became rich from the production of sugar and slaves were brought from Africa to work in the fields. After slavery was abolished some East Indian laborers were imported to take over the field work.

Today, the intermingling of the races has produced an interesting blend of people who live in harmony together.

During its colonial history Martinique, the northernmost Windward Island, was nearly always in French hands. Today it is still part of France and therefore a member of the European Community. The language and ambience are French, and while not essential, it certainly helps to speak a few words of their language.

St. Lucia, St. Vincent and Grenada are now all independent nations with a British tradition. Each has its own laws and customs. The official language is English, though the dialect can be hard to understand when locals talk fast among themselves. In St. Lucia, Patois, an Afro-anglicized French, is widely used, as well as English.

These countries are small nations by any standards, with populations of around 100,000 each. Recently there have been moves to form a union, but the process is in a very early stage and it is hard to foresee the outcome.

The Windwards are a joy for the sailor. Good trade winds ensure exhilarating passages and delightful anchorages abound. The weather is pleasant year round, the people are friendly, and there are few annoying regulations. You are free to sail and enjoy some of the most beautiful islands on earth.

Welcome to the Windwards!

SMMA headquarters

14

Cumberland Bay

ALL ABOUT THE ISLANDS

Fishermen, Mayreau

Currency

In Martinique the currency is the French franc which varies widely in comparison with the US dollar (between four and nine francs to the dollar). You get the best rates at the change places in Fort de France and Anse Mitan, rather than at the banks. Some tourist shops offer up to a 20% discount on purchases made with traveler's checks.

In the other islands the currency is the Eastern Caribbean (EC) dollar at a fixed rate of 2.67 to one US dollar. The banks usually give a better rate than the shops or taxi drivers, though most people are willing to take US dollars. You get a lot of EC dollars for the US ones, but they are much more quickly spent. Oh well, "EC come, EC go," or as Jimmy Buffet said: "It's much more fun to spend money with pictures of flowers and palm trees on it than money with pictures of green old men."

Tourist season

Charter and hotel rates vary with the time of year. Most people want to come down when it is cold up north, so the winter months (November to April) are the high (expensive) season; the rest of the year is low season. Restaurant and bar prices are generally the same year round. During the quietest months (September and October) some small hotels close down and go on holiday.

What to bring

Nearly all visitors bring too much luggage and do not realize that it is almost impossible to stow hard cases on a yacht. Only soft bags should be used. One of my charterers once arrived without luggage, the airline having spirited it away. Rather than wait, he bought a bathing suit, two pairs of shorts and a shirt and wondered why he had ever bothered packing anything else.

If you need prescription drugs, bring an ample supply and make sure they stay in your carry-on bag.

Life is very informal down here and even in the best of eating places men can get by with a pair of slacks and a sports shirt, women with a simple dress.

Local etiquette

Clothing. Unlike many other western seaside towns, people in the Caribbean will look somewhat askance at you if you wander away from the beach in a bathing suit or, perish the thought, a bikini. Away from the beach, even in that tiny waterfront village, people generally wear at least a shirt and

pair of shorts or skirt. In the major towns people dress much as you would if you were going to your local town.

For women toplessness is accepted in some places, particularly in Martinique. I notice it occasionally now on the larger resort beaches in some of the other islands, but elsewhere it is frowned upon. The easiest thing is to see what other people are up to. Complete nudity is best confined to really secluded beaches or anchorages.

Greetings. Manners here are different and great store is set on greetings: "good morning" or "good afternoon" (or in Martinique "bon jour" or "bon nuit"). It is considered rude to approach people with a question or to transact business without beginning with the appropriate greeting.

Tipping. Everyone likes to be tipped, but it is not always expected. In restaurants where no service charge is added, a 10% tip is normal. If service has already been included (as it is by law in Martinique) a little extra is appreciated but not essential. Taxi drivers do not normally expect to be tipped, but if they go out of their way to help you, you can add a few dollars to the fare to show your appreciation. If you get help from kids carrying your suitcases they will expect an EC dollar or two.

Water skiing, jet skis

Local laws require that a water ski vessel have at least two people on board. Water skiing or jet-skiing within 100 yards of a beach or in harbors where yachts are anchored is strictly forbidden. St. Vincent and the Grenadines has some enlightened environmental laws and jet skiing is completely forbidden throughout the country.

Drugs

Marijuana grows in the Windwards and is part of the local "Rasta" religion. It is, however, illegal, as are all other mind bending substances except alcohol and tobacco. Laws are very strict and those caught can expect yacht confiscation and up to life imprisonment (a longer vacation than you may have intended).

Suntanning

Whatever the season, the sun is intense and adequate protection is essential. It is advisable to bring down plenty of sunscreen (15+) and use it from the start, building up exposure slowly. The tops of your feet are vulnerable, so light cotton socks are important. Loose long-sleeved cotton clothing, hats and sunglasses are essential. Heavy burning can still take place on cloudy days and in shade.

Markets

All the main islands have great open air fruit and vegetable markets. These are always colorful, but Saturday morning is the best and busiest time with the greatest selection (Friday in St. Lucia). Never be afraid to ask about things you do not recognize. The market ladies are helpful and will tell you how to cook different vegetables. Some things are not what they appear to be. For example, many fruits which look like bananas to the untrained eye are starchier versions, known as plantains and bluggoes, which have to be cooked. (For more local food information, see our section on tropical food.)

Transport

If you don't like to hoof it, you have a choice between taxis, buses, communal taxis, and self-drive rent-a-cars.

Taxis are plentiful and come in all shapes and sizes. For long trips some bargaining is usually possible. In any case, always ask for the fare in EC dollars (or French francs) before you start. If you think you are being quoted too high a figure, try another driver.

Colorful, noisy and cheerful, the buses in the English speaking islands are the mainstay of the transport system. They often bear such names as "Trust no Man," "De Bad Ride," "In God we Trust," and similar reflections. Not only is this an inexpensive way to travel, but you get to experience some local life. Some buses are huge custom-built wooden affairs, others are mini-buses. Whatever the type they are not for the claustrophobic, for there is always room for one more on a local bus. Just when you think the whole thing is packed to bursting, the driver's assistant manages to create a tiny square of spare air and, like a conjuror, he whips out yet another seat – a pullout piece of wood that is jammed in to take the extra person. Most buses have stereo systems and the drivers like to run them, like their buses, at full-bore. The buses are a wonderful example of the kind of service you can get with free enterprise. If you are carrying heavy shopping and wish to go off the normal route, this can be negotiated. In some islands buses will stop to pick you up anywhere, in others (including St. Lucia) they are only allowed to pick up at designated stops. Buses do get rather few and far between after dark, and may be very limited when going to a distant spot. Before taking off to the other end of an island, make sure there will be a bus coming back.

If you arrive by air at a reasonable hour, without too much luggage and can make it to the nearest main road, St. Lucia's Hewanorra Airport and the airport in St. Vincent are on bus routes, and Martinique's airport is on a communal taxi route.

Bus in Carriacou

BUGS, BEASTS AND PLANTS

Don't let the cockroaches bug you

Now, for the first time, we will discuss the unmentionable: the indomitable cockroach thrives. If you are on a yacht, the odds are that eventually you will find yourself face to face with one of these miniature, armor-plated monstrosities. No need to panic. Despite their off-putting appearance, they are quite harmless, make good pets, and in reasonable quantities are not a general reflection of the cleanliness of the boat. A good dose of spray will keep them out of sight for a couple of days (this will be done automatically on a skippered yacht). If you are on a boat with a bad infestation, the permanent cure is as follows. First, give a good spray to reduce the numbers (not necessary if you only have one or two). Then, using a mortar and pestle, grind equal quantities of boric acid and white sugar together and distribute freely under drawers, in bottoms of lockers, etc. This will normally give at least six months of cockroach-free living. Some people prefer to mix the boric acid into a gooey mess with condensed milk because they can then stick it on walls and ceilings. I have also found some large versions of the "Sticky Box" to be very effective. Cockroaches generally arrive on board as stowaways in cardboard cartons or amid fruits and vegetables. It is essential to keep special "cockroach free" crates and boxes on board and transfer all incoming supplies into them. Examine lo-

WELCOME TO POWER BOATS
THE PLACE FOR YACHTS

VERY ATTRACTIVE RATES ON WORK AND STORAGE

FACILITIES

- 50 ton marine hoist
- Telephone and fax services
- Free water and electricity
- Mast removal
- Refueling dock - gasoline & diesel
- Laundromat, toilets & showers
- Restaurant & grocery
- Woodwork. upholstery & electrical shops
- Sail repair loft & marine store
- Stern-to docking
- Self contained apartments
- Stockists of AB dinghies

SERVICES

- Skilled and semi-skilled labour for sanding, painting, welding, woodworking, engine repairs, fiberglassing
- Sail and rigging repairs
- Very comprehensive machine shop work for propeller repairs and all aluminum, stainless steel and bronze repairs
- Osmosis repairs using state-of-the-art
- Peeling machinery & drying methods
- Gelcoat restoration

AND REMEMBER

- Trinidad is out of the main hurricane belt
- Teak is grown in Trinidad and is readily available at excellent prices
- Bona fide crews are allowed to work on their boats free of charge

Power Boats Mutual Facilities Ltd.,
P.O. Box 3163, Carenage, Trinidad, W.I.
Tel: (868) 634-4303 Fax: (868) 634-4327
E-mail: pbmfl@powerboats.co.tt
VHF: ch.72 call "Power Boats."

Power Boats

cal fruits and vegetables before you stow them. So much for the bad news. The good news is that the boat variety, known as the German cockroach, is relatively small, quite unlike the huge shoreside monsters that grow up to two inches long and are aptly called "mahogany birds."

Mosquitoes are not usually a problem on board because of the breeze, but jungly anchorages or enclosed lagoons on the lee of the large islands are occasionally buggy. If you find yourself in such a bay, you can always resort to the mosquito coil. This is not a contraceptive device for mosquitoes but a spiral of incense-like material that burns slowly and puts the mosquitoes to sleep. It is effective, but you should be warned that it does not usually kill the bugs and, should the coil go out before you awake, they will be up first and you will be breakfast.

In the evening beaches can be buggy, especially on a still night in the rainy season (July to November). Worse than mosquitoes are the minute sand flies known as "no-see-ums." Any brand of bug repellent will help prevent your sunset barbecue from becoming a free-for-all slapping match.

Dangers

Perhaps we should start with the **rum punch**. This delicious concoction, a mixture of rum and fruit juice, is available in any waterside bar. It can be positively euphoric in small doses and lethal in large. Strongly recommended at sunset, but be warned that the potency is often stronger than the flavor would suggest.

There are poisonous **scorpions** and **centipedes** on the islands, but these are not generally deadly and luckily are rare. Still, take a good look at that old pile of twigs and leaves before you sit and take care when picking up coconut husks to burn for your barbecue.

A real danger is the **manchineel tree** *(Hippomane mancinella)* which grows abundantly along some beaches. This pretty tree with yellow-green apples is toxic. The leaves can produce a rash like poison ivy. It is all right to take shade under the tree, but never stand under it in the rain and avoid

using the branches for firewood, or that song "Smoke Gets in Your Eyes" may take on new meaning. If you eat the apples they will cause blisters from stem to stern and are very dangerous. I once knew a couple who had a most romantic barbecue on the beach. They used the branches on their fire and lay on the leaves. The next morning they woke up with bunged-up red eyes and rashes in some unfortunate places. They had to stay in bed and delay their charter for two days. Seagrapes, which often grow near

manchineels, are quite harmless.

Martinique and St. Lucia are also home to a deadly snake, the **fer de lance**, which is thankfully very rare. St. Lucia has been listed as having a fresh water liver fluke. This is supposed to have been eradicated, but you might want to restrict your fresh water swimming to the fast streams well above habitations.

The main dangers in swimming and snorkeling are negligent and speeding fishermen, yacht tender drivers and water taxis.

Barracuda, fun to see and not considered dangerous

We have had some serious accidents over the years so swimmers and snorkelers should be aware of small craft movement in their area at all times. Lesser dangers include **sea urchins**. These are spiny creatures whose prickles penetrate and break off on contact. This is quite painful, especially for the first few hours. They are virtually impossible to pull out once embedded as they break into little pieces. It is best to leave them in and treat them with hot lime juice, as the acid helps dissolve them.

There are **sharks** and **barracudas**, but unlike their cousins in the movies, they have yet to attack anyone in these waters unless harassed and so are not considered dangerous here. There is no question that spearfishing can excite these fish. I have dived and snorkeled at night with no problem, but since so few people swim at night,

it is impossible to assess how safe it is. Despite their reputations, moray eels are short sighted and timid, but it would be pushing your luck to stick your hand into holes in rock or coral. Some corals are poisonous, so it is safest to look and not touch. Coral scratches can become infected. If you get one, scrub it well with soap and fresh water. **Stinging jellyfish** are rare, but do exist, and occasionally the swimmer may feel a mild tingling from minute animals known as "sea ants."

A good book on dangerous marine animals would certainly list some more horrors, but the truth is that harm from any of these is extremely rare, and provided you watch where you put your hands and feet, and keep an eye on the sea conditions and current, snorkeling is safer than doing the weekly ironing and a lot more fun.

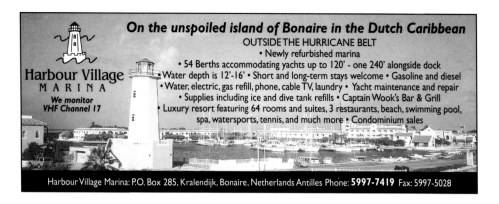
PEOPLE

Taxi drivers

Taxi drivers are often colorful characters, owners of highly individual cars, and they have a fund of local knowledge. In St. Vincent and Grenada some reach beyond the normal bounds of the job. They often acts as a kind of commission agent as well, running around shopping for yachts or hotels, tracing and sending on lost luggage, obtaining hard to find parts, arranging and officiating at weddings, and even arranging funerals. There is almost nothing some taxi drivers won't attempt. In Martinique, only a few of the drivers speak English though they will bear with your French, sometimes with a sense of humor. (A friend once asked one in her best French if he was a taxi. "Oh, no" he replied, pointing at his car, "I am a driver; this is the taxi.") Unfortunately, among the good ones there are an overenthusiastic few who will bully or confuse the unwary passenger into going on a tour he or she really does not want. There is one basic rule: always discuss and agree on a price before you embark on a taxi ride and make sure you are both talking in EC dollars or, in Martinique, francs.

Boat vendors

At some point there will be a thump on your topsides and a voice shouting "Hey skip, want some limes? Any laundry then? How about a coconut boat? It sails very good." You are in islands with a great spirit of free enterprise – better get used to it. From the skipper's point of view the most harrowing thing is trying to persuade these vendors that you really do not want several hundred pounds of rough wood and exposed nail heads (a local dinghy) banging your topsides. The vendor's cheerful cry of "no problem, skip" does nothing to remove the scratch.

The problem is further exacerbated because in some areas the competition is so

keen that you may be approached two miles from port. This most often occurs in the Soufriere/Pitons area in St. Lucia and the Cumberland/Wallilabou area in St. Vincent. In these areas it is quite a useful service because it is necessary to tie to a palm tree, owing to the depth of water. However, most vendors you meet way out will want you to tow them in. It is unwise to tow these heavy boats a long way and there are always line handlers close to the shore, so refuse these long distance offers. You can tell them your insurance does not allow for towing. When you get closer, come to a standstill and negotiate the price before handing over any lines. (I offer a set fee of $10EC on a "take it or leave it" basis.) When finally at anchor, put out at least two big fenders and make sure any local boats coming alongside stay on them.

You will probably be offered, at various times, jewelry, fruit, scrimshaw, model boats, ice and live music. It is worthwhile looking at what is offered. All the jewelry is handmade and some items are attractive.

No one minds if you do not buy. Some vendors can be a bit persistent, but usually a firm, confident and clear message that you are not interested is enough. Before you buy, please note that buying coral jewelry and turtle shell is unkind to the environment and most countries prohibit their import.

One service I would definitely avoid is the self-appointed "harbor pilots." Excellent though they may be in a small, "two bow" sailing boat, most of these youths have neither the training nor experience required to put them in charge of an expensive yacht. I have seen one charter boat put on a reef, and others anchored too close to other yachts or moorings. I am surprised at how many people will hand over the helm to youths who offer to "show dem de way." Better to trust your own judgment and charts and refuse the services of these youths, asking them to stand clear till you are anchored and have put fenders over the side. They may then prove quite helpful in taking out a second anchor.

Vendors are part of the local color and endemic to undeveloped countries with struggling economies. They are usually friendly, helpful and can add interest to your trip. Very rarely you might get one who is too pushy and boards the yacht uninvited. In such a case you should insist they get off, and if you have any further problems, try to get help on the VHF and, if necessary, move.

Sometimes in the Soufriere and Cumberland anchorages kids use your dinghy as a swimming platform. I have given up trying

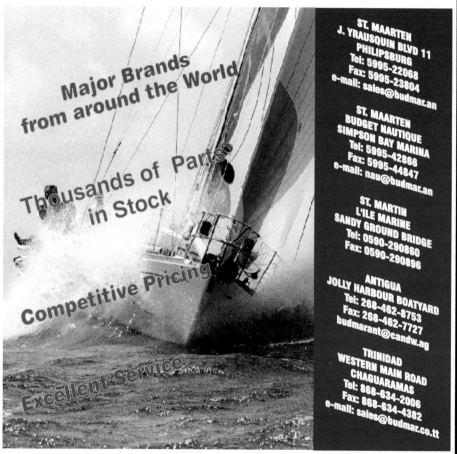

to stop them; I give them a dollar to clean it instead.

People have paid youths to "watch their dinghy". This has resulted in the creation of an unnecessary service, with the dinghy watchers often being rude. Lock your dinghy on with a cable and refuse all such services. Make sure your locking line is at least 16 feet long so that you do not block others approaching the dock.

Some kids beg. "It's my birthday, what are you going to give me?" is a favorite line. It is important to bear in mind that wages for an unskilled adult may only be $30 to $50 EC a day. If young kids end up getting three times that much liming around the docks, begging from tourists, or getting grossly overpaid for watching dinghies, they skip school and it is hard for them to adjust later when they need to go out to work. Further, once you accept alms from someone you are no longer their equal, so by giving to normal healthy kids you are demeaning them, helping to build up future resentment. By all means employ kids and find something useful for them to do. That helps the economy, but just throwing money around is bad for everyone. For those who like to give away money, there are a few beggars who have handicaps. Local associations for the handicapped are also happy to accept donations.

"Tiefs"

Most islanders and yachtspeople are very honest, but obviously there are shady characters, too: thieves, con men and extortionists. Dinghies and outboards are sometimes stolen at night. It is hard to say how many, because no one wants to admit that his dinghy disappeared after that final rum punch because the "rabbit" lost its way while going through the "hole" to make the bowline. There have been cases when a dinghy is returned the next day and the finders demand huge sums for the "rescue." Occasionally some fisherman runs short of money for rope and gets tempted in Wallilabou or the Pitons by all those lines tied to a palm tree. Boats occasionally get robbed when people are ashore. The thieves are mainly looking for cash and easily saleable items. Never have large amounts of cash. Use traveler's checks (universally accepted) and credit cards. Insure valuables such as cameras and binoculars. This way if you do get affected the results will not be as bad.

There are a few who will provide a service and then demand outrageous sums. Therefore always ask the price before accepting any service, including taxis. Make sure you are both referring to EC dollars. Many a delighted taxi driver has agreed, for example, that the fare is "twenty-five dollars" and been offered $25 US rather than EC. One can hardly blame him for accepting it. Worse though are those cases where you think they are talking EC and after the event

---

PROTECT YOURSELF AGAINST PETTY THEFT

If you take the following precautions, you are unlikely to be badly affected.

✔ Lock up when you leave the boat, and leave someone on board at night in main towns like St. George's, Castries and Kingstown.

✔ Lock your outboard onto your boat at night.

✔ Lock your dinghy to the dock by day and onto your yacht by night.

✔ Be cautious about inviting strangers on board.

✔ Do not bring large amounts of cash; use traveler's checks and credit cards instead. Do not leave cash on the boat. Insure valuables such as cameras.

✔ Don't leave things unattended on the beach or in the dinghy in public places.

you find they meant US.

When you are thinking of walking at night or hiking into remote places, it doesn't hurt to ask around first, especially if you are alone or with just one other person. Keep in mind that while the islands are generally safe, there are isolated incidents, as there are anywhere in the world. Occasionally someone turns bad and goes on a robbing spree, doing a "your money or life" bit with the aid of a cutlass. Usually they run amok for a month or two before they get well and truly nailed. Once they are put away everything reverts to normal. For current information on where there are problems, ask in any charter company office; also, read the free newspaper, Caribbean Compass, which often highlights areas that are a problem.

PHOTOGRAPHY

The light in the Windwards is so bright that colors often photograph better in the early morning or late afternoon. There is enough light for you to be able to use slow speed film (ASA 64 or 100). This changes if you venture into the rain forest where the light is poor and you need fast film. Slide film can be hard to come by in the islands, so if this is what you use, bring plenty with you. Sea shots will come out much better using a polarizing filter. If you don't have one, it is worth getting one for your trip. You can watch the colors change as you twist the filter. Keep an eye on the sky as well as the sea, as it will turn grey at some angles.

It is only polite to ask when you want to photograph someone. Local attitudes can be a little strange. People with cameras sometimes become a focal point for frustrations and feelings of being exploited. If you try to take a crowd scene, someone will often object and, funnily enough, that person might not even be in the picture. Vendors who deal with tourists are usually happy to say "yes," especially if you are buying something. Those with a Polaroid "now-for-now" camera who are willing to give some prints will have the greatest success.

FISHING

Trolling for fish is fun, means free food, and those you catch yourself always taste better. The simplest gear is adequate – about 150 yards of 80 to 100 lb. test line, a wire leader, swivel, hook and lure. Pink and white seem to be the fishes' "in" colors recently. It is necessary to feel the line every few minutes to see if you have caught anything (a clothes pin can be rigged as a telltale), and every 40 minutes or so it should be hauled in for a weed check. Fish never go for a weed lure. Fish are easily cleaned and scaled, but if you have never done it before, hire a local to show you how with your first fish.

Any fish you catch out in open water will almost certainly be good to eat. Fish poisoning, common farther north, is a rarity here. One might be suspicious of a really large barracuda who could be down from up north visiting relatives, but smaller barracuda (around five lbs.) are considered excellent eating. If you have no luck fishing, it is often possible to buy fish from the local fishermen. Do not be offended if they offer you dolphin. This is a delicious fish and no relative of Flipper.

The lobster season is usually from the first of October to the end of April. During this time lobsters may be bought from local fishermen and the most likely places to find them are Mustique, Union, the Tobago Cays and P.S.V.

It is against the law to buy lobster out of season, those less than nine inches long, or lobsters bearing eggs at any time, and the fines are steep. You may be offered one, but please refuse.

There is adequate medical care for most ailments in all the larger islands and any of the hotels or charter companies will help you get in touch with a doctor. There is a doctor and a good little clinic in Port Elizabeth in Bequia which stands by on VHF:74 and responds to emergency calls. Mustique is a good place to get sick. There is an excellent small clinic, situated next to the airport in case you need further treatment. In emergencies remember that all cruise ships stand by on VHF: 16 and carry doctors on board. If you have a life threatening situation that needs hospitalization or includes serious head injuries, plan on immediate transport to Martinique or Barbados. You can call the Martinique hospital (596-55-20-00/51-51-52) for a helicopter ambulance. (See also the air charter companies in our directory.) For diving accidents needing decompression call: Martinique (596-50-20-00) or Barbados (246-436-6185) for immediate evacuation. For lesser emergencies:

Martinique: (clinic): (0) 596-71-82-85

St. Lucia: Dr. Soni, surgery: (758) 452-6002; home: (758) 452-8116; Rodney Bay Medical Clinic (Dr. Beaubrun): (758) 452-8621/0179 is close to the Marina. If you think you may need tests or multiple services then call Tapion Hospital (758) 459-2000, which is a kind of medical shopping mall with all kinds of doctors and testing services.

Grenada: Dr. Michael Radix, surgery: (473) 444-4850, 440-4379; home: (473) 443-5330; St. George's School of Medicine: (473) 444-4271

St. Vincent: Maryfield Hospital (highly recommended by some of our readers), Gunn Hill, Kingstown: (784) 457-2598/2929, or use the Botanic Hospital: (784) 457-1747

Bequia Hospital: (784) 458-3294, VHF:74 (24 hours)

Mustique: (ask for clinic) (784) 458-4621

ENTERTAINMENT AND SPECIAL EVENTS

Carnival, St. Vincent

Green flash

In the evenings, sunset brings an opportunity to look for the elusive "green flash." This happens as the sun disappears below the horizon. For about a second (blink and you've missed it) the very last bit of the sun to disappear turns bright green. To see this you need a clear horizon and the right atmospheric conditions. Some say rum punch helps. Binoculars make it a lot clearer. Photographers will need a big telephoto lens and an auto drive wouldn't hurt.

Entertainment

The most popular form of evening entertainment is the "jump up." This usually happens in one of the bars or hotels and takes the form of a dance, most often to a live band. If enough rum flows, everyone does indeed "jump up." Both Martinique and St. Vincent have casinos, but these are very low key. Most of the larger hotels offer evening dancing with a floor show. Some hotels serve Sunday lunch to the accompaniment of a steel band. You can dance, swim or just enjoy the music.

Special events

There are a variety of local occasions for entertainment and partying. If you happen to be here at the right time, they are worth investigating.

Carnival started as a riotous bacchanal before Lent. Carnivals feature costumed parades, calypso contests, steel bands and days of dancing in the street. Martinique and St. Lucia still have theirs before Lent, but St. Vincent and Grenada have switched. Check our information on holidays at the beginning of each island section.

Sailing events. Martinique has a fun week in early June with races from port to port around Martinique and plenty of good food and etertainment. Ask about joining in at Puces Nautiques. If you are here on July 14th, the French national holiday, you may see pirogue races around Fort de France. Pirogues also feature in each coastal village during celebrations for its patron saint. Anyone interested can get a list from the local tourist office.

St. Lucia's Pitons Regatta is in the second week of February and includes four days of racing out of Rodney Bay.

Bequia's Easter Regatta is well worth attending. It includes yacht races, local "two-bow" fishing boat races, model boat races and cultural shows.

The Grenada Sailing Festival is held in early February. It offers a program of race events backed by a well organized social program. All entrants are welcome, from serious racing boats to live-aboards.

The Carriacou Regatta (weekend before the first Monday in August) is a local event featuring races for small fishing boats and the larger cargo carrying sloops. These are some of the finest sailing vessels made in the islands. Ashore there is plenty of fun.

Continuous sunshine and balmy trade breezes, right? Well, not too far wrong.

There are two seasons, the dry and the wet, but they are not always well differentiated. During the dry season (February to June) there will often be weeks of clear sunny weather broken only by an occasional small rain shower. In the wet season (July until January) there will still be plenty of sunshine, but with more frequent showers and occasional rainy days with no sun. There is very little temperature difference between the seasons; you can expect 78° to 85° Fahrenheit year round.

The winds are nearly always from the northeast to southeast at 10 to 25 knots; calms are rare. The wind tends to strengthen around the northern ends of islands. Rain usually arrives in intense squalls which can be seen coming from afar. Sometimes these squalls have a lot of wind in them (40 knots or more); often they do not. There is no way to tell before they arrive. Infrequently, a squall or cold front can produce winds from the westerly quadrant, making the usual anchorages uncomfortable.

During the winter months cold fronts farther north sometimes produce swells that reach the Windwards. These northerly swells can make anchorages which are open to the north or west rolly and occasionally untenable.

Visibility varies from an exceptional low of five miles to a high of over 50 miles. The hazy days are caused by dust from Africa. Sometimes reddish traces may be found on the cabin and decks. On hazy days avoid dust stains when doing the laundry by wiping off the lifelines before hanging out the washing.

The hurricane season is from June until October. The months of June, July and October only produce about one hurricane every three years for the whole western Atlantic including the Caribbean Sea and Gulf of Mexico. During August and September the

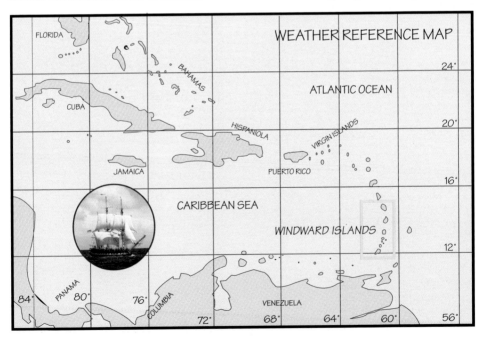

number is around five a year. Hurricanes frequently start well out in the Atlantic Ocean, often on the latitude of the Windwards, but then they usually swing north and pass through the Caribbean higher up. Very few hit the Windwards and sometimes years go by without one in this area, but it is essential to listen to the forecasts. Try Barbados Broadcasting Corp. with a weather forecast after the 0700 morning news. If you are in Grenada, Radio Grenada has a forecast at about the same time. Radio Kayac in Carriacou puts out weather at 0725 and 0915. You can also try Gem Radio with news and weather updates on the hour. Otherwise use your boatphone or a local phone and call a met office: St. Lucia (758) 545-6550, St. Vincent (784) 458-4477, Mustique (784) 458-4621 [ask for Mustique information services], Grenada (473) 444-4142.

Here are some terms you will hear on the radio and what they mean: "Intertropical convergence zone" affecting the area. This is not any kind of "low," but you may get some rain squalls or cloudy weather. "Tropical disturbance," "tropical wave" and "upper level trough" are poorly organized weather systems associated with rain squalls of varying intensity. A "tropical depression" is an organized weather system with sustained winds of up to 35 knots and rain. Sometimes these can be very nasty and other times they turn out to be nothing. A "tropical storm," on the other hand, is definitely something to be avoided as it has lots of rain and sustained winds of 35 to 63 knots. Once the sustained winds become more than 64 knots it is called a hurricane.

Hurricane winds can come from any direction, so be prepared to run for one of the hurricane holes: Cohe du Lamentin, Trois Ilet, or better still, Cul de Sac Marin in Martinique; Rodney Bay Lagoon or Marigot Bay in St. Lucia; the mangrove swamp in Tyrrel Bay, Carriacou, and in Grenada either in the Lagoon at St. George's or Port Egmont.

During one of the very few hurricanes that we did get, a charter party was advised by their company to make at once for a safe harbor to ride it out. "Oh no," they said "we

LOCAL RADIO
For news, views and weather

A M
Radio Guardian (Trinidad) ----- 610
Radio Trinidad -------------------- 750
Radio Grenada ------------------- 535
(weather after 0700 news)----
Barbados Broadcasting Corp - 900
(weather after 0700 news)
St. Vincent Radio ---------------- 705
St. Lucia Radio ------------------- 660

F M
Capital Radio (Grenada) ------- 90
Radio Kayak (Carriacou) ------- 106
 (weather 0725 & 0915)
Gem Radio* (St. Lucia) -------- 93.7, 94.5
Gem Radio* (Trinidad) --------- 93.1
Gem Radio* (Dominica) ------- 93.3
 (weather on the hour)
Radio Caraibes (French) ------- 89.9
Radio Martinique ---------------- 92, 94.5

* Marine weather daily at 0730 and 0930 & on Wednesdays a marine news follows

HAM & SSB
Antilles emergency net weather on 3815 kHz LSB at 0635 AST and 7163 kHz LSB at 0640 AST.
Caribbean SSB weather net on 4003 kHz at 0815 (local time)
8104 kHz at 0830
8107 kHz at 1815, only when there is a warning.
English Harbour Radio on 8297 kHz just after 0900.

VHF
Sam taxi in St. Vincent gives forecasts on VHF:06 at 0900 &1730.
In Martinique, COSMA gives forecasts in French at 0730 and 1830 on VHF:11

have confirmed flights out and don't want to miss them – we will make it in time." They sailed north from St. Vincent to St. Lucia, but by the time they reached Soufriere, it was raining cats and dogs, and the wind was howling, so they anchored and went ashore. The boat soon began to drag and the skipper,

35

aided by a local fisherman, tried to re-anchor. They managed to get their anchor line caught in the prop so they could not use power, and it was blowing too hard to make sail. In the end they drifted all night through the hurricane, and were rescued, after the winds fell, by a French coast guard boat off Martinique. I suppose the moral of the tale is that it is amazing what you can get away with, but better not to try.

NAVIGATION

Tides and currents

The tidal range is around two feet, not enough to be critical except in a few places. An equatorial current sets to the west northwest. This current is affected by the tide when you are within a few miles of land. A counter current begins about one hour before low water and offsets the equatorial current and can run up to one knot to the east. This continues for about four hours. Skippers of boats that are very slow to windward can make use of this to help them when sailing between islands. However, it is a mixed blessing because the counter current usually sets up much rougher seas.

Charts

Those needing charts have a choice between British Admiralty (B.A.), U.S. Defense Mapping Agency (D.M.A) and yachting charts. U.K charts are much more expensive in the U.S. and vice versa. If you are buying new charts you should make sure they are based on WG 84 data so they can be used with Global Positioning Systems (GPS).

For yachting charts there are the Imray Iolaire charts and the Nautical Publications Chart kits, both now based on WG 84 data, and both in full color. The Imray Iolaire charts are printed on plastic which lasts just about forever and you can get them wet. However, vigorous rubbing will take the color right off them, so experiment a little before you cover them with temporary pencil lines. In the unlikely event you need to

CHARTS OF THE WINDWARDS

Nautical Publications charts ■ ■ Caribbean 3 Guadeloupe to ■ □ Martinique □ □ Caribbean 4 St. Lucia to Grenada Each kit contains 7-9 charts most of which are printed on both sides. They include general coverage, island charts and detailed harbour plans. **Imray Iolaire charts** ■ Imray B Martinique to Trinidad ■ Imray A4 Guadeloupe to St. Lucia ■ Imray A30 Martinique, incl. plans: Fort de France, Trinite, St. Pierre, Marin, Francois, Pte. du Bout Imray A 301 East Coast of ■ Martinique Imray B1 St. Lucia, incl. □ plans Imray B30 St. Vincent, □ Bequia and Mustique, incl. plans of all major anchorages	□ □ Imray B31 Bequia to Carriacou, incl. plans. □ □ Imray B311 Canouan to Carriacou □ □ Imray B32 Carriacou and Grenada, incl. plans **Defence Mapping Agency charts** ■ DMA 25001 Eastern Caribbean Sea ■ DMA 25524 Martinique ■ DMA 25525 Plans: St. Pierre, La Trinite ■ DMA 25526 North & West Coasts of Martinique ■ DMA 25527 Fort de France □ DMA 25521 St. Lucia □ DMA 25528 Plans: Castries, Vieux Fort, Marigot, Rodney Bay □ DMA 25484 St. Vincent □ DMA 25483 Plans: Kingstown to Calliaqua, Admiralty Bay □ □ DMA 25482 Bequia to Carriacou, incl. Tobago Cays plan □ □ DMA 25481 Grenada, incl. plans **British Admiralty charts** ■ BA 956 Guadeloupe to Trinidad	■ BA 371 Northern Martinique, incl. plans ■ BA 494 Southern Martinique, incl. plans □ BA 1273 St. Lucia □ BA 197 Marigot to Pte. du Cap □ BA 499 Plans: Vieux Fort, Castries, Marigot, etc. □ BA 791 St. Vincent □ BA 799 Plans: Kingstown to Calliaqua, Admiralty Bay □ BA 793 Bequia to Canouan, incl. plans □ □ BA 794 Canouan to Carriacou, incl. plans □ BA 795 Grenada to Carriacou, incl. plans □ BA 797 Grenada □ BA 799 Plans: South Coast & St. George's Area ■ General ■ Martinique □ St. Lucia □ St. Vincent/Grenadines □ Grenada/Carriacou

dispose of them, they should be treated as plastic, not paper. These charts are sold individually, so you can tailor your collection to your needs. The format is regular chart size and most charts include several detailed harbor plans.

The Nautical Publications Charts come in kits and cover several islands. They are printed on traditional paper, and, in most cases, printed on both sides. Each kit includes planning, island and detailed harbor plans. The format is relatively small (23.5" by 16.5") so you never need to fold them. One of the delightful things about these charts is that they include very detailed land information as well as nautical information. On a price per chart they are very inexpensive as kits. They are also available

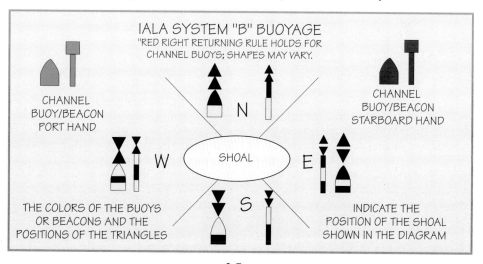

IALA SYSTEM "B" BUOYAGE
"RED RIGHT RETURNING RULE HOLDS FOR CHANNEL BUOYS; SHAPES MAY VARY.

CHANNEL BUOY/BEACON PORT HAND

CHANNEL BUOY/BEACON STARBOARD HAND

N

W   SHOAL   E

S

THE COLORS OF THE BUOYS OR BEACONS AND THE POSITIONS OF THE TRIANGLES

INDICATE THE POSITION OF THE SHOAL SHOWN IN THE DIAGRAM

individually, but as the price per chart is so much higher this is only worthwhile if one of your old ones blew over the side. Each kit comes in a handy plastic see-through envelope which you can take into the cockpit with the current chart on top. This also ensures (as a friend of mine found out), that rather than losing one chart over the side, the whole kit can blow over, so make a little hole in the plastic and tie them down. We have agreed to help users of these charts by cross-linking them to this guide.

Charterers might like a general chart of the Windwards for plotting their cruise.

Buoyage

All the islands now use the IALA B buoyage system. Main channels are marked with red and green buoys or beacons with red to starboard when entering: in other words "Red Right Returning." Other shoals and channels are indicated by black and yellow buoys or beacons coded both with respect to color and triangulation (using cones) as shown in the diagram on page 37.

Lights and buoys in the Windwards may be unreliable. Lights sometimes do not work, buoys can go adrift and beacons can lose color and cones. In short, treat navigational aids with great caution.

GPS

GPS is the biggest leap in navigational science since the invention of the chronometer. Now we can always know our precise position anywhere in the world. Accurate though this system is, there are limitations. I have noticed occasional inaccuracies up to a tenth of a mile, even when the GPS suggested the accuracy should have been better. Therefore I would not advise using a GPS to navigate reef-strewn passages at night or in poor visibility. Many of the older charts were created on unspecified formats, and inaccuracies of up to half a mile may occur. Most newer charts are based on WG 84 data and work with GPS. The charts in this book are on GPS grids. These were created using a Garmin 50 on WG 84 data, using much interpolation. No guarantee is offered about their accuracy, but I would be interested to hear how accurate readers find them. There

GPS POSITIONS

Approximate locations - for more accurate locations see sketch charts: see also navigation text.

MARTINIQUE	deg min (N)	deg min(W)
St. Pierre (off main dock)	14 44.5	61 10.7
Case Pilote (0.1 miles west of harbour wall)	14 38.4	61 08.5
Fort de France (0.1 miles south of cruise ship dock)	14 35.7	61 04.5
Pointe du Bout (northern end of anchorage)	14 33.7	61 03.4
Grand Anse D'Arlet (just outside a line between the points)	14 30.0	61 06.0
Petit Anse D'Arlet (middle of bay)	14 29.2	61 05.2
Cul de sac Marin (entrance)	14 26.7	60 54.0
St. Anne (western part of anchorage)	14 26.2	60 53.2
Baie Des Anglais (entrance)	14 24.9	60 49.8

ST. LUCIA	deg min (N)	deg min(W)
Pigeon Island (0.1 miles west of Pigeon Island)	14 05.5	60 58.2
Rodney Bay Lagoon (entrance)	14 04.7	60 57.4
Castries (entrance)	14 01.2	61 00.5
Marigot (entrance)	13 58.1	61 01.9
Anse Cochon (center of bay)	13 55.6	61 03.6
Anse Chastanet (0.2 miles southwest of reef off Gd. Caille Pt.)	13 51.5	61 05.2
Off Gros Piton (0.1 miles west of Gros Piton)	13 48.5	61 05.0
Off Vieux Fort (0.75 miles southwest of dock)	13 43.0	60 58.0

ST. VINCENT	deg min (N)	deg min(W)
Cumberland Bay (center of entrance)	13 16.0	61 15.8
Wallilabou (center of entrance)	13 14.9	61 16.5
Bottle & Glass (0.1 miles to the west of Bottle and Glass)	13 14.4	61 16.9
Petit Byahaut (0.1 miles southwest Petit Byahaut Point)	13 10.9	61 16.2
Ottley Hall (entrance)	13 09.5	61 14.9
Kingstown (center of bay)	13 09.0	61 14.0
Fort Duvernette (0.1 miles southwest of Point Duvernette)	13 07.6	61 12.4

GRENADINES	deg min (N)	deg min(W)
Bequia, Devil's Table (at beacon)	13 00.7	61 15.1
Bequia, West Cay (just off western end of West Cay)	12 59.5	61 17.6
Bequia, Friendship Bay (0.1 miles south of Hilaire Point)	12 59.1	61 14.0
Mustique, Britannia Bay (center of bay)	12 52.8	61 11.5
Canouan, Charlestown Bay (center of bay)	12 42.7	61 20.2
Canouan, Glossy Hill (just west of Glossy Hill)	12 42.2	61 21.4
Baline Rocks (0.4 miles west of Baline Rocks)	12 39.5	61 23.0
Tobago Cays (0.1 miles west of Petit Rameau)	12 38.2	61 21.8
Mayreau, Salt Whistle Bay (0.1 miles west of bay)	12 39.0	61 23.7
Mayreau, Saline Bay (0.5 miles west of the Saline bay)	12 38.0	61 24.5
Union, west of Grand de Coi (0.25 miles west of Grand de Coi)	12 35.0	61 25.0
Union, Chatham Bay (0.25 miles west of Miss Irene Point) .	12 35.5	61 28.0
PSV, Mopion Channel (0.2 miles north of center of channel)	12 32.9	61 24.1
PSV (0.5 miles west of the dock)	12 32.0	61 23.5
Carriacou , north end (0.25 miles westnorthwest of Rapid Pt.)	12 32.0	61 27.0
Tyrrel Bay (entrance)	12 27.5	61 30.0

GRENADA	deg min (N)	deg min(W)
Off north end (1 mile north of David Point)	12 15.0	61 40.0
Halifax Harbour (entrance)	12 06.7	61 45.0
Dragon Bay (entrance)	12 05.2	61 45.9
St. George's (0.25 miles west of entrance)	12 02.7	61 45.7
Point Saline (just off tip of land)	12 00.2	61 48.3
True Blue (entrance)	11 59.6	61 46.2
Prickly Bay (entrance)	11 59.3	61 46.0
West of Porpoises rocks (0.25 miles west of Porpoises)	11 58.6	61 45.9
St. David's harbour (entrance)	12 00.6	61 40.7

is also a table of GPS positions for planning purposes. You cannot just punch these numbers in and sail safely there; land and shoals will probably be on your line of approach, depending on your route.

CUSTOMS & IMMIGRATION

The Windwards contain four separate countries: Martinique, St. Lucia, St. Vincent (including the Grenadines to PSV); and Grenada, which includes Carriacou and Petite Martinique. Each has its own customs regulations and it is necessary to clear in and out of each country. On arrival you should anchor in a port of entry and hoist a yellow flag. After that you can go ashore in search of customs and immigration officers. Passports, ship's papers and three to four copies of your crew list are required. In Martinique and St. Lucia the crew list forms are supplied and in St. Vincent they are available for a nominal fee. Grenada sometimes has them, but better take your own. Make three copies, include the yacht's name, tonnage and home port, along with the names of all crew members, their nationalities and passport numbers. When clearing, always take your previous clearance with you. Customs and immigration officers will refuse to deal with anyone not wearing a shirt. Charges and other details are given under island and harbor headings.

Dogs

So you've brought your pet all the way over the ocean and now you want to take it for a walk? Well, here is what you can expect from the local authorities. In Martinique and Grenada if you have a rabies vaccination certificate handy when you clear in, you can walk your dog ashore. St. Vincent and St. Lucia are both rabies free and animals are not allowed ashore under any circumstances.

Few people realize that dogs in the Caribbean are subject to a deadly little heart worm. Check with a vet for appropriate counter measures before leaving, or as soon as you get here.

PROTECTING THE ENVIRONMENT

Most visitors are courteous and well behaved. With the increasing volume of yachts in the area, it definitely helps if people are considerate. This area has been reasonably free of loud noises, including drunken raucous laughter, stereo equipment, endlessly running generators and loudly clanking halyards. Luckily, there is plenty of room in most anchorages, so those who want to make noise or need to run generators for much of the time, can just stay well away from everyone else. Most of us have to run our engines at sometime during the day, but let us at least leave the hour around sunset free so everyone can enjoy it in peace. One disturbing exception to this has been the increase in windmills. Most of these are quiet and unob- trusive, but a few can be heard well over a 100 yards away. They can destroy the natural peace of many a quiet anchorage. Further, the people who own them seem to think that, because they are not using fossil fuels, they are on the side of the angels and can do no wrong. They run them 24 hours a day without giving any consideration to those who might find the noise irritating. If you have not yet bought a windmill, I suggest you consider buying a quiet one or, better still, try solar panels. If you already own a noisy one, please try to anchor to the back of the fleet, and when your batteries are charged up, stop the blades.

Right now you can don a mask and snorkel and dive over the side anywhere in the

MILEAGE CHART

This table is approximate and offered as a guide to planning. Distances sailed are often in excess of those shown due to wind and current.

From \ To	Ft. de France	Anse Mitan	Gd. A. D'Arlet	St. Anne	Rodney Bay	Castries	Marigot	Pitons	Vieux Fort	Wallilabou	Kingstown	Young Island	Admiralty B.	Friendship B.	Mustique	Canouan	Mayreau	Tobago Cays	Union L.	P.S.V.	Hillsborough	Tyrrel Bay	St. George's	Prickly Bay	Mt. Hartman B.
St. Pierre	12	14	16	30	42	45	47	56	67	90	97	99	105	115	122	127	130	133	136	139	159	165	166	172	173
Ft. de France		3	7	21	33	37	39	47	57	83	90	92	98	108	115	120	123	126	130	132	152	158	159	165	166
Anse Mitan			6	20	32	36	38	46	57	82	89	91	97	107	114	119	122	125	129	131	151	157	158	164	165
Gd. Anse D'Arlet				15	26	30	32	41	52	77	84	86	92	102	109	114	117	120	123	126	146	152	152	158	159
St. Anne					21	26	30	39	50	76	83	85	91	101	108	113	116	119	123	126	146	152	152	158	159
Rodney Bay						5	8	18	29	55	62	64	70	80	87	92	95	101	108	113	133	135	140	140	141
Castries							4	13	24	50	57	59	65	75	82	87	90	95	101	119	123	135	140	140	141
Marigot								10	21	46	53	55	61	71	78	82	87	89	93	120	125	131	135	135	136
Pitons									11	36	43	45	51	61	65	69	75	82	86	96	126	130	135	135	136
Vieux Fort										34	41	43	49	59	66	71	73	76	79	83	114	119	121	131	132
Wallilabou											7	9	15	25	32	37	40	43	47	50	77	81	84	114	116
Kingstown												2	9	19	27	32	35	38	42	45	75	80	84	114	116
Young Island													8	11	16	27	32	35	38	45	75	80	85	119	120
Admiralty Bay														7	9	15	25	27	32	37	83	86	114	116	122
Friendship Bay															7	19	25	32	37	40	79	83	86	116	120
Mustique																14	18	20	24	27	83	86	96	126	131
Canouan																	7	7	6	10	14	19	61	66	67
Mayreau (Saline Bay)																		4	4	7	9	12	42	47	48
Tobago Cays																			4	7	11	14	44	49	50
Union (Clifton)																				4	7	10	40	45	46
P.S.V.																					7	9	39	44	45
Hillsborough																						4	34	39	40
Tyrrel Bay																							30	35	36
St. George's																								7	8
Prickly Bay																									2

Laughing gull

Tropic Bird

Windwards and find the seabed pretty clean. Let's keep it that way.

Fishing and hunting

The days have gone when we could jump over the side, bristling with knives and festooned with spearguns long enough to be sold by the yard, to decimate the local fish population. Spearfishing has proved too damaging and new laws have been passed to control it. By the time this guide comes out, it will be illegal to spearfish almost anywhere from St. Lucia to Grenada. It is worth noting that compliance not only helps the environment, but that illegal fishing fines exceeded $100,000 during the first couple of years they were enforced in St. Vincent and the Grenadines. Hunters should note that all cows, goats and sheep, even on remote uninhabited islands, are privately owned. They are often put out to graze and left for months on end. They should not be harmed.

Garbage

Our record on yacht garbage is terrible. Yacht garbage has totally overwhelmed the land facilities of the Grenadine islands, and we have to cut down on what we bring ashore. The best way to do this is to buy things with as little packing as possible and use returnable bottles. Always take along your own shopping bags and avoid all those plastic ones.

In addition yachtspeople have caused considerable degradation by letting locals "dispose" of their garbage. **Never give garbage to vendors**. Some will offer to dispose of it for a fee. However, the person offering to take your garbage has no proper means of disposing of it. The good ones try to burn it, but combustion is never complete and the remains are left strewn around. Others dump your garbage in holes in the bushes and the worst take it to the nearest beach, rummage through for items of interest, and abandon it. You are responsible for your own garbage. If you give it to someone else for a fee, they are considered your employee, and if they litter with your garbage, you are legally liable.

Food waste in all its forms should be dumped at sea in deep water. Carrying organic food matter from one island to another as garbage is a dangerous practice. Island agriculture is very sensitive as we saw recently when an inadvertently introduced pink mealy bug spread rapidly through some of the Windward Islands and cost millions of dollars in lost or unexportable produce. Organic matter may contain fruit flies, cockroaches, fungi and other potentially dangerous pests. So take care when transporting and disposing of fresh fruit and vegetable matter. In addition, it is unwise to transport things like woven palm hats and baskets between islands.

No plastics, including bags and bottled water containers, must ever be thrown at sea. Leatherback turtles eat jellyfish and many have been found dead, their stomachs filled with plastic bags. Take the plastic bags ashore and let the turtles eat the jellyfish. Smelly bags can be rinsed in the ocean before storing. Other items that should never be thrown out at sea include string and fishing line which might be eaten, or which might form a tangle trap somewhere, plastic lined cardboard cartons (juice cartons, etc.) and tin foil. These can all be rinsed in seawater before stowing. Similarly, anything that could be the least bit toxic, including aerosol sprays and chemicals, should never be dumped at sea.

Royal tern

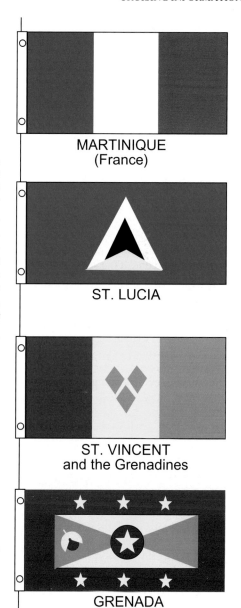

MARTINIQUE
(France)

ST. LUCIA

ST. VINCENT
and the Grenadines

GRENADA

Most of our garbage consists of paper, cardboard, cans and bottles. Should we throw these at sea? Ideally, no. The ocean is not a dumping ground, and if we are not very careful where we dump such garbage we can damage reef structures. On the other hand, we should not take these items ashore and dump them in the Grenadines where the facilities are totally inadequate. So what to do? As far as possible, keep the garbage for an adequate refuse facility in one of the larger islands. Martinique has plenty of places to put garbage and you will find adequate facilities in Rodney Bay and Marigot Bay in St. Lucia, and in GYS, Spice Island Marine and Secret Harbour in Grenada. Dirty cans and other food containers should be rinsed before stowing so they do not stink up your boat.

If you are unable to do this then it is probably marginally better to dump nonreturnable bottles, cans, shredded paper and cardboard out far from land, with no islands or reefs in the lee, in water over 600 feet deep, than it is to pile them in a heap on land where they are not being collected. Paper and cardboard will eventually dissolve (though we do not know about the toxicity of the inks printed on them). Cans and bottles will sink and sit on the sea bed which, in deep water, is mainly sand or mud. Nothing should ever be dumped near a reef or in an anchorage.

Another form of degradation occurs when yachtspeople accept offers from locals to "fix up a barbecue" on shore. While not wishing to deprive locals of a livelihood by this method, I would point out that in popular spots, like the Tobago Cays, the resultant mess from litter has been dreadful and that enough charcoal has been mixed with the sand to turn it grey in places. So if you barbecue ashore (with or without local help)

dispose of everything properly yourself. You cannot assume it will be done for you, even if you are paying for your meal.

Save our reefs

In minutes anchors can destroy what nature has taken generations to build. A coral structure is a colony of millions of minute animals called polyps. They are fragile and reefs grow very slowly. Never anchor your yacht on coral, always on sand. If there is any doubt, have someone snorkeling when you drop your anchor. Dinghy anchors also do harm, so you need a sand anchor for your dinghy and you need to anchor on the sand beside the coral, never on the coral itself.

When snorkeling or diving, be careful of coral structures. Do not stand, bump into, get swept onto or grab coral structures. Even a small amount of damage can open a coral structure to predation from sponges and algae. Don't wear gloves when diving and snorkeling and never take anything from the reef.

Eco-purchasing

Few people realize how powerfully their dollars speak and one of the very best things you can do for the environment is to spend wisely.

Dollars spent on such items as wood carvings, jewelry made from decorative local seeds, banana craft, straw goods, woven grasses and anything made from coconut shells will really help the economy and the environment. Jewelry made from conch shells is also okay as these are caught for their meat, and the shell is normally thrown away. (However, check importation regulations in your home country.)

Avoid buying coral and turtleshell products. Considerable damage to reef structures is done by youths who take corals to sell to the jewelry makers. The hawksbill turtle, most often killed for its shell, is an endangered species, as are all Caribbean sea turtles, and importation of turtle shell is forbidden in most countries. These items are sold mainly to yachts, so let us say "no" to these vendors and support the turtles and reefs. If you visit during the lobster season and are buying lobsters, always turn them over to see if they have eggs underneath (easily seen as red caviar). If they do, refuse to buy them.

Another problem, harder to deal with, is that in some places vendors build illegal structures ranging from bars and small boutiques to squatter camps in order to service the yachting trade. These in themselves degrade the environment and are only constructed to satisfy the needs of the yachting community. So look around you, see what effect your money is having and likely to have. Do spend money but spend it wisely.

SCUBA DIVING

"It's fantastic. I could breathe underwater just like a fish, and fish swam up and looked at me. What an incredible feeling."

"It's the greatest sensation I've ever felt. When we swam back with the current it was just like gliding through a beautiful garden!"

These are typical comments from first-time divers who find that diving is the most exciting thing they have ever done. No wonder – it is the closest most of us will ever come to visiting a strange planet. Not only that, under water we are weightless and seem to fly. Like birds we can soar, hover and dive down to see anything of interest.

The underwater world is full of wonders – tall soft waving "plants" that are really colonies of tiny animals, sponges which look like ancient urns, in colors ranging from yellow to a psychedelic luminous blue. Huge schools of fish swim by, unconcerned about our presence. Little squids move by jet propulsion, turtles and gentle giant rays glide with elegant ease.

Yet many people are put off diving because they are under the impression it is complicated and difficult. Nothing could be

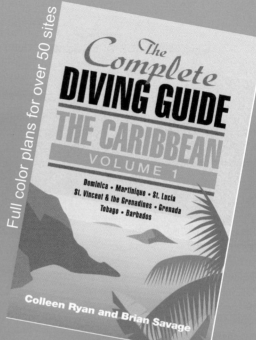

parrotfish

go for your first dive. A resort course only qualifies you to dive under the close supervision of an instructor. If you are staying in the same place, you can keep going on dives with the instructor without further training but what if you change locations? If you keep a log book of your dives, you may find another instructor on another island willing to take you down, but many will want you to redo the resort course. Once you go home and stop diving, you must take another course before starting again. If you take to diving, it is much better to become fully qualified.

farther from the truth. With modern equipment, diving is very simple and with one of the popular "resort courses" you can be diving in half a day. In fact, the problem most divers have is to avoid boring their non-diving friends to distraction with tales of undersea adventure.

Equipment

Experienced divers will want to bring their own masks, fins and regulators. A really good comfortable B.C. (buoyancy compensator) might be worth bringing, too. As for the rest, forget it. There is no point in humping tanks and weight belts. Far better to rent them here. Those without any equipment don't need to worry. The dive shops will supply everything and it is usually excellent up-to-date gear. In many parts of the world you have to wear a protective "wet suit" against the cold, but in the Windwards the water is warm enough that for most of us this isn't necessary.

Courses for learners

Anyone who just wants to give diving a go can do so very quickly with a "resort course." It will take one whole morning or afternoon. First you get a one-hour talk which tells you in simple language what diving is all about. Then you try out the equipment in shallow water and, lastly, you

trumpetfish

First dive

Wherever you take a resort course the instructors will choose a site which is easy but interesting enough to attract aficionados. A typical example is Devil's Table in Bequia. The rocks and coral start at 12 feet and slope down to about 35 feet deep. You enter the water and feel a bit nervous, but you breathe out and gently sink. Soon your attention turns outwards. Large pillar corals rise from among the rocks. They look fuzzy but if you brush them ever so lightly with your hand, the tentacles withdraw, leaving them looking like rocks. You stop to examine some pretty shells clinging to a waving sea fan and to your surprise a tiny damsel fish shoots up and tries to chase you away. He's protecting his patch, and you don't scare him; it's then you learn that you can even laugh through your regulator. There is

a great deal more to see: brightly colored parrotfish and angelfish, moray eels staring from their holes, strange looking arrow crabs and brightly banded coral shrimp. You enjoyed it? Good! It can count as your first dive toward full certification.

Certification

If you've ever thought about getting certified, or if you try a dive and like it, then it makes sense to get certified on your holiday. If you get certified at home, the chances are that it will be in a swimming pool with nothing more interesting to look at than tiled walls. Your open water dives are likely to be in some frigid grey lake. Furthermore, you will probably have to buy or rent equipment which is normally included in the course price down island. In the Caribbean you can train at a cost not much greater than the dives alone. The course includes all equipment; you do everything in open water; the dives are fantastic – and you can take home a diving certificate as well as your memories. There are several diving associations which have accredited diving instructors who can train you and give you a certificate. These include Padi and Naui which are equally good. A full diving course in the islands takes about four or five days, and includes a couple of hours of instruction each day followed by a dive, during which you increase your practical skills.

You do not have to stay in one place for the time it takes to get certified. Dive St. Vincent (which includes Grenadines Dive) and Dive Bequia work together so you can start a certification course in any of their locations and continue it as you sail through the islands.

For qualified divers

Some people, especially those chartering

pufferfish

yachts, prefer to rent gear and go off diving by themselves. Others prefer to join a dive with professional instructors. At least for your first few dives, I recommend going with the dive instructors. They know all the good sites, the hidden caves, the special ledge where angel fish live, and maybe they know where there is a tame octopus, seahorse or frogfish. A good instructor is also a good guide and can often point out many things that would otherwise be missed, which can add interest to your dive. Perhaps the most important reason is that many good dive sites are in places that can only be reached with a powerful dive boat rather than a dinghy. I have worked with many charterers who have tried it both ways and noticed that those who went with dive instructors had a much better time than those who went on their own.

The diving in the Windwards varies markedly from island to island and from one dive site to the next, so enthusiasts will want to try diving in several different spots. We will mention the good sites and their accessibility in the text under each anchorage section. Dive shops are listed in our directory.

MARTINIQUE

Regulations

The main customs office is in Fort de France, but clearance may be found in Marin and St. Pierre. Martinique is free to many countries, including the UK and the US, but yachts from some countries are charged on a per ton /per day basis. Yachts present in Martinique waters for more than six months in one year are liable to import duty. (You can avoid this by special permission if you want to leave your yacht in Martinique while you fly abroad.) Visas are not currently necessary for EEC members or US citizens. Other nationals should check to see if they need a visa. Customs in each port has its own opening times which are given in the harbor sections. There are no overtime fees.

Shopping Hours

Shops are normally open 0800-1200 and 1500-1730, Monday through Saturday. Many offices are closed on Saturday. The large supermarkets (and many smaller ones) open at 0800 or 0900 and stay open till 1900.

Holidays

Jan 1st - New Year's Day
Jan 2nd - Recovery Day
Carnival - Monday and Tuesday, 40 days before Easter. 15th-16th Feb 1999 and 6-7th March 2000
Easter Friday through Monday. 2-5th April 1999 and 21st-24th April 2000
May 1st - Labor Day
May 8th - Victory Day (1945)
May 22nd - Abolition of Slavery
May 28th - Ascension Day
July 14th - Bastille Day
August 15th - Virgin Mary Day
Nov 1st - All Saints Day
Nov 11th - Victory Day (1918)
Dec 25th - Christmas Day

Telephones

Card telephones are placed all around Martinique. You need a card to make a call. These are available at post offices, change houses, and most newspaper stands. You need to insert a card even for a reverse charge or telephone card call, but the card is not charged. Dial: 00 00 11 for USA direct and 00 596 11 for an international operator. You can also dial direct and your telephone card gets charged. Dial 00 to get out of the country and then the country code and number you want. Most Martinique call boxes have their number posted, so you can also call your party and have them call you back. All Martinique numbers are ten digits and start with 0596. If you are calling Martinique from abroad, leave off the first 0.

Transport

Martinique has a few suburban buses. For other places you can take a communal taxi, "TC". They are found on most town squares and run on fixed routes, mainly to and from Fort de France. They are reasonably priced. There are also taxis. Typical taxi rates in French francs are:

Airport - Fort de France	80
Airport - Anse Mitan	160
Anse Mitan - Golf course	50
Fort de France - Euromarche	60
Short ride	50
Full day tour	1500
By the hour	200

Rental cars are available (check our directory). You can use your own license. Drive on the right.

MARTINIQUE

Petit Anse D'Arlet

Martinique is the largest of the Windwards and, apart from a few short spells under the British, has been French since it was colonized. It is a part of France and feels it, with excellent roads and a thriving economy. Nearly every bay has a wonderful government-built dock ideal for leaving your dinghy. Fort de France is a busy city, bustling with shoppers and cars. The smaller towns are quieter and some look so clean they could have just been scrubbed. That typically French smell – a blend of Gitane smoke, pastis and well-percolated coffee – wafts from bars and cafes.

You can get almost anything done in Martinique – from galvanizing your boat to having stainless steel tanks made. The sailmakers are first rate, the chandleries are magnificently stocked, restaurants and boutiques abound. In short, when you have had enough deserted beaches and raw nature, Martinique is the place for a breath of civilization. And the island has enough excellent and varied anchorages for a week or two of exploring. Some have fashionable resorts, others are sleepy waterfront villages, plus there are deserted bays with excellent snorkeling. Well marked hiking trails make walking a delight.

The Empress Josephine grew up in Martinique on a 200-acre, 150-slave estate near Trois Ilets. A strange quirk of fate links Josephine and Martinique to the Battle of Trafalgar. In 1804 Napoleon was master of Europe, but the British still had naval supremacy and largely controlled Caribbean waters. However, ships were always scarce and some bright spark noticed that Dia-mond Rock on the south coast of Martinique was just about where they would station another British vessel if they had one, so they commissioned the rock as a ship. It was quite a feat to climb this steep, barren, snake-infested pinnacle, and equip it with cannons and enough supplies and water for a full crew of men. But they succeeded and for some 18 months H.M.S. Diamond Rock was a highly unpleasant surprise for unsuspecting ships sailing into Martinique. Napoleon was incensed; this was after all the birthplace of his beloved Josephine. Brilliant as he was on land, Napoleon never really understood his navy or its problems and considered his men to be shirkers. Consequently he ordered them to sea under Admiral Villeneuve, to free the rock and destroy Nelson while they were about it. Villeneuve slipped out under the British blockade in France and headed straight for Martinique. Lord Nelson, with his well trained and battle-ready fleet, smelled blood and bounty and hurtled off in hot pursuit. However, poor information sent him on a wild goose chase to Trinidad so Villeneuve was able to liberate the rock and return to France, prudently keeping well clear of Nelson.

Napoleon was none too pleased with Villeneuve because the British fleet was still in control of the high seas, so he was ordered to report in disgrace. Villeneuve preferred death to dishonor so he put his ill prepared fleet to sea to fight Nelson at the Battle of Trafalgar. Ironically, Villeneuve, who wished to die, survived the battle, while Nelson died.

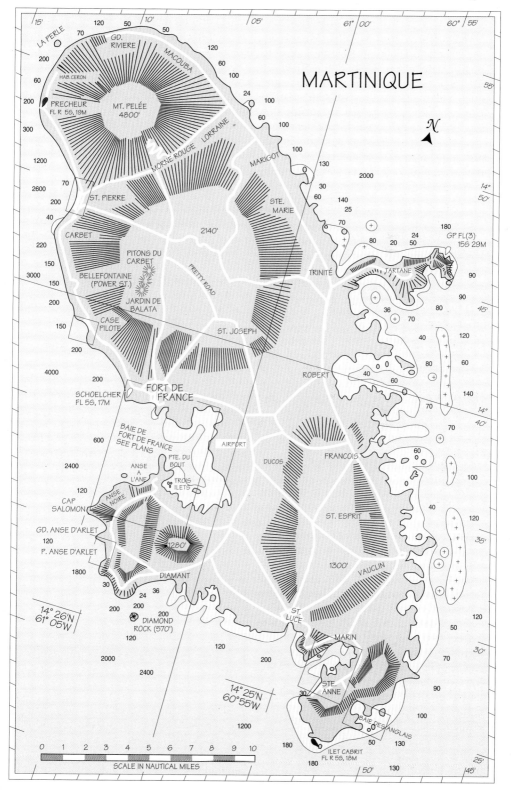

MARTINIQUE

N

15' 120 50 10' 50 05' 61° 00' 60° 55'

LA PERLE 70 GD. RIVIERE 120
MACOUBA 60
200 100
HAB. CERON 24 100
60 200 PRECHEUR MT. PELÉE 60 100 55'
FL R 5S, 19M 4800' 100
300 MORNE ROUGE LORRAINE MARIGOT 100
1200 130 2000 14°
2600 70 ST. PIERRE 60 140 50'
200 30 25
40 2140' 70 180
CARBET 80 20 24 GP FL(3)
220 PITONS DU 50 15S 29M
150 CARBET TARTANE 90
3000 BELLEFONTAINE 36 45'
150 (POWER ST.) 70 90
200 JARDIN DE 80
BALATA 40 120
150 CASE TRINITÉ 60
PILOTE ST. JOSEPH 80
200 ROBERT 40 60 140
4000 200 70 14°
SCHOELCHER 70 40'
FL 5S, 17M FORT DE
FRANCE
BAIE DE
600 FORT DE FRANCE AIRPORT 70
SEE PLANS FRANCOIS 60
2400 ANSE DUCOS 100
A
L'ANE 40
120 PTE. DU
CAP BOUT TROIS ST. ESPRIT 120
SALOMON ANSE ILETS 35'
NOIRE
GD. ANSE D'ARLET VAUCLIN
120 1300'
P. ANSE D'ARLET 1280'
1800 120
30 DIAMANT 120 50 30'
24 36 ST.
200 200 LUCE 70
14° 26'N 200 MARIN
61° 05'W DIAMOND 90
ROCK (570') STE. 100
120 120 ANNE
30 BAIE DES ANGLAIS
2000 200 50 130
2400 120
14° 25'N 180
60° 55'W 1200 ILET CABRIT 130
180 FL 5S, 18M

0 1 2 3 4 5 6 7 8 9 10
SCALE IN NAUTICAL MILES

Navigation

The south coast of Martinique between Ste. Anne and Diamond Rock has several shoals extending up to a half mile offshore. Fish traps are plentiful and two or three are often tied together. It is best to stay in several hundred feet of water, outside the heavily fished area. The current here usually runs to the west so if you are cruising to Martinique from St. Lucia, it is easier to go first to Marin and Ste. Anne, leaving an easy downwind trip to Fort de France. If you do visit Fort de France first, the beat to Marin is in protected water and can be exhilarating.

The west coast (excluding the Bay of Fort de France) up to St. Pierre is mainly steep-to, and a quarter of a mile offshore clears any dangers.

The Bay of Fort de France has many shoals, especially at its eastern end. Check the charts and instructions given under the appropriate section.

ST. PIERRE

St. Pierre lies at the foot of Mt. Pelée volcano, not far from where European settlers wiped out the last of the Carib residents in 1658. It is said that before the last ones died they uttered horrible curses, invoking the mountain to take its revenge. Mt. Pelée, in true Caribbean fashion, took its own sweet time until Ascension Day, the 8th of May in 1902.

At this time St. Pierre, with a population of 30,000, was known as the Paris of the Caribbean and was the commercial, cultural and social center of Martinique. The wealth of the island lay in the plantations and the richest of these surrounded St. Pierre. Ships would take on rum, sugar, coffee and cocoa and enough was sold to make several of the plantation owners multi-millionaires. There were also enough cheap bars, brothels and dancing girls to satisfy the sailors.

The volcano gave plenty of warning. Minor rumblings began early in April and, before dawn on the 2nd of May, a major eruption covered the city with enough ash to kill some birds and animals. Later the same day, Pierre Laveniere, a planter with an estate to the south of St. Pierre went to inspect his crops with a party of workers and they were swept away by a vast avalanche of volcanic mud. On the fifth of May it was the turn of the Guerin Estate, one of the richest in the area, just a couple of miles north of St. Pierre. A torrent of volcanic effluent, including mud, lava, boiling gasses and rocks, estimated to be a quarter of a mile wide and a hundred feet high completely buried the estate.

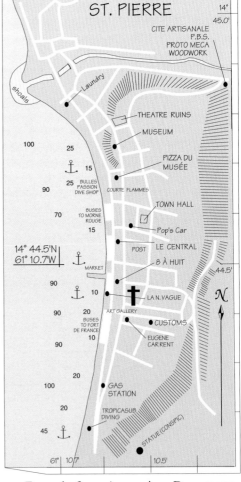

Even before Ascension Day many people had been killed in and around St. Pierre. So why did people stay? Governor Mouttet, on the island for less than a year, couldn't cope with the responsibility of

ST. PIERRE

evacuating Martinique's most important city. He desperately wanted the problem to go away and was encouraged to sit tight by most of the planters and business leaders who would have suffered financial losses if the city were evacuated.

Evacuation would also have affected the coming elections in which black voters were seriously challenging the status quo for the first time. A committee was put in place to monitor the volcano and those in charge enlisted the support of the local paper, Les Colonies, to persuade people that there was no danger, despite the deaths. A few individuals had the sense to leave, but for the rest the destruction of St. Pierre was unimaginable.

There were many eyewitnesses to the disaster. People were approaching from Fort de France for the Ascension Day church service when they saw heavy, red smoke from the volcano descend on St. Pierre. Rather than continue, they climbed the surrounding hills to see what would happen next. The end came at two minutes past eight in the morning. The side of the volcano facing St. Pierre glowed red, burst and released a giant fireball of superheated gas which flowed down over the city, releasing more energy than an atomic bomb. All that remained were smoking ruins. An estimated 29,933 people burned to death, leaving only two survivors, Leon Leandre, a cobbler who was in his cellar, and the fa-

mous Cyparis, imprisoned for murder in a stone cell.

Today many ruins remain. Post-disaster buildings have been built on to old structures so nearly every new building shares at least one wall with the past. Ruins also form garden walls, and many have been tidied up as historical icons. A museum in a modern building up a small hill, depicts that era and the tragedy. It stands on top of old walls that are artistically lit up at night, making an enchanting backdrop for those anchored below.

Navigation

St. Pierre makes a good overnight anchorage except when there are heavy northerly swells. There is an adequate shelf on which to anchor, about 25 feet deep, on either side of the town dock. The dropoff is very steep, so make sure you are well hooked. Occasionally you have to move for local fishermen who have been known to move unattended yachts. You will not be in their way close to the dock or behind the fishing fleet at the northern end of the harbor. A conspicuous statue on the hill at the southern end of the beach is lit at night.

Regulations

You can clear in and out here but the officers are often away on duty. If the office is locked in the morning, try in the afternoon, or vice versa. As a last resort, catch a communal taxi to Fort de France (about 40 minutes away) and clear in there.

Services

There are some excellent services in the Cite Artisanale on the edge of town. Celestin's PBS is the only propeller and stern gear specialist in the Windwards. They balance, rebuild and repair broken propellers of all materials, they can fix and repair shafts and they stock cutlass bearings, stern glands and anodes. They are sales and service agent for France Helices and can supply anything related to boat propulsion. They will pick up and deliver to Martinique's other marine centers. Christopher, who works in the store, speaks English.

Jean-Michel Trébeau trained as an aviation machinist in France and now has a first rate shop, Proto Meca close to PBS. Anything you can break he can fix, be it in stainless, aluminum, or bronze. He welds these metals and does all kinds of machining. He can rebuild your engine and resurface the block. In the same compound you will find three carpenters.

Back in town, two laundry/dry cleaner establishments will take care of your wash; Lacapress is south on the front street, L'auxiliaire is near the river mouth.

Ashore

The waterfront area is being renovated. An elegant replica of the old financial center will soon become the tourist office. The new dock is perfect for dinghies and you can also come alongside to take on water with permission from the town hall. The gas station at the foot of the dock which sold cube ice is currently closed, ice is available at the gas station to the south of town. There are a couple of banks, a pharmacy, and a good little 8 à Huit supermarket which closes for lunch and half an hour earlier than its name suggests. It also opens Sunday mornings. System Cash near the cathedral offers a more limited range but includes quantity discounts. The market is most active on Friday and Saturday mornings. Shops in St. Pierre now include clothing boutiques, souvenir shops and places selling local fabrics.

Photographers can have print film developed in an hour at Imaphot along the waterfront road heading north from the dock.

The museum gives a historical perspective and is open daily 0900-1200 and 1500-1700. There is a small admission charge. Among the most interesting places to visit are the theater ruins beyond the museum and the prison where Cyparis was jailed, which is just below the theater.

Finding a meal ashore is no problem. Raymonde Pousset cooks superb pizzas to the latest music in his old wood-fired oven at Pizzeria du Musée [$C-D]. Sit inside, or watch life go by on the road from outdoor tables where you can also smell the pizzas as they cook. Lucretia's Courtes Flammes [$C-D, closed Sunday] is a small restaurant with tables both inside and outside, facing the bay. Lucretia speaks English and serves Créole food at a very reasonable price. Le Caraibes [$B-C, closed Monday] is very popular come sunset with its tables right out on the new waterfront promenade. They serve meals and have entertainment quite frequently. Next door is Tai Loong, a Chinese snack bar. On the other side of the road, La Vague [$B-C] has an impressive waterfront location and you can get a reasonable meal here at lunch or dinner. La Taverne Créole [$B-C], on the road to the museum, offers crepes, salads and barbecued food, while next door is Royal Bellevue [$C], a Chinese restaurant. The entertaining new Parisien-owned Paris-Montmartre [$C-D] is on the road to the gas station and La Mouillage [$B-C] is right by the gas station.

Le Central [$B-C] and Habitation Josephine [$B-C] both serve Créole food, and open for lunch, but dinner is by reservation only.

St. Pierre sits amid the most magnificent scenery in Martinique, so if you are thinking of sightseeing, this is an excellent place to begin. Rental cars are available from Eugene Garage, Budget and Pop's Car.

There are many sights to see. The following places are marked on maps available at no charge from the tourist office. Maps of hiking trails are usually posted by the parking areas. Plantation Ceron, north of

St. Pierre

Precheur, escaped the volcanic eruption and is a fine example of what the plantations were like before 1902. One hundred and forty francs buys you an excellent meal and all the food comes from the estate, including freshwater crayfish. As a perfect antidote to boats, spend as long as you like wandering around the shady estate gardens built along a river. Habitation Ceron is owned by Louis and Lawrence DesGrottes, and Louis used to run a charter yacht out of Union Island. Afterwards you can return to the road and head north till it ends. A footpath continues some miles along the coast in the shade of the forest.

In the mountains to the south of St. Pierre, there is an extraordinary walk along the Canal de Beauregard. Built by slaves in 1760 this canal brought water around a steep mountain to supply the distilleries of St. Pierre. It is most interesting to start at the bottom end of the canal and walk towards the source. The canal is fairly level, often shady, and easy, though only for those with a head for heights, for you walk along the outer canal wall which is about 18 inches wide and the panoramic views are often dizzyingly precipitous.

If the weather is clear, the energetic should hike up Mont Pelée. A road takes you to within a mile and a half of the summit. Turn right just at the entrance to Precheur on the Chameuse Road. Non-hik-

ers can enjoy the view from the top of the road.

The rainforest starts behind St. Pierre and you can drive past the conspicuous volcanic observatory right into the mountains. When you reach the main crossroads in the middle of the rainforest, turn south and look for a tiny road, barely the width of a car, which goes to St. Joseph. It may be marked "impassable," but adventure down it as far as possible.

Gorges de la Falaise are dramatic waterfalls in a narrow canyon on the east side of Mt. Pelée. The hike takes about an hour and a half and it is closed in heavy rains.

If you have kids you may enjoy the butterfly farm which is set in a ruined distillery just before Carbet. Nearby is a museum about Gauguin. It includes letters, documents, artifacts and a whole show of imitation Gauguin paintings.

Water sports

Twelve wrecks of ships that sank in the tragedy of 1902 are nearby, most within dinghy range of the anchorage. The best way to find them is to dive with a local dive shop. Otherwise, watch the local dive boats which visit them frequently. They vary in depth from 30 to 150 feet. In addition, the north coast has the best diving in Martinique, with dramatic walls, canyons and reefs, and many more fish than you find in the south.

Regis and Nicha run Bulles Passion from a convenient spot at the ruins right below the museum. They fill tanks and go diving daily at 0915 and 1415. Check with them and they will be happy to pick you up from your yacht. Bulles Passion is a Naui shop and they offer all kinds of courses. Regis speaks English.

Tropicasub Diving [VHF:16, closed Monday] is based right on the beach. Owners Françoise and Lionel Lafont dive twice daily, at 0930 and 1500. Since the number of places is limited, call in advance on the VHF. Françoise speaks English well.

If you are diving on your own, there is an easy dive right off the beach in front of the big wall under the museum. A good reef with a dropoff from 40 to 90 feet, is decorated with old anchors, a huge old chain draped over the coral, and plenty of fish.

Case Pilote is a delightful small fishing town whose pretty church is one of the oldest in Martinique. There is a picturesque little fishing port with an active fish processing plant which buys fish from boats that come from as far away as Venezuela. This place is charming and unspoiled and the locals have no intention of becoming another yacht haven. Anchorage outside the port is limited by the needs of the active fishing fleet and when the fishermen put out seine nets at about 0500 hours they will wake anyone they feel to be in their way. To avoid this, anchor well inshore on the northwest side of the bay (see our sketch chart). Go in as close as you dare, drop your hook, then back down and use a second anchor to keep your stern to any swells and to stop you from riding up on the beach. Or anchor just round the headland off the next small bay to the northwest in about 25 feet of water and use your dinghy to go to the port.

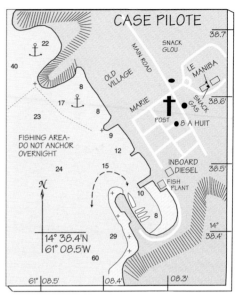

Regulations

There are currently no customs in Case Pilote, so you must clear in at a port of entry. If you are staying here for more than a few hours, you should visit the police station with your ship's papers, including your inward clearance.

Services

Frank Ågren's Inboard Diesel is right at the entrance to the port. Frank is the main Volvo Penta dealer for the Windwards. He does warranty work and can supply spares somewhat more cheaply than you may pay in other islands. He has a hot line to the factory and, being Swedish, he speaks the same language as the engine. Anyone having Volvo Penta problems should give him a call. Those visiting Frank can come inside the port where he has a couple of reserved spaces. Frank and Christer, his second in command, speak perfect English and are happy to work on other brands of inboard diesel. New equipment is now being added for the testing and repair of electrical problems including all brands of starter and alternator.

Next door, Marc Eugene at Renovboats offers first class fiberglass repairs and spray painting. He also works in the Fort de France haul-out facility.

Case Pilote

Expansion of the fishing port with fuel pumps and customs are eventually planned. Meanwhile, diesel can be fetched from the gas station in jugs.

Ashore

Case Pilote is charming and quiet. The church is worth a visit and it is pleasant to stroll around the town. For topping up provisions visit 8 à Huit, whose name gives you their weekday hours. For a breakfast of fresh French bread and croissants, visit Snack Bar de La Plage right on the waterfront. Manager Bertrand will greet you with a big smile.

Snack le Pilote [$D] in the main square opens from 0800-1500 and 1700-2000. They serve tasty daily specials and in the evening they also fire up the pizza oven. They sell telephone cards.

For a fancier dinner, visit Le Maniba [$B-C, closed Sunday and Monday]. It is small and a little formal (wear long trousers). Owner Monique Rangon specializes in French/Créole food at reasonable prices. Her filet of fish in maracudja (passion fruit) sauce is excellent. The maître d' speaks English.

Water sports

Diving and snorkeling off the headland just south of the marina are very good. Huge rocks rise from 70 feet and the whole area is filled with brightly colored sponges, corals and fish. If you don't have your own gear, contact the Case Pilote Diving Club. For those interested in wildlife, there is a bat cave in the cliffs behind the snorkeling area.

FORT DE FRANCE

When approaching Fort de France from Cap Salomon it is hard to see at a glance exactly where the harbor is, as the whole surrounding area is built up, including a huge hotel and some apartment blocks at Schoelcher, a couple of miles west of Fort de France. As you approach, you can iden-

tify the main yacht anchorage by the prominent slab-sided fort wall and all the yachts at anchor.

Fort de France is the largest and liveliest city in the Windwards. It is fun to shop here and you are in the center of many yacht services.

The Government has built a large new cruise ship dock. Customs and immigration have their premises in the adjoining compound.

To keep yachts out of the way the government has allowed a small anchorage area which we show on our sketch chart. When cruise ships are not expected on the dock, yachts anchor in a considerably wider area.

Holding in the bay is fair in soft mud. Frequent ferries make the anchorage rolly. Those who prefer a quieter spot should clear in here and then sail over to Anse Mitan, Anse a L'Ane or Trois Ilets which are connected to town by efficient ferries.

Those seeking repairs can find a work

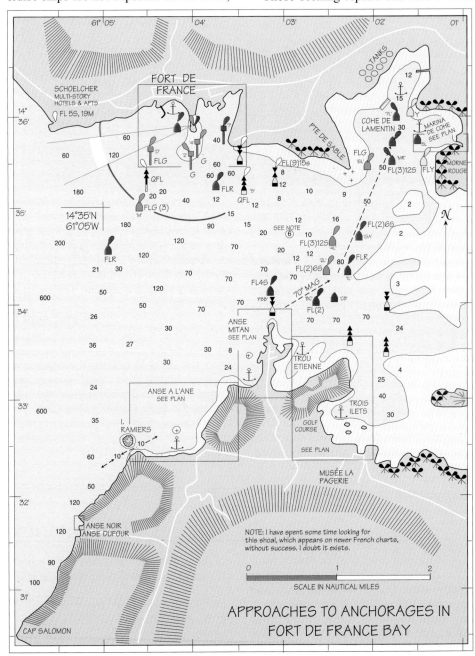

NOTE: I have spent some time looking for this shoal, which appears on newer French charts, without success. I doubt it exists.

SCALE IN NAUTICAL MILES

APPROACHES TO ANCHORAGES IN
FORT DE FRANCE BAY

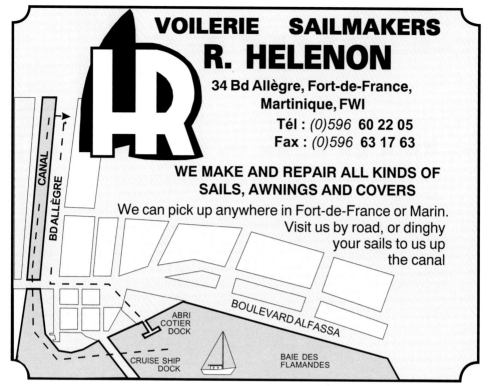

berth in the Baie de Tourelles. If you are heading east (or southeast toward Anse Mitan), keep well clear of the shoals off the fort. It is possible to cut somewhat inside the green buoys, but to be on the safe side, go around them.

Regulations

The customs and immigration office is in the new cruise ship compound. If the gate right on the waterfront is closed, there is another round the back. (I have noticed that those adverse to walking edge their way into the compound round the rocks past the gate.) Customs open daily 0730-1100, 1430-1700, including holidays. There are no overtime charges.

Services

There is a good dinghy tie-up at the Abri Cotier dock. There are bins for garbage nearby. For cooking gas, take a taxi in the morning to Antilles Gas in Zone Industriel Californie. You can get fuel and water in the new CBS dock in Baie de Tourelles, along with many other services which we describe in this section.

Helenon is a good, reliable sailmaker with many years of experience in Martinique. He will repair your sails or make new ones, along with awnings and biminis. He is conveniently located and easily found upstairs next to Littoral at 32 Blvd. Allègre (the canal road). You can dinghy up the canal to the outside of his shop where there is a ladder going up the wall. He will help hoist your sails over the wall or he will collect them from anywhere in Fort de France. He will also come collect sails or measure for a new sail in Marin. Helenon has a monster machine that can sew any thickness of cloth, even a cruise ship sail.

Sea Services on Rue Deproge is Martinique's largest chandlery with a wide range of products, including International Paints, 316 stainless fasteners, Plastimo tenders and liferafts, charts and guides. They stock a good range of electrical equipment from wire and connectors to solar panels, Ampair wind generators, diesel generators, fridges, watermakers and batteries. They have doubled the size of their shop and now have deck shoes, a little nautical clothing, many decorative nautical items and furniture. Owners Jacques and Ciarla speak perfect English (Ciarla is English Canadian), so people having problems with French come by to seek advice on anything and everything. Jacques loves to do rigging and they have a full rigging service, from a dinghy locking line upwards. Their on-the-spot swaging works for up to 12mm wire and they do larger diameters by order. Sea Services is open weekdays right through from 0830-1730 and on Saturdays from 0830-1230. If you are down island and need something, give them a call, they can take your order, arrange credit card payment by fax, and Fedex it to you. Sea Services regularly deliver anti-fouling

paint to all Martinique haul-out facilities.

You can find excellent buys at Plus Nautique, a shop with second hand, discounted and discontinued goods, as well as many new brands including Narwhal inflatables, Facnor roller furling and their own brand of anti-fouling. It is hard not to stay for hours, poking around looking for bargains, and the range is immense. Shackles, second hand sails, "pack away" motor bikes, new snorkeling gear, old pulpits, bits of teak, pumps, diving gear, stoves, a good selection of new stainless fittings, tubing, plus many sizes and types of rope are all on display. You can leave unwanted gear here for sale on commission. Prices of second

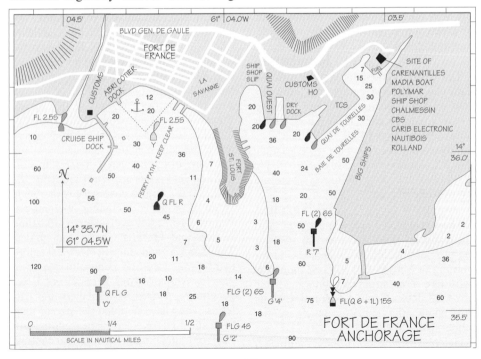

FORT DE FRANCE
ANCHORAGE

To Baie de Tourelles

Fort de Image

hand stock vary considerably, depending on the owner's evaluation. Sorting out the best bargains is part of the fun. Plus Nautique has a catalog which includes many of their regular products and they will Fedex orders anywhere in the Caribbean. To find Plus Nautique, walk down Rue de la République till you cross the big Blvd. du Général de Gaulle. The road soon comes to a T-junction. Turn left on the road before the T-junction and look out on your left hand side.

Barnacles bugging you? Need a new stainless fuel tank? There is a new, clean yacht services compound in Baie de Tourelles which should solve all your problems. You can dinghy there, bring the yacht or check it out on foot. The walk to Quai de Tourelles is about ten minutes from town. Head past Quai Ouest on the main road out of town. Turn right immediately after the big customs (douanes) building which is on the right side of the road. Follow the road and turn left at the junction. This leads you to the new basin. At the heart of this compound is the haul-out run by CareneAntilles who also have the larger facility in Marin. Dredging is planned in the canal past the travel lift slip where it is currently shoal.

look after your yacht while you go away.

Michel Lelande's Ship Shop chandlery is on the premises, with everything you need for your haul out as well as general marine hardware, diving, fishing and snorkeling gear. Michel speaks English, is happy to help with sending faxes and is a major yacht mail drop: Ship Shop, Baie des Tourelles, 97200 Fort de France. Michel also runs Servi-Marine to carry out any repairs or work you may need

M. Josefa's Coopemar started as a basic fishermen's cooperative to get better prices on nets, lines and other fishing gear. As fishing has become more sophisticated so has their range of products and now they have all kinds of things which will appeal to yachtspeople from fishing gear through to electronics and antifouling.

Jean Pierre and François Chalmessin can work wonders with stainless and aluminum, including argon welding, bending, building and machining. Whether you have a broken winch or want a new pulpit or water tank – they can do it. They are also wizards at fixing most marine cooking stoves.

Also into metal work is Jean-Michel Rolland who has tig and mig welders and can fabricate in aluminum, stainless and bronze.

Troublesome engine or gearbox, or want to upgrade your machinery with new equipment? Go talk to Pierre and his wife Nichol at Madia Boat. They can help sort out your problems. Pierre is an agent for BMW, Yanmar, Perkins and Ford, and works on all other makes of motor (both normal and turbo-charged), including Volvo, Holset, Garrett and KKK. They are also agents for Hurth, Borg Warner and Twin Disk gear boxes and will work on other types. Pierre is a boating man himself, with a high speed jet motor boat he uses for fishing and trips to the Grenadines.

Alain Belat [VHF:16, 68] is the man to visit for electronic equipment or repair. At his company, called Carib Electronic Engineering, he keeps Navico and President electronic gear in stock and repairs most brands.

Richard Dupin at Nautibois will have a go at fixing anything wooden, from replanking

The haul out has a 30-ton marine hoist and everything you could need in the way of work. Language is not a problem as most people speak some English. If you have trouble finding anyone, go to Max at Polymar and he will help. Polymar is a complete fiberglass shop. They will do anything from repairing your hull or refinishing it with a top quality spray paint job, to custom building hard tops or tanks. Polymar builds a good line of dinghies and they also sell marine ply which can be bought cut to size. Resins, paints, foam and a little marine hardware are available, plus they can fill diving tanks and they sell Scubapro gear.

Jean Luc Cassius de Linval at CBS runs the fuel dock, selling diesel, gasoline, ice, and oils. Jean has an outboard shop and is agent for Mariner and Mercury, though he stocks spares for, and will repair, all makes. The major part of this shop is in Marin but he can accept work and organize new engines from Baie des Tourelles. Jean is also a yacht broker, he rents cars, including some inexpensive older models, and he will

Madia Boat

Repairs - Sales
Réparations - Vente

Engines :
Yanmar Mercruiser
Perkins Volvo

Gear Boxes :
Hurth Borg-Warner
Twin Disc

Centre de Carénage -Baie des Tourelles
97200 Fort-de-France
Tél : (0)596 **63.10.61 Fax :** (0)596 **63.48.70**

Polymar

Quai Ouest 97200 Fort-de-France
Tél: (0)596 70 62 88 Fax: (0)596 60 10 97
e-mail   polymar@sagi.fr

Materials
Marine plywood, glass cloth and rovings,
resins and paints

Workmanship
Specialists in polyester and epoxy
construction and repairs

Paintwork
Spray painting

Construction
Sailing, rowing and outboard dinghies
and tenders

Diving
Dive tank refills. Dive equipment and
accessories (SCUBAPRO)

Salvage
Recovery and flotation

Travelift 25 tons
Rack storage
Electricity 220 v - 380 v

CARENANTILLES
CARENAGE CENTER
Tel : 0596 63 76 74 - Fax : 0596 71 66 83

Fort-de-France
Baie des Tourelles
e-mail : carenmarin@mail.sasi.fr
(Credit cards accepted)

Complete haul-out and repair facilities
Gas, fuel, ice, water, (all services).

• **Global Impex**   Tel: 0596 72 83 927
Agent Mariner, Mercury, Bayliner, Wellcraft.   Fax : 0596 72 48 85

• **Polymar**   Tel: 0596 70 62 88
Glass fibre construction, repairs and painting.   Fax: 0596 60 10 97

• **Servimarine**   Tel: 0596 73 73 99
Haul-out, painting, technical assistance.   Fax: 0596 70 13 02

• **Carib Electronic Engineering**
Electricity and electronics. Tel: 0596 60 07 00/Fax: 0596 63 60 14

• **Cadet-petit**   Tel: 0596 63 79 17
Electricity - rewinding alternators, starter motors, etc.

• **Nautic-Bois**   Tel: 0596 71 95 74
Fitting-out, carpentry and repairs in wood   Fax: 0596 71 82 33
and epoxy.

• **Rolland** Jean-Michel   Tel: 0596 71 49 28
Repairs, aluminium and stainless welding.

• **Madia Boat**   Tel: 0596 63 10 61
Marine engineers.   Fax: 0596 63 48 70

• **Coopemar** Tel: 0596 73 37 54-Fax: 0596 63 76 63
Provisioning and chandlery cooperative of Martinique.

• **Chalmessin**   Tel: 0596 60 03 79/596 60 03 75
Fabrication in aluminium and stainless steel.   Fax: 0596 63 49 67

• **Shipchandler**
Baie des Tourelles.   Tel: 0596 73 73 99 - Fax: 0596 70 13 02

• **Caraibes Boat Services**
Fuelling, etc..   Tel: 0596 7173 91- Fax: 0596 71 73 96

• **Snack L'Orient**   Tel: 0596 71 51 86
Restaurant / Bar.

a hull to building fine interior joinery. He is also familiar with the West-epoxy wood construction system.

An inexpensive restaurant in the compound makes life easy while you work.

If you are too long, wide, heavy or ugly to haul elsewhere, you can arrange to be slipped alongside a ship in the huge Martinique dry dock which will take anything up to a cruise ship. Camaco, a paint shop and liferaft repair depot, is next door.

Also in this area, on Quai Ouest, is Multicap Caraibes [VHF:68], the largest boatyard in the Windwards. You will see their ferries crossing Fort de France Bay and their fast catamaran yachts chartering up and down the islands. They also build a variety of custom dive boats, fishing boats and racing yachts. Multicap Caraibes build and repair in foam core, wood/epoxy, aluminum or steel to the French Bureau Veritas standard. They are the main repair station for large multihulls, and they have their own 60-ton crane to bring them out on the quay. They will also haul out problem boats, such as racing boats with exceptionally deep keels. Famous single-hander Isabel Autissier hauled her boat here with its draft of about 12 feet and stepped off her boat into one of the upstairs windows. They regularly repair aluminum masts. Christian Hernandez runs the yard and as part of their repair service they have a good mechanical workshop, but they will only work on Volvo, Lombardini, Nanni, Man or Baudouin inboards and Suzuki outboards. They keep a good range of new inboard engines and outboards in stock. Multicap Caraibes also has a chandlery shop. You will be helped by Jocelyne who speaks good English. They have a broad selection of materials and fittings, including sheets of marine ply, resins, cloth, Andersen and Fredericksen winches, electrical panels, anchor winches and light fittings. They are agents for Caribe dinghies, Northern Lights generators and Sea Recovery desalinators.

If you want to fix your own Perkins engine, spares may be available from Madia Boat, Mecanique Plaisance or at Croquet, out by Euromarché not far from the big

MULTICAP CARAIBES

Construction and repairs

Yachts, workboats, 6-30 meters.
Sail and power, multi and monohulls.
Bois/epoxy, fiberglass, aluminium and steel

Engineering & Repair Shop

Volvo, Lombardini, Baudouin.
Northern Lights Generators, Suzuki Outboards, Sea Recovery Watermakers

Materials

Sicomin epoxies,
Glass fibre, carbon fibre, Kevlar.
Aluminium & stainless tube,
bar and plate.

Chandlery
(Fredericksen/Andersen)

Hatches, winches, windlasses, blocks, deck fittings, sterngear, etc...

Tél : (0)596 71.41.81 Fax : (0)596 71.41.83
VHF 16/67

Caterpillar sign. Manager Jean Trudo speaks perfect English. The Volvo Penta parts store is on Rue J. Cazotte north of La Savanne.

Injectors or injection pumps need servicing? Martinique Diesel, near the airport, is the place to take them. They service all kinds except Caterpillar and Cummins and have a vast stock of filters, separators and other parts.

If you need something transshipped through customs, check with Jean Marc Berté at Quai de Tourelles.

Ashore

(See our Fort de France plan and Fort de France anchorage chart.)

Changing money in Fort de France is now easy at the best rates, thanks to efficient little change places like Change Caraibes, which is at the Savanne end of Rue Ernest Déproge and opens weekdays 0800-1730, Saturdays 0800-1230. Another money changing shop, called Martinique Change, is at the Blvd. Allègre end of Rue Victor Hugo, and yet another is at the La Savanne end of the same road.

Littoral, at 32-34 Blvd. Allègre, lies next to the canal where many of the local fishing boats tie up. Wander in and peruse their wonderful selection of fishing equipment, probably the largest in Martinique, along with snorkeling gear, ropes, diving knives and some yacht chandlery.

Bricogite, next to Sea Services, is a useful hardware and do-it-yourself shop. They carry a big range of tools, materials, electrical wire and fittings. In addition, they keep a stock of interior and exterior grade ply which they will cut into squares and sell by the meter.

SCIM, on Rue François Arago caters to many kinds of sports enthusiasts and their shop includes a corner with fishing gear. A larger range of marine stock is kept at their store near Euromarché at Dillon. They have the Evinrude sales and repair agency and keep many models in stock.

Anyone need personal protection? Armes Levalois on Rue Déproge sells small spray cans of CS gas.

Provisioning in Martinique is a pleasure. When you are ready to stock up on duty free stores, including wines, beers and liquors, try The Caribbean Supplier (TCS) [VHF:72] on Quai de Tourelles. While there, you can visit the Sea Explorer, their duty-free visitor's shop with jewelry, watches and gifts. TCS will deliver your order to the Abri Cotier dock so you can take it on board after you have cleared out.

The nearest good supermarket in town is Match which has one branch upstairs in a department store and another farther up Rue de la République. Super H is the largest store in town with good cheese, paté, meat and produce sections. The open air market in the front offers the best selection of fruits and vegetables. None of these stores currently delivers, but Super H will call you a taxi. Leader Price, opposite Sea Services, is a good sized market and has bargain prices on cans and dry goods. For a first rate butcher, try Tailame, they will vacuum pack and freeze your purchases for you.

For the fun of shopping in a really big supermarket, you will need to visit the malls out of town where small shops surround gargantuan, modern supermarkets,

called hypermarchés. Buses go to all these from the western end of Blvd. du Général de Gaulle, by the cemetery, or you can take a taxi from in front of La Savanne. Ask the supermarket staff to call a return taxi for you.

The closest is La Ronde Pointe in the Schoelcher direction and it can be reached via the Schoelcher Communal Taxi which leaves from the Abri Cotier dock. The energetic may prefer to walk: it is rather uphill but half an hour will get you there at an easy pace. Close by, the Bellevue Commercial Center has a first rate wine shop which is owned by Alain Nicholas. He used to be a restaurateur and can provide helpful advice on his wines. In the same center you will find Jacky's Surf Paradise, with everything for windsurfing. The Cora Mall at Cluny is in the same direction but somewhat farther.

Euromarché is in the other direction, at Dillon, on the road to the airport. Considerably farther down the same road is La Galleria, a mall with a Hyper U supermarket and about 16 other shops. For a selection of case lots of foods at wholesale prices, try Leader Price much farther along the road that passes Euromarché.

There are numerous restaurants in Fort de France. We will mention a few. Jean Dogue's Le Pub [$C-D], across the road from the side of Sea Services, is an English style pub with friendly staff and the latest music at night. They have an inexpensive lunch menu every weekday and their nightly special (Wednesday to Saturday), served with a glass of champagne and a glass of wine, is increasingly popular.

The Crew [$B-C, closed Saturday and Sunday evenings] is reliable, easy to find and relatively inexpensive. They serve good French food, and while it is crowded with businessmen for lunch, it is usually easy to find space there at dinner.

Le Planteur [$C, closed Sunday and for lunch on Monday] is upstairs on Rue de la Liberté, with pleasant views over both La Savanne and the harbor. They serve good Créole food. At noon the air conditioning is a blessed contrast from the midday heat.

West Indies [$C-D, closed Sundays] is a pleasant upmarket bar and ice cream parlor which also serves meals. A great place to sit comfortably outside and watch life go by. They have live music most nights after 2100.

For fancier quality at a price to match, try El Racor [$A-B] on Rue Lazare Carnot, north of La Savanne, which opens for lunch from Monday to Friday and for dinner from Tuesday to Saturday.

At the other end of the scale, trucks parked on the east side of La Savanne towards the northern corner in the evenings put out plastic tables and chairs and serve barbecued conch, chicken, rice, stews and more.

Several other places are open only for lunch. Fancy a smoked salmon sandwich? Then Lina's [$D] on Rue Victor Hugo is just the ticket, with elegant sandwiches and salads and wine by the glass in a pleasant air-conditioned house with seating on two floors. Leave some room for dessert and excellent coffee.

Many take their lunch in the main market (between Rue Victor Hugo & Rue Antoine Siger), among the bustle of people selling

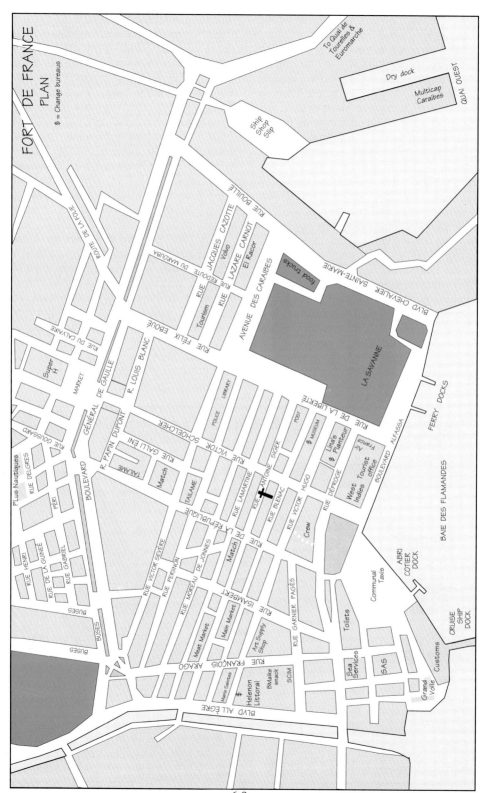

fruits, tropical flowers, exotic alcoholic drinks, souvenirs of all kinds and straw goods. Tables are set out both at one end of the market and upstairs. About half a dozen small restaurateurs [$D] offer typical Créole meals at a bargain price. There is also a fresh fruit juice stand where you choose your fruit and watch it being juiced.

Marie Saintes [$C] is a small but fine Créole restaurant which is very popular with the locals, so go early. Another less crowded lunch spot is Bmalke Snack [$C-D] which serves food with a Syrian flavor.

Wherever you eat, beware of those little green peppers. They are often put beside the food as decoration, and they are the hottest of hot.

Fort de France is the place for both fashionable shopping and souvenir hunting. There are two handicraft markets, one right on La Savanne and the other on Rue de la République near Rue Moreau de Jonnes. You will find everything from jewelry to handbags, paintings and varnished palm fruits. Half the artists and carvers in Haiti must be kept busy whipping out an over-whelming number of coconut trees, banana plants, fruits and models in balsa wood. These are available all over town.

When it comes to shopping, Fort de France is the only place in the Windwards for Paris fashions and stylish clothing shops. Start by wandering down Rue Victor Hugo from La Savanne. As you cross other roads, turn now and again when tempted. Return by Rue Blenac and if it all gets to be too much, try Au Printemps which takes up the corner between Rue Antoine Siger and Rue Schoelcher. This is a department store, where everything is laid out so that it is easy to see.

If you are spending some time in Martinique, pay an early visit to the main tourist office. They will answer your questions and fill your arms with informative maps, books and brochures. Make sure you ask for their dining guide. A second tourist office on Rue Lazare Carnot has detailed information on Fort de France.

Do you have photos to develop? Photo First develops print film and does E6 slide processing (Fujicolor and Ectachrome).

The quality is normally good.

History buffs should visit the little pre-Columbian museum on Rue de la Liberté [closed Saturday afternoon and Sunday]; architecture buffs the Schoelcher Library.

Fort de France is a convenient starting point to see the island as there are buses and communal taxis that go to all major towns and villages. Currently most of them start right outside the (old Abri Cotier) dinghy dock, If you are going to the airport, take the "Ducos" car. The charge is less than ten francs. Most of the suburban buses go from the western end of Avenue Général de Gaulle. These include buses to Dillon, Balata and Didier. Buses to Lamentin go from the east side of La Savanne. Taxis may be found by La Savanne.

The Caribs called Martinique "Madinina" (Island of Flowers). To see a superb flower collection, take a trip to Jardin de Balata, a privately owned and perfectly maintained garden high in the mountains behind Fort de France, near the Pitons de Carbet. These gardens are the result of over 20 years of work by the owner, Jean Philippe Those, aided by a team of gardeners. There are acres of carefully laid out tropical plants, a small stream and ponds. The views south toward St. Lucia and St. Vincent and north into the rain forest are excellent. Enjoy the lush vegetation at several small seating areas. The entrance fee is about 30 francs per person, but it is the kind of place where you could happily spend an hour or two. A bus to Balata leaves from the western end of Blvd. Général de Gaulle. Now that there is a bypass around Fort de France, Le Jardin de Balata is also accessible by rental car from Anse Mitan or Fort de France. This makes it possible to continue your exploration north through the rain forest, returning by a coast road.

If you are in Martinique in early June and would like to get to know some local sailors, join in for the big race and party time of the Banana's Cup. It is sponsored by Multicap Caraibe and Plus Nautiques and arranged by the yacht club. Either can give you details.

RIVIÈRE SALÉE

Rivière Salée is an industrial area back from the sea. However, there are several businesses here that work with yachts. West Indies Nautic Distribution (WIND) is run by Bruno and Isabelle Marmousez. They specialize in paint, epoxy system 3, polyester resins, fiberglass materials and the latest cores. Paints and varnishes include Awlgrip and Epifanes and the tools for applying them. They also sell Seajet antifouling. Their prices are excellent, they are very knowledgeable about their products and can give good advice on epoxy. You don't have to visit Rivière Sallée personally. Pick up their catalog at either Littoral, Le Ship, Mecanique Plaisance or Plus Nautiques, or call Bruno on the phone (he speaks excellent English) and he will happily deliver to your boat.

Pierre Leandre at ETPI is the man to see if in need of metal coatings. He can sandblast and prepare any metal, then galvanize, chrome, cadmium plate or polish it. Pierre can hot dip or spray hot metals so you can galvanize your entire yacht if you wish. He has a machine shop and fixes winches or any other broken part. Pierre Leandre, Sr., his father, spent some years in Canada and speaks perfect English. They do excellent work.

North Sails is represented by Gianni Bruno at Tech Sails Voilerie. This is a one-man operation run by Bruno who is very pleasant to deal with. Bruno speaks just enough English – if you speak slowly. He will collect your sails for repair anywhere in Martinique and he does canvas work such as biminis and awnings. He has a connection with Andrew Dove's North Sails in Guadeloupe and can order new North Sails.

COHE DE LAMENTIN

(See also our "Approaches to Anchorages in Fort de France Bay," page 60)

This murky backwater is only of interest if you need to get close to the airport, are hiding from a hurricane or an ex-wife, or need a place to leave your boat while you go away.

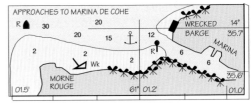

To approach from Anse Mitan, start by the black and yellow buoy just off Pte. du Bout and head about 70 degrees magnetic which will join you to the main channel. Leave all the red buoys to starboard and the green ones to port. From Fort de France, head east, going outside the green buoys marking the shoals off the fort, then head about 130 degrees magnetic until you join the main channel from Anse Mitan to Cohe de Lamentin. The troublesome shoal is the one extending from Pte. des Sable. The water on this route is mainly 10 to 12 feet deep, but watch for unmarked wrecks or obstructions.

Marina de Cohe is a somewhat strange,

quiet, hot creek tucked in the mangroves. It should be generally safe as the grounds are patrolled by dogs that make the hound of the Baskervilles look like a playful puppy. As you approach, be sure to leave the red buoy off Morne Rouge to starboard. The entrance to the marina is hidden down a small creek which is marked by a wrecked barge. Stay center channel and do not cut the corner on the southern shore, which is where most people go aground. Yachts of around six-foot draft can get in.

There is another dock (usually full of local boats) tucked up in the top corner of Cohe de Lamentin.

TROIS ILETS

For a charming and photogenic town, not yet overrun with visitors, visit Trois Ilets. Most houses are old, built of wood or stone, and capped with fish-scale tile roofs. There is a handsome square between the church and the town hall and if you are thinking of becoming ill, you will not find a prettier hospital. This pleasant area offers several scenic, quiet and secure places to

anchor, some of which are protected enough to ride out a hurricane.

Approach from Anse Mitan by leaving the black and yellow buoys off Pte. du Bout and Pte. de la Rose to starboard. Give the shoals along the coast between Pte. de la Rose and Pte. Angboeuf reasonable clearance. You find the easiest anchorage by following the coast in from Pointe

Angboeuf and anchoring off the golf course. There is one four-foot shoal, but otherwise the approach is easy. The approach into town is between the islands. A line between Pte. Angboeuf and the dark-roofed shelter on the waterfront is helpful and the new green buoy makes the approach easier. Approach the buoy from east of the above-mentioned line and, after rounding the buoy, turn a little east again to avoid the shoals off the island to the west.

Ashore

More yachts use this port now that there is a ferry to Fort de France. It runs about once an hour, starting at 0610 and the last

ferry leaves Fort de France at 1745.

A short walk into the town will find you most essentials: a local market (open every day), a post office, a butcher, boulangerie and patisserie, pharmacy and a couple of general stores. There is a tourist office in the market square and should you wish to rent a car, the woman at the tourist office will send you in the right direction. The four restaurants are delightfully welcoming and friendly. Two face the main road through town. Les Passages du Vent [$D] is owned by Laurence, the artist who painted all the pictures on the walls. Her talent shows in the appealing renovation of her restaurant's pretty old stone buildings. Seating is either inside or out in an enclosed courtyard. Her menu is not huge but has plenty of choices, including Créole and French dishes and

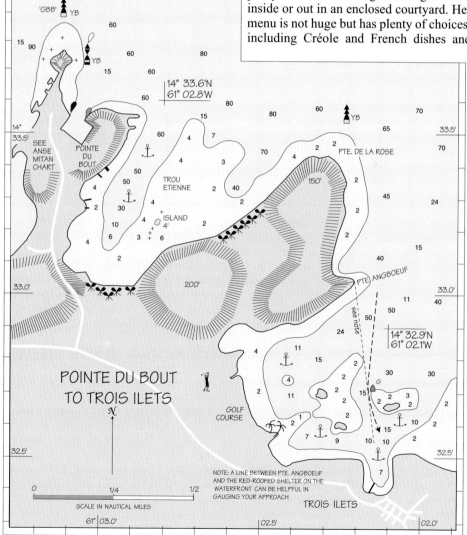

POINTE DU BOUT TO TROIS ILETS

73

Trois Ilets

homemade pasta dishes.

Green [$D] has a large patio with a view of the street. They are open every day except Sunday from 0930 to 2200 to serve Créole food at an affordable price. Their specialty is skewered meats and seafood. Rue Trois Chandelles runs east from the church. Walk down and look left to find Restaurant Reverbere, a pleasant, informal family-style local restaurant whose menu offers a full selection of Créole food, plus a few Asian, African and American dishes. Esther, one of the family, speaks some English. You will pass Le Bomaki on the waterfront as you walk into town. Look for an informal bamboo structure. Owners Kiki and Bolo offer local dishes and brochettes. They usually have live music on Fridays and Saturdays.

This is one of the few places in the islands where you can play golf overlooking your yacht in the bay below.

TROU ETIENNE

Just occasionally, the weather goes crazy and storms from afar create huge swells which make both Fort de France and Anse Mitan untenable. If this happens, pop round to the other side of Pte. du Bout and anchor in Trou Etienne. As you come from the west, leave both yellow and black buoys to starboard and as you enter the bay, do not go too close to shore. There are many moorings and the water is either rather deep or too shallow. If you are anchoring on chain, choose your spot carefully. Docks and roads are private, but there is a small public access path just north of the hotel. The hotel is quite conspicuous. See also our Anse Mitan chart.

ANSE MITAN

Anse Mitan was one of the original tourist areas in Martinique. It is part of the Trois Ilets district, and the head of the peninsula is called Pte. du Bout. There are beaches, boutiques, restaurants, lots of life and it's a great place for people watching. Several ferry services run to Fort de France. Some operate out of the marina at Pte. du Bout, others from the Langouste Dock on Anse Mitan. (This one also services Anse a L'Ane). Both use high speed ferries. There is a discount when you buy a return ticket, but then you must return with the same company and this may take longer. Marina ferries start at around 0600 and finish at about 2300. They run regularly between 0700 and 1900, often about every 15 minutes. There is an hour-long lunch break after the 1300 ferry. From the Langouste Dock most ferries run at either ten to the hour or on the hour. They return from Fort de France at half past the hour (except 1320

instead of 1330). Times change, so check the notice boards on the docks.

Anse Mitan is attractive to yachts, and though there are often around a hundred boats at anchor, it is not overcrowded.

When approaching Anse Mitan, the main danger is the reef lying 200 yards west of the Bakoua Dock. Yachts are often anchored all around this reef. It is marked by a small red and black buoy. Anchor anywhere among the other yachts. Holding is good in sand, but poor on patches of coral. Leave a couple of hundred feet in front of the beach clear for swimmers and leave the channel clear for the ferry. The no-anchoring areas are marked by yellow buoys, which occasionally stray.

On those very rare occasions, when there is a bad northwesterly swell, go to the other side of Pte. du Bout to Trou Etienne, or to Trois Ilets.

Services

The Ponton du Bakoua [VHF:16, 68] is a good service-oriented, mini-marina on a single dock with berthing space along both sides. Yachts of any size with a maximum draft of 16', can come along the outside.

The inside is limited to yachts drawing less than six and a half feet. Take some care on the approach to the inside as rocks come out a fair way from shore. There is one rock in particular that makes one of the spaces suitable only for catamarans. Manager Olivier Carniaux speaks English and if you call on the VHF he will help you find your way in. France Caraibes Charter is based here. At the end of the dock a cleverly-designed octagonal fuel dock accommodates several yachts at one time. Diesel fuel (duty free for charter yachts which have cleared out), cube ice, gasoline and water are all available. Le Ponton Restaurant is described later. Along the dock there is water and 220-volt/50-cycle electricity. Full communications services, a laundry service, French cooking gas, showers and toilets are available. The marina office sells wine, beer, spirits, juices and soft drinks, if ordered in advance.

Somatras Marina (Marina Pte. du Bout) [VHF:9] is a small marina offering stern-to berthing with water and electricity. Short and long term berths are now often available. There is no fuel dock. Just behind the

Anse Mitan

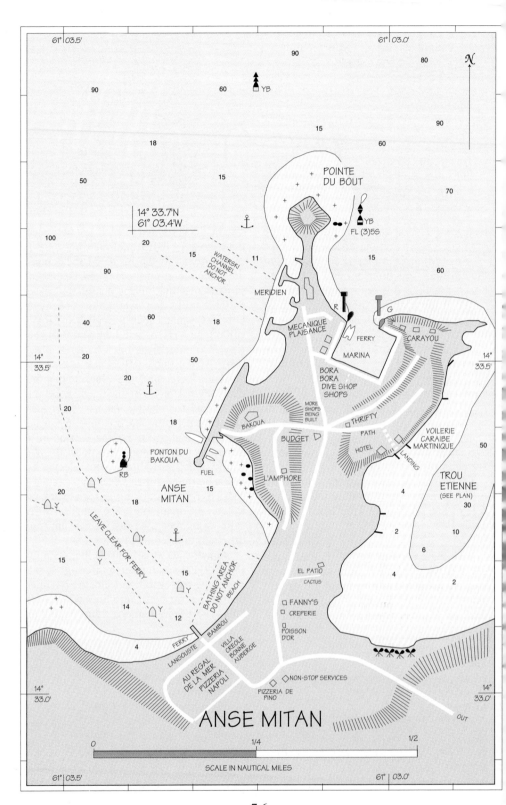

61° 03.5'   61° 03.0'

90   80

90   60   YB   N

15

18   90   90

15   60

50   POINTE
                        DU BOUT   70

14° 33.7'N
61° 03.4'W   YB
                                                    FL (3)5S

100   20

90   15   WATERSKI   11   15   60
                    CHANNEL
                    DO NOT
                    ANCHOR

40   60   18   MERIDIEN

20   60   R

20   MECANIQUE   G
                    PLAISANCE   CARAYOU
14°   50   FERRY
33.5'   MARINA   14°
20   18   33.5'

20   18   BORA
                                  BORA
                                  DIVE SHOP
                                  SHOPS   MORE
18   SHOPS   VOILERIE
                    BAKOUA   BEING   THRIFTY   CARAIBE
                                  BUDGET   BUILT   MARTINIQUE   50
            PONTON DU   PATH
20   BAKOUA   FUEL   HOTEL
         RB   LANDING
                                        L'AMPHORE   TROU
         ANSE   ETIENNE
20   MITAN   15   4   (SEE PLAN)
         Y   30
18
              Y   2   10
         Y   6
15   15   EL PATIO
         Y   CACTUS   4   2

14   Y   12   BATHING AREA   FANNY'S
                          DO NOT ANCHOR   CREPERIE
                    BEACH
         Y   POISSON
                    FERRY   BAMBOU   D'OR
4   LANGOUSTE   VILLA
                                  CREOLE
                    AU REGAL   BONNE
                    DE LA MER   AUBERGE   NON-STOP SERVICES
14°   PIZZERIA   14°
33.0'   NAPOLI   PIZZERIA DE   33.0'
                               PINO

                    ANSE MITAN   OUT

0   1/4   1/2

SCALE IN NAUTICAL MILES

61° 03.5'   61° 03.0'

LEAVE CLEAR FOR FERRY

marina, Pointe Service Laverie or Clean Cool can take care of your laundry, whether you want to do it yourself in their machines or have them do it for you. They open all day every day from 0730-1930 except Sunday when they close at midday. This marina is the base of the charter companies Star Voyage and Loca Boats. Loca Boats rents small power boats as well as yachts.

Patrice Caillot's Mecanique Plaisance is a complete shop and repair facility for everything to do with diesel engines on pleasure boats. They are agents for Perkins, Volvo, Westerbeke and Yanmar and keep a full line of yacht engines and generators in stock. Their shop sells everything from cutless bearings, shaft materials and stern glands to plumbing bits, alternators, electrical parts, gaskets, engine spares and a complete range of Racor filters. Patrice works mainly on the makes of engine he sells. He guarantees his work, and his equipment includes a complete machine shop. Part of the shop contains chandlery. This chandlery is connected to their larger chandlery in Marin, so if you don't see what you need, ask, they can bring it in. Patrice, his wife Viviane, and some of their staff speak English.

Hervé Lepault's Voilerie Caraibe Martinique [VHF:16] is a full sail loft where you can get anything made or repaired, from a new main to a bimini or sailboard cover. He has a department that specializes in boat cushions. Hervé builds sails with the well known French Incidences label and guarantee. The sails are computer designed in France with the latest technology and built in Hervé's loft. Hervé speaks English and if you call him from Anse Mitan on the radio, he will come by your boat and pick up your sail and deliver it back later. You can also visit his loft in Trou Etienne by foot or dinghy. (Look for the only dock with dinghies tied to it.)

Gottfried Strasser's Non-Stop Services offers all kinds of mechanical repairs, including engines, electrics and hydraulics. Gottfried is also a wizard with auto-pilots. He speaks English, French

and Spanish as well as his native German. He is the agent for several brands of marine equipment including Simrad, Robertson, Data Line, Shipmate and Hundsted. You can visit his office (look in the back of the big buildings next to Pizzeria de Pino) or call him on his mobile phone (0596-45-67-89).

Dominique Rousselon offers a complete sales and repair service for mechanics, electrics, electronics, air-conditioning, and refrigeration. He is agent for Sea Recovery, HRO and Aquaset watermakers, and Kohler Generators. You will find him in his Anse Mitan office at Ponton du Bakoua early in the morning till about 0830 and late in the afternoon after 1700.

You can change money at Martinique Change by the marina. They also sell telephone cards and are agents for DHL.

Ashore

The Bora Bora Supermarket is compact but complete. It is open all day every day, except Sundays and holidays when it is open mornings only. If you are buying a large

amount they will deliver it to the waterfront. It is the cheapest place to have a cold beer. Albert, the manager, speaks English. For fresh produce go to Jardin Créole, a greengrocer by the beach. For a really huge provisioning consider renting a car to drive to one of the giant supermarkets.

One of the delights of Anse Mitan is to stroll over to Deli France or Boule de Neige next door and have a breakfast of French coffee, fresh croissants and pain de chocolat. You can pick up your bread at Deli France and it is well worth returning to Boule de Neige later in the day for one of their wonderfully decadent ice cream specials. They also serve crêpes and are open till 2200.

The whole of Pointe du Bout is full of trendy little boutiques. There are more every year and you can find attractive clothing, jewelry, handicrafts, souvenirs, magazines and books. For those going on charter there are two flower shops down by the marina. There is also a pharmacy, massage parlor/beauty salon, two hairdressers and a shop that sells and develops film.

Anse Mitan is devoted to satisfying those on holiday, so there is plenty to do. This is a great place to rent a car and explore the island.

Once you hit the road there are plenty of roadside attractions. Not far away is a scenic 18-hole golf course where you can rent the gear you need. Opposite is La Pagerie Museum, the original home of Empress Josephine. Most of the old estate house burned down when she was three years old, but you can still see the old kitchen and the remains of the sugar mill on the plantation where she lived until she was 16 and left for France. Farther down the road, past Trois Ilets village, are a sugar cane museum and some potteries.

A few restaurants stand out among the dozens that line the streets. The hungry sailor cannot beat Fanny's [$C-D], a Créole restaurant which has become almost legendary for offering the best value for money. Her Créole cooking is excellent and very inexpensive. A menu is posted outside which nearly always includes fish, chicken and either shrimp or freshwater crayfish (ecrevisse). In addition, a changing daily special menu often has such delights as duck in pineapple sauce or filet mignon. Lobster is usually available, though it costs more. Shorts are acceptable and the outside tables are the most pleasant in the evening, though during lunch on a hot day the inside air conditioning may be preferred. It is currently open for lunch and dinner (starting 1900) every day except Wednesday. To get there from La Langouste dock, walk down the beach until you see the road on your right. Fanny's is right across the road. Do not mistake it for Le Corosol which is next door and offers a menu for about the same price, but is not the same. If you do not understand the menu, Fanny and some of her staff speak English.

For something more sumptuous and expensive, Régal de la Mer [$A-C] is attractive with a large tank of live lobsters kept in full view at the entrance. Everything from smoked salmon to ostrich meat are on the menu, including freshwater crayfish

ANSE MITAN

reef

Chez FANNY
Cafétéria Créole

Good food at the best price.... with a smile!

Anse-Mitan (facing beach car park) Tel :*(0)596* 66 04 34 *Ask for FANNY*

flambéd in aged rum or mixed seafood cooked in saffron sauce. Cheaper menus that will not break the bank are available.

Le Ponton at Ponton du Bakoua [$C-D, closed Sundays] has the most convenient location and is pleasantly laid out right on the dock. They open at about 0900 for coffee, and Happy Hour is 1800-1900. You can eat well here for a reasonable price and the range runs from sandwiches and specials at lunch to a well prepared dinner, sometimes enlivened by a musical group.

For the pleasure of sitting on the beach and watching scantily clad beautiful people, check out the snack bars Le Tam Tam [$C-D], Barracuda [$C-D] or the Hemmingway Pub [$A-D}. If you prefer to watch people clad in designer clothes, try one of the four restaurants by the marina. You get to sit in the open and watch all the strollers on the sidewalk. Le Marine is the oldest and has the best spot.

Two pleasant Italian restaurants offer pizza and pasta. Pizzeria Napoli [$C-D] has an attractive outside dining room and Pizzeria de Pino [$C-D] is on the road that runs back from La Langouste. Both have wood fired ovens and chefs that spin the pizzas in full view to amuse the kids.

There are several snack bars and restaurants down the road close to Fanny's, including Le Toucan, Cactus (Spanish cuisine), Chez Melin and O'Malley's Pub. Heading down the main road to the Anse Mitan Dock, Aux Poisson D'Or [$B-C] and La Villa Créole [$A-B] can both serve a good, but not cheap, Créole meal.

There is plenty of entertainment in Anse Mitan, though cover charges are often 100 to 200 francs. Some quite elegant floor shows depicting local life are often performed at the major hotels. A copy of "Choubouloute," available everywhere, will have the latest schedule. Both the Carayou and the Meridien have discos. One of the cheapest places for entertainment is the Bambou, a rough and ready beach hotel. They have entertainment here most nights and you can just go in and buy a drink.

Water sports

Sub Evasion (Subchandlers) is an excellent dive shop in the marina, open every day, but closed Monday mornings. It is in the square behind the restaurants, under the Bora Bora. Jean Jacques Aleci and Karine both speak English and are very helpful. They sell and rent a wide range of snorkeling and diving gear, including compressors. They have two new, covered, high-speed dive boats which enable them to offer all the best dives in Martinique. The boat for the more experienced divers leaves the marina at 0900 and 1430. The larger boat goes out on all-day trips. An underwater seawalk is available for those who want to keep their glasses on and their faces dry. They are happy to fill tanks and advise on dive sites. If you dinghy into the marina with your tanks in the middle of the day, it is easy to park your dinghy near their shop because all the day charter boats are out. Sub Evasion also has a shop in Marin, and on the land side they run land safaris in four wheel drive vehicles to remote areas.

ANSE A L'ANE

Anse a L'Ane

reef

Just around the corner from Anse Mitan is Anse a L'Ane, a sweet little bay with a charming beach. It makes a pleasant anchorage and is a lot quieter than Anse Mitan. It is serviced by the high speed ferries to Fort de France which run about once an hour. Check the times on their notice board.

Right in the middle of the bay, about one third of a mile offshore, there is a reef about four feet deep which is hard to spot. You can pass on either side to anchor in about 12 feet, sand bottom. Last time I passed it was marked by a yellow buoy of unknown reliability. Make sure your anchor is well dug in and leave plenty of room for the ferries which come into the dock. Anse a l'Ane is open to the northwest and should be avoided in times of heavy ground swells. When approaching from Anse Mitan, give

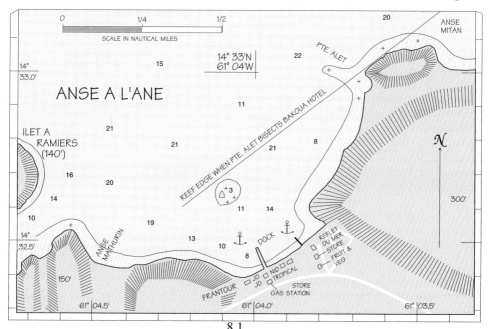

the first headland a wide clearance as it is all rocky and at Pte. Arlet shoals stick out 270 yards (see chart). When heading toward Cap Salomon from Anse a L'Ane, there is about 10 to 14 feet of water between Ilet a Ramiers and the mainland, enough for most yachts to pass.

Ashore

Anse a L'Ane is a holiday area, though much less built up than Anse Mitan. The beach has kept much of its original charm with seagrapes and palm trees providing shade. You can leave your dinghy on the inner end of the ferry dock and there are garbage bins ashore. There is a gas station on the main road and two small food stores, one opposite the gas station and the other on the road behind Reflet du Mer. Farther down the same road is Pomme Canelleis, a greengrocer who also sells tropical flowers and smoked chicken.

Ready for a meal out? For lunch you cannot do much better than Le Nid Tropical [$D], a snack bar which also sells pastries and ice cream. The advantage of this place is its superb location right on the beach look-ing at the bathers and the ocean.

Pignon sur Mer [$A-B] serves fine Créole food. The Calalou [$B-C] at the Frantour Hotel offers a beach bar lunch and elaborate dinners with entertainment most nights. Visit for the Martinique Ballet on Wednesdays. Check out the quaint, hand carved, wooden merry-go-round in the garden. Chez Jo Jo [$C] is an inexpensive restaurant and the local hot-spot, with live Zouk music most nights. It is informal and shorts are fine. Across the bridge, Reflet du Mer [$C] is cute and inexpensive. Not far away, opposite the gas station, is Ti-Calebasse [$B] which is good for fish, especially on Fridays. There are two Chez Ginette's. One is right on the main road near the beach, the other about 600 yards up the hill to the south. Both are good, but it is best to book in advance for the up-the-hill Chez Ginette.

Water Sports

The dive shop Corail Club Caraibes at the Frantour Hotel has several instructors who speak English.

ANSE NOIRE

Anse Noire is a tiny, deeply indented bay about half way between Ilet a Ramiers and Cap Salomon. It should be avoided in northerly swells, but is otherwise well protected. Small colorful cliffs rise on the southern headland and there is a steep hill on the northern one. Palms line the black sand beach at the head of the bay and a large fancy dock juts out from the beach. Behind the beach a steep jungly valley rises into the mountains. Anse Noire is a popular day time anchorage, especially on the weekends, but usually is deserted and peaceful at night. The wind swings in all directions. Just south of Anse Noire is a small fishing village called Anse Dufours with a white sand beach. Anse Dufours is a good lunchtime anchorage, but do not stay overnight as you will be in the way of the fishermen.

Ashore

It is pleasant just to sit and watch the kingfishers and other birds on the cliffs. An

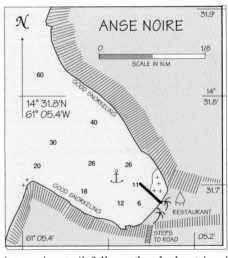

interesting trail follows the shady strip of riverine forest up the river behind the beach (river bed in the dry season) right up to the main road.

Hidden behind the vegetation, Restaurant Anse Noire [$C, closed Mondays] has more the feeling of the Pacific than the Caribbean with its tall thatched roof and wooden benches and three rental chalets. Owners Viviane Eglantine and Claude Castex offer an excellent seafood menu. Their fish, grilled and served whole covered in herbs with a separate sauce, is delicious, as is their lobster. They only open for lunch.

Alternatives are Desir's Sable D'Or [$C-D, closed Tuesday] which specializes in fresh seafood and Créole meat dishes at reasonable prices. To get there, climb the steps up the cliff and walk a short way up the road. For lunch there is also Snack Chez Nini [$D] in Anse Dufours.

Water Sports

The snorkeling around the bay and headlands is excellent. There are small walls, crevices and rocks decorated with sponges, tube worms and anemones which attract a large variety of smaller fish. Electric rays, octopuses, squid and a variety of sea cucumbers are often found here.

GRAND ANSE D'ARLET

Grand Anse D'Arlet is a picturesque fishing village set on a white sand beach which houses a fleet of dug out fishing pirogues. It is becoming popular with tourists and the northern corner has a touch of the Riviera, with brightly colored beach umbrellas. A fancy new walkway runs behind the beach. Yachts should anchor on either side of the bay to leave the center free for the fishermen. This area may be marked by yellow buoys. Avoid sailing too close to the center of the village as a shoal area extends seaward several hundred feet. The best spot is in the southeastern corner of the bay which has a sand bottom eight to 30 feet deep.

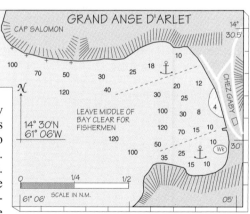

Services

Veve Cariabes is a small laundry along the beachfront walkway. If you need water, check out the dive shop Localizé. They have a floating hose from their shop in about six feet of water. They use it to supply their own boats but have been known to sell to visitors.

Ashore

There are several small food stores ashore which sell ice. When you get to the dock turn in either direction and you will come to one.

Something to look forward to in this bay is a meal at Chez Gaby [$C, closed Sunday night and all Monday], a small, informal and clean restaurant just behind the main dock. It is run by Gabrielle, originally from Germany, and her husband, Marcel, who spent many years working there. Here you can enjoy a fine French/Créole meal at a good price. Seafood is always featured and they often have lobster in their holding tank.

Otherwise, Coco Banane, Bidjoul, Tamarin Plage and L'Abrepain all offer inexpensive meals. At the northern end of the beach, behind all the fancy Mediterranean style sunshades, is Quai Sud [$B-C], open lunchtime only, and Ti Sable [$B-C].

Cars can be rented from the beach and the coast road from Petite Anse D'Arlet, which winds over the hills to Diamant, offers spectacular views.

Water Sports

Snorkeling is interesting all along the southern shore and between Grand Anse D'Arlet and Petite Anse D'Arlet. Divers can join Plongée Passion on either of their two daily dives at 1000 or 1430. Localizé specializes in day-sailing/diving trips.

You can rent small craft, including Hobie cats, from the northern end of the beach by Ti Sable.

GRAND ANSE D'ARLET

PETITE ANSE D'ARLET

The village of Petite Anse D'Arlet is photogenic, with some lovely old houses and a picturesque church right near the waterfront. A handsome promenade follows the waterfront. It makes a good overnight anchorage when the wind is not too far in the south. When approaching town, look out for the rocks to the west of the dock. Some are visible but others extend some yards seaward. Anchor in one of the sand patches off the town dock.

There is also an anchorage at Anse Chadière in the southeastern corner of the bay which is suitable for a quick dip or snorkel. Approach with caution as isolated rocks extend about 100 feet offshore. Anchor in the sand bottom at 10 to 12 feet.

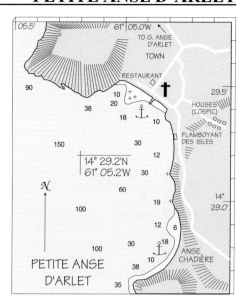

Ashore

Ashore you will find a couple of tiny shops, artists' studios, a post office, gift shops that rent cars and the modern pharmacy, Bernis. Snack Mac Roger has tables both on the beach and at the end of the promenade where you can eat inexpensively. A restaurant set in a quaint old house in the town was being rebuilt in 1988 and yet unnamed (just follow the road that runs back a bit to the west of the church). Otherwise, the fancier Le Flamboyant des Isles [$B, closed Sunday night and Tuesday] has a splendid view across the anchorage. For lunch, gravitate to the plastic chairs set out on the beach in the shade of two tamarind trees. Sandwiches and local meals are available from mobile vendors.

Water sports

The snorkeling is good in Anse Chadière. It may be worth giving scuba a go here as well.

THE SOUTH COAST OF MARTINIQUE

There are no good anchorages along Martinique's south coast until you get to Ste. Anne. There are some shoals along this coast that extend up to half a mile. There is deep water (over a hundred feet) outside these shoals. It is best to stay in this deep water to avoid the numerous fish traps at lesser depths.

As long as you don't get too far offshore, the sail east to Ste. Anne is usually a brisk beat to windward in protected water.

STE. ANNE

The white buildings of Ste. Anne stand out clearly against the surrounding green hills. Above the town is a prominent shrine with a walled path leading up to it. Anchor anywhere off the town. The buoyed area off the beach is reserved for swimming and dinghy sailing. Or eyeball your way south and anchor off the Caritan Hotel. The water depth is ten to 20 feet and holding is good in sand. There are shoals close to shore between Ste. Anne and Anse Caritan. If you are arriving here from abroad you must first go to Marin and clear customs. Customs do sometimes check.

Ashore

Ste. Anne is a delightful seaside town, small and peaceful, yet big enough to have a town square. There are two main streets, one along the waterfront and a parallel one at the back. If you turn left along the front street you can climb over the hill to a popular beach which stretches all the way to Club Med. Turn right along the front and you pass two small supermarkets which are ample for topping up your stores. Opposite is L'Epi Soleil, a boulangerie/patisserie good for coffee, sandwiches and snacks. Walk through the store to a pleasant sitting area right on the waterfront. Farther down the street on the right is a fish market, then a few steps more is a market with handicrafts and fresh fruits and vegetables. A little farther down the road is a T-junction. Just before this junction is an unmarked building where they make fresh bread and Danish and they open very early in the

morning. Let your nose be your guide.

Other businesses in town include boutiques and handicraft stores, a pharmacy and a bookstore. There is a curious walk up to the shrine on the top of the hill.

Hikers should take the road towards Anse Caritan and then follow the marked forestry trail that goes all the way along or just behind the shore to Anse des Salines. Anse des Salines is one of Martinique's finest palm-backed beaches and very popular, so ideal for people watching. Those who prefer a more private setting will pass several fabulous smaller beaches along the way which are too far from a car park to be popular.

Ste. Anne is a fine place to eat out. Les Tamariniers [$B-D, closed Tuesday evening and all day Wednesday] is a cute

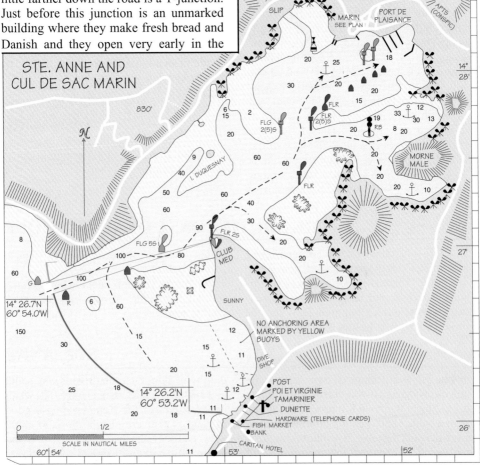

STE. ANNE AND
CUL DE SAC MARIN

SCALE IN NAUTICAL MILES

CUL DE SAC MARIN

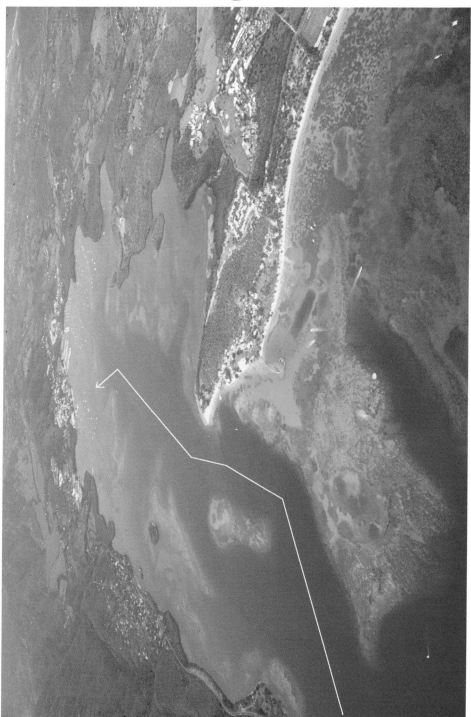

restaurant with a picturesque exterior surrounded by flowers. Jean Claude Edmond cooks tasty French/Créole food and adds artful touches to his more expensive dishes by decorating them with flowers.

Restaurant Anthor [$C-D] on the front street and L'Outre Mer [$C-D] on the back street both turn out fair Créole meals and in addition they cook pizzas. La Dunette [$C] has an open dining room facing the sea under a blue striped awning, and is a perfect place to stop for a beer or ice cream. Pause Café and Le Rendez Vous are both inexpensive and down near the market. If you turn left on the main road past the market you come to several more places, ending with the elegant Manoir de Beauregard.

Those who prefer something more up-market should try Poi et Virginie [$A-B, closed Monday], well known for first rate seafood served in a dining room which hangs out over the water. There are also many more restaurants and snack bars behind the long beach which stretches from Ste. Anne to the Club Med.

Water sports

A good place to start snorkeling or diving is at the second red buoy in the channel toward Marin. Snorkelers can follow the shallow part of the reef and divers can head south into deeper water where they will find a large collection of sponges, including some unusual shapes. This is a good place to see corallimorphs, pencil urchins and small colorful reef fish.

Thierry Theroude is the owner of Histoires D'Eau, the local dive shop at the Ste. Anne end of the beach. They dive twice daily, at 0930 and 1430.

Small sailing catamarans and sailboards are available for rent on the beach.

MARIN

Marin is a pleasant small town and an important yachting center. There is a large marina, a haul out facility and many other yacht services. Where else in the Windwards can you walk into two mechanic's shops and view several makes of marine engines on show and ready to install? This is the main base for the Martinique charter industry; The Moorings, Stardust, Sunsail, Star Voyage, Catana, Tropical Yacht Services, Chimere Yachting and Petit Breton all have bases here.

Navigation

Cul-de-Sac du Marin is a vast, deeply indented bay, surrounded by hills and lined with mangroves. It is full of shoals that are often visible in good light. The whole area is a gunkholer's dream and the best place to be in Martinique during a hurricane. The entrance channel is well marked by buoys and beacons. After you pass Club Med, head for the apartment buildings behind the forest of masts until you see the pair of red and green beacons in the middle of the bay. Pass between them, leaving the red one to starboard and the green one to port. Follow the channel in leaving the red buoys to starboard. There are shoals in the "no anchor-ing" area off Marin Beach, so avoid navigating through it.

If you are going between Marin and Ste. Anne, turn on the second red buoy which marks the long reef that extends to the west of the southern part of Club Med. Avoid the 6-foot shoal that lies east of the outer red buoy.

Regulations

Marin is a port of entry and a customs officer is available at his office in the marina every morning. He usually arrives about 0730. He is occasionally there in the afternoon.

Anchoring is forbidden in the swimming area marked by yellow buoys in front of the beach.

Services

Services in Marin are in two locations, each easy to reach by dinghy. Some are close to the town waterfront and the marina; others are over by CarenAntilles, the large slipway.

SAEPP [VHF:9], generally known as the Port du Plaisance Marin, is the only size-able marina in Martinique. Managed by Eric Jean-Joseph, it is good, friendly and inexpensive. SAEPP plans a large extension for

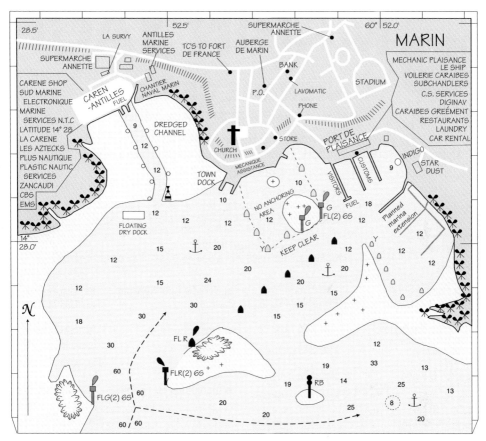

visitors which we show on our plan. Eric hopes to complete construction by the time this guide comes out, so there should be plenty of room for everyone. You can get diesel, gasoline and water on the fuel dock daily: 0830-1230 and 1500-1800. On Friday and Saturday they stay open through lunch. Dockage is available with 220-volt/ 50-cycle electricity (110-volt transformers are also available). There is space for yachts up to 80 tons and 140 feet long. Ask in the office if you need to get money changed. Since most of the charter companies are based here, there are many marine services right in the marina, as well as two car rental agencies.

On the street side of the Marina you will find a branch of Voilerie Caraibe Martinique owned by Hervé Lepault, whose other shop is in Pointe du Bout. New sails by Incidence, the well known French sailmaker, are computer-designed in France and sewn here. Hervé also has an upholstery department for boat cushions. Turn around time is good because if this shop gets overwhelmed by work, they can truck sails needing repair to Pointe du Bout.

Near the marina office you will find a branch of Patrice Caillot's Mecanique Plaisance. Their shop is new and shiny with a good range of new Perkins, Volvo, Westerbeke and Yanmar engines and generators in stock at competitive prices. The shop also sells a full range of spares for most things mechanical, including all kinds of filters for fuel and oil. They repair all the brands they carry and will try to help out with other makes of engine when they have time. They guarantee their work.

Le Ship, which is part of the Mecanique Plaisance group, is a great chandlery with an ever increasing stock. You will find stoves, heads, anchors, chain, rope, charts, pumps, stoves, electronics and all kinds of yacht hardware.

MARIN YACHT

CARENAGE CENTER
YACHT REPAIR AND STORAGE YARD

Ancienne Usine du Marin
Long term berthing and dry storage -Travelift 45 tons - Dry dock: 1000 tons
Voltage 220V - 380 V

■ **Carenantilles**
Haul-out - Long or short term stay -Restaurant/Bar/Facilities
Tel: 0596 74 77 70   Fax: 0596 74 78 22
e-mail : carenmarin@mail.sasi.fr   VHF : canal 73.

■ **Latitude 14°28**
Boatbuilders and repairers - Tel: 0596 74 78 58 / 45 50 96   Fax 0596 74 78 58

■ **Carene Shop** Tel: *0596* 74 74 80
Marine Paints and Chandlery. Fax: *0596* 74 79 16

■ **Plus Nautiques** Tel: *0596* 74 62 12
Shipchandler new and
used items. Fax: *0596* 74 70 52

■ **La Survy** Tel: *0596* 74 63 63
Sale & repair of inflatables
& life raft.. Fax: *0596* 74 63 00

■ **Crater Tony** Tel: *0596* 74 66 60
Aluminium and stainless
welding and fabrication. Fax: *0596* 25 65 49

■ **Caraïbe boat Services** Tel: *0596* 74 70 30
Fuelling. Fax: *0596* 74 70 31

■ **Plastik Services** Tel: *0596* 74 70 37
Fibreglass work. Tel: *0596* 25 07 69
 Fax: *0596* 74 70 43

■ **Martinique Sud Sablage** Tel: *0596* 74
 0 37
Sand blasting Fax: *0596* 74 70 43

■ **Frédéric Moser** Mobile: *0596* 45 54 30
Marine refrigeration Fax: *0596* 74 66 63

■ **Antilles Marine Services**
Sales and repairs Tel: 0596 74 70 78
of inboard engines Fax: 0596 74 63 71

■ **Sub Marine Electronique** Tel: 0596 74 65 56
Electronics - sales and repairs 0596 45 68 04
 Fax: 0596 74 76 62
Catorc Miguel Tel : 0596 76 79 39
Glass fibre work Mobile : 0596 25 52 91
Les As Teck Tel : 0596 74 72 85
Marine carpentry/cabinet maker Fax : 0596 74 72 85
Entretien Multi Services Tel : 0596 74 80 00
Inboard engine maintenance and repairs
 Fax : 0596 74 78 77
Nautic Services Tel : 0596 74 70 45
Painting & antifouling 45 60 61

■ **Restaurant la Carène** Tel: 0596 74 66 60
(Cards accepted)

HARBOUR

PORT CAPTAIN'S OFFICE
Capitainerie: 8:30 / 12:30 am - 3:00 / 6:00 pm

Bassin Tortue 97290 LE MARIN
Phone: *0596* 74 83 83 - Fax *0596* 74 92 20
(Cards accepted)

14 Charter Boat Companies - Sailmaker - Ship Chandlery - Rigging - Customs and Immigration Clearance - Restaurant - Provisioning - Laundry - Boutique - Taxi Car rental - Glassbottom Boat "AQUABULLE"

■ Mecanique Plaisance   Tel: *0596* 74 68 74 / Fax: *0596* 74 68 78
Sales, repairs and spares for auxiliary engines.

■ Station Maritime "'TOTAL"   Tel: *0596* 74 86 11 / Fax: *0596* 74 92 20
Fuelling

■ C.S. Services   Tel: *0596* 74 91 13 / Fax: *0596* 74 91 74
Electricity - watermakers - solar panels

■ Voilerie Caraïbes   Tel: *0596* 74 88 09 / Fax: *0596* 74 87 94
Sailmaker - Sail repairs - awings - cushions - ect ...

■ Diginav   Tel: *0596* 74 76 63 / Fax: *0596* 74 76 62
Marine electronics

■ Restaurant-bar Mango Bay !!   Tel: *0596* 74 60 89

■ Sub Evasion   Tel: *0596* 74 63 65
Dive equipment.

40 moorings buoys
400 stern -to -berths

Looking East over Cul de Sac Marin, I. Duquesnay just right of center

Upstairs on the same floor as the marina office is Jacques Fauquet's Diginav electronics shop. Jacques speaks English, is pleasant to deal with and fixes all types of electronic equipment. He also keeps Furuno, Brookes and Gatehouse, Navico and Autohelm equipment in stock. He can set you up with a satellite communication system.

Caraibes Greément is a full rigging service run by Philippe Leconte. Philippe can handle any rigging problem you may have, from replacing a stay to a complete re-rig of your yacht, even including a new mast. They are agents for Lewmar, Navtec, Profurl, Spectra, Richard and Harken. Anything they do not have can be shipped in on short order. They are happy to work on your yacht and make repairs aloft. Look for them in Tropical Yacht Services, downstairs in the marina on the road side.

On the same floor as the marina office, Dominique Rousselon offers a complete sales and repair service for mechanical systems, electrics, electronics, refrigeration and watermakers. He is agent for Sea Recovery, HRO and Aquaset watermakers, and for Kohler Generators. He also stocks batteries, paints and other supplies from WIND. If you wander into his shop you will find all kinds of electrical components, water filters, spares, and more. Dominique is in his shop from 0900-1700; otherwise you can find him in his Anse Mitan office.

Jose Boutigny at Mecanique Assistance [VHF:77] sells and installs Yanmar engines and repairs all makes of diesel and their accompanying electrics. He has a launch and can easily make boat visits. Like most of the people working on yachts, he can speak English. His office is on the waterfront near the small dinghy dock on the beach.

Max Montabord is a helpful refrigeration technician who does a lot of work for Star Voyage. He speaks enough English to talk about refrigeration problems and can fix all brands. Max also sells new Frigoelectric systems.

Natalie Voilerie is a new sailmaker above Stardust Charters.

Blatman and Laverie is a small laundry conveniently placed right behind the marina. Otherwise, Kirk and Nichol Charles' Lavomatic is just a short walk from the marina or the dock on the beach. They open daily from 0800 to 1900.

CarenAntilles [VHF:16/73] is a large haul out facility with a fuel dock and many support services. We show their location on our sketch chart. You can easily visit by dinghy, but avoid blocking the fuel dock. CarenAntilles can take boats with up to 23-foot beam with their 65-ton travel lift and larger vessels up to 48 feet wide, 130 feet long and 1000 tons on their floating dry dock. The dredged channel to the lift is nominally 11 feet, but it shoals somewhat between dredgings. Both sides of the channel are buoyed though you must be careful to stay in the middle of the channel. The storage area is large enough to take about 200 boats and this is a good place to leave your yacht in dry storage. Rates depend both on how long you need to be ashore and the current parity between the franc and other currencies. Fax them for a rate sheet. You can do your own work on the slip, or if you prefer, there are workshops that can do it for you. Facilities include toilets, showers and a restaurant. The yard manager Pierre speaks some English. CarenAntilles is surrounded by many support services which we mention below.

Carene Shop owned by Herve Ferrari, is right in the CarenAntilles compound and is a good chandlery which aims to provide everything you might need on the slip. Paints, antifoulings, epoxies, polyesters, cloths and all the tools necessary for their applications are carried as well as zincs, through-hulls, hoses, marine batteries, Caribe inflatable dinghies and more.

In the same building, upstairs, is Plus Nautiques, the bargain basement and nearly new shop of the marine industry. They also carry an ever widening range of regular chandlery. You can find great bargains here on all kinds of marine hardware and diving gear. They often have both inflatables and rigid dinghies in stock, and they sell their own brand of anti-fouling which they have tested extensively. Plus Nautiques is open weekdays, 0900-1300 and 1430-1730, and on Saturday mornings.

Jean Luc Cassius de Linval at CBS runs the fuel dock, selling diesel, gasoline, ice, oils and he may add cooking gas sometime soon. Jean has an outboard shop and is agent for Mariner and Mercury, though he stocks

spares for, and will repair, all makes. Jean can haul large yacht tenders (up to 30') and he is a yacht broker. He rents cars, including some inexpensive older models, and will look after your yacht while you go away.

Talba Gaston's Martinique Sud Sablage (Nautic Services) in the CarenAntilles compound is the place to get your boat's antifouling, epoxy or coal tar priming done. Gaston has a sandblaster. He also polishes hulls. In addition, he ships yachts long distance and makes the cradles for them. Gaston does commercial diving and rents scuba gear, usually to yacht parties going on charter.

Three workshops in the compound do all kinds of fiberglass repair, osmosis treatment and topside paint jobs. Camille Pancaldi at Plastik Services, Miguel Cartorc at Zancaudi and Michel Baudouin at Latitude 14° 28'.

For woodwork see Lionel and Vincent at Les As Tecks, who evidently have a sense for puns as well as wood.

You can bring your electrical problems to Frantz Larochelle's Sud Marine Electronic, also in the compound. He fixes everything electrical, including starters and alternators. He stocks Autohelm, Navcom, Incastec and Eagle electronics and will repair these brands. He can look at other electronic problems, but may not have the spares.

You will be in good hands with Yvon Icare at Antilles Marine Services who is an

excellent mechanic, a diesel specialist who speaks English. He is agent for Nannidiesel and Man engines and keeps a good range in stock from 10 h.p upwards. For larger engines he stocks Iveco. He is an agent for Hurth and ZF drives and Dessalator watermakers. He has been so successful that he now generally only works on these brands. He is happy to sell new engines and watermakers which he keeps in stock. His shop is way in the back of the buildings you see as you walk past Chantier Naval Marin.

Frederic Moser at Tilikum does a good job with electrics and refrigeration. Try asking for him at Antilles Marine Services.

Eric Guyon at EMS [VHF:16] is a good general mechanic who speaks English and works on all makes of diesel engine. He also welds stainless, fills scuba tanks, fixes alternators and starters, sells batteries and looks after yachts when owners go away.

Those with inflatables will be glad to know that La Survy offers a repair service. It is run by Maurice Phillias, Pascal and the rest of his family and they have over 30 years of experience. Their modern shop is temperature and humidity controlled and they will fix any kind of inflatable. They also repair and are warranty agents for Zodiac, Bombard and Plastimo. They keep Zodiac tenders and liferafts in stock.

Chantier Naval du Marin, next to CarenAntilles, is owned by Endrik Holzinger from Germany. He does custom fiberglass construction. He will build anything from a water tank to a power cruiser. You can also ask him about repairs and he will come and sort out your electrics. He is agent for Steyer diesel engines.

Miguel Trobrillant works in a container in back of Chantier Naval du Marin. He has tig and plasma welding and fabricates, welds and polishes stainless and aluminum and makes many bimini frames.

Ashore

Provisioning in Marin is good. Jean-Michel Annette runs the two big supermarkets in the area, both called Supermarché Annette. The larger one is just behind CarenAntilles in a mall whose other stores include a fishmonger, book shop, photo store, gift shop and a boulangerie/

patisserie and rotisserie where you can eat lunch. This is the only hypermarché in Martinique within walking distance of your boat and is more than ample for a large provisioning, with good meat, cheese and wine sections. There is even Cash du Sud, a separate wholesale department. It is a fairly long walk to Supermarché Annette from the marina, but you can dinghy to CarenAntilles and walk up. A little local Marin bus goes round and round the town and passes by this supermarket. The other Supermarché Annette is right in town, an easy walk up from the marina. It is a good sized market, light and airy with a broad selection of meat, frozen fish, and fresh produce. Both Annette supermarkets offer free delivery to the waterfront in Marin for all yachtspeople. You can arrange this with the cashier or at the welcome desk. Should you prefer to shop without leaving the marina, Annette has a little office in the marina called Martinique Plaisance. Armande Domi will give you their provisioning list in English or French, complete with prices. You can tick off what you want and have it

delivered. Or fax your order in advance and they will bring anything they do not stock from outside.

Marin has many good inexpensive restaurants where you will be welcome in shorts. Smart, pleasant and airy, Indigo [$B-C] is a new custom built floating restaurant offering waterfront seats all around. You can look out from your table and watch the fish jumping outside. The service is pleasant and the food first rate, with the best choices of Créole food as well as grilled meats and fish. They are open daily for lunch and dinner and there is a cocktail bar. Their tourist menu is good value and they are popular, so book or go early.

Mango Bay [$B-D] is right in the marina with a pleasant view over the yachts. This is an excellent place to come for breakfast and lunch as they also own the adjoining Deli-France with fresh bread being baked much of the day and excellent sandwiches, croissants and pain au chocolat available. Their bar is a gathering place in the evenings for many of the yacht crews, with cheerful music. Daily specials, as well as pizzas and ribs, are served for both lunch and dinner.

If you want to get away from the water and experience something really local and interesting, visit The Auberge du Marin [$B-D] in town. It is quaint and entertaining with lots of atmosphere and is very popular with the French yachting crowd in the evenings, so it is best to go early (dinner starts at 1930), or call, or pop up and make a reservation. Gerard and Nadine Michelon offer good French style family cooking at a very reasonable price. The menu is in French with an English translation. The Auberge du Marin is open every night and most days for lunch.

La Masure [$C-D] has a pleasant outside seating area where you can watch the world go by as well as an air-conditioned dining room. They offer an inexpensive menu and on Fridays and Saturdays serve brochettes with live music.

On the waterfront, the Lagon Bleu, above the yacht club [$A-B, closed Monday night and all day Tuesday], is a smarter restaurant

with a perfect location looking over the bay. Their excellent French cooking includes a variety of both meat and seafood dishes.

La Carene [$C-D] is upstairs right in the CarenAntilles compound, with a good view of the harbor. Proprietor Daniel Louis-Sidney keeps it inexpensive and good value.

Restaurant La Paillote Cayali [$C-D] has a great location right on the beach in Marin. Sit out next to the waves and eat a variety of local specialties at reasonable prices. Open every day all day.

Marine Mouillage [$D] is right behind the marina restaurant. They do a brisk lunch trade with tasty local specials, and are open as a bar in the evenings. On Thursdays they have a happy hour from 1800-1900 followed by barbecued food.

Water sports

Sub Evasion (Subchandlers) have a dive shop here: It is a good retail store and in addition you can rent equipment for your cruise (including compressors) or go for a dive with them.

THE EAST COAST OF MARTINIQUE

This guide covers all the most frequently used anchorages but does not include most of Martinique's east coast. This area is pleasant and interesting, but it is also tricky, with many reefs and shoals in water that is often difficult to read. The charts that are available are short on details where it matters and over the years it has claimed more than its fair share of hulls. Adventurous cruisers who wish to visit should buy the Trois Rivières guide to Martinique by Jerome Nouel. It is in French and English with excellent color photographs and is the only guide that covers this area well. We do include Baie des Anglais, the closest east coast anchorage.

Baie des Anglais

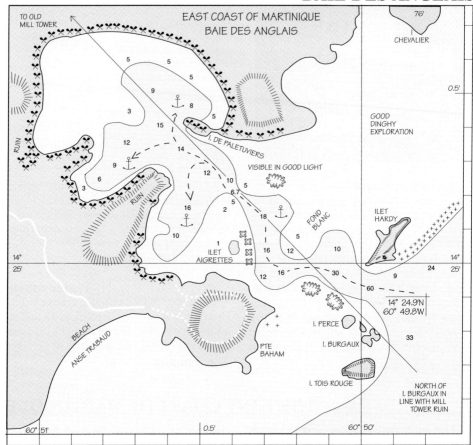

The wine locker is full, you are stuffed on restaurant meals, you've seen enough elegant boutiques to last a lifetime. What next? Consider a few days of quiet recovery in Baie des Anglais. Baie des Anglais is less than three miles up Martinique's east coast. It is a large mangrove lined bay, with some small beaches and several little islands for dinghy exploration. There are no restaurants, no shops, and while there may be another boat or two, you may have it to yourself.

The navigation is tricky and Baie des Anglais should only be visited in relatively light trade winds (10-15 knots). The entrance is down wind and down sea. Enter between Ilet Hardy and the group of islands which include Ilet Perce, Ilet Burgaux and Ilet Tois Roux. Ilet Hardy has a distinctive rock knoll on its southeastern shore. Once

past Ilet Hardy, look for the two reefs to the northwest of Ilet Perce and pass fairly close to them. (You will also be able to see Fond Blanc to starboard.) Note that there are quite a few isolated rocks just to the east of Ilet Aigrettes. By now the seas should be relatively calm and you will find there is a large daytime anchoring area about 20 feet deep to the west of Fond Blanc between Ilet Aigrettes and the visible reef on the other side of the channel.

Your strategy from here on in depends on your draft, the size of your engine, the strength of the wind and whether your insurance premium is up to date. You have to cross a bar of soft mud in unreadable water with the wind right behind you. For boats of less than six-foot draft there will probably be little problem. For boats of six and a half-foot or seven-foot draft, the width of deepest channel is very narrow, and at low tide sounds out at about seven and half feet. The only seamanlike thing to do is to anchor in the deep water and sound out the channel with a lead line in your dinghy. As you look at Ilet de Paletuviers you will see an old mill tower just behind it a little to its left. A range I found helpful is to be on a line between the northern edge of Ilet Burgaux and this old mill tower. The deepest water is probably a hair to the southwest of this line. Once over the bar you have plenty of water and many perfectly protected anchoring spots. Inside Ilet de Parletuvier is the most popular. If you dinghy over to the shore near Ilet Aigrettes you can find a way through to Anse Trabaud, a lovely but fairly popular beach. Dinghy exploration is also good up to Ilet Chevalier.

Go to Baie des Anglais well provisioned, because should the wind and sea get up while you are there, seas break across the entrance and you may have to wait a while to get out.

· PIGEON ISLAND ·

PASSAGE BETWEEN MARTINIQUE AND ST. LUCIA

Northbound

The passage between St. Lucia and Fort de France is usually a fast reach. A course of due north from Rodney Bay usually gets you close to the lee coast. It doesn't hurt to be a little offshore when you arrive as the wind tends to follow along the coast and is fluky close in. If Martinique is visible at the outset, it will appear as two islands, because the low-lying land in the center is not visible from St. Lucia. As you approach Martinique, Diamond Rock stands out as a clear landmark.

If you are heading for Ste. Anne, you can often make it in one tack, but be sure to head up a bit to allow for current as you cross.

Southbound

The southerly passage from Anse D'Arlet is sometimes a pleasant reach. At other times it can be hard on the wind. As the wind flows round the land, you will be pointing high as you follow the coast. It often pays to motor sail to stay reasonably close to shore before setting off across the channel. If sailing, it may pay to sail fast on the southerly tack and hope to play lifts later. When you see St. Lucia, head for the highest (rather rounded) mountain in the north end of the island until you begin to make out the distinctive shape of Pigeon Island, a clear double peak joined by a slope. The higher twin mounds of Mt. Pimard and Mt. Flambeau (see Rodney Bay

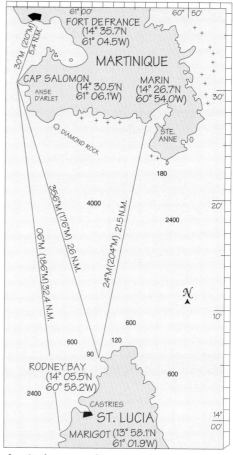

chart) also sometimes stand out.

The sail from Ste. Anne to St. Lucia is usually an easy reach.

Regulations

St. Lucia has customs offices in Vieux Fort, Marigot Bay, Castries and Rodney Bay (Soufriere to be included soon). The entry charges in $ EC are as follows. All yachts pay $15 navigational aids, $10 pratique (up to 100 tons) and clearance fees according to length; $5 for under 40 feet and $15 for over 40 feet. In addition, yachts on charter which are less than 40 feet pay $20; between 40 and 70 feet, $30 and over 70 feet, $40. For stays of less than three days, you can clear in and out on arrival. You can get permission for stays up to six weeks from the customs officer on arrival. Extensions are arranged with the main customs in town. You can overnight in the Soufriere area on your way out. Those clearing out of normal office hours (weekdays 0800-1215, 1330-1545) will be charged a reasonable overtime fee. St. Lucia has strict environmental laws. Most coastal areas are now protected, and spearfishing, damaging corals, buying coral, turtle shell products or out-of-season lobsters (lobstering season is 31st October to 31st April) are strictly forbidden. Fishing without a license, is forbidden. Sports fishing boats must have a license. but sailing yachts are generally allowed to troll a line or handline for pleasure. No scuba diving (except for underwater work on your yacht) may be done without a qualified guide. Pets are not allowed ashore. Fines are severe.

Holidays

Jan 1st and 2nd
Carnival - Monday and Tuesday, 40 days before Easter. 15th-16th Feb 1999 and 6-7th March 2000
Easter Friday through Monday. 2-5th April 1999 and 21st-24th April 2000
Feb 22 - Independence Day

May 1- Labor Day
Whit Monday (24th May 1999 & 12th June 2000)
Corpus Christi (3rd June 1999 & 22nd June 2000)
First Friday in August
October (variable) - Thanksgiving
December 13th - National Day
Dec 25th and Dec 26th

Shopping hours

In St. Lucia most shops open 0830-1230, then 1330-1600. Saturday is half day and most places close by noon. Banks close by 1500 except Friday when they open till 1700.

Telephones

There are card phones all over the island. You buy phone cards in selected shops. For the USA dial 1 + 10 digits. For other overseas calls, dial 011 + country code + number. For operater calls, dial 0. For ATT dial 1-800-872-2881. When dialing from overseas, the area code is 758 followed by a 7-digit number.

Transport

Inexpensive ($1.50-$6 EC) buses run to most towns and villages. If you are going a long way, check on the time of the last returning bus. Taxis are plentiful. Sample taxi rates are:

	$EC
Rodney Bay - Vigie	40
Rodney Bay - Castries	40
Rodney Bay - Hewanorra	160
Castries - Hewanorra	120
Castries - Marigot	60
By the hour	52
Short ride	10

Rental cars are available (check our directory). You will need to buy a local license which costs $30 EC. Drive on the left.

ST. LUCIA

Marigot Bay

St. Lucia, the largest of the English speaking Windwards, is mountainous and lush, with many beautiful white sand beaches. Tropical rain forest covers the steep slopes of the center and gives way to cultivated agricultural land around the more moderately sloping coastal fringe. Bananas are the principal crop. For sheer physical beauty, the area around Soufriere and the Pitons is outstanding.

St. Lucia offers excellent sight-seeing and hiking. You can see most of it by bus or a rental car. Adventurous travelers willing to combine driving with hiking will want to rent a four-wheel drive vehicle and explore some far away corners like Grand Anse or Anse Louvet on the windward shore. Organized tours are available through most travel agents and this is an easy way to see St. Lucia. All day tours cost in the region of $40 US and include lunch, drinks and transport from your nearest dock. Popular tours are round the island tours, plantation tours, where you get to see the backbone of the St. Lucia economy at work, and the rainforest tour which involves hiking across the middle of the island. For those interested in nature, the National Trust runs tours to Frigate Island and the Maria Islands, as well as turtle watches.

St. Lucia has been developing at an amazing rate over the last few years and offers an excellent full service marina with haul out facilities and a large choice of restaurants and shoreside activities. St. Lucia is a major charter center, with charter companies in Rodney Bay and Marigot Bay.

Yacht security is taken seriously by the Marine Police who listen 24 hours a day to VHF:16. They are currently based in Vigie, and will respond to requests for help.

Navigation, west coast

Between the northern tip of St. Lucia and Rodney Bay there are several shoals and no anchorages, so it is best to keep clear.

Rodney Bay offers several anchorages which are dealt with in detail below.

Barrel of Beef is a low lying rock about a quarter of a mile off the southern side of the entrance to Rodney Bay. It is marked by a white light which flashes every five seconds. The water is deep enough (about 18 feet) for most yachts to pass inside it.

Between Barrel of Beef and Castries, the coast sweeps back in a large bay containing Rat Island. This bay is full of reefs and shoals and best avoided. On leaving Rodney Bay the normal route is to pass inside Barrel of Beef and head directly toward Castries Harbor.

Tapion Rock forms the southern entrance to Castries Harbor. There are some rocks close by, so give it a reasonable clearance. Two miles south of Castries, Cul de Sac Bay is a huge depot for Hess Oil. It is well lit and makes an obvious landmark by day or night. There is a buoy in the middle of the entrance to this bay which flashes at night.

From Cul de Sac Bay to the Pitons the island is mainly steep-to and a quarter of a mile offshore clears all dangers. There are a few rock hazards lying up to 100 yards or more offshore. The worst is a sizable rock patch off the southern end of Anse Chastanet which should be given wide clearance.

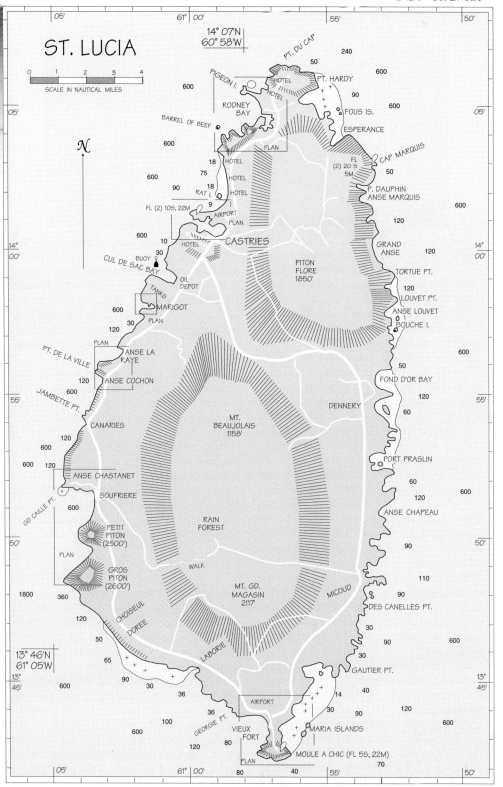

ST. LUCIA

14° 07'N
60° 58'W

SCALE IN NAUTICAL MILES
0 1 2 3 4

N

PT. DU CAP
240
50
PIGEON I.
600
HOTEL
HOTEL
PT. HARDY
90
FOUS IS.
600
RODNEY BAY
ESPERANCE
BARREL OF BEEF
600
PLAN
CAP MARQUIS
50
FL (2) 20 5
5M
18
HOTEL
75
HOTEL
P. DAUPHIN
ANSE MARQUIS
90
RAT I.
18
HOTEL
600
9
120
FL (2) 10S, 22M
AIRPORT
PLAN
600
CASTRIES
GRAND ANSE
120
10
HOTEL
14°
00'
CUL DE SAC BAY
BUOY
30
PITON FLORE
1850'
TORTUE PT.
120
OIL DEPOT
120
LOUVET PT.
TANKS
ANSE LOUVET
BOUCHE I.
600
MARIGOT
30
PLAN
600
120
PLAN
PT. DE LA VILLE
ANSE LA RAYE
FOND D'OR BAY
50
120
ANSE COCHON
120
JAMBETTE PT.
600
DENNERY
60
600
CANARIES
120
MT. BEAUJOLAIS
1158'
600
120
PORT PRASLIN
ANSE CHASTANET
60
600
SOUFRIERE
120
ANSE CHAPEAU
GD CAILLE PT.
600
RAIN FOREST
PETIT PITON
(2500')
90
PLAN
WALK
110
GROS PITON
(2600')
MICOUD
90
1800
360
MT. GD. MAGASIN
2117'
DES CANELLES PT.
120
CHOISEUL
DOREE
30
50
LABORIE
90
600
65
30
13° 46'N
61° 05'W
90
30
GAUTIER PT.
36
40
600
AIRPORT
14
36
30
90
120
100
GEORGIE PT.
VIEUX FORT
80
600
MARIA ISLANDS
120
PLAN
MOULE A CHIC (FL 5S, 22M)
70

105

Pigeon Island

Rodney Bay is over a mile long. At the northern end an artificial causeway connects Pigeon Island to the mainland, providing the whole bay with protection. In the old days, when Europeans used to entertain themselves by sailing around in wooden boats taking potshots at each other, Pigeon Island was the main base for the British navy in this area. It was ideally situated, being in sight (on most days) of Martinique, the French main base. There used to be a fort, hospital buildings, barracks and storerooms. Now it is conserved by the St. Lucia National Trust as a delightful park. There are shady gardens and the fort has been partly restored. The climb to the top is well rewarded by the views. Strategically placed signboards tell you about the history. Near the causeway the old officers' barracks have been rebuilt to house a new interpretation center. The audiovisual recreation of the Battle of the Saintes is well worth the entrance fee, and in addition there are natural history, Amerindian, and other historical exhibits, many of them interactive where you press buttons and watch things happen. You can even take an electronic quiz to find out how much you have learned, and buy souvenirs in the gift shop.

There is a small entry charge to the park and interpretation center. This helps finance the National Trust, which works to preserve the environment as well as historic sites. The anchorage off Pigeon Island is good or you can dinghy here. Jambe de Bois [$D] is in the building that Snowball's Restaurant occupied way back before the causeway was built. It is open for lunch, snacks and drinks.

Rodney Bay Lagoon is a large and completely protected inner lagoon which is entered via a dredged channel between Reduit Beach and Gros Islet village. This is lit by port and starboard lights at the entrance and by range lights which make an excellent aid to good night sight. The lagoon is the home of Rodney Bay Marina.

Outside the lagoon, to the south of the channel entrance, is Reduit Beach, one of St. Lucia's finest beaches and the home of the St. Lucian Hotel and the St. Lucia Yacht Club.

Many yachts tie up at a marina . Otherwise the three main anchorages in the area are: inside the lagoon (dredged to 8-10 feet), to the southeast of Pigeon Island, and off Reduit Beach. Some people also anchor off Gros Islet village. The outside anchorages occasionally become untenable in northerly swells.

Regulations

Rodney Bay Marina is a port of entrance and a good place to clear in. If you plan to stay in the marina, you can go into a berth (see below) and walk down to the customs office. If you plan to anchor, clear in at the marina by using the customs slip which is opposite the customs office. It is about half way down the outer dock and marked by a yellow post. Customs are normally open daily from 0800 to 1800, but you pay overtime after 1600. Entry charges are $30-40 EC, depending on the size of boat. Details of fees are given at the beginning of this chap-

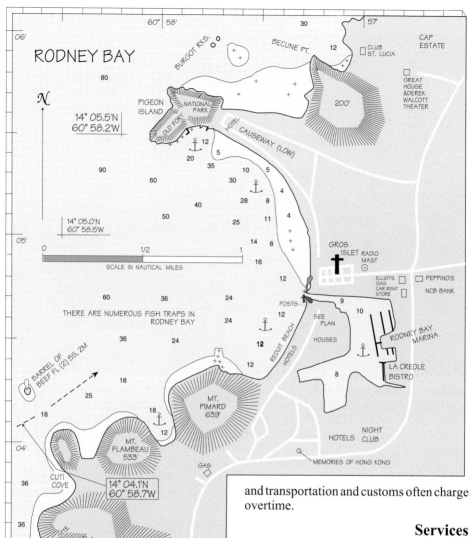

RODNEY BAY

14° 05.5'N
60° 58.2'W

14° 05.0'N
60° 58.5W

SCALE IN NAUTICAL MILES

THERE ARE NUMEROUS FISH TRAPS IN
RODNEY BAY

14° 04.1'N
60° 58.7'W

and transportation and customs often charge overtime.

Services

Rodney Bay Marina [VHF:16] is large and pleasant, with lawns and coconut palms, as well as offices and shops. Manager Cuthbert Didier is very helpful. There is a convenient bus to town and a plethora of restaurants close by. Call for a dock space and, if you cannot get through, choose a spot and hope for the best. Eight foot draft is no problem. A Swan 65 at 9' 3" can make it in comfortably on a good high tide. Boats of up to 10-foot draft have managed to enter on unusually high tides. If in any doubt, sound out the channel before entering. Some berths on "B" dock are reserved for charter yachts. The outside of "A" dock has easier access and is the only space suitable for really large

ter. In addition to those fees, some officers charge $25 EC for a permit to anchor in either Anse Cochon or Jalousie which are not designated ports of clearance. These permits are good for one designated day only.

If you are too deep to enter the lagoon you can anchor outside and dinghy in.

Shipping in parts? Note that invoices and all shipping papers must be marked "for transshipment". Even though items are duty free, there are charges for documentation

yachts, so there is a minimum fee rating here of 45 feet. Dock services include ample water and electricity (220-volt, 50-cycle; transformers for 110 volts can be arranged) and cable TV. (Rental TVs may be available in the office.) Pleasant features in the marina include hot showers, two banks, a first rate chandlery and an electronics shop. You can use Rodney Bay Marina as a postal drop and send faxes. USA-direct telephone line to the States and several public card and coin phones make communications easy. There is garbage disposal.

Apart from the main office, there is a Rodney Bay Marina Services office. It is run by Rosemary Cowan, with technical support from Ian Cowan. Here you can buy block ice, get your laundry done, fill all kinds of LPG gas and source anything from the tiniest widget to a brand new engine. This is all brought in duty free and delivered to your yacht hassle free. You can arrange to have your boat looked after while you are away and come here for day-workers as well as mechanics, refrigeration and other technicians. Rosemary keeps a record of these independent workers and can find the right one to suit you. Here, too, is the Sail Loft at Rodney Bay Marina managed by Ince and his team who repair sails and make biminis, covers and awnings. New sails come from Doyle Sails in Barbados. The Sail Loft is also agent for Furlex roller furling gear, and they can always help with rigging problems.

Rodney Bay Marina Boatyard [VHF:68], managed by Ian Cowan, is St. Lucia's largest haul out facility with a 50-ton yacht hoist and room for about 120 yachts in long term storage and another 20 having work done on them. Labor is available or you can do the work yourself. The yard can handle any size job from a quick haul to a complete osmosis treatment and respray. The yard does fiberglass, woodwork and painting and has a 10-boat work dock for lifting and working on engines. They also work on mechanical problems. Here, too, is the fuel dock. Duty free fuel is available for anyone who has cleared out. Just show your papers.

Cube ice is available from the liquor store, the Bread Basket and the mini-market at the Mortar and Pestle.

108

Sparkle Laundry [VHF:16] in Gros Islet will collect and deliver from your yacht.

Ulrich at Destination St. Lucia is very helpful. His crew can help to get your boat repaired, your refrigeration cooling and your engine back working. They will look after your yacht while you go away and they undertake all kinds of yacht management and will charter suitable yachts. A German language book swap is available in their reception.

The Bistro [VHF:67] offers stern-to dockage with water and electricity (220-volt, 50-cycle). Bistro offers a mail drop with full communications services including e-mail, is a charter boat agent, runs a yacht brokerage and does limited yacht victualling including some frozen meals.

La Creole also has a large docking area in front of the restaurant. Waterside Landings is a small, quiet dock with about 15 berths in the inner part of the lagoon. They have water, electricity and cable TV, but no other services. The ownership is changing, so check them out and see what is happening.

Cay Electronics [VHF:09], with stores in St. Lucia, Antigua, B.V.I. and the U.S.A. is efficiently run by Richard Tinley. He offers sales and service for all your electronics, watermakers, generators, refrigeration and electrics, including alternators and starters. New stock includes electronics, gel filled batteries, water pumps and a wide range of spares. He can quickly obtain anything that is not on hand.

Rodney Bay Marine Hardware [VHF:16 "RBSS"], part of Rodney Bay Ship Services, is owned by Lucian Greg Glace and managed by well known St. Lucian yachtsman Ted Bull. It is one of the best stocked chandleries in the Windwards. Avon Tenders hang from the roof, and you can get a Johnson outboard backed by the full service facilities. Huge deep cycle batteries rub shoulders with watermakers, Stat Power inverters, International paints, solar panels and windmills. You will find anchors, chain, rigging, fittings and ropes, along with snorkeling gear, barbecues, shipwear for shore and a book swap. Everything is duty free for non-St. Lucian yachts. By agreement with the boatyard,

110

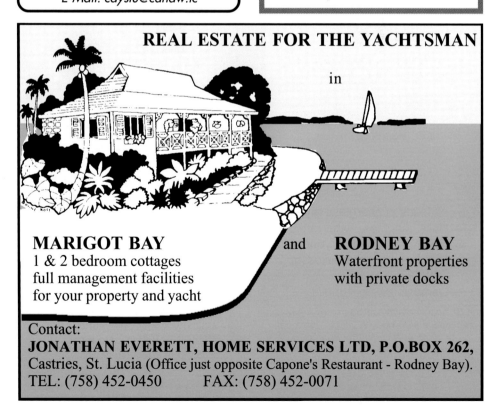

they do not sell antifouling.

Johnson's Hardware have a large store just opposite the marina. They keep a good stock of marine basics at reasonable prices. Their range includes deck gear, rope, chain, anchors and fenders, fastenings, electrical fitting, lights, wiring and fuses, paint and sandpaper, fishing and snorkeling gear, fuel and oil filters and outboard accessories. They can special order just about any marine hardware you might want duty free. In addition they keep a good selection of general and household hardware including power tools.

Cox Marine are the fiberglass specialists with years of experience in all kinds of repairs and construction for the yachting trade. Whether you need a quick-fix job, a new dinghy, a major repair or a paint job Richard Cox is the man to contact.

Port to Port [VHF:16, Charlie Victor] is owned by Vialva Cyprian, a St. Lucian who originally came from Trinidad and has worked with boats for many years. He fixes any kind of diesel engine or gearbox and also works on all marine systems including water makers, hydraulics and heads. He will happily take care of your starter motor or alternator problem, though he farms this work out to specialists. Cyprian will also help with charter yacht provisioning or arrange to take care of any other problems yacht owners may have. If you want to see him, call him on the radio.

Ryte Weld Enterprises, 100 yards up the side road past Johnson's Marine Hardware, is managed by Lawrence and they weld all metals, including aluminum and stainless, and machine and fabricate them to your specifications. They can make you a new shaft or check your old one.

Other people who have workshops outside the area and pay house calls to Rodney Bay include: Andrew Tyson, cabinet work; B&L Upholstery Clinic (cushions and drapes); Remy and Parris Enterprises, (woodwork, recaulking, fiberglass repairs and fixing broken tape decks and radios); and Trevor Joseph for sail repairs and canvas work. Vergel Joseph is a good general mechanic who worked for the Moorings for many years. He now has his own small work-boat and can

113

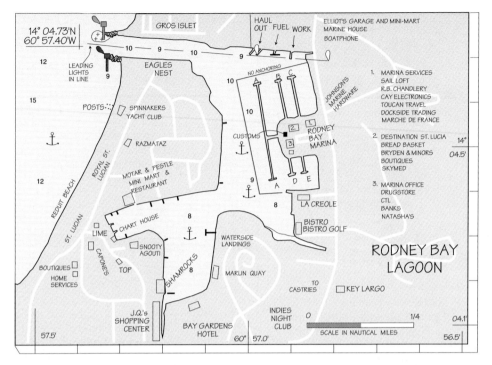

The map shows: 14° 04.73'N 60° 57.40'W, GROS ISLET, HAUL OUT FUEL WORK, ELLIOT'S GARAGE AND MINI-MART, MARINE HOUSE, BOATPHONE, LEADING LIGHTS IN LINE, EAGLES NEST, NO ANCHORING, SPINNAKERS YACHT CLUB, POSTS, RAZMATAZ, CUSTOMS, RODNEY BAY MARINA, JOHNSONS MARINE HARDWARE, MOTAR & PESTLE MINI MART & RESTAURANT, ROYAL ST. LUCIAN, REDUIT BEACH, ST. LUCIAN, LIME, CHART HOUSE, SNOOTY AGOUTI, CAPONES, TOP, SHAMROCKS, WATERSIDE LANDINGS, MARLIN QUAY, LA CREOLE, BISTRO, BISTRO GOLF, KEY LARGO, TO CASTRIES, BOUTIQUES, HOME SERVICES, J.Q.'s SHOPPING CENTER, BAY GARDENS HOTEL, INDIES NIGHT CLUB, RODNEY BAY LAGOON, SCALE IN NAUTICAL MILES, 0 1/4

1. MARINA SERVICES
   SAIL LOFT
   R.B. CHANDLERY
   CAY ELECTRONICS
   TOUCAN TRAVEL
   DOCKSIDE TRADING
   MARCHE DE FRANCE

2. DESTINATION ST. LUCIA
   BREAD BASKET
   BRYDEN & MINORS
   BOUTIQUES
   SKYMED

3. MARINA OFFICE
   DRUGSTORE
   CTL
   BANKS
   NATASHA'S

visit you wherever you have a problem in St. Lucia. Some businesses in the Castries area also pay marina visits. These include Chris Kessell for surveys, alternator and electrical repairs and International Marine Diesel for engine work.

Windward Island Gases, just beyond Glace Motors, tests scuba tanks and can fill most kinds of gas bottles, including CO_2, argon, helium and nitrogen.

Two first rate travel agents in the area will get you home safely. Right in the marina nothing could be more convenient than to walk into Jane Tipson's Toucan Travel [VHF:16]. Ask for Kathy, Craig or Carina.

They often have special rates for trips to the U.K. and U.S.A. and they also arrange car rentals and island tours to help you get to know St. Lucia better. They offer e-mail and fax service and act as an information agency for tourism.

Travel World is owned and run by Joycelyn. Her office is in American Drywall, but you don't even have to go near the office; just call Joycelyn on the phone and tell her what you want: tickets, car rentals (through Cool Breeze) or tours and she will arrange everything and deliver your tickets to you. Joycelyn is helpful and enthusiastic and works hard to get the best rates which has earned her many

dedicated customers.

If you wish to rent a car, CTL [VHF:16] is right in the marina. They not only rent cars but offer e-mail, internet and faxing and copy services.

If you are looking for somewhere inexpensive to stay while you recommission your boat, La Panache Guest House is a 10 minute walk down the Cas en Bas road, but it has a very pleasant garden atmosphere and overlooks the whole Rodney Bay area. Owner Henry Augustin turns out a first rate satisfying home meal at dinner time for only $35 EC. Non residents can also eat at La Panache, but you have to let Henry know in the morning.

Rodney Bay Marina is also home to Sky Med an insurance company that offers, for a yearly premium, medical evacuation and a full range of support services.

Ashore

Rodney Bay ferry runs around the lagoon from about 0900-1600. You can call them on VHF:16.

Rodney Bay Marina itself is a small shopping center. Le Marche De France is a conveniently placed supermarket offering a selection of meats, vegetables, and canned and dry goods as well as wines and cheeses from Martinique.

The Bread Basket sells fresh bread, croissants and baked goods, and Bryden and Partners is a fully stocked liquor store with some basic stationery supplies as well. Their Marina store is a small outlet for their much bigger Castries branch, so if you do not see what you need, ask and they will deliver. Several other small supermarkets are in the area. In the inner lagoon, the Mortar and Pestle has a well stocked mini-mart, with cube ice, some fresh vegetables, meat, wine, beer and soft drinks. They open weekdays 0800-1900, Saturdays 0700-1600, and Sundays and holidays 1000-1300. You can park your dinghy right outside.

Elliot's Convenience Store and gas station is just a few minutes walk in the Gros Islet direction from the marina gates and is open every day. About three miles in the other direction is Glace supermarket which is open weekdays from 0630-2030. Their stock includes some hardware items like sandpaper.

A big new J.Q.'s shopping center was nearing completion in the southern part of Rodney Bay, accessible through a passage by Shamrock Pub building. J Q.'s has several other large supermarkets including one on the road to town, near the airport and a dollar bus ride away. They have the widest variety of food products and are best for a major provisioning. The new supermarket in Rodney Bay should be similar.

There is no need to go to Martinique to stock up on wines. Caribbean Chateaux are the St. Lucia wine specialists, and they can deliver duty free to your yacht. They stock spirits as well as a huge selection of wines. Give them a call or go visit them. Their office and storehouse is on the left hand side of the main road between the airport and Rodney Bay, not too far from the airport roundabout, just past American Drywall.

The Gablewoods Shopping Center is about half way between Rodney Bay Marina and Castries. This complete mall includes the large Julie'n Supermarket, a post office, pharmacy, Radio Shack, music center, M&C Hardware, and Sunshine Bookstore – the best bookshop in St. Lucia with international papers, local books, guides and more. Also here are an optician, a complete medical center and a variety of shops selling clothing, linen, handicrafts, jewelry and office supplies. The Sea Island Cotton Shop has a particularly cheerful selection of clothing and handicrafts. Another good reason to visit is Choice Meats and Delicatessen, with meat, some fish and lambi. In addition, their black forest cake is rumored to be addictive. Of importance in Gablewoods Mall is Chateaux des Fleurs, a shop selling flowers which also provides elegant fruit, cheese and wine hampers. They offer good service and delivery to the marina, Vigie or Marigot can be arranged at reasonable rates. Should shopping time run over the lunch hour, there is a restaurant and complete arcade of fast foods.

Several specialty stores are essential for those running charter yachts, and good for others to know about. For quality meats visit the new branch of Maison Salaison in Gros Islet which has top of the line cuts or try Island Foods in the Massade Industrial Es-

tate. Admac is a wholesale outfit in Sans Souci, not far from Vigie Creek, part-owned by an ex-charter skipper. They import smoked salmon, gravlax, creams, coffee, juices, yogurt and more. Charter yachts should call or drop by for a price list. Those whose tastes run to these quality foods, but do not need wholesale can call for a list of their retailers.

Shops around the marina include Jane Tipson's Pieces of Eight, a delightful shop with everything from local books, including cruising and nature guides, videos and paintings to unusual gift items and objets d'art. You can buy your postcards with stamps here and after you have written them, you can drop them in their mail box.

Colleta II has casual and beach wear as well as evening wear and accessories. The Drug Store sells everything from sunglasses and sun lotion to aspirin, beach balls and telephone cards.

Dockside Trading, upstairs over the marina supermarket, is run by yachtsman Don Baker. Here you will find Trekker shorts that will follow you through countless seasons of hard work, excellent sailing hats, water filters, wind chimes, artistic souvenirs, and Caribelle Batiks. Don keeps a good bookswap going and his assistant cuts hair.

Start the day in the marina anytime after 0730 at Nick's Bread Basket [$D] for coffee, with a full cooked breakfast or plate of fresh croissants. Return at lunch for a really good ham and cheese sandwich or one of their special lunch plates, followed by ice cream or cake.

If pizza is your thing, you will love Key Largo [$C-D], run by an enthusiastic young St. Lucian/Italian family. It is just a few minutes walk from the marina (be very careful of the traffic) or a minimum taxi ride. The pleasant Italian style building features a wood-fired brick pizza oven, presided over by Carlo from Rome. Key Largo is open for lunch and dinner and kids are welcome. The real Italian pizza is consistently by far the best in St. Lucia, pasta (evenings only), salads, sandwiches, ice creams and freshly ground espresso coffee are also served. Nightly happy hour is from 1730-1830.

The Marina's After Deck [$C-D] is a cheerful bar/restaurant popular with the yachts-people as a hangout. Arrive for happy hour from 1830-1930, and stay for the nightly barbecue. You can choose your atmosphere; Inside it is noisy and cheerful, outside it is peaceful and quiet with seating around the pool with a view over the bay. The menu is simple but nicely done; barbecued fish, chicken, conch or steak all served with rice and a variety of local vegetables. Manager Sancha creates a pleasant atmosphere with friendly staff. They have a band on Thursdays and often bring in a steel band or other live entertainment on other occasions.

Natasha will welcome you at Natasha's [$D] a friendly coffee bar, regular bar and boutique which is open from breakfast till night.

The Rodney Bay area offers a large variety of bars and restaurants. Dinghy tie up is available at the Bistro, Shamrocks, Snooty Agouti, The Lime, and the Mortar and Pestle. There is much to see, so if your time is limited you could try a tour, coordinating happy hours as you go. Here is a run down of what you will find:

One side of Bistro [$B, closed Thursdays] is a long, cheerful bar and restaurant over-hanging the water. Behind is their burger park [$D], with a professional 18-hole miniature golf course (lit at night). The burger park side has an informal, easy garden atmosphere. Families come to play miniature golf, parents bring their kids to enjoy the small playground. The A-frame burger hut menu includes rotis, fish 'n', chips, salads and vegetarian quesadilla as well as both fish and traditional burgers. Childrens' birthdays are specially catered. It's the best fast food in St. Lucia and their fishburgers are cooked to perfection. On the restaurant side, sailors can enjoy these inexpensive items from the waitress service on the dock right over the water. Owner Nick is a sailor and designed it that way. Arrive from 1700-1900 for happy hour and select from the blackboard of happy hour specials. The dock merges into the waterfront restaurant with its neatly laid tables and here fancier fare is served. The wide-ranging menu has an excellent selection of seafood including perfectly grilled fish and dolphin steamed in

119

banana leaves. Meat eaters will enjoy the ribs and steak au poivre. Try to leave room for one of their delightful desserts. The restaurant is popular, so booking is advisable.

You no longer have to go to Martinique for French Creole cooking. You can find it at La Creole at prices which are very competitive even with the French islands. La Creole [VHF:16, $B-D] is between the marina and The Bistro. The owner has successfully mixed nautical paraphernalia and plants to create a pleasing atmosphere. The whole restaurant is one long wooden balcony with a pleasant view over the marina. The food, all made from fresh local ingredients, emphasizes sea food with fish, freshwater crayfish, shrimp, lambi and lobster. For meat eaters there are steaks, chicken and goat. For those heading south, this is a great place to get a taste of Martinique before you go.

Dinghy down to the Snooty Agouti [$C-D] in the inner lagoon with its own dinghy dock. Treat this delightful place as your own private club. Sit upstairs amid wood,

flowers, paintings and books and drink coffee, eat cakes, or come by at meal times for inexpensive but good light-meal specials. Relax in an armchair, there are always plenty of magazines to read. Browse the internet or send e-mail. Snooty Agouti is a combination bar, cyber-coffee shop, art gallery and boutique, the creative inspiration of Jane and Barbara Tipson. They often feature free wine-tasting evenings, fashion shows and special art shows. Drop by and ask about coming events.

When John and Suzie Wright wanted to open a different kind of a restaurant, a real East Indian restaurant seemed a sure winner. Both had Indian connections, and no truly East Indian restaurant yet existed in the Windwards. The result is Razmataz [$B-D] opposite the Royal St. Lucian Hotel. A pivotal decision was to bring in Dependra Bahadur as a partner. Dependra is from Khatmandu in Nepal and he cooks like an angel. Since many fruits and vegetables from India were introduced to the Caribbean long ago, fresh ingredients are no problem. A tandoori oven is kept going 24 hours a day

The Bistro

BURGER PARK AND MINIATURE GOLF

Bistro, a great place to meet up with friends in a relaxed and comfortable atmosphere just a short walk from Rodney Bay Marina. A perfect waterfront setting for sundowners and dinner with choices from our light Dockside and Bar Snack Menu through to the full A La Carte selection. Fresh seafood is always available with the fishermen pulling right up to our dock.

Open six nights a week from 5:00 p.m
Closed Thursdays. Reservations 452 9494.

And yes, families are welcome! The Burger Park on the same property is an ideal place for kids who can play on the flood-lit miniature golf course,and order their favourites from hot dogs to burgers, while you relax at The Bistro!

Open six days a week from 11:00 a.m. to 10:00 p.m.
Closed Thursdays. Take Out: 452 0811
e-mail: bistro@candw.lc

and the food is reasonably priced and excellent. For preference, reserve in advance and ask for a table on the patio. John often brings out his guitar and sings country music and on Saturday nights a belly dancer usually makes an appearance. The bar has a happy hour from 1700-1900, darts and French boules are available.

Capone's is an art deco restaurant in 1920's Miami style. Smart and snazzy and cool inside [$A] with efficient service and excellent and inventive Italian food, it will appeal to those wanting the best for a special night out. Outside [$C-D] is pleasant, casual and popular among both locals and visitors with an inexpensive menu for everyday eating.

Right on the waterfront with its own dock, Nick's Charthouse [$B-C] has a cheerful decor with lots of jungly plants. Nick is always on hand and greets guests personally; the service is excellent and the food consistently good. Specialities are steak, seafood and ribs, but on a lucky night you can get freshwater crayfish. Happy hour is 1700-1800, when a few regulars gather to sample Nick's collection of well over 100

rums. The Charthouse is often full so reservations are advisable.

Nick also runs Pizza Pizza [D], next door under the Snooty Agouti. This place is very popular with families and kids because of the playground with a trampoline and outside park like seats. They serve pizza, pasta, and salads. Their pizzas are American style with plenty of cheese and topping and rated very highly judging by the popularity of the place.

Near Nick's you will see an odd sort of floating bar called the Sip 'n Dip. I don't advise dipping while it is parked in Rodney Bay, but the sipping is excellent in a convivial atmosphere where you are bound to make some friends. Food is planned.

Shamrocks [$C-D] is the local pub with draft Guiness, cheerful loud music and pool tables. Tie your dinghy up right outside. Owner Steve Gasson opens up about 11 am and keeps going till people leave. Happy hour is 5.30-6.30. Food is simple and inexpensive. Live musical entertainment is usually on Wednesdays and Saturdays, Thursdays is Karaoke, beer swillers turn up on

Pigeon Island

Mondays for the 60 oz. pitchers of Heineken and you can party any night.

The Lime [$B-D] offers Caribbean cuisine in a pleasant atmosphere. It is very popular, so reservations are advisable, but you can often get in without one. For late night entertainment they have a small night club/disco.

Spinnaker's [$B-D] has a great location right on the beach by the yacht club. It makes a perfect place to stroll to for lunch where they serve cheap and cheerful light lunches, featuring tasty rotis, chilis and hamburgers. Dinners are informal and less expensive than in many of the surrounding restaurants. The main feature is the carvery - a choice of meats, local vegetables and salads, buffet style. But they also offer local catch of the day, a seafood skillet and lobster. Happy hour is 1800-1900 daily.

Those hankering after Chinese food should try Memories of Hong Kong [$C-D], a well run Chinese restaurant with full take-away service and a happy hour on Fridays from 1800-1900.

Erwin fell in love with St. Lucia when he was visiting from his native Switzerland. He returned as a resident and now owns Top [$B], which serves both exotic Caribbean specialties and international food. Items include lobster soup and lamb chops with whisky sauce. Large paintings by local artist St. Omer adorn the walls and are also for sale. Happy hour is 1800-1900, two for one.

Whispering palms, traditional Caribbean chairs and decor and dockside tables feature at Julie Betts' Mortar and Pestle [$B]. Julie offers exotic Caribbean specialities and national dishes from a host of islands. Expect a peaceful atmosphere and a pleasant mixture of both local and visiting customers. If you are in a party mood, turn up on Tuesday for a barbecue and minstrel band, Thursdays for Jazz or Sundays for a steel band.

Miss Saigon [$C-D] should suit those who like far-eastern specialties. It is run by Myrna from the Philippines and includes both a dining room and take out service. The food is good and inexpensive.

Eagle's Nest [$C] is built right on the channel into Rodney Bay. It has a romantic pleasant atmosphere and serves excellent seafood at a reasonable price

The St. Lucian Hotel has two restaurants and nightly entertainment. Tuesdays to Saturdays the young can jump up to their Splash

THE GREAT HOUSE

RESTAURANT - ST. LUCIA - A FEW MINUTES FROM RODNEY BAY
TEL: (758) 450-0450 FAX:(758) 450-0451

Open: Afternoon Tea 4:30 p.m. to 5:30 p.m. Happy Hour 5:30 p.m. to 6:30 p.m., Dinner 7:00 p.m. to 10:00 p.m. (last order). Closed Mondays. To avoid disappointment, call us to book your table.

Elegant dress, please

Colonial enchantment and pure elegance. With friendly staff, professional cuisine, soft elegant ambiance and a fantastic view. The a la carte and Great House value menu ($99 EC) has creatively transformed traditional French cuisine by adding the spicy creole touch of the islands into a famous style unique at the Great House.

---

disco and for Sunday lunch they offer a buffet and steel band.

For a special night out the place to visit is The Great House [$A] in Cap Estate. The restaurant is set in a grand old colonial style estate house, and everything has been done to enhance the ambiance of old style luxury. The food is traditional French modified by a touch of spicy Creole. Next door the Derek Walcott theater regularly puts on cultural shows from dancing and music to theater. You can enquire about the program from the Great House.

The small town of Gros Islet is picturesque and very local. It is within walking distance of Rodney Bay and you can get a good meal at O'Reilly's [$C]. This cute restaurant is tiny, so if a group is going, it is best to call O'Reilly and let him know you are coming. You sit out at a table on the street and watch life go by as you eat fresh Creole seafood with all the local vegetables.

One night you wouldn't go to eat in a Gros Islet restaurant is Friday when the village is closed to traffic and everyone dances in the streets, or wanders from bar to bar. All along the street there are stalls selling such goodies as barbecued conch on a skewer and barbecued fish and chicken. If you like to eat sitting down, the lovely old Scottie's Bar right in the center of town puts chairs out on the street. In recent times Friday night at Gros Islet has attracted undesirable elements; to be safe, go in a group or by cab or bus and return the same way. Stay in well lit areas.

If all that eating has left you with a heavy feeling, you can burn up some calories horse riding at Trims. Then for a thrilling sky high view of the anchorage (you can take your camera), try a parasailing ride with Jacobs. Golfers should know that just north of Rodney Bay on Cap Estate is the St. Lucia Golf and Country Club where you can enjoy a round of golf and get to know local golfers. If you like St. Lucia so much that you want to buy a house or piece of land, speak to fellow yachtsman Jonathan Everett at Home Services, near Capone's.

Water sports

The water in front of the St. Lucian Hotel is completely flat and good for beginner

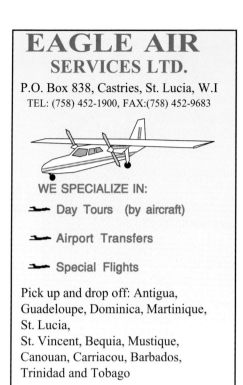

windsurfing. Boards are available for rent at the hotel.

There is reasonable snorkeling around Pigeon Island. New Scuba sites are being found in the north. If there is not too much surge, Pigeon Island offers a pleasant dive to 60' with stag horn coral, sponges, and brightly colored parrot fish. Barrel of Beef has boulders, sponges and colorful reef fish including sargent majors.

Buddies Scuba, in the marina , is run by Ian, though Berni is usually sitting behind the desk waiting to help you. They have a purpose built 30-foot dive boat with a bimini shade and they dive daily. They will fill tanks, though they do not rent equipment.

Dolphin Divers is over by Shamrocks. You can buy or rent gear here, get tanks filled and have equipment serviced.

Windjammer Landings

Windjammer Landings is a brand new upmarket villa development just south of Rodney Bay. The anchorage is tricky so those who want to go in there by boat should contact the managers and they will provide a guide. It is also just a short cab ride from Rodney Bay. They have a particularly good Sunday jazz brunch and you can get your fill of fire eating and limbo on Thursday's Caribbean night. Windjammer Landings has boutiques, a full diving facility, and entertainment several nights a week.

Castries Market

CASTRIES AND VIGIE

When entering Castries Harbor, the only danger to avoid is the shoal that extends to the west of Tapion Rock. There are two main anchorages: Vigie Creek and close to Castries town itself. Neither location is particularly scenic and both are noisy, but they are conveniently located for shopping and services. Of the two, Vigie is more secluded, but farther from town.

Castries Town

Castries has burned down twice and was most recently rebuilt in the early 1950's. Some post-disaster architecture lacks charm, but there are lovely old buildings around Derek Walcott Square and along Brazil Street that escaped the fire. The area between Peynier Street and Chausee Road along Brazil, Micoud, Chisel and Coral Streets has an interesting Creole atmosphere, with balconies, gingerbread, old and new buildings.

Regulations

Castries is a port of entry, though it is much easier to clear in Rodney Bay or Marigot. The officials insist that entering yachts come straight to the customs dock, or if there is no room, to the anchorage east of the customs buoy.

Services

Water is available at the dock and ice may be bought from one of the plants in town.

Valmonts has a Yamaha dealership opposite the fire station. They sell duty free outboards to yachts in transit at good prices. They also keep a good range of spares and will fix your broken Yamaha. Ray's Refrigeration will fix your freezer.

The big bus station is behind the local produce market. All routes are numbered. 1A is Gros Islet, 2H is Vieux Fort, 3D is Soufriere.

Ashore

St. Lucia's local market ranks among the best in the islands. It occupies several buildings as well as outdoor areas and spreads to both sides of the road. It vibrates with color and excitement as hundreds of local vendors sell their wares. Spend an hour or two here enjoying the scene and take the opportunity to stock up on local foods, t-shirts, coal pots, straw work and handicrafts. The market includes a street of tiny food stalls, each owning a single outside table. Here you will find the cheapest

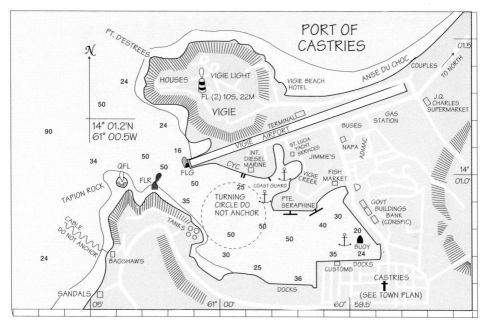

PORT OF CASTRIES

and tastiest local food in the island. A ferry links the market with Pointe Seraphine, the duty free shopping mall where you will find over 17 pleasantly laid out tourist shops. (Take your boat papers with you for the duty free.)

The best supermarket in town is J.Q. Charles on W. Peter Boulevard. Bryden's is a good liquor store and will deliver large orders to the marina. They also have a big pharmacy and stationery store on Bridge Street. For the best meats visit Maison Salaison.

You will find general hardware at Homecenter, Valmonts and J.Q. Charles. If you need acrylic sheet or synthetic canvas, then J.N. Baptiste is the specialist. For auto-stores try Johnson's and Bandag.

The new La Place Carenage Mall is the in-town duty free mall. About a dozen shops offer handicraft, jewelry and more. Don't miss Noah's Arkade, over the road, for handmade items. Art lovers should visit the Artsibit Gallery. A trip out to Bagshaw's clothing factory is well worth the short taxi ride from town. Their large showroom is in a lovely setting overlooking the sea.

Secrets Wine Bar [$D] is owned by Maurice and Steven, both St. Lucians who have spent much of their lives in the UK. Their food is very inexpensive and available

from 1000 to 2300 daily. Their baguette sandwiches with many different fillings make a fine lunch. Good local food, including fresh snapper, is also available. They have a daily happy hour from 1700-1830 with lower priced drinks including a wide variety of beers. Yachtspeople come by to watch the big games on their large TV system.

There are plenty of local snack bars. The Aft Deck [$D]in La Place Carenage serves good local lunches on a pleasant balcony overlooking the bay. Kimlin's [$D] on Derek Walcott Square serves good local food very inexpensively, cafeteria style. The Pink Elephant [$D] on William Peter Boulevard is airy and pleasant with daily specials and snacks, including rotis. The most stylish downtown restaurant is Rain's [$B-C] in Columbus Square. Set in a lovely old Caribbean building you can sit on the balcony and watch life unfold below. They have a good menu with plenty of choice and Dora the manager will see you are content.

Two hillside restaurants on the Morne have magnificent views over Castries. San Antoine [$A] is unmatched for elegant ambience. Originally built as a grand residence in the 1880's, it was converted to a hotel in the 1920's, then burned to the

PORT OF CASTRIES

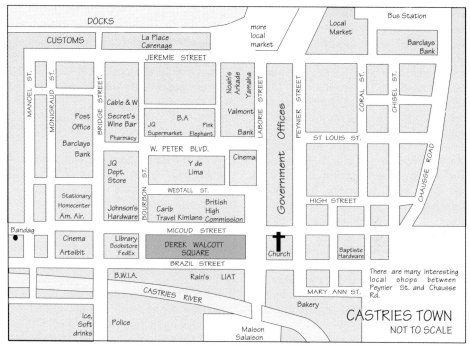

CASTRIES TOWN
NOT TO SCALE

There are many interesting local shops between Peynier St. and Chausse Rd.

ground in 1970, leaving only massive stone walls with lovely arches. It has been beautifully recreated without regard to cost and has a sumptuous atmosphere. The other famous restaurant on the Morne is Chef Harry's Green Parrot. Harry is a superb MC who gets everyone dancing and having fun. Call in advance and go when he has entertainment.

Vigie

There is a light on Vigie Hill (group flashing 2 every 10 seconds) which is helpful in identifying Castries Harbor at night.

You can anchor either inside or outside Vigie Creek, but leave room for the large brig Unicorn, which takes out day charter-ers from here. Anchoring here before clearing customs will incur the full and expensive fury of officials.

Services

Castries Yacht Center (CYC) [VHF:16] is a relatively inexpensive, full service haul out facility using a 35-ton travel lift, with accommodation for both short term haul outs and long term storage. There is a perimeter fence and 24-hour security, showers, and a marine chandlery to cover haul out needs, including paint, zincs and safety gear. Do your own work, or they can do it for you. Fiberglass repairs are available and power tools may be rented. CYC sells water and duty free fuel. A snack bar will keep you going and inexpensive apartments are available nearby.

In the same yard as CYC, International Diesel and Marine Services is a really comprehensive diesel shop. Run by Derek Morton, a fully qualified British diesel engineer, they have a small machine shop and equipment for fully servicing fuel injection pumps and injectors. They are agents for CAV and Perkins and can arrange spares for most brands of engine at short notice. They offer every kind of service, from routine maintenance and repair to a complete rebuild.

St. Lucia Yacht Services (SLYC) [VHF:16] is a ramshackle marina, home to a few local boats. Their fuel dock is fine and they offer water, fuel and car rentals. You can talk to them about docking, but look at the docks first. Although apparently well protected, St. Lucia Yacht Services can suffer from a surge in a hurricane or other large weather system. There is a mechanic shop on the premises. Inside the fading exterior of their long building you will smell the fresh bread from CMC Exclusive Bakery. You can buy freshly made white and whole wheat bread.

Christopher Kessell [VHF:16 call sign "Chrisalis"] is the local yacht surveyor. He also does excellent work on yacht electrics and can help with light machining. His prices are reasonable and you can arrange for him to come and visit you in Rodney Bay or Marigot.

A short walk on the road to town is Leroy James' big NAPA agency which stocks loads of filters, parts, sprays, seals, polishes and tools. They are agents for Evinrude outboards and offer full sales and service. In addition they stock OMC inflatables, ropes and some marine hardware.

Ashore

A good reason for coming into Vigie is to visit one of the two excellent restaurants that grace its shores. The Coal Pot [$B] has a very romantic setting right on the waterfront in an old boat storehouse, which is suitably nautical. The restaurant is run by Sonia and Michel whose cooking is superb,

Welcome to Paradise

Nestled in beautiful Marigot Bay, twenty minutes by road or eight minutes by sea from Castries, offers you a little bit of paradise. In style it gives you a homely feel but not without all the luxuries of the standard resort. Phone for details of room rates or just come for the day and dine in our famous Doolittles Restaurant by the sea's edge.

email: sluone@sluonestop.com   website: http://www.marigotbeach.com/
voicemail: (758) 451-4973

P.O Box 101 • Castries, St Lucia, West Indies • Tel: (758) 451-4974 • Fax: (758) 451-4973

with the emphasis on seafood. This is one of the best restaurants in St. Lucia and those who are seriously interested in food should visit either by cab or boat. They are open for both lunch and dinner and, as it is popular, reservations are advisable. Soon they plan to open the Mango Moon Fitness, a well equipped gym with instructors, and Art Cafe, a coffee house where you can admire local art.

Jimmie's Restaurant [$B-C] has a tropical garden setting by the waterfront with a view across the bay and is conveniently situated at St. Lucia Yacht Services. Jimmie's is one of St. Lucia's best seafood restaurants with some excellent recipes (try the Harbor Catch). Jimmie is a St. Lucian who has spent years in the catering trade and really knows the business. He offers an interesting light lunch menu, and best of all he keeps the atmosphere informal; it is the kind of place where you can feel comfortable just going for soup and dessert.

MARIGOT BAY

Marigot Bay is another of the Caribbean's spectacularly beautiful anchorages, completely sheltered and affording a perfect backdrop to that sunset rum punch. It lies about a mile south of Hess Oil's huge tanker depot at Cul de Sac Bay. By staying fairly close inshore and watching for a prominent house with a conspicuous red roof on the hill of the southern entrance, you should not miss Marigot. However, it is so well

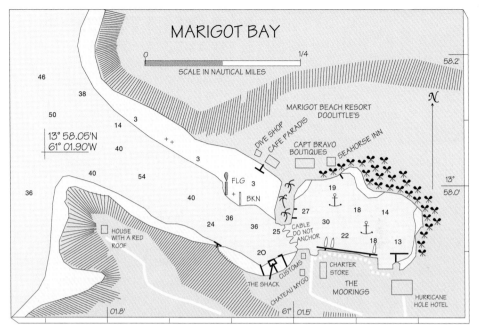

MARIGOT BAY

SCALE IN NAUTICAL MILES

0   1/4

46
38
50
14 3
13° 58.05'N
61° 01.90'W   40
40
54
36
40

MARIGOT BEACH RESORT
DOOLITTLE'S

DIVE SHOP
CAFE PARADIS
CAPT BRAVO
BOUTIQUES
SEAHORSE INN

FLG 3
BKN

HOUSE
WITH A RED
ROOF

24   36
36

27
25 CABLE
DO NOT
ANCHOR
30
22
19
18   14
18   13

58.2'
13°
58.0'

20
THE SHACK
CHATEAU MYGO
CUSTOMS

CHARTER
STORE
THE
MOORINGS

HURRICANE
HOLE HOTEL

01.8'   61° 01.5'

tucked away that a British admiral is reputed to have hidden his fleet here, disguising the masts by tying coconut fronds in the rigging. The pursuing French sailed right by.

Favor the southern side of the channel as you enter. This is not always easy as many yachts anchor on this side of the channel. Pass close to them or you will touch the shoal that extends a long way out from Marigot Beach Resort. A green marker and orange and white striped beacon mark the shoal. Leave these to port as you enter. Anchor anywhere in the inner harbor, where holding is fair in soft mud. Depths are 18 to 24 feet. Costly and delicate underwater electric cables and water pipes cross right at the entrance to the inner harbor. Anchoring is strictly forbidden here.

You may well be approached by vendors in boats who frequently offer bananas of dubious provenance at twice the price of the Mariner Market. So far I have politely refused all offers and have been left in peace.

Regulations

Marigot Bay is an official port of entry, with customs and immigration. Linus Leon, the man in charge, is friendly and helpful. He is usually there from 0900-1200 and 1300-1700. There is a five-knot speed limit in the harbor.

Dinghy docks are outside the customs house, close under Hurricane Hole Hotel and directly in front of Cafe Paradis. Dinghies must not be tied to the yacht docks.

The only place to dump garbage is in the facility behind the customs/police station. There is a small charge.

Services

The Moorings Marina is secure, pleasant and offers short term dockage, electricity, water and ice. The Moorings stand by on VHF 16 & 25 from 0800 to 1630. VHF channel 25 is the working channel and has a much greater range. Contact Hurricane Hole Hotel [VHF:25] outside working hours. Diesel and gasoline (ask about duty free fuel) are available on The Moorings fuel dock next to the customs dock.

The Moorings have inexpensive showers and free toilets upstairs above the Mariner Market. Anchored yachts are asked to use the shore toilet facilities. This is the base of The Moorings charter company with a fleet of 40 yachts for bareboat or skippered charter.

An inexpensive 24-hour ferry service connects all parts of the bay. Tickets are refundable against drinks at the Cafe

Paradis on the far shore.

Taxi Service Marigot [VHF:16] is a cooperative of the local taxi drivers who wait near customs.

Ashore

Marigot has very much come to life in the last two years and now there are half a dozen excellent restaurants for eating ashore.

On the south shore is The Moorings Hurricane Hole Hotel [VHF:25], with a swimming pool and the elegant Hurricane Hole Restaurant where you can peruse their gourmet menu. For lighter fare a less expensive Patio menu is available at the bar. Happy hour is nightly from 1730-1900, two for the price of one. They offer evening cabaret acts several times a week in season. While here, visit The Moorings boutique with a full range of swim and casual wear, local books and holiday essentials.

The Mariner Market is a well stocked mini-market with a wide range of French and other wines. They bake fresh French bread daily and often have smoked salmon in stock. It is open in season from 0800-1800, except Sunday when it closes at 1630. In the summer time it closes a couple of hours earlier.

Right near the customs is Chateau Mygo. This restaurant is new, though it replaces the old Mama Sheila's [$D], and is run by her daughter. The new building is much more elegant than the old. Hopefully she will continue with the Mama Sheila tradition of great home-style Caribbean Indian food at unbeatable prices, offering the best value in the bay. This restaurant has just opened and is definitely worth checking out. Mama Sheila still occasionally caters to private parties at her house on request. But she does not serve alcohol.

The Shack [VHF:16, $B-D] hangs out over the water on stilts at the entrance to the inner harbor. Manager Shauni, from Guiana, runs a happy hour from 1700-1900, with two for one and plenty of good cheer. It is popular with both yachties and local residents. Stay for a seafood (including lobster) or steak dinner at reasonable prices. When the crowd gets going, the chef comes out and gives a limbo show. Also a guitarist makes an appearance from time to

Marigot Bay

time. Captains bringing a party of five or more get their dinner free. You can tie your dinghy to the bar and are welcome to use it as a dinghy dock at any time. The Shack also does a good buffet lunch.

On the north shore is Marigot Beach Club [VHF:16, $B], run by Dave from England. The whole area is known as Doolittles after the movie that was made here. Dave plans to rebuild all the docks on the east side of his spit, so docking may be available by the time this guide comes out. When this is done full communications including mail (c/o Marigot Beach Club, P.O. Box 101, Castries, St Lucia) will be available. His Cafe Paradis restaurant is pleasant, comfortable and right on the waterfront. Happy hour is 1700-1900 nightly with entertainment from time to time. This is a great spot for a pleasant relaxing meal, and the setting is unbeatable.

Behind Cafe Paradis are several shops, boutiques and businesses. Here you will find Captain Bravo, a store selling fishing gear and chandlery. This is a good place to buy flags, cruising guides and a handline to keep you in fish while you cruise.

JJ's [VHF:16, $B-C] is up the hill and local, cheerful and rowdy in character. JJ serves excellent conch, chicken and fish to the accompaniment of loud music. If you call and let him know you are coming, he will arrange free transport from the customs at about 1930. If you decide to go, you should definitely do this as people walking up and down the hill have occasionally been mugged.

Walk about a mile to the main road to catch a bus to town for $2 EC. On the return journey most bus drivers are willing to bring you all the way to the customs dock for $5 EC.

Water sports

Rosemond's Trench Divers [VHF:16] is in the Marigot Beach Resort complex. It is owned and run by St. Lucian Rosemond Clery who is one of the best-qualified divers in the Windwards. He also happens to be a boxer and retired as the Caribbean welterweight champion. Rosemond is an

enthusiastic diver and underwater photographer who teaches diving at all levels, including specialty courses. He is helped by three instructors and two dive masters. They are happy to rent gear and fill tanks.

Rosemond's Trench Divers take regular trips to Anse Cochon and Soufriere (for details of the dives, see the water sports sections for these areas). They are happy to take you diving from your yacht anywhere down the leeward coast. You can arrange a rendezvous over the radio. However, if you are in the Soufriere area you will probably have to telephone.

Other water sports in Marigot are run by **Cosmos William** who rents small craft from kayaks up to 21-foot Impulse sailing boats. He organizes snorkeling trips and rents snorkeling gear. In addition he runs a water taxi which is the fastest way to get down to Soufriere or back up to Castries. No to visit Soufriere on your own yacht? Cosmos is the man to talk with.

ANSE COCHON

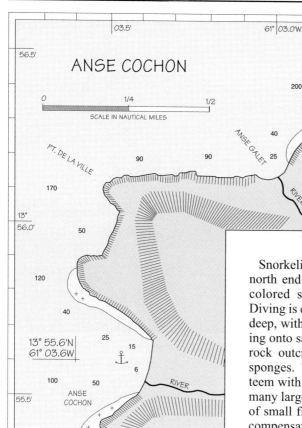

Water sports

Snorkeling off the rocky headland at the north end of the bay is fair with brightly colored sponges, corals and parrotfish. Diving is excellent. The water is 25-40 feet deep, with a coral and rock slope descending onto sand. Out on the sand are isolated rock outcroppings covered in corals and sponges. These underwater fairy castles teem with small fish. Though there are not many large fish, the abundance and variety of small fish and reef creatures more than compensates. There is also a wreck of the Lesleen-M in the middle of the bay. It is a 160-foot freighter and lies in 67 feet of water. It was deliberately sunk in 1986 to make a dive site and it has attracted an exceptional collection of invertebrates, many of which are uncommon elsewhere. Just south of Anse Cochon is Rosemond's Trench, a delightful dive that starts between two small canyon walls. There are many sponges and invertebrates with a colorful selection of reef fish. St. Lucia only allows diving with a local dive shop, so make contact with Rosemond's Trench Divers and he can pick you up in the bay.

Anse Cochon is a small bay with an attractive deserted beach. Many day charter boats make brief stops here on their day tours. It lies about three miles south of Marigot. First you pass Anse La Raye, then there is a rocky headland. Anse Cochon is tucked up in the corner just past this headland. It is the first beach after the headland. There are rocky patches to the south end of the beach, but there is no problem anchoring off the middle. If you get hooked into sand, rather than weed, you can find excellent holding in about 12 to 25 feet of water. Your boat may swing around so take care if you have an anchor that can trip itself. Anse Cochon makes a good daytime anchorage and overnight stop in settled conditions. Anse Cochon is also a fishing priority area, so move if the fishermen ask you to.

Soufriere, The Hummingbird anchorage is at the top

Soufriere is a small, picturesque town set amid a scenic wonderland dominated by the towering twin Pitons. Its exceptional beauty will enthrall hikers and photographers. The marine side is a magnificent marine park.

When approaching Soufriere from the north, beware of the shoal which extends out from the south side of Anse Chastanet.

Regulations

The whole area shown on our sketch chart is part of the Soufriere Marine Management Area (SMMA) under the direction of Kai Wulff. The SMMA [VHF:16/8] regulates all anchoring, diving and fishing activity here. The only anchoring area is by the Hummingbird (see below); otherwise, pick up a mooring – small blue and white ones are for yachts up to 70 feet, large blue and white ones are for yachts over 70 feet and orange buoys are reserved for dive boats. We will deal with these below area by area. There are charges for being in the Soufriere Marine Managment Area. The basic rate allows you to stay for two nights and is $27 EC for a vessel up to 40 feet; $40 EC up to

70 feet and $54 over 70 feet. Inexpensive weekly rates are also available. If there are not enough moorings, the SMMA will direct you to anchor. You can pick up any available mooring; a park ranger will come by to collect the fees. Park rangers carry identification and give official receipts. Put your mooring line through the loop on the mooring rope, do not put the loop on the mooring rope on your cleat. All fees go towards paying for the maintenance and upkeep of the park. As in the rest of St. Lucia, spearfishing, damaging, taking or even buying coral, sponges, sea urchins (dead or alive) is strictly forbidden, as is the dumping of garbage, oil, etc. Fishing is also forbidden in some areas. The Marine Park staff are very helpful with finding taxis, giving weather alerts and making yachts feel welcome. They have an office on the waterfront near the craft market.

Security in the SMMA is generally very good, though they do occasionally have theft problems, which only seem to occur when one particular individual is out of jail. The trouble is he has scored considerable funds on a couple of occasions and now has

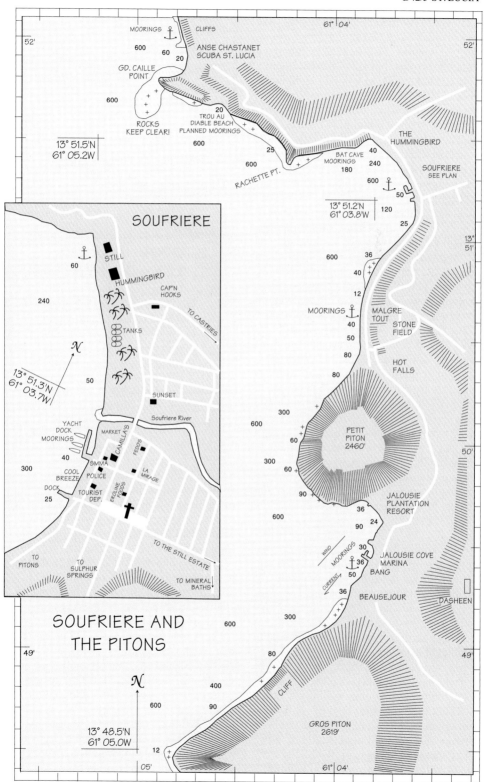

MOORINGS ⚓ CLIFFS

600 60 20

ANSE CHASTANET
SCUBA ST. LUCIA

GD. CAILLE
POINT

600

52'

13° 51.5'N
61° 05.2W

ROCKS
KEEP CLEAR!

20
TROU AU
DIABLE BEACH
PLANNED MOORINGS

600

RACHETTE PT.

61° 04'

52'

THE
HUMMINGBIRD

25

BAT CAVE
MOORINGS
180

40

240

600 ⚓

600

50

SOUFRIERE
SEE PLAN

13°
51'

13° 51.2'N
61° 03.8'W

120

25

600

36

40

12

MOORINGS ⚓

40

50

80

MALGRE
TOUT

STONE
FIELD

HOT
FALLS

SOUFRIERE

⚓
60 STILL

HUMMINGBIRD

240

CAP'N
HOOKS

TO CASTRIES

N

13° 51.3'N
61° 03.7'W

TANKS

50

SUNSET

Soufriere River

YACHT
DOCK
MOORINGS

40

MARKET

CAMILLA'S

FEDO'S

SMMA
POLICE

LA
MIRAGE

EROLINE
FOODS

80

300

600

60

300

60

90

36

PETIT
PITON
2460'

90 24

300

COOL
BREEZE

DOCK

25

TOURIST
DEP.

TO THE STILL ESTATE

WIND

MOORINGS

CURRENT

⚓
30
36
50

36

JALOUSIE
PLANTATION
RESORT

JALOUSIE COVE
MARINA
BANG

50'

TO
PITONS

TO
SULPHUR
SPRINGS

TO MINERAL
BATHS

BEAUSEJOUR

600

300

DASHEEN

SOUFRIERE AND
THE PITONS

N

13° 48.5'N
61° 05.0W

600

400

90

80

CLIFF

GROS PITON
2619'

49'

12

05'

61° 04'

49'

a lawyer to try to keep him at liberty. Ask any official water taxi driver about the security situation. Harassment is mainly a thing of the past, but should anyone annoy you, contact the SMMA [VHF: 16/8] or the police [VHF:16]. Take a description of the person and the name of their craft.

Anyone scuba diving must be accompanied by an accredited dive guide. If you have your own equipment the SMMA can put you in contact with a guide, which is a relatively inexpensive option. If you do not have your own equipment you can go with one of the dive shops. Snorkeling is open and free.

Soufriere is an official port of entry, though customs were not yet available as we went to press. There is no problem staying here on your last night before you leave and you can get a temporary permit to moor from the police station if you want to overnight here before clearing in properly.

The Soufriere Water Taxi Association [VHF:16] is a very professional group of properly equipped and insured water taxis. They offer many sightseeing and snorkeling tours around the area and run people to town or Vigie airport, saving considerable time over the twisty land road. They also sell ice, arrange beach barbecues and deep sea fishing. Associate members include yacht guides who will tend your stern line and are licensed to sell fruits and souvenirs. In the hurricane season they will keep you abreast of the latest weather.

Anse Chastanet

Anse Chastanet is a delightful cottage hotel built on a hill which slopes to the sea. Several yacht moorings are available off the cliffs just north of the beach. There are rocks just south and north of the moorings so approach with caution. While often reasonably peaceful, this area can be untenable in times of a northerly swell. A dinghy dock is planned near the moorings.

The Anse Chastanet beach bar is a congenial lunch spot and one can browse in the two boutiques. For dinner, they have a restaurant up the hill where the emphasis is on Creole and international seafood. Anse Chastanet is also accessible by dinghy or by the road from Soufriere, or you can hire a

water taxi to bring you over.

Water sports

Scuba St. Lucia at Anse Chastanet [VHF:16] is one of the largest dive operations in the Windwards, with two resort courses and four dives daily. It has a range of facilities, from an equipment shop to photo and video labs. They do not fill tanks. Scuba St. Lucia takes divers on the Anse Chastanet Reef for their first dive. This dive is usually done at 1100. It is best to turn up half an hour before and remember to bring your diving card. If you are not certified, resort courses are available and these usually start at around 0900.

The Anse Chastanet reef is a flawless reef that extends seaward from the beach. The shallower parts are good for snorkeling and the diving is excellent along the length of the reef which slopes from about 30 to 80 feet. Sheet coral, fungus corals, solitary corals and brain corals are abundant, as are a delightful variety of sponges, from the azure vase sponge to large barrel sponges. The water is clear and reef fish abound, with

clouds of brown and blue chromis, along with sergeant majors, brilliantly colored parrotfish and goatfish. All kinds of jacks and snappers cruise just off the reef.

Trou au Diable

This beach lies between Gd. Caille Point and Rachette Point. Moorings are planned here. Sand covers much of the anchorage but there are lovely coral gardens, ideal for snorkeling and diving, both to the east and west. If approaching this area from Anse Chastanet, be particularly careful of the reef off Gd. Caille Point.

Hummingbird anchorage

This is the most comfortable anchorage in the SMMA. There are no moorings but you can anchor in the northern part of the bay – the area is marked onshore with signs. Take a line stern to the shore. You must move if requested to do so by fishermen, but this is rare. A few moorings have also been placed in the area of the bat cave. You will have to get a stern line ashore and find a tree to tie up to. Watch out for prickles.

Ashore

The Hummingbird Restaurant [VHF:16, $A-B] is the most elegant and charming of Soufriere's restaurants, featuring a wall made of pottery coal pots, wonderful hand carvings and an exquisite view across the pool to the Pitons beyond. The food is a blend of French and Creole cuisine, with seafoods a specialty. Owner Joyce gets much of her business from yachts and welcomes them warmly. So much so that a skipper bringing in a party of four or more gets his or her fish or chicken dinner (any style) free. They arrange beach barbecues for groups of ten or more.

Hot and cold showers are available, and Joyce will arrange taxis and tours for her customers at a fair local rate. The staff will help customers with telephone calls or faxes during normal office hours; They will help you get rid of well-wrapped garbage. Batiks, hand made on the premises, feature in a small shop. Rooms are available. For those that like to watch the waves lap the shore, Joyce opens the Hummingbird's Bamboo Beach Bar for entertaining sunset

Soufriere Beach

or moonlit cocktails.

If you are eating at the Hummingbird, call on the VHF just before you go ashore and have Harry, the uniformed security guard meet you on the beach. He will help you pull your dinghy to the hotel entrance and he will watch it.

The Still Beach Resort [VHF:16, $C-D] is another restaurant, to the north of the Hummingbird. Of modern design, The Still has both an inside dining room and a large very open patio with a superb views. The patio is perfectly delightful in the cool of the morning and evening. The helpful and friendly staff offer good sized portions of local food (much of it from the associated Still Estate) at reasonable prices. They are happy to help out with local and overseas telephone calls.

A short distance behind the Hummingbird lies Captain Hook's Hideaway [$C-D], a small, cheap and cheerful restaurant good for local plates and snacks.

The Hummingbird anchorage is just a short walk or dinghy ride from town.

Water sports

Snorkeling is good all the way between the anchorage and Trou au Diable Beach. If you snorkel in shallow water off the beach in front of the Still Beach Bar you are likely to see streams of bubbles rising to the surface – they are from a minor underwater volcanic vent.

Soufriere town

The town of Soufriere was the set of the movie "Water," starring Michael Caine, and it has many charming old Creole buildings with balconies and gingerbread. Much has been done recently to upgrade the town and waterfront.

You can go stern to the specially constructed yacht dock right outside the police station. Keep your yacht a good distance from the dock as swells can come in suddenly. There is a dinghy dock at the end, and there is a landing charge of $5 EC per person for using it.

Ashore

The area has many points of interest and you may want to go to the new tourism center close by the waterfront for details.

Ben taxi stands by on VHF:16. He is a knowledgeable guide and will happily take you on a tour of the area. You can find him at his music store. He also owns a small gift shop.

Cool Breeze gas station can supply gas or diesel to the dock. They also have a reasonably priced car rental agency for those who like to explore on their own. They deliver their cars all over the island.

In town you will find a great little supermarket, sparkling clean with an ample array of foods to provision your boat. We were pleased to see they had local frozen fish on sale. It is called Eroline's Foods and is open

welcome to the

HUMMINGBIRD RESORT

VHF Channel 16
Telephone:(758) 459-7232
Fax:(758) 459-7033

Batik Studio
exclusive designs at reasonable prices

JOYCE (YOUR HOSTESS)

Gourmet Restuarant
With a perfect Pitons view
Open breakfast, lunch and dinner
(breakfast 7-10 am)

The Yachtsman's Favorite Bar
Our guards will watch your
dinghy and your yacht.

Hot and cold showers
Overnight Accommodation

143

Monday to Saturday. Normal hours are 0800-1800, but on Saturday it stays open till 1900. If you buy more than you can carry, they will deliver it back to the boat for you. There is also a pharmacy and drug store called Clarke's.

For a local restaurant visit Camilla's [$C], upstairs with a balcony overlooking the street. This artistically designed restaurant serves local meat, seafood and vegetarian specialties The staff are pleasant and friendly and the seafood is fresh, good and reasonably priced. Should you need somewhere to stay, Camilla also has a guest house.

Otherwise try Fedo's New Venture [$C-D]. It is very small and you would not go for the ambience, but Fedo is an excellent chef and can produce a first class meal. The Sunset Bar [$D] is a cheap and cheerful upstairs restaurant that cooks pizzas and local meals. La Mirage was still being constructed but it was planned to be a new restaurant run by John, Mary and Janice Lamontagne.

The Still Estate [$C], just out of town, is a large restaurant offering good local food and they have a handicraft boutique.

Up in the hills to the north of town Jo Allain's La Haut [$C] with a hilltop view over the area is open for lunch; dinner is only by special arrangement.

If you visit just one place in this area, it should be the Dasheene Restaurant at Ladera Resort [$A-B]. The view here, straight down the valley between the Pitons, is exquisite, probably the most spectacular in the Caribbean. It is hard not to exclaim "wow" when you first see it. There is a swimming pool and bar with a friendly atmosphere. They serve both lunch and dinner. I would recommend lunch so you can see the view, though dinner on a moonlit night can be spectacular. They keep a first class chef making the dinner a fitting accompaniment to the view. The energetic can walk up to Dasheene from between the Pitons. You can also take a taxi or the Vieux Fort bus from Soufriere. It is a long but pleasant walk back down.

The Sulphur Springs, between Ladera Resort and Soufriere look like a scene straight from hell, with barren, brightly colored earth, bubbling pools and huge spurts of steam. More scenic and pleasant are the naturally hot Diamond Baths built by Louis the 16th (a fair walk or short ride out the back of town). Take a few dollars and your towel, and you can luxuriate in these baths set amid a well-tended tropical garden. Start at the top where the indoor baths are the hottest and most therapeutic, then graduate to the outside pools.

The rain forest area near Morne Fond St. Jacques offers exquisite views for walking or hiking. The road is sometimes bad so you may have to ask around to find a taxi driver willing to take you there. You are required to have a guide and pay a fee when hiking in the rain forest reserve, but walking on the road leading to it, amid the lush vegetation with hidden glimpses of the Pitons below, is also beautiful. For hikes into the rainforest call the Forestry Department [450-2231]. They have knowledgeable guides in the Soufriere area that can arrange to come and take you on a rain forest tour. (They can provide transportation from the nearest dock). One of the most interesting is a two and a half hour loop tour to the Maho waterfalls. Take your bathing things for a shower in the fall and a swim in the pool above it.

Malgre Tout

The Marine Park has put moorings towards the southern end of the beach. You will need to take a line ashore. I recommend using only members of the St. Lucia Water Taxi or Yacht Guide Association. Agree on a price in advance. ($10 EC is fair.) If you would prefer to do it yourself, say so.

Just above the anchorage you can see the new Stonefield Estate [$B-C] managed by Cybelle Brown. This elegant family run hotel has a lovely restaurant area with a swimming pool and view over the yachts. Trails lead to some excellent examples of Carib petroglyphs. If you walk uphill to the concrete Jalousie road and keep going up hill, the estate is to your left and is marked.

There is an interesting small hot waterfall

on Jah I's land, with a nominal entrance fee. Walk back from the beach to the road and turn toward Petit Piton and you will see a sign to the waterfall. Get permission from Jah I in his small wooden house. This is the best hot shower available, and an unbeatable value.

Diving and snorkeling is good around Petit Piton.

Between the Pitons

Moorings are available in the area shown near Bang and the Jalousie Hilton Marina. If your maneuvering skills are insufficient to pick up a mooring, you will have offers from local water-taxis and others to help. Do not feel obliged to accept such offers. Note that the wind and current can be strong in this area and that the current is sometimes against the wind. This area is sometimes calm, sometimes rolly, and it can change with the tides.

The beach between the Pitons is now part of Jalousie Hilton [$A]. This is one of the Windward's fanciest and prettiest resorts. Their Jalousie Hilton Marina [VHF:16] is not a marina, but it does have docks capable of taking just about any size of yacht stern-to. Water is on the dock and telephone, electricity (220-volt, 50-cycle), and fuel should be available by the time you read this. Dinghies may be left inside the main dock. Bang is also planning a dinghy dock (see below).

Ashore

The Jalousie Hilton [$A] is open to the public and has four restaurants with a bevy of excellent international chefs. Whatever your choice you will not be disappointed. The Pier, by the Jalousie Cove marina, is open for dinner (specializing in seafood). The Plantation is open for dinner. Bayside (which is on the beach) and The Verandah open for lunch. If you are here on a Sunday don't miss the Sunday Brunch. They offer a wonderful selection starting with suchimi, and a variety of their own delicious home smoked fish. Take your time and eat in many small courses rather than one big one; you can go back again and again and get a little taste of everything.

There is a full spa with a massage center,

Plus -BUPA GIFT SHOP

We jerk every day and twice on Sundays

Tel and Fax:758-459-7864
Beau Estate, Soufriere

facials, hairdressers, saunas, and hot tubs. You can pay a day fee for use of the beach chairs and facilities including some watersports, the tennis courts, kids' learning center, pool tables and other hotel amenities. All kinds of tours and rental cars can be arranged at the hotel. There are several boutiques both in the main building and down by the marina office. A coffee shop and small gourmet/provisioning foodstore is planned next to the marina office.

Right next door to Jalousie, but completely separate is Bang [$B-C], a charming place owned by the eccentric English Lord Glenconner. Having spent years involved with the very upper crust of international society, including the development of Mustique, Lord Glenconner has grown Caribbean roots and his latest venture is a collection of five artistically designed local houses. These include a rum shop, boutique, and a restaurant. Bang is inexpensive and entertaining, where locals and visitors can mix under the seagrape trees in com-

Jalousie Hilton Marina

is ideally located between St. Lucia's two landmark mountains, the Pitons, which slope down to meet the sea in position 13° 49' 35"N/061° 03' 50"W with the superbly designed Hilton Resort & Spa, located on 325 Acres of lush tropical forest, 114 elegant villas, four bars, four restaurants, spa, scuba, tennis and lots of entertainment. The marina is fully equipped, with hot water showers, electricity, gas, diesel fuel, water, provisioning, laundry & dry cleaning and helicopter services.

For further information call Jalousie Marine Manager on:
Tel: (758) 459-7666

fortable open shelters built along the shore. The simple menu is cooked to perfection; starters include christophene au gratin and fish cakes, the main course is local fish and meat, barbecued in Jamaican jerk sauce and served with local vegetables.

Bang opens sometime around mid-morning and lunch is available around noon. However, most people come for dinner. Jump-ups are often arranged on Mondays and Wednesdays. The boutique has excellent buys on a variety of mainly Indian handicrafts. The toilets have showers which you are welcome to use. Guides are available here if you wish to climb Gros Piton. They plan a dinghy dock and when this is in operation, you should use this rather than the Jalousie dock when visiting Bang.

Water sports

Dive Jalousie [VHF:16] is run by Vitus, one of St. Lucia's best instructors. He will pick you up from your yacht and take you diving, Tank rentals are available by the week and you can get tanks filled as you head south. All kinds of courses are available. Radio communication is hard from Hummingbird and Malgre Tout, so call on the radio and make arrangements before you get in the shadow of the Pitons or use a telephone.

The dive around the base of Petit Piton is one of St. Lucia's greatest. Start from close to the beach and explore at whatever depth you feel comfortable. There are wonderful sponges, good coral formations and an extraordinary variety of fish. Sometimes huge schools of fish make magical patterns in the sunlight. Apart from reef fish such as angelfish, blue chromis, parrotfish, scorpionfish and damselfish, there are lots of hunters out there; jacks and snappers swim in fair sized schools and occasionally one sees a monster. The snorkeling here is also quite good. Another good site for both snorkeling and scuba is under Gros Piton just below the prominent cliff. A sloping drop off with plenty of fish and coral goes down to great depths. There are sometimes currents in this area.

The trip from the Pitons to Vieux Fort is a tough one against both wind and current. There are reefs extending about half a mile offshore between Choiseul and Laborie, so this coast is best given a good clearance. There are no good anchorages until you reach Vieux Fort.

VIEUX FORT

Vieux Fort

As the beaten track becomes trampled these days with the arrival of more and more boats, Vieux Fort gains charm by virtue of being away from it all. The town, with its old wooden buildings and large fishing fleet, has a quaint attraction. The anchorage is well protected, and a long walk (or short ride) away is one of the Caribbean's most magnificent windward beaches, a beach so long you can guarantee a mile or so to yourself. I would recommend this stop to those who want to get away from the obvious charms of the tourist spots and savor something really local. It is an obvious pickup or drop-off point for those arriving or leaving from Hewanorra, St. Lucia's largest airport.

Navigation

The sail to Vieux Fort from the Pitons is a beat to windward, often against the current. It takes about two hours in a weatherly boat. Keep well clear of the reef that stretches about half a mile offshore between Choiseul and Laborie.

You can anchor either in the first bay southwest of the main ship harbor marked on our chart, or off the town to the northwest of the port. To approach the town anchorage, leave the green beacon to port, head slowly for the Kimatrai Hotel on the hill and choose your spot.

Getting ashore and leaving the dinghy is a problem. The main port is run by the St. Lucia Marine Terminals. They are not really geared up to dealing with yachts but have been quite helpful. They are completing some major new dock construction and plan to keep a place where you can tie your dinghy, so take a look or ask. You can also

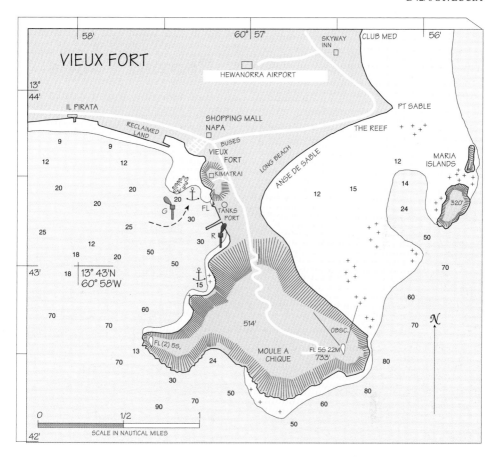

beach your dinghy among the fishing boats. However, a few people have complained that local youths demand large sums to guard your dinghy.

Regulations

Vieux Fort is an official port of entry and customs may be found at the head of the large ship dock. You will probably have to travel two miles to the airport to clear immigration, though you might get lucky and catch an immigration official visiting the port. By compensation, no port fees were being collected – no guarantees it will stay that way.

Services

Telephone calls may be made from any of the hotels.

Cooking gas is available at the gas depot just outside the port. Dinghy over to town to get outboard gasoline where all the fishing boats are beached.

Some nautical hardware is available from the Napa shop in the mall.

Ashore

Shopping is excellent. A good supermarket has opened in a mall by the roundabout. The even bigger Gabblewoods South is a few miles beyond Il Pirata. Fruits and vegetables in town are good and less expensive than in Castries. Mike's Frozen food offers a first-rate selection of meats as well as frozen vegetables. If you are buying more than you can carry he will happily deliver.

There are two restaurants ashore that make Vieux Fort a pleasant destination. The Kimatrai [$C-D] stands on the hill over the yacht anchorage. You can walk up from the ship dock. Head toward town, keep bearing left and look for a sign. The Kimatrai is an old fashioned kind of hotel, cool and breezy, with a marvelous view of the harbor. It is open all day and is a great place to hang out, relax, write postcards, catch up on your diary or watch cable TV. It has the perfect location for sunset. The meals are very inexpensive and excellent value; their fish Creole is delicious.

Il Pirata Restaurant [$B-C, closed Monday] is a superb Italian restaurant run by an Italian family. Their pasta is all homemade and cooked perfectly. Their Zuppa cake is out of this world. If you don't feel like a full meal you can eat inexpensive pastas and pizzas. The service is friendly and the waiters wear cheerful pirate uniforms. You are welcome to use the showers. Il Pirata lies a mile west of the town of Vieux Fort. Walk or taxi the mile from town, or take a bus heading toward Choiseul or Laborie. There is a Club Med farther afield, east of the airport.

If you plan to put in some beach time, try hanging out at The Reef [$C-D] on the windward beach. They have a pleasant bar/restaurant open both lunch and dinner serving local dishes at reasonable prices. Their menu includes seamoss and coconut water, saltfish bakes, lambi, lobster and squid. They also rent windsurfers.

East of Vieux Fort are the Maria Islands, a nature reserve and home to a species of lizard and a snake unknown anywhere else in the world. You can call the National Trust to arrange a guided trip. The energetic should hike up to the Moule a Chique light-

house for the view.

There is a great art and craft center at Choiseul, accessible by bus or taxi, which has baskets, carvings, seed jewelry, pottery, and household items made from natural local materials.

Soufriere Street

150

Northbound

The northbound passage between St. Vincent and St. Lucia can be hard on the wind and hard on the body. The north end of St. Vincent is unbelievably gusty on occasion and more than a little bumpy. It is not unusual to have gusts of 30 to 40 knots. These will steady down about six miles offshore. It pays to be prepared. I often do this trip single-handed and am not over fond of it, but find the easiest way to do it is as follows: Motor sail close up the coast under reefed main and engine and wait until the full force of the wind hits before deciding what to do. If you are comfortable under main and engine, keep going that way until the wind steadies down. Otherwise, if you have roller furling, just unroll a little of the jib until it gets calmer. The main thing is not to arrive at the north end with too much canvas, where reducing sail can degenerate into hanging onto flailing dacron as the boat bucks about and tries to throw you over. Once you get about five miles north of St. Vincent, wind and seas generally become much more constant and you can adjust sail accordingly. The current will set you to the west, so head up if possible. It is going to be a long day, so plan to leave early from Cumberland Bay or Wallilabou, as that will make it seem shorter.

Southbound

The southbound trip is usually a lovely broad reach. If you cannot see St. Vincent from St. Lucia, a course of 208° magnetic should start you in the right direction. Most people know how far they like to go in one day. I personally favor starting at the Pitons and stopping in St. Vincent. Nature lovers will favor Cumberland or Wallilabou and those who like waterfront bars can clear customs in Wallilabou or Barrouallie and continue onto Young Island Cut. If you plan to go all the way to Bequia, make sure you allow plenty of time.

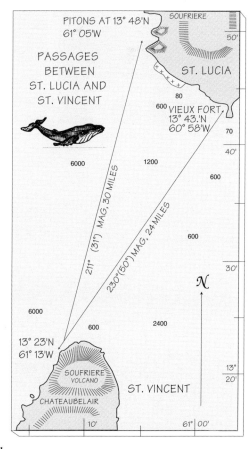

VINCENT & THE GRENADINES

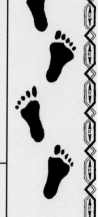

Regulations

St. Vincent, together with the Grenadines, make up one country. The main customs stations are Wallilabou, Kingstown, Bequia and Union Island. In a pinch you can find customs in Mustique and Canouan.

There is an entry charge of $10 EC per person. Yachts on charter are charged $2 EC per foot per month. You may stay as long as six months. Those clearing outside normal office hours (weekdays 0800-1200, 1300-1600) will pay an overtime fee.

No jet skis, aquascooters, or similar craft are allowed anywhere in St. Vincent and the Grenadines.

You are welcome to fish, but only for your own consumption. You can troll when sailing, or hand-line at anchor or from the shore, but not in protected areas where all fishing is forbidden. Protected areas include: The northeast coast and Devil's Table in Bequia, Isle de Quatre, all Mustique, the eastern coast of Canouan, all of Mayreau and the Tobago Cays, the whole of Palm, PSV and the surrounding reefs. Spearfishing is strictly forbidden to all visitors. Buying lobster out of season (the lobstering season is 1st October to 31st April) is also illegal, as is buying a female lobster with eggs (easily seen as red "caviar" under the tail), or any lobster less than 9" in length. Corals must not be damaged. Fines run at around $5000 EC.

Holidays

Jan 1st - New Year's Day
Jan 2nd - Recovery Day
Jan 22nd - Discovery Day
Easter Friday through Monday.
  2nd-5th April 1999, and 21st-24th, April 2000
First Monday in May - Labor Day
Whit Monday (24th May 1999, and 12th June 2000)

Carnival - 2nd Monday and Tuesday in July
1st Monday in August - August bank holiday
October 27th - Independence Day
Dec 25th - Christmas
Dec 26th - Boxing Day

Shopping hours

Most shops open 0800-1200 and 1300-1600. Saturday is half day and most places are closed by noon. Banks normally open weekdays till 0800-1200, 1300-1500, and on Fridays 0800-1200, 1500-1700.

Telephones

Card and coin phones may be found all over the island. You can buy cards for the phone in post offices and selected shops. For overseas calls dial 0 + country code + number. Dial 115 for an overseas operator or 1-800-872-2881 for an ATT USA direct line. When dialing from overseas, the area code is 784, followed by a 7 digit number.

Transport

There are inexpensive ($1.50-$6 EC) buses running to most villages. If you are going a long way, check on the time of the last returning bus. Taxis are plentiful. Sample taxi rates are:

	$EC
Kingstown - Airport	20
Kingstown - Young Island	25
Airport - Young Island	20
Kingstown - CSY/Bimini	30
Short ride	10
By the hour	40

Rental cars or motorbikes are available (see our directory). You will need to buy a local license which costs $40 EC. Drive on the left.

ST. VINCENT

North St Vincent,
Troumaker Bay
foreground
Chateaubelair Island
behind

St. Vincent is an island of towering mountains, craggy peaks and dramatic precipices. Everything is dressed in a tangle of dense green forest. St. Vincent's steep and wild terrain was among the last to be settled by Europeans. At the time Columbus sailed through the islands, St. Vincent was inhabited by amber colored Caribs who had migrated from South America and had a more poetic name for the island: Hairoun, which means "home of the blessed." They were a fierce tribe who had wrested the land from the previous and more peace loving residents, the Arawaks. While the other islands were being exploited by the newly arrived Europeans, a slave ship was wrecked off Bequia and the Caribs took the slaves as their own. However, these slaves were a fierce and warlike tribe and gave the Caribs lots of problems. To control this, the Caribs decided to kill all the young male black children. This caused a revolt among the slaves who killed those Caribs they could, stole their women and ran into the hills. They kept the names the Caribs had given them, followed some Carib customs and became known as the Black Caribs. Over the years they took control of the land from the original Caribs and put up fierce resistance to British settlement. Finally, in the late 18th century, they were defeated by a superior British force and shipped en masse to Honduras.

The northern end of the island is dominated by Soufriere, a 3000-foot volcano. I had a friend who was anchored under the volcano in April 1979 with an amateur geologist on board. Together they scaled the volcano and peered into the depths. The geologist declared it was safely dormant. That night, which happened to be both Friday the 13th and Good Friday, there was a rumbling from the very bowels of the earth and it erupted with a massive cloud that landed dust hundreds of miles away. It created a murk in the area so thick they couldn't see to the bow of the boat and had to leave completely blind, steering by compass to get away. The eruption, which lasted for some days, was Soufriere's second since 1902. The other was in 1973. As you sail by you can see some rivers of dark volcanic matter that flowed down from the summit. Despite the absence of any warning, everyone left the area in time and there were no casualties. The enthusiastic can hike up Soufriere and it is unquestionably one of the Windwards' best and most exciting hikes. Starting on the Windward side there is a clear trail that starts in farmland and goes through rain forest, montane forest, and then into an area where only tiny plants can survive. The top is often in cloud, and you need a little luck to see down into the crater or get the views over the island. The wind often blows a gale at the top and it is cool and damp, so take a rain jacket. You have to be careful not to get blown down into the crater which is a sheer thousand foot drop with no guard rail. Take lunch with you and eat it near the top, as the longer you spend there, the more likely you are to get windows in the clouds and see

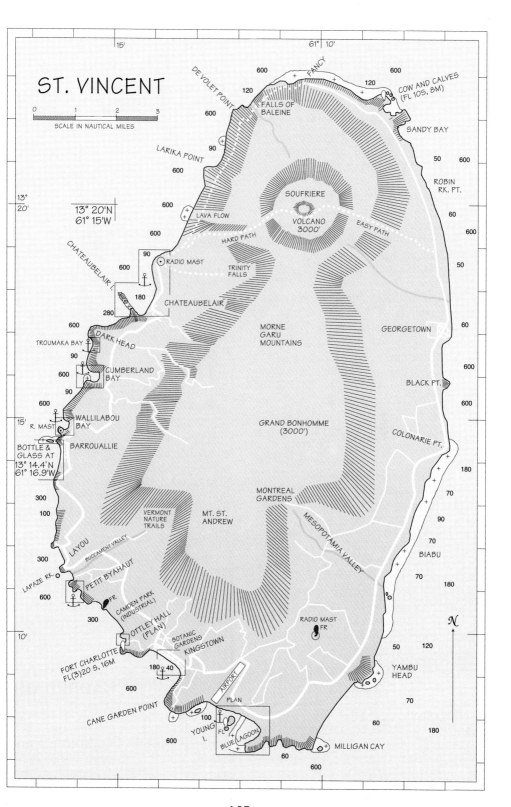

ST. VINCENT

SCALE IN NAUTICAL MILES
0 1 2 3

13° 20'N
61° 15'W

DE VOLET POINT

FANCY

FALLS OF BALEINE

COW AND CALVES
(FL 10S, 8M)

SANDY BAY

LARIKA POINT

SOUFRIERE

ROBIN RK. PT.

LAVA FLOW

VOLCANO
3000'

EASY PATH

HARD PATH

CHATEAUBELAIR I.

RADIO MAST

TRINITY FALLS

CHATEAUBELAIR

MORNE
GARU
MOUNTAINS

GEORGETOWN

DARK HEAD

TROUMAKA BAY

CUMBERLAND
BAY

BLACK PT.

WALLILABOU
BAY

R. MAST

GRAND BONHOMME
(3000')

COLONARIE PT.

BARROUALLIE

BOTTLE & GLASS AT
13° 14.4'N
61° 16.9'W

MONTREAL
GARDENS

MESOPOTAMIA VALLEY

VERMONT
NATURE
TRAILS

MT. ST.
ANDREW

BIABU

LAYOU

BUCCAMENT VALLEY

LAPAZE RK.

PETIT BYAHAUT

FR

CAMDEN PARK
(INDUSTRIAL)

OTTLEY HALL
(PLAN)

RADIO MAST

FR

YAMBU
HEAD

FORT CHARLOTTE
FL(3)20 S, 16M

BOTANIC
GARDENS

KINGSTOWN

AIRPORT

PLAN

CANE GARDEN POINT

YOUNG I.

FL

BLUE LAGOON

MILLIGAN CAY

N

into the crater. The crater is an impressive cone with a huge smoking volcanic dome in the middle. Call any taxi driver for details. The crater rim is at 3000 feet; the mountains to the north attain 3800 feet.

In St. Vincent it seems that neither God nor man was completely sure they wanted tourism, for it lacks tourist type resorts, the acres of white sand beach and the convenient, easy anchorages of the Grenadines. In compensation, this very beautiful island remains unspoiled and you can drive or hike amid exotic, almost theatrical, scenery. Its fierce, uncompromising form is the perfect scenic complement to the appealing and gentle Grenadines farther south. Those doing a round trip from St. Lucia who only wish to stop one way are better off visiting St. Vincent on the way north, as this makes the windward north bound trip shorter.

Try to see some of St. Vincent's interior, which is totally wild. Roads run up both of St. Vincent's coasts, but none goes all the way round or crosses the middle. Climbing the volcano or a boat trip to the Falls of Baleine are recommended. I also like Montreal Gardens in the Mesopotamia Valley. Perched upon the very threshold of the mountains, they are at the end of the road. They are not well maintained, but that perhaps is part of the charm. There are little paths, dense vegetation, a river, and broad views. The gardens are a perfect place to spend an hour away from it all, communing with nature. (Reorganization of Montreal Gardens may come soon.) Those who like to be more organized can take a tour of the Botanical Gardens and Fort Charlotte. The Botanical Gardens are the oldest in the western hemisphere, and it was here that Captain Bligh brought the breadfruit tree after the mutiny on the Bounty fiasco. A direct "sucker" descendant from his original

tree is on display. You will find many youths to guide you through the gardens; one or two are good and entertaining, but negotiate fees in advance. There is also a pre-Colombian museum on the grounds of the Botanical Gardens open only on Wednesdays (0945-1145) and Saturdays (1600-1800).

Navigation, west coast, north to south

Navigation along this section of the coast is straightforward as the land is steep-to except for the clearly visible Bottle and Glass rocks near Barrouallie. A quarter of a mile offshore clears all other dangers.

CHATEAUBELAIR

Chateaubelair lies at the southern foot of Soufriere, St. Vincent's volcano. The coast here is rugged and photogenic with dramatic hill and mountain outlines, cliffs and beach. In settled weather it can be a dream. But, in times of northerly swells, Chateaubelair can be untenable, so great caution must be used during the winter months when dangerous northerly swells often arrive without warning. A steep cliffy slope covered in palm trees lies along the eastern half of the bay. This is the calmest and most scenic place to anchor. There is an ample anchoring shelf 20-40 feet deep. Don't anchor too close to shore as rocky patches extend in places. The bottom is sand but some of the boulders you see tumbling into the sea along the water's edge have made it onto the sand, so if you anchor on rope, snorkel on your anchor. There is also a good sandy anchoring shelf with excellent holding in front of the Beach Front Restaurant, though just to the northeast of the restaurant there is a deep hole. A rock lies in the middle of the channel between Chateaubelair Island and the mainland. There is a navigable passage just south of this rock (between it and the mainland) some 35 feet deep. There are rocks around, so only attempt it in good light. If you do anchor in Chateaubelair be prepared to move for fishermen if they ask. You can dock your dinghy at the town dock (swells permitting).

Ashore

Most people here are naturally friendly in the nicest way. Try to keep it that way; treat people with friendly respect, don't encourage too many locals to become boat vendors and do not give to those who beg.

Esron Thompson's Beach Front Restaurant [$D] is a conspicuous building on the beach. He and his wife Gail will cook you the most wonderful fresh fish at very reasonable prices which are geared to the local market. For preference eat upstairs under the shelter with a panoramic view of the bay. But watch out as you get towards the top of the stairs – the third one from the top is a little higher than the rest and likely to trip you up. Esron may well send out Felix in his rubber dinghy to invite you to visit his restaurant and give you a ride in.

Chateaubelair lies in the heart of some of St. Vincent's best hiking. The volcano is a full day's hike, Trinity Falls are a four-hour round trip, but you can get a taxi most of the way. The Darveo Falls are a pleasant 40-minute hike away. Take your bathing things. You can swim at Trinity Falls and take a good shower at the Darveo Falls. Wherever you go it will be in beautiful scenery. Taxi tours and walking guides are also available at Beach Front Restaurant.

Water sports

The whole of Chateaubelair Bay is an invitation to snorkel. Interesting boulders and rocks abound. For divers, Chateaubelair Island is magnificent; you can find a good dive almost anywhere on it. On the western side a steep wall has been sculpted by the sea into a rich pattern of ravines, hollows, and tiny caves which are home to eels, soapfish and other creatures. It is decorated by a variety of black corals including wire coral. Giant gray angelfish often gather over the sand at about 90 feet. There is also a reef 40 feet deep where huge structures, covered with a colorful mixture of corals, rise from

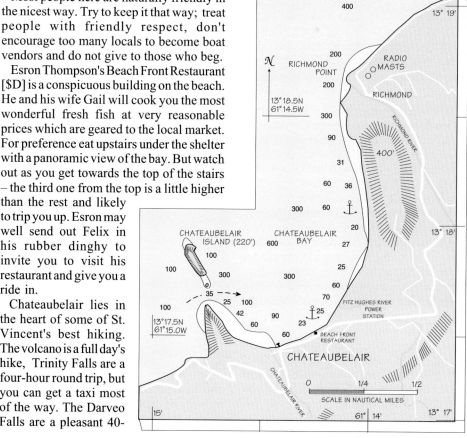

the sand like fairy castles. Pufferfish swim by with what look like broad smiles on their faces. Huge schools of tiny silver fish catch the sun in a brilliant display. You will see a good variety of brightly colored reef fish and creatures such as Christmas tree worms, snake eels and maybe an octopus. On the northern end of the eastern side, a dramatic wall plunges to about 130 feet, with elegant soft coral formations. Further south diving is less deep but equally pretty.

TROUMAKA BAY

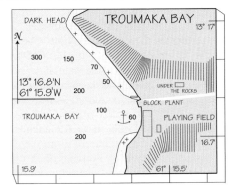

This small bay only has room for a handful of yachts. It is well protected except in bad northerly swells. Steep hills ashore afford panoramic views for energetic walkers. There is good snorkeling all along the northern shore. The water here is deep – you begin to think the bottom does not exist as you approach the beach – so bow or stern to the beach or block plant landing dock is essential. There are a couple of mooring posts on the beach, and you can also run an anchor ashore.

Ashore

There is a small block plant and a communal playing field along the shore. Perched on the slope near some massive ruined foundations is Under the Rocks [$D], a tiny local bar owned by Alstar Mars who owns much of the hillside. You can drink here all day long at regular prices which are lower than most happy hours and Alstar will be delighted to cook you a local meal at a very reasonable price, though he needs a couple of hours notice.

CUMBERLAND BAY

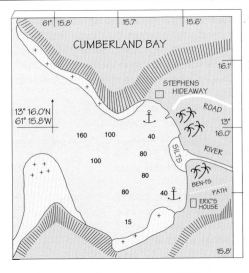

This deep and enchanting bay is part of an estate in the heart of St. Vincent's wildest and richest land. A forest of coconut trees and bananas flows down the valley to the beach. At dusk a flock of cattle egrets roosts in nearby trees, and at night the tree frogs set up a rich throaty chorus. Sometimes the bay becomes a boiling mass of jumping tuna and fishermen can often be seen with their seine nets waiting patiently. Cumberland is unspoiled by tourism. There are many here happy to take you on a tour or feed you, but it is all so unsophisticated that it still has the charm of an untouched settlement. For the cruising sailor there is a river to do a fresh water clothes wash. Enter toward the north of the bay to avoid the large rocky shoal which extends from the southwestern part of the bay. Cumberland is very deep and you will need to anchor bow or stern to a palm tree. There will be many eager to help. Do not tow anyone into the bay; wait till you get right in and choose one of the people inside the bay itself.

Cumberland Bay

Regulations

There is no customs at Cumberland Bay, but you can clear in or out at Wallilabou or Barrouallie, which are close by.

Ashore

Although many of the locals look like bad guys in a spaghetti western, for the most part they couldn't be nicer and more helpful.

You can buy vegetables from Maxwell, fish from Joseph and crayfish from his brother, Uncle Sam. Carlos sells attractive calabash ornaments which he handpaints himself. Other locals you will meet include Dande, Zaquie and Sydney. Sydney guides people on walks and Kiki sells jewelry. New people are turning up on the waterfront. You will have to be their judge. Under no circumstances should you do business with anyone you find aggressive or objectionable in any way.

The old hands are good about not overwhelming yachtspeople when they arrive, and they generally keep an eye on the bay but very occasionally, in the wee hours after they have gone home, dinghies have been known to go missing and once or twice the lines tied to the palm trees have been stolen. It is therefore advisable to keep the outboard on deck, the dinghy locked to the boat, and to use an older piece of line across the beach.

The largest restaurant is Stephens and Stevens Hideaway [VHF:68, $C], right on the beach. Mr. and Mrs. Stephens are well known characters in the area. You can check out their prices when Mr. Stephens comes by the boat or you can call them on the VHF. Mrs. Stephens cooks a great crayfish and callaloo soup as well as local mutton, chicken and goat. Stephens and Stevens Hideaway has electricity from their own generator.

The house at the other end of the bay belongs to Eric, a well traveled Vincentian who is retiring to go fishing. He may one day open a bar and meanwhile will always give good advice to passing yachts. He has placed a few posts on his wall to take stern lines.

Bennett has just opened a new little beach bar called Ben-I's Place [$D], which is occasionally open. It is a small bamboo and wood affair with a few outside wooden seats. Bennett serves beer and rum punch and if you give him a little notice he will cook you a simple fish or chicken barbecue with rice and local salad at a very reasonable price. There is currently no electricity at Ben-I's, just small oil lamps. This makes it a wonderfully romantic place to sit, meet other yachtspeople and watch the day fade into night to the serenade of crickets and tree frogs. Bennett also has a van and he does tours, including the volcano, Vermont Nature trails, Trinity Falls or straight into the rain forest up the water pipe road. Ask him for prices; they sounded inexpensive to me.

Maxwell is an old hand at beach barbecues; just ask him in advance.

You should definitely take a walk here. An easy one is up the hill to the north which gives you a great view of the anchorage. Walk back to the road, turn left and keep going. (Unless you land at the north side of the bay, you must ford a small river, but that is part of the fun.)

Wallilabou is a picturesque bay about a mile south of Cumberland with a pleasant waterfront restaurant and hotel. Enter in the middle of the bay and pick up the moorings put down by the Wallilabou Anchorage Restaurant, or anchor where there are not moorings, and tie bow or stern to the wall or trees. The situation here with regards to the boat-vendors has vastly improved. However, it is up to us to keep it this way, and if it deteriorates again it is we, the yachts, who will be to blame. Men in rowing boats still approach you from as much as three miles away asking to take your stern line ashore and want you to tow them to Wallilabou. Refuse all such offers. If you do tow them, and their boat overturns (a likely scenario, it has happened to me), you could be liable for their boat and any personal damage. In any case, there are always plenty of line helpers in Wallilabou itself. Wallilabou has a boat vendors association – deal only with members who wear conspicuous official badges. Line handlers Joel, Myran, and the twins, Ron and Ronnie, are helpful. The going rate for someone to help you with your lines is $10 EC. You may enjoy buying fruits and vegetables on display by Jahman and others, but if the offer is to "go fetch you nice oranges/bananas/mangos", beware, the quality of the product rarely matches the description.

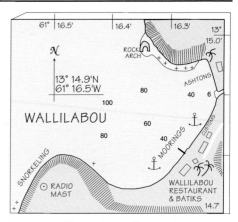

Regulations

Customs clearance is available daily between 1600-1800. Moderate overtime is usually charged. You can also clear in (without paying overtime) earlier in the day in Barrouallie at the police station.

Services

Steve and Jane Russell, who run the Wallilabou Anchorage Restaurant, are keen to attract yachting customers. They have a good dinghy dock and offer free moorings, showers and inexpensive water via a long hose from the dock. A phone is available as is block and cube ice and overnight accommodation. They will help you dispose of well wrapped garbage. (Do not give it to the boat vendors.)

Ashore

The Wallilabou Anchorage Restaurant and boutique [VHF:68, $C-D] has a delightful location where you can eat looking out over your yacht. Steve, who is from St. Vincent, and his wife Jane from England are very pleasant and usually in the bar in the evenings. The restaurant serves generous portions of local style food, particularly fish and shrimp. Happy hour with cheaper drinks is

1700-1800. You can meet a parrot, buy brightly colored locally made batiks, and admire a small collection of old Carib artifacts. They usually have a lively little band on Monday nights in season, and by special request.

There is a small but photogenic waterfall, good for a hearty shower, about a mile up the road. The walk through the lush countryside is quite delightful and the falls are easy to find. (Just get to the road and turn left; look for the falls on your right.)

This is also a good place for exploring St. Vincent. The rain forest is close by, and the Vermont Nature Trails are not too far away. Arnold Chambers, the owner and driver of Chambers Taxi Service [VHF:16, 68], is the local taxi driver. He is personable and

friendly and will be happy to take you to town or on a tour. If you don't see him, ask for him in the restaurant.

Ashton's Country Style [$C-D] is a small restaurant/snack bar at the far end of the beach. They can cook a good fish meal at a reasonable price. The dinghy dock is still in the planning stage, so you have to beach your dinghy. They have live music on Wednesdays and Fridays in season when things are busy enough.

Water sports

Snorkeling is interesting around the southern headland of Wallilabou. As we went to press, a local dive shop had opened in Ashton Country Style. Well worth checking out, the diving in this area is excellent.

BARROUALLIE

Barrouallie is easily identified by the conspicuous Bottle and Glass rocks. It is a picturesque local town with a few quaint buildings. The main reason to stop here is to clear in or out. However, the anchorage is pleasant and good enough for an overnight stop. Those who prefer can move on to Cumberland, Wallilabou, Petit Byahaut or Young Island Cut. Some people anchor in one of the bays to the north and visit by dinghy.

Navigation

If you are coming from the north give a reasonable clearance to the last visible rock in Bottle and Glass as there is an underwater rock that extends seawards a few hundred feet. Anchor between the town dock and Pint Rock. There is an adequate anchoring shelf for a quick stop in about 25 feet of water. For overnighting it would be advisable to get one anchor hooked in the shallow water, drop back and set another in the deeper water, holding the boat bow to the beach. You can tie your dinghy to the town dock. You do not need any boat boys here.

Regulations

You can clear in or out at the police station opposite the playing field. The police seem very efficient and friendly

here and are not currently charging overtime even on weekends. Clearance is also possible in Wallilabou between about 1600-1800. It is not possible to clear in Barrouallie during the hours the customs officer is in Wallilabou. Barrouallie clearance is immigration only, but it seems to work. For entry you may need to pay some fees at the next proper customs station.

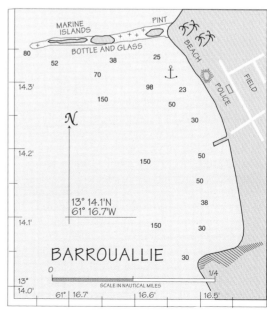

This small and delightful bay usually makes a good overnight anchorage, though it can be uncomfortable in some sea swells. A stern anchor may cut the roll. Ashore there is a small beach backed by hills with several conspicuous peaky outcroppings of rock. If you are coming from the north you pass the village of Layou, then Buccament Bay (just after the island called Lapaze Rock), then the next headland is Byahaut Point, a distinctive rounded headland with a diving flag sometimes flying from the top. Pass the headland, head into the bay and pick up a mooring or anchor outside the moorings. Do not anchor inside or among the moorings as they are all hooked together by underwater chain. If you are coming from Kingstown, Byahaut Point is the furthest headland you see after you leave Kingstown Bay, after Camden Park, Questelles and Clare Valley. Ashore Petit Byahaut looks private; you mainly see some small green roofs poking out of the vegetation. If you are coming from abroad, Chuck and Sharon at Petit Byahaut will run you to Wallilabou to clear in for a fee.

PETIT BYAHAUT

SCALE IN NAUTICAL MILES

Ashore

Petit Byahaut [VHF:68, $B], approachable only by sea, is a delightful small resort where guest accommodations are in luxurious tents under roofs. It is owned by Chuck and Sharon, originally from Canada and California. They have four moorings available for yachts. If you use their moorings, there is a $15 US-a-night-fee, deducted from your bill if you are eating dinner ashore. The restaurant is excellent in a beautiful setting of flower gardens with the sea beyond. Special overnight rates are available when there is room. The beach changes, so call for information on the best place to land your dinghy.

Chuck and Sharon organize great hikes, and it is a safe place to leave your boat. Their most popular energetic all day hike is the volcano. You travel by taxi up the lee side of the island, taking in the sights such as the Mesopotamia Valley, and climb the volcano along the easiest route. For the less vigorous there are lovely nature trails at Vermont which you can visit with knowledgeable guide Elroy. They also arrange hikes to Trinity Falls (2.5 hours each way). You can also hike over the headlands, but get an OK from Chuck or Sharon before you wander over their property. Remember, guests stay in tents, so if you take a wrong turn the expression "dropping in on someone" could take on a new meaning.

Petit Byahaut

"like no other place"

www.outahere.com/petitbyahaut
e-mail: petitbyahaut@caribsurf.com

(784) 457-7008 TEL/FAX

photos: Carol Lee

Water sports

Snorkeling and diving between Petit Byahaut and Buccament Bay is superb and easily accessible by dinghy, though the current is strong. Petit Byahaut has a dive shop, fills tanks and rents gear. Chuck is an excellent dive master and knows all the best sites. It is best to arrange the evening before for a dive the next morning.

Dinosaur Head is the face of Byahaut Point that faces the anchorage. There is a 120-foot wall covered in coral, sponges and seafans. You swim through large schools of tangs and see queen angelfish, eels, snappers and spotted drums.

The Bat Cave is a short dinghy ride away and can be done as a dive or a snorkel as long as the swells are slight. There is about three feet of water at the cave entrance. You can find somewhere to anchor your dinghy outside and there is good snorkeling in this area. Inside the cave it is quite dark, but you can see the bats which cling by the hundreds to the cave walls and roof. Crabs climb up among the bats. You catch a glimpse of the tunnel which leads off to the left because you can see a hint of light at the end of it. This tunnel is about 30 feet long and about four feet wide. You rise and fall on the swells and if the swells are bad it could be dangerous. The tunnel leads out into a fissure about 30 feet high and 40 feet deep. Below, the water is a brilliant blue. You swim out through the fissure and divers go down to two huge rocks at 80 and 130 feet which are covered in sponges and corals and teeming with all kinds of fish. The ascent is up a wall textured with nooks and crannies. If you do the Bat Cave dive, it is most important not to disturb the bats. Two species live here, fishing bats (*Noctilio leporinus*), which eat fish and insects, and the St. Vincent fruit eating bat (*Brachyphylia cavernarum*) which was thought to be extirpated and is endangered. So swim quietly through the cave, without talking or splashing, and under no circumstances take flashlights or flash photographs.

Ottley Hall lies just to the west of
Kingstown, on the far side of Fort Charlotte.
Here you will find a new yachting facility.

Services

This new yard has a 35-ton travel lift, a 200-
ton ship lift and a dry dock capable of
handling anything up to 65 meters long, 15
meters wide and six meters deep. Special
covered sheds on rails can be rolled over
yachts on the hard or in the dry-dock so that
respraying and repainting can be done out
of the rain. There is a fuel dock and long
term storage for smaller yachts. There is a
marina area in front of the work space,
which is fine under most conditions for an
overnight stop, but swells do get in, and it
can occasionally be unpleasant.
The mini mart is run by Gourmet Food
Service. But this is just a small part of their
provisioning business. Gourmet Food
Service provides wholesale foods to yachts
and resorts all through St. Vincent and the
Grenadines. They have a full range of foods,
liquors and wines; anything they do not have
they buy wholesale. They also provide a full
range of fresh produce.

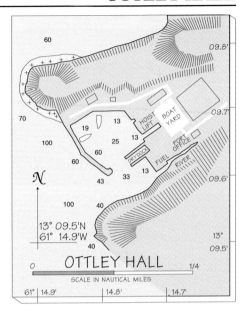

Ashore

The boatyard was running in a very low-key
mode. The storage and haul out parts are
fully operational, but the labor force was
minimal. Check it out for yourself and see
if it suits. The marina is a short taxi ride
from Kingstown

KINGSTOWN

Kingstown, St. Vincent's capital, has some
charming corners with old stone buildings,
cobblestone sidewalks and handsome
arches. The market is colorful and the
shopping for both tourist items and
provisioning is good. More yachtsmen
currently visit Kingstown by road than by
sea; taxis and buses are readily available
from both Young Island Cut and Blue
Lagoon. Up to now Kingstown, as an
anchorage, left a lot to be desired. The
anchorage was not scenic, youths tended to
overwhelm visiting yachts and there was no
secure place to leave a dinghy. This will
change with completion of the new cruise

ship facility whose planned completion is
fairly early during the life of this guide. We
have marked the new facility on our sketch
charts; work was well under way as we went
to press. Part of the dock is earmarked for
yachts and as things stand, yachts may still
anchor off. It is too early to predict how
well this project will work for yachts, but it
is likely to be a vast improvement.

Regulations

You can clear customs in Kingstown, but
it is more cumbersome than elsewhere: you
have to deal with customs and port authority
and then go down to immigration at the

The passage inside Chateaubelair Island, looking northeast

other end of town. Yacht clearances are a sideline in these offices and there are sometimes lines of people doing other business. It is much easier to use the yacht facility in Wallilabou, or use Sam Taxi Service to do it all for you.

Services

There is an excellent small dock where you can take on fuel and water right opposite the fish market, provided there is no swell. It is run by the Fisherman's Cooperative. You can make contact by calling St. Vincent Signal Station [VHF:16] for a phone relay. Pull along the west side of the dock where it is 15-30 feet deep. Water here is inexpensive and available from 0700-1900. The diesel and gasoline pumps open about 0800. Ice is available in the fish market.

KP Marine, owned by Paddy Punnett, is the sales and service agent for Yamaha and outboards in St. Vincent are duty free. Paddy a keen boating man himself, can give you good advice whatever your problem. KP Marine is not far behind the ferry docks (see our sketch charts). Paddy expects to expand into general yacht chandlery soon, so check him out

Carlton King runs a first rate machine shop 150 yards from the Botanical Gardens towards the Prime Minister's residence.

Whatever you break, he can probably fix, including stainless, cast iron and aluminum.

See also "Services" under Young Island Cut and Blue Lagoon.

Ashore

There are many supermarkets to choose from, but the biggest and most convenient is Greaves which stays open till 1700 Monday to Thursday and 1900 on Fridays. Its subsidiary by the airport opens till 2000 nightly, except Thursdays and Fridays when it opens till 2100 and Sundays when it opens from 0700-1300. Greaves, in town, offers a charter yacht discount and delivery to Young Island Cut is negotiable. New products include delicatessen meats, French cheeses and whipping cream. The Marketing Board often has good deals, especially on produce. The local market is lively and colorful with many local ladies eager to offer you excellent buys in local produce. Marion Mills' T & M is a good wine and liquor shop.

St. Vincent Sales and Services is a modern shop in a new building conveniently placed opposite the ferry dock. They sell both auto spares and some marine hardware. They are a NAPA jobber and have excellent buys on filters. Rope, chain, anchors and boat batteries are available. They can make

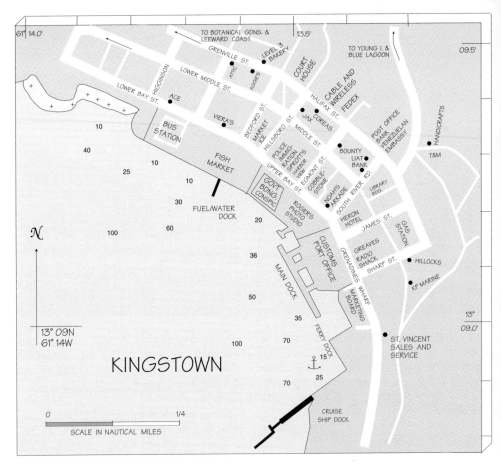

KINGSTOWN

hydraulic hoses while you wait.

Radio Shack on Bay Street looks more like a regular housewares store than an electronics outlet, but if you need something, ask, they may have it and they can bring in anything in the catalog. For more general hardware, try Ace just beyond the bus station. Ace often has good buys on silicone seal, 5200, sandpaper and tools. Sprotts has an excellent selection of tools and household hardware. Trottman's has a good range of electrical supplies and there are several lumber yards and plumbing and hardware stores around town.

If you are shopping for fun, take a walk along Bay Street. Pop into 96 Degrees for casual wear. Next look in at Noah's Arkade, a delightful shop with a wide range of Caribbean handicrafts and literature. The crafts side includes brightly colored batiks, ornaments, gifts, sculptures, household items, t-shirts, and clothing. The book selection ranges from children's books and fiction to nature, cooking and cruising guides, all with a local flavor, and many are unavailable outside the region.

At the Cobblestone Inn there is an arcade with more shops, such as Alexanders, which sells duty-free porcelain, china, crystal, jewelry, and perfumes, and Giggles, a clothing boutique. Upstairs in the new Sprotts department store, Sprotties Silk Screen Shop offers delightful clothing and household items, all made from their own silk screened fabrics.

There are several department stores including Laynes and Jax and there is a local handicraft center. Roger's Photo Studio on Bay Street sells film and does one-hour processing.

The Heron Hotel serves a wonderful breakfast at a reasonable price and is a

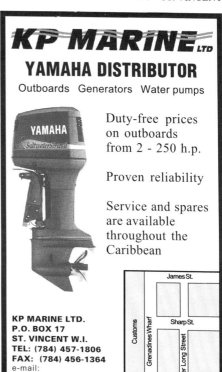
favorite with the "ferry from Bequia" crowd. Come back again for lunch or dinner in this old-style, friendly hotel which offers good food at a reasonable price.

You can choose a lunch spot to suit your mood: we mention just a few of many. Clean and inexpensive, The Bounty [$D] is perfect for light snacks (rotis and small lunch plates). When you go in, head straight up to the cash desk, select and pay. They give you a slip which you hand over the food counter. Then you sit down and the food arrives. You must know this because if you sit first, nothing happens. The Bounty is upstairs on Egmont Street and owners Tracy and Tony run a continuous exhibition of local art which is for sale. Chams is a sweet inexpensive courtyard restaurant on Halifax Street on the opposite side of the road from the post office. They serve rotis and local dishes. Le Cafe de Paris is upstairs in the Alliance Francais, in the beautifully restored old library building. Popular with students, they serve French and local snacks. In Aggies Bar and Restaurant [$C-D, closed Sunday lunch] you can find good local food in a

friendly atmosphere. If you want something cooler, more spacious and social, then go to Basil's in the Cobblestone Inn [$C-D], where you can get a first rate lunch buffet, or climb up the stairs to the Rooftop Restaurant [breakfast and lunch only] for a breezy open atmosphere with a view. Harbour View [$C-D] is a new top floor restaurant serving first rate local food; Indian curries, fish broth and rotis; they have occasional live music at night.

St. Vincent nightlife

Those who like to go out on the town should try The Attic, an attractive jazz club in Kingstown which occasionally has good visiting groups. Level Three is a bar and restaurant geared to the middle aged crowd with oldie goldie music. The Alliance Francais puts on many good French cultural shows. Wander into their headquarters in the restored library building and ask for details. See also the Aquatic Club in Young Island Cut.

THE SOUTH COAST OF ST. VINCENT

Navigation

The current along this coast is predominantly westward, up to two knots. It reverses weakly for a few hours which can create choppy seas.

When leaving Kingstown heading for Young Island, give the headland a good clearance as there is a submerged rock about 200 feet south of its eastern end.

There are two good anchorages close together: Young Island Cut and Blue Lagoon. Both are well serviced by bus and taxi to town. The nearest large supermarket is near the airport. If you visit the Calliaqua fish market around 1600, you have a chance of meeting the fishermen as they return with

the day's catch. For cooking gas, go to the filling station just before the airport (a short bus or taxi ride). Both anchorages are within dinghy reach of each other, so read about services and shore facilities for both anchorages.

Young Island Cut

YOUNG ISLAND CUT

Young Island Cut is a favorite with yachtspeople. The anchorage lies in clear water between Young Island and the mainland. At night the lights of Young Island take on a fairytale look and a convivial array of bars and restaurants follows the shore. It is conveniently placed for anything you might want to do in St. Vincent.

Young Island is open and easily entered from the west. The channel to the east of Young Island is narrow, curves, and is best given a miss, even with the new beacons. You have to anchor with care. The current sweeps through both ways and the center of the cut goes as deep as 65 feet. There is good holding in the north or western parts of the anchorage, but it occasionally rolls. Anchoring bow and stern is essential or your boat will swing with the change of current and bang into someone else. The sea bed close to Young Island offers poor holding. Young Island's electrical cable carries 11,000 volts, enough to make your whole boat glow, so anchor well clear or better still use a mooring.

Moorings are available in Young Island Cut. These are a great help as anchoring here is not easy. The present system of unauthorized moorings is managed by two taxi drivers who feel that if you rent one of their moorings, you should also take their taxi. Rivalry between the two has sometimes caused minor problems. Avoid two boats competing for your business when you arrive, call on the VHF and book your mooring in advance. Mooring rates are $10 US up to 100 feet and $20 US over 100 feet.

Services

Sam Taxi Tours [VHF:68] is one of those who rents out moorings. Sam also offers a whole range of yacht services and is agent for Windjammer and some other cruise ships. He does yacht clearance which is very convenient if you want to come straight to Young Island. He charges $50 US for

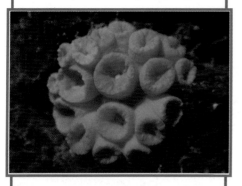

yachts up 100 feet, $100 US for yachts up to 149 feet and $200 US for yachts over 150 feet. His crew do laundry and fill gas bottles. Sam Taxi Service handles communications and many skippers get their spares sent here, which Sam can clear through customs. Sam Taxi Tours also rents cars, and has a fleet of taxis for scenic or shopping trips. He puts out a weather forecast at 0900 and 1730 (announced on VHF:16/68 given on 06), and arranges duty free fuel bunkering for larger yachts.

Charlie Tango [VHF:68] is the other moorings man and Charlie also runs a full taxi and tour service and will help in any way he can.

Some yachtspeople visit town by bus to clear customs.

The Aquatic Club [VHF:68] sells water and ice from their new dock. Just pull alongside, but keep an eye on the current.

If you have a mechanical problem, contact Howard's Marine [VHF:68]. They are a sales and service agent for OMC outboards and Yanmar inboards, though they are happy to fix all makes. You can buy your new inboard or outboard here and they expect to stock more general yacht chandlery soon. They were planning an ambitious fuel dock next to the customs dock to sell diesel, gasoline and water. They already haul out small power boats and were planning to rebuild the railway to take yachts up to 100 feet and be suitable for catamarans.

Verrol at Nichols Marine has an efficient mechanized workshop where he repairs and reconditions alternators and starter motors in a few hours. They come back looking and working like new. Verrol also does aluminum and stainless welding. Call him on the telephone and he will come and sort out your problem wherever you are in St. Vincent. (In Bequia you can leave things for him with GYE or Sam Taxi Tours.) Verrol's workshop is in Belaire, just behind the airport, which is closer to the south coast than town. A few houses down from Verrol is Oscar's Machine Center, a good new machine shop. They can do all manner of jobs here on all kinds of metals and can resurface engine blocks or fix your old winches. They work quite closely with

YOUNG ISLAND CUT

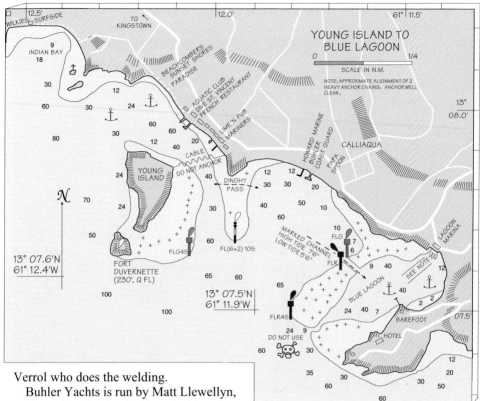

Verrol who does the welding.

Buhler Yachts is run by Matt Llewellyn, a Vincentian who lived and worked for some 30 years in British Columbia. It is in Calliaqua. They build fiberglass yachts, especially large catamarans for the charter industry. They can also do any kind of custom construction to order, including tanks. They have the technical ability and equipment on hand for all kinds of fiberglass repair jobs and spray painting. Check them out if you have a boat problem. Matt is very helpful.

Ashore

Young Island Cut is lined with restaurants and is a good place to bar hop and eat out. Take your time, wander along and peruse the menus till you find the one that suits you. The premier place for gourmet food is The French Restaurant (known as "The French") [VHF:68, $A-B]. Prices are on a par with other good restaurants and owner Jacques and his staff make you feel like important guests. Their cuisine is excellent – as good as you will find anywhere in the Windwards, with the emphasis on a variety of seafoods, and the French is a perfect

place to eat lobster (in season). Choose your own right out of their pool. Lunch is light, delightful and very inexpensive. Reservations for dinner are advisable.

The Mariners [$A-B] has just reopened and has a lot going for it; a perfect location right on the waterfront (they don't mind customers using their dinghy dock on a regular basis and it is the best and most hassle free along the front). The staff are professional and helpful while retaining their island warmth of welcome. The atmosphere is romantic with candle light and the sea, and the food is first rate. I hope it lasts.

The Lime 'n Pub [$B-D] is informal. You can relax, play darts, meet people, and prop up the bar with draft beer in an iced mug. Owner Dave Dunn serves a huge variety of food so he has something for everyone. For the cheap and cheerful crowd there is English pub food, rotis, burgers, "gourmet" pizzas, ice cream and espresso coffee. (The bon vivant will find a large menu.) The Lime 'n

174

the FRENCH RESTAURANT

Famous throughout the islands for its gourmet cooking

at Villa (Young Island Cut),
St. Vincent

The French Restaurant is unanimously acclaimed to be the best restaurant in the Grenadines. We have the original live lobster pool in St. Vincent. You choose your own lobster. The only restaurant in St Vincent to earn ☆☆☆☆ in The Best Hotels, Restaurants and Shops in the Caribbean '94 -'95.

Open every day for breakfast, lunch and dinner.
Free meal for a skipper with a party of 6 persons
Reservations advisable in season

Tel: (784) 458-4972, Fax: (784) 457-4930, VHF channel 68

Pub is managed by Desiree and Andrew. There is a dinghy dock and occasional live music.

Beachcombers [VHF:68, $B-D] is an intimate restaurant where the view of the anchorage and sea beyond is framed by almond trees. Seafood, local specialties and snacks are available. Beachcombers also has rooms for rent and a popular health spa with sauna, steam room, Turkish bath, aroma therapy, facials and a gymnasium.

Stilly's Aquatic Club is where the action gets heavy on Friday, Saturday and holiday nights into the early hours.

Paradise Inn [$C-D], offers local food and occasional barbecues with live music.

Across the water with a good dinghy dock, Young Island Resort [VHF:68, $A] is a delight of tropical flowers and trees and is well worth a visit for a sundowner. They have a steel band and other entertainment on a weekly basis (call for details). If you wish to dine at Young Island Resort, make reservations in advance.

If you look back from the anchorage you see a large building at the end of the beach to the west of Young Island Cut (Indian Bay). This is the Grand View Beach Hotel, one of St. Vincent's grandest family owned traditional hotels. There are a couple of reasons to visit. Down on the beach, Surfside [$B-D] owned by Bob Demmons, serves a variety of snacks and meals just about all day long. The open air dining room facing the sea is very informal and a pleasant place to relax around the bar. Up the hill the hotel pool has one of St.Vincent's great views atop a cactussy knoll. You can take a drink and eat a light lunch here, then return for dinner to Wilkie's [$A-B] the hotel's main restaurant. They have a great chef who offers a variety of a la carte menus which change daily.

For an adventure in inexpensive local food, wander down the road to Papa Spoon's Rasta Ranch [$D] on the Calliaqua playing field. He serves good all-natural food in calabash bowls and sells beer and fresh juices.

Boutiques include the Young Island Dock Shop and The Lime 'n Pub boutique.

Anyone needing an inexpensive night ashore can check out Chez Norris, run by Danni from North America and Norris from St. Vincent. Set in a residential area in the hills behind Blue Lagoon it gets a good breeze and has a down-to-earth friendly home atmosphere. Danni runs a full yacht provisioning service and can find practically anything you need, and Norris has an 8-seater taxi for tours.

Fort Duvernette stands behind Young Island, a monument to the ingenuity of the soldiers of a bygone age who managed to get cannons up to the top. There is a place to tie the dinghy, and 250 steps take you to the cannons. The panoramic view is your reward. Fort Duvernette was used in the late 18th century when the settlers were fighting off the Black Caribs from inland. You will notice that cannons face in both directions.

Water sports

Diving in St. Vincent is really wonderful. The rugged shoreline is equally dramatic

BLUE LAGOON SHOWING POSITION OF MARKED CHANNEL

177

below the surface. Walls and reefs that drop far deeper than any sane person can dive are common, fish are everywhere – feeding in schools, tucked under rocks and hiding in sponges.

Dive St. Vincent [VHF:68] is run by Padi/Naui instructor Bill Tewes. Bill has been here about a decade and is on nodding terms with most of the fish and sea creatures. He has the honor of appearing on a St. Vincent and Grenadines postage stamp in full diving regalia, part of an underwater series that features his photographs. He has stations in Young Island Cut, and Union Island and is associated with Dive Bequia. Dive packages good in all these places, or learn-as-you-go full certification programs, are available. Bill also offers trips to the Falls of Baleine. Charter skippers should know that Bill can pick up a group from a yacht heading north, take them to the Falls of Baleine as the yacht powers up the coast and deliver them back at the north end of the island.

Those diving on their own will find the base of Fort Duvernette easily accessible, though you do have to be careful of the current which tries to sweep you out to sea. Anchor your dinghy to the west of the Fort Duvernette dinghy dock. Follow the base of Fort Duvernette down. Almost as soon as you begin you will be surrounded by large schools of brown chromis. At 40 feet you find yourself in a pleasant area of house-sized boulders with nooks and crannies where eels, shrimps and angelfish hide out. Large schools of sergeant majors hug the rocks while offshore jacks, mackerels and schools of margates patrol.

Other even better dives are best done with a local dive shop as the anchorages are dangerous for yachts and local knowledge about the currents is essential. Bottle Reef under Fort Charlotte starts at 25 feet. You descend along the foot of an underwater rock headland. On your right is a gentle slope of coral decorated by sponges and many smaller soft corals. On the left the headland turns into a sheer wall adorned by deep water sea fans. There are small bushes of black coral in several colors. At the bottom we found several cherub fish. These little critters, the smallest of the angelfish, are only a couple of inches long. You round the bottom of the headland at 100 feet and ascend through huge schools of grunts and even larger schools of brown chromis that seem to explode into a variety of patterns all around. There is always a chance of finding ancient bottles. A curious current pattern here makes it possible to have the current with you the whole way.

Kingstown South is on the south side of Kingstown Harbor. You can see by looking at the sheer cliffs above and the schooling chromis below that this will be an interesting dive. The descent is down a steep slope and this is the place to look for the unusual red banded lobster. This colorful little crustacean is clearly marked in bands and spots of red, white and gold. Unlike other Caribbean lobsters, it has claws, though they are tiny. We saw one when we finished

our descent and three more later, as well as a slipper lobster and the more normal spiny lobster. We circled slowly anti-clockwise up the slope looking at sponges, corals and big rocks. You often see large pelagic fish swimming out toward the sea. Among the many reef fish you will meet are spotted drums and filefish.

New Guinea Reef is on the east side of Petit Byahaut. This spectacular dive takes you down a wall to 90 feet where large black corals occur in bushes of white, pink, dark green, light green, brown and red. All three black coral species are here. Fish include black jacks, parrotfish, French angelfish and occasional sightings of the rather rare frilled goby, frogfish and sea horses. An overhang near the bottom makes this dive visually spectacular.

BLUE LAGOON

Blue Lagoon is a pleasant anchorage with a beach and plenty of palm trees. You can lie comfortably, protected by land and reef. The main shoals between Blue Lagoon and Young Island are marked by large beacons (see sketch chart). These are in fairly shallow water, so do not cut them too fine.

The opening of the west entrance is marked by two large beacons. After that head straight across the reef into the deep water. Depths in the channel vary with the tide from about five foot nine inches to about seven and a half feet. Call Lagoon Marina or Barefoot Yacht Charters on VHF:68 to ask about the state of the tide. Do not attempt to use the deeper south entrance as it is dangerous and has gotten many a yacht in trouble. The anchorage is quite deep, so be prepared to use plenty of scope. You will need a stern anchor to keep your stern into the small swells. If you anchor in the region of the two old mooring chains (see our sketch chart), use a trip line in case your

anchor gets hooked on one. You can also come stern-to at either of the yacht facilities.

Services

The Lagoon Marina and Hotel [VHF:68] is small and personal and the base of both Sunsail and the TMM charter company. The Hotel and docks are operated by Sunsail. Electricity (110/220-volt, 50-cycles) can be arranged at the dock. Top up on water, fuel (both diesel and gasoline) and ice. Services include showers, laundry and communications. When available, rooms are offered at special rates. Manager Mike Tinson is very helpful and will sort out your mechanical or electrical problem. TMM charter company manager John West is happy to give advice and a helping hand to any yachtspeople with problems. They also manage yachts and will hold faxes.

Mary Barnard's Barefoot Yacht Charters [VHF:68] is a charter company which welcomes visiting yachts. They offer full communications, a full travel agency, an air charter service, diesel, water and ice. They usually have room for visiting yachts to tie up overnight at their dock, or they can rent them a mooring just off their base.

Ashore

The Lagoon Marina's Green Flash bar has a perfect view over the harbor and their restaurant [VHF:68, $A-C] offers well prepared Creole and international food. They also have a boutique selling local handicrafts, books and souvenirs as well as essentials like suntan cream.

Barefoot's Restaurant [VHF:68,$B-C], set in the open amid the rocks overlooking the sea, is quaint and intimate. Good pastas and food with a local flavor.

Blue Lagoon is a good place to leave your boat while you explore ashore. If you decide to do this by taxi, Robert of Robert Taxi [VHF:68] is a real gentleman and very reliable.

NORTHERN GRENADINES PASSAGES

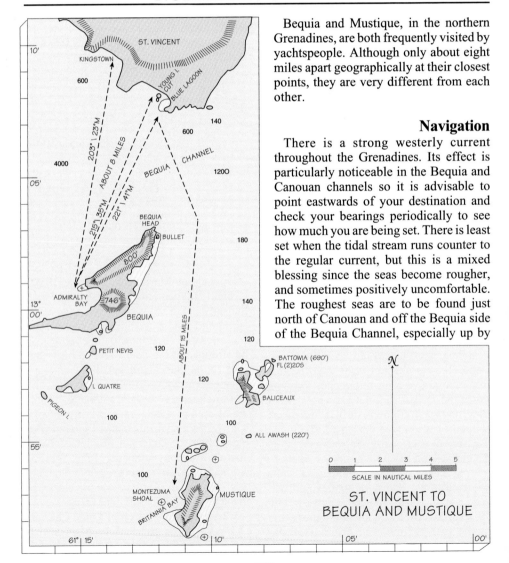

Bequia and Mustique, in the northern Grenadines, are both frequently visited by yachtspeople. Although only about eight miles apart geographically at their closest points, they are very different from each other.

Navigation

There is a strong westerly current throughout the Grenadines. Its effect is particularly noticeable in the Bequia and Canouan channels so it is advisable to point eastwards of your destination and check your bearings periodically to see how much you are being set. There is least set when the tidal stream runs counter to the regular current, but this is a mixed blessing since the seas become rougher, and sometimes positively uncomfortable. The roughest seas are to be found just north of Canouan and off the Bequia side of the Bequia Channel, especially up by

ST. VINCENT TO
BEQUIA AND MUSTIQUE

Bequia Head. It is not unusual for the current to be going in two different directions on opposite sides of the channel.

St. Vincent to Bequia

The passage from St. Vincent to Bequia is usually pleasant off-the-wind sailing. Although Admiralty Bay is hidden till you get quite close, you can usually see the headland that you have to round because it stands out against the more distant land behind. Look behind you to see which way you are being set by the current, and make adjustments so you stay on course. Big seas can lead to a little exciting surfing and one often covers the eight or nine miles in about an hour and a half. Be prepared for the Bequia Blast after the lee of Devil's Table. Many drop their sails here, but if you fancy an exhilarating short beat, keep going. When sailing in you might notice what appears to be a madman zooming around your yacht standing up in a tiny inflatable, being badly bounced by the waves. Fear not, it is just Tim Wright who makes his living taking marine photographs. If he takes your yacht's picture he will probably bring a proof for you to see. There is no obligation to buy. And, yes, he has flipped over and lost his camera gear at least once. If you want to be sure Tim comes by your boat, you can always call him [VHF:77] and let him know when you will be sailing by.

Sailing the other way is a different matter. To make Young Island or Blue Lagoon from Admiralty Bay you normally have to tack to windward against a foul current. It usually takes two hours and can take three or more. It is generally quicker to tack or motor sail up the Bequia coast and then shoot across from Anse Chemin, the bay just southwest of Bequia Head. This is fine in calm weather, but on rough days one can sail straight into a range of liquid mountains near Bequia Head. If the seas are rough, head straight over to St. Vincent and then work back up the coast.

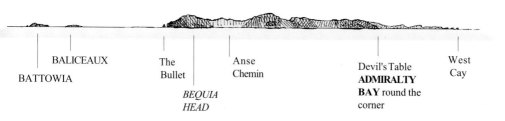

BATTOWIA   BALICEAUX   The Bullet   *BEQUIA HEAD*   Anse Chemin   Devil's Table **ADMIRALTY BAY** round the corner   West Cay

Approaching Bequia from St. Vincent

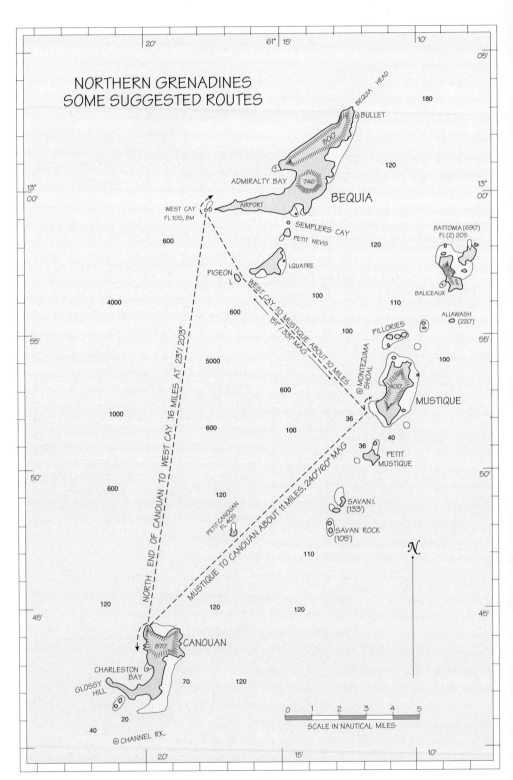

NORTHERN GRENADINES
SOME SUGGESTED ROUTES

BEQUIA HEAD

BULLET

800

ADMIRALTY BAY   746

BEQUIA

180

120

WEST CAY
FL 10S, 8M   AIRPORT

SEMPLERS CAY

PETIT NEVIS

I.QUATRE

PIGEON
I.

600

600

4000

600

5000

600

1000

600

600

120

600

120

PETIT CANOUAN
FL 40S

BATTOWIA (690')
FL (2) 20S

BALICEAUX

100

110

120

120

ALLAWASH
(220')

PILLORIES

100

100

MONTEZUMA
SHOAL

400'

MUSTIQUE

100

36

40

36

PETIT
MUSTIQUE

SAVAN I.
(133')

SAVAN ROCK
(105')

110

120

120

120

WEST CAY TO MUSTIQUE ABOUT 10 MILES
151° / 331° MAG

NORTH END OF CANOUAN TO WEST CAY 16 MILES AT 23° / 203°

MUSTIQUE TO CANOUAN ABOUT 11 MILES, 240° / 60° MAG

N

870'   CANOUAN

CHARLESTON
BAY

GLOSSY
HILL   70   120

20

40   ⊕ CHANNEL RK.

0 1 2 3 4 5
SCALE IN NAUTICAL MILES

13°
00'

13°
00'

55'

55'

50'

50'

45'

45'

20'   61° 15'   10'

20'   15'   10'

05'

St. Vincent to Mustique

The trip between St. Vincent and Mustique is about 15 miles, and in good going it takes two and a half to three hours. The seas around the north end of Bequia can be very rough, but one often gets an exhilarating reach. Whether you are sailing north or south, keep well off Bequia Head and The Bullet as the current pulls you down that way. Otherwise just strap everything down, hang on tight and ride 'em!

Bequia to Mustique

Most people approach Mustique from Admiralty Bay. The easiest way is to round West Cay and sail out between Pigeon Island and Isle de Quatre. As you approach Mustique, Montezuma Shoal is a real danger. It is marked by a beacon placed right on the middle of the reef. Pass either side but keep at least a quarter of a mile clear of the beacon. The beacon is red and black, but if you get close enough to see the colors you will probably run aground.

There are passages between Semples Cay and Petit Nevis, and between Petit Nevis and Isle de Quatre, but they can be very rough and the current extremely rapid. Furthermore, there is a reef extending well south of Petit Nevis, so serious thought should be given to prevailing conditions before choosing either of these routes. It is an easy seven-mile reach from Friendship Bay to Mustique or back.

Bequia to Canouan

As you round West Cay (Bequia) and head south, it will be possible to see Petit Canouan; if the visibility is good Canouan itself will be in sight. Glossy (Glass) Hill, the southwestern point of Canouan, is joined to the rest of the land by a low isthmus which stays below the horizon till you get quite close, so Glossy Hill appears initially as a separate island.

Mustique to Canouan

This trip can be a rolly run with the wind right behind. I often tack downwind to make it a reach.

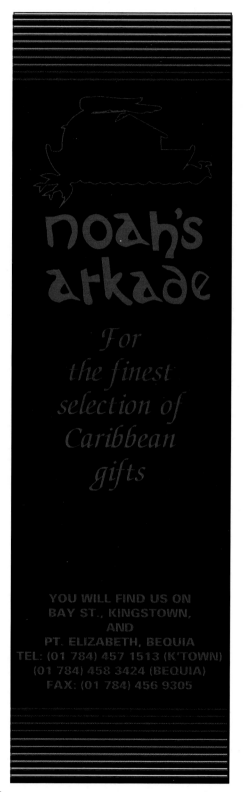

Bequia Boats

Regulations

Port Elizabeth is a port of entry for St. Vincent and the Grenadines. The procedure is simple, though the lines are sometimes long. Customs are open weekdays at 0900-1200, 1300-1500 and 1530-1800. On holidays they are open 0900-1200 and 1530-1800. Fees are given under St. Vincent. Those clearing out of normal office hours (Monday - Friday, 0800-1500 and Saturday before noon) are subject to reasonable overtime fees.

Jet skis and the like are strictly forbidden, as is spearfishing, throughout the Grenadines (see St. Vincent).

Shopping Hours

Office and bank hours are as for St. Vincent. Most stores open from 0800-1200 and from 1400-1700.

Telephones

Card and coin phones may be found near the tourist office. You can buy phone cards in the post office and Solana's. Dial 1-800-872-2881 for ATT USA direct. See also St. Vincent.

Holidays

See St. Vincent.

Transport

There are inexpensive buses which run to many parts of the island. (Ask in the little tourist office on the quay.) Taxis are plentiful and reasonable. Sample taxi rates are:

	$EC
Most rides	15
Longer rides	20

Rental jeeps and motor bikes are available (see our directory). You need to buy a local license which costs $40 EC. Drive on the left.

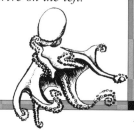

BEQUIA

Bequia has long been a favorite of yachts-people. Isolated enough to remain relatively unspoiled, yet lively enough to be stimulating and entertaining, it provides a blend of the old and new that many find perfect. It is well connected with St. Vincent and the other Grenadines both by the new airport and by the cheaper and more traditional ferries. The Admiral makes four trips on weekdays: the first ferry normally leaves Bequia at 0630 and the last returns at 1900. Some yachtspeople leave their boats anchored in Bequia and take a ferry over to visit St. Vincent. Check the free Caribbean Compass newspaper or the tourist office behind the main dock for the latest ferry schedule. The traditional sailing schooner Friendship Rose which served as the Bequia ferry for many years, has now been refitted as a charter boat.

Bequia is an island of sailors and boats. Linked to the outside world mainly by the sea, the old traditions still go on. Boats are built on the beach in the shade of palm trees. Everything from little "two bow" fishing boats to grand schooners are built by eye, using only simple hand tools. A big launching is always a festive occasion with rum flowing freely, music playing and hundreds of brightly dressed people helping to roll the boat down the beach into the sea. Bequians travel all over the world on cargo vessels and quite a few have ended up owning their own. Some are intrepid fishermen who venture all over the Grenadines in little open boats.

The island used to be an active whaling station, and though the tradition is now dying out, Bequians still make an occasional foray during the whaling season, between February and April. At this time of year humpback whales leave their northern feeding grounds and head south to mate and bear young. Few people are left in Bequia with the skills necessary to hunt them — a daring feat in an open sailing boat, using hand thrown harpoons. On the rare occasions that they make a kill, the hunters tow the whale to Petit Nevis for butchering.

Bequians are a proud people, descendants of settlers who came from North America on whaling boats, from farms in Scotland, from French freebooters and from Africa.

Bequia's main harbor is Admiralty Bay. There is a harbor on the south coast called Friendship Bay, and a daytime anchorage at Petit Nevis.

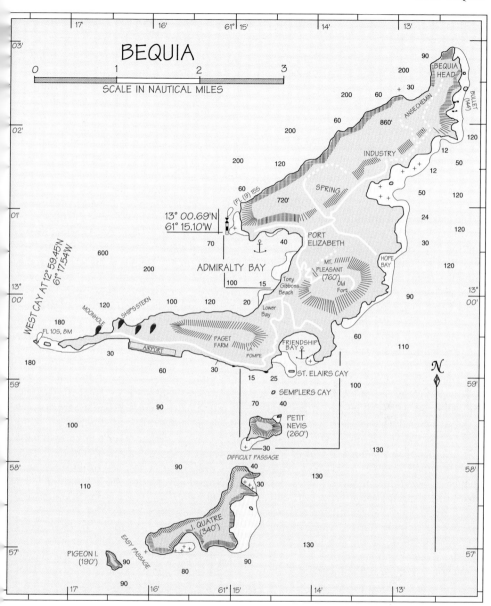

BEQUIA

SCALE IN NAUTICAL MILES

0   1   2   3

WEST CAY AT 12° 59.45'N 61° 17.54'W

13° 00.69'N
61° 15.10'W

BEQUIA HEAD

BULLET (144')

ANGECHEMIN

INDUSTRY

SPRING
720'

860'

(FL (9) 15S)

PORT ELIZABETH

ADMIRALTY BAY

MT. PLEASANT (760')

Old Fort

HOPE BAY

Tony Gibbons Beach

Lower Bay

MOONHOLE

SHIPS STERN

FL 10S, 8M

AIRPORT

PAGET FARM

LA POMPE

FRIENDSHIP BAY

ST. ELAIRS CAY

SEMPLERS CAY

PETIT NEVIS (260')

DIFFICULT PASSAGE

I. QUATRE (340')

EASY PASSAGE

PIGEON I. (190')

N

187

Admiralty Bay is a huge, well-protected bay with Bequia's town, Port Elizabeth, at its head. Small hotels, bars, restaurants and shops spread from town along the southeastern shore, strung together by a tiny path along the beach that threads its way along the seashore. On the northern shore are the workshops of several yacht services, all within an easy walk of Bequia Marina.

Navigation

The entrance to Admiralty Bay is straightforward. As you approach from the north and the bay begins to open up you can see two fine beaches, Lower Bay and Tony Gibbons (aka Princess Margaret) Beach, separated by a distinct headland. East of Tony Gibbons Beach it becomes more built up, starting with the Sunny Caribbee Plantation House and continuing to town.

Approaching the bay, allow plenty of room for Devil's Table, a reef which extends a good way from shore: it is marked by a yellow and black beacon. The beacon is on the outer part of the shoal, so allow plenty of room when you go round. Once in the harbor, take care not to hit the shoals that lie offshore between the eastern end of Tony Gibbon's Beach and the Green Boley. Yachts anchor inside some of these shoals, so it looks like tempting empty space. If entering at night, avoid the unlit, heavy metal buoys near Bequia Marina. These are used for big ship tie-ups, and the large plastic one has a hose running ashore.

Anchor well clear of the local ferry channel to the main dock. The ferries are large and need plenty of turning room. It is advisable to keep out of their way at all times. Yachts may not tie up to the ferry dock or the dinghy dock.

There are many places to anchor. Many choose up in town off the Frangipani Hotel. The water is deep and it takes lots of anchor line and sometimes a couple of tries to get hooked in the muddy sand.

The area by the Bequia Marina is calm. Avoid anchoring on the wreck which is at 13° 00.67'N, 61° 14.47'W. There is about 12 feet of water over it, but it has tied up many an anchor. Some yachts anchor off the Old Fig Tree and Sunny Caribbee. Enter inside the shoals by following a line between the ruined fort and the Sunny Caribbee Plantation House. The anchorage is eight to ten feet deep, shoaling toward the shore. Sometimes this is a beautiful spot, calm as a lake, the water decorated with floating pink blossoms from the white cedar trees that line the shore. Yet in times of northerly swells it can be untenable. On the shallow banks on both sides of the harbor (8-20 feet) you are anchoring on a mixture of hard sand and lumps of dead coral. The holding is generally poor. You need to let out ample chain and make sure you are holding.

Tony Gibbon's Beach is one of the easiest and prettiest anchorages, yet within a reasonable dinghy ride to town. Holding is good in sand. It occasionally becomes rolly in northerly swells, when landing a dinghy on the beach can be hazardous. Lower Bay

ADMIRALTY BAY

is also easy and picturesque though a little further away.

Some moorings are available. Call African Pride on VHF: 68 (most moorings on the south side) or Daffodil (moorings on the north side) on VHF: 67 for this service. Be careful accepting other offers as you may be rented a mooring belonging to someone else. If you get a receipt you should be OK. It is smart to snorkel on any mooring and to make sure it is okay.

Regulations

Port Elizabeth is a port of entry. Customs and immigration are both in one building, along with the Post Office, right behind the ferry dock. While the main office is being rebuilt (completion around the middle of 1999) the entry is on Back Street. In this temporary location it can be crowded, so only the skipper should go in. Customs are open weekdays 0900-1200, 1300-1500, 1530-1800, and weekends 0900-1200 and 1500-1800.

There is a five-knot speed limit in the harbor. This applies to dinghies, tenders and water taxis as well as yachts and ships. If you need to speed into town, do so only in the main shipping channel in the center of the harbor. Currently fast small boats are the most serious danger to life and limb in this harbor. We have already had one death and several maiming accidents. Is five minutes worth it?

Services

Bequia has excellent yacht services. Bequia Marina [VFH:68] and slip run by Neil Saunders offers stern-to docking with shore power for about 8 yachts. Pull along-side to take on water, diesel, and cube ice, and you get the best prices in Bequia here. Laundry and showers are available. Bequia Marina has a marine railway, the only haul out facility in Bequia. It can haul yachts up to 40 tons, 35-foot beam and 8-foot draft. Multihulls are welcome.

Although it is a little more expensive, the easiest way to get water and fuel is to call Daffodil Marine Services [VHF:68].They will deliver it alongside in a mobile service station. Their water comes from their own large desalinization plant. For gasoline go to the Shell station in town.

An overworked garbage collection bin stands near the head of the market dinghy dock. Never accept offers from local youths to "take your garbage."

Two places will help sort out your mechanical problems. Tyrone Caesar at Caribbean Diesel [VHF:68] is a first rate diesel mechanic. He spent nine years as an engineer on cargo carriers, then several more working in Miami for many large organizations, including Cummins. His experience covers all sizes of engine from giants to lightweights, and he knows Detroit Diesels, GM's, Perkins and Yanmar particularly well. He can bring in most parts in three days. Tyrone is good at basic electrical trouble shooting, and knows when to pass the job on. He can also arrange for refrigeration repairs. Tyrone's workshop is behind the church.

Peter Roren's Fixman Marine Engineering [VHF:16] is a full repair facility for any boat problems, from a clogged head to a broken engine. Peter sailed here from Norway with Maryanne on Fredag, a large boat

they built themselves. After years of adventure and misadventure, including a sinking and two dismastings, Peter seems to have found his metier fixing other people's problems rather than sailing into his own. He has a well-equipped work shop with a lathe and can do light machine work. He can weld stainless and aluminum. He deals with all kinds of mechanical, electrical and most electronic problems and is the Autohelm agent. Peter offers a complete sourcing and shipping service for anything from a new engine or mechanical part to any kind of electronics or hardware. He arranges the delivery to be free of hassle and duty. Fedexed parts usually take three days. Peter handles breakdowns for many charter companies, including The Moorings and Stardust.

There are two places that specialize in recalcitrant outboards. Grenadine Yacht Equipment (GYE) [VHF:16, 68], in a new building close to Bequia Marina, is the sales and service agent for Evinrude outboards and accessories. They also repair all other makes of outboards. GYE can fill gas

bottles (including French ones) and have a yacht chandlery including an excellent stock of brass pipe fittings, stainless steel hardware, rigging wire, rope, epoxy, marine ply and Danforth anchors, marine accessories and parts. You can send a fax or make a photocopy here. Owners Daniel and Missy Foulon speak French, Dutch and English.

Maxwell Stowe's Max Marine [VHF:68] is in Bequia Marina. It is a full sales and service agent for Mariner Outboards and carries chandlery including guides, charts, flags, resins, paints, cleaners and some hardware. Maxwell can arrange for the repair of any kind of outboard and he is agent for the popular AB Inflatables.

Daniel Refrigeration Service [VHF:68] will help get your beers cold again. Daniel studied both refrigeration and air-conditioning in the states, he can fix all systems and rebuild compressors. Should you need new installation Daniel can order it and do the joinery work necessary for building in a new freezer box. Call him to arrange a visit.

Andrew Mitchell's East Coast Yacht Refinishing [VHF:68] does maintenance

and top quality topsides spraying using modern two-part polyurethanes. You can find Andy at the Papa Mitch buildings. While Andy will go to a yard to spray your yacht out of the water, he has done many fine jobs in the water alongside the dock at Bequia Marina. Under the name Handy Andy, Andy rents both motor bikes, mountain bikes, and mechanical mules as well as a water tour and taxi service by speedboat.

There are four places for sail and canvas work, all good. Three of them are to be found on the road close by Bequia Marina.

Turbulence Sails [VHF:16] is run by a charming Frenchman called Richard. He is often to be found making high tech sails from mylar and polyester for the local "two bow" boats looking for an edge to win them the next race. Richard and his team can make new sails and they are agents for Doyle Sails in Barbados. They also handle repairs and do canvas work. Richard offers a complete spar and rigging shop. He can solve all your problems and doesn't mind

working up at the top of your mast. Turbulence Sails is agent for Profurl and Harken and they install many of these systems.

Grenadines Sails is owned by Avell Davis, a Bequian who has spent years making sails both in Bequia and Canada. Avell is the North Sails representative and works with Andrew Dove out of Guadeloupe to get you a fast quote for a new North Sail. Avell has a wide range of experience from his training in traditional handmade sails under Lincoln Simmonds, to modern high tech ones. New awnings, covers and alterations can easily be done in the loft.

Allick [VHF:68] is up the hill behind town. He is local, low key, personable, thorough and reasonably priced. He nearly always has the materials on hand for repair jobs, and you can ask him about new sails, awnings, cushions and covers. Contact him on VHF:68, his son Barbin comes by in Starlight watertaxi to pick up jobs.

Bequia Canvas [VHF:68] does just about everything but sails: interior and exterior cushions, awnings, covers, even tote bags.

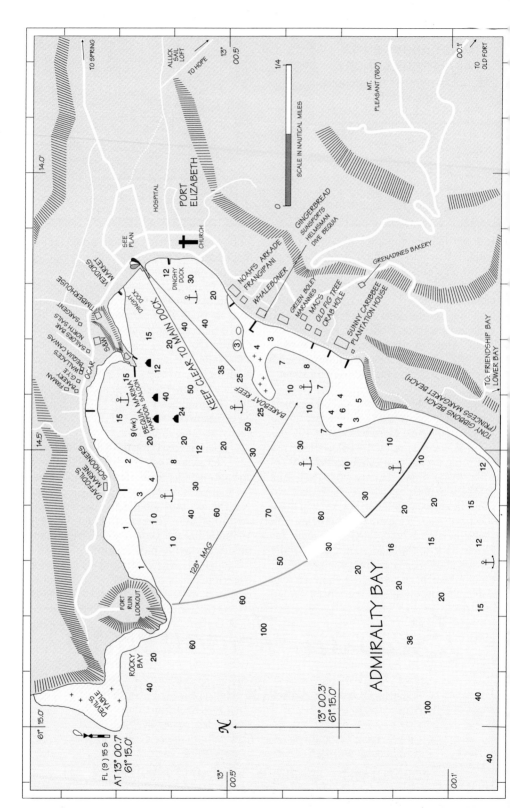

ADMIRALTY BAY

194

It is an efficient operation run by Carol Farrington from the U.S. They keep a wide range of materials, including closed-cell foam. Go to their shop next to Wallace's fishing tackle store, or if you call them on the radio, Carol will come to your yacht to discuss the job.

Bequia also has many shipwrights and carpenters.

Nowhere in the Caribbean is better than Bequia for getting laundry done. One call on the radio [VHF:68] brings a rapid collection service to your yacht and same-day delivery at fair prices. Three companies offer this service: The Lighthouse, Papa Mitch and Daffodil Marine. All have water taxis and will also deliver ice, beers, soft drinks or whatever else you need. Lighthouse and Daffodil will send and receive faxes. In addition, The Lighthouse [VHF:68] has a land taxi, showers by their office and has an apartment to rent.

Block ice is also available from GYE, The Old Fig Tree and the Gooding's house behind Bequia Marina. Cube ice may be found in the Shoreline Mini-market, Kingfisher Cafe, and the Frangipani.

Frangipani Yacht Services [VHF:68] are open weekdays from 0830 to 1300 and 1400 to 1700. They have a mail drop, telephone, fax, e-mail and will help in any way they can. You can have mail sent here. Sam Taxi Tours [VHF:68] lies on Back Street next to the Vinsure building. He offers a full communications service, and will make airline reconfirmations. Iconet in the Sailor's Bar offers a bank of computers for e-mail and surfing the net. There is a travel agency at the Gingerbread called Grenadine Travel [VHF:16,68].

Bequia is the home of Caribbean Compass, the free waterfront paper for the southern islands. The editor, Sally Erdle, has drawn for this Sailor's Guide since its inception.

Taxis in Bequia are inexpensive and sight seeing in Bequia is highly recommended. Gideon has two taxis, works well with the yachts and is always listening to VHF:68. He also has four-wheel drive rentals.

Water taxis are always available, just call on VHF:68.

Ashore

David de Lloyd's Bosun's Locker is a fine chandlery where you can buy most items duty free. It is the sole agent for Simpson Lawrence and has a good line of their manual and electric windlasses. David also sells Avon inflatables, wind generators, toilets, stoves, and has a good stock of Blake and other paints, along with Marina rope, anchors, chain, pumps of all kinds as well as pump parts. All the usual yacht necessities are here including Admiralty Charts. He also carries nautical gifts.

Le Ron's General Store has resins, clothes, inexpensive shackles and some hardware and Bequia Venture hardware store includes a few marine items.

You've been hanging a line over the stern for miles, but never have any luck? Get Wallace's, near Bequia Marina, to recommend a lure, or sell you a made up rig. New owners Jergen and Bip both have biology backgrounds and Steadman Wallace is often around to give local tips. Wallace's has

expanded into more general chandlery including a big selection of ss screws and bolts, safety gear, snorkeling equipment and rope. While the chandlery selection is not big, the prices are reasonable. The Wallaces keep a book swap here. The price of using this is to make a small contribution to the Sunshine School for disabled kids.

Nowadays Bequia has become quite a good place to stock up on provisions. Doris Fresh Food [VHF:68,16], a complete small air-conditioned supermarket where you will find excellent meat, cheese, good wines, local chutney, gourmet items, including smoked fish, and some fresh produce. Baked goodies include Hearty Russian bread, which tastes good and keeps well, making it popular with those setting out to sea. Fresh French bread is baked daily as are croissants during the season.

The Food Mart over by Daffodil's is another small supermarket with deli meats and cheeses. It is air conditioned and small tables enable you to lunch in the cool on sandwiches and salads.

S&W is the largest of the supermarkets

and they have a good selection of dry goods, cans, cheese, wines and liquor. The smaller Shoreline [VHF:68] is convenient if you are using the Frangipani dock.

You can also buy fruit and vegetables in the new market block. The selection is good, but those who don't like high pressure salesmanship prefer the quieter stalls which you will find dotted around the main street. Joan has a stall right opposite Doris.

Few people realize that Daphne bakes her own bread, as does Mac's Pizzeria, Kingfisher Cafe and The Harpoon Saloon. When it comes to bread and baked goods, excellent cooked breakfasts and lunchtime sandwiches consider the Bequia Bakery. If you dinghy to the Crab Hole and walk up to the main road and turn right it is a little way up the hill on your right with a great view of the harbor. The Whaleboner sells yogurt and fresh milk from their own cows, as well as bread and cookies. The Gingerbread Coffee shop has baked goods, coffee, wine, caviar and gourmet items. Maranne's has yogurt and home-made ice cream.

The waterfront in Port Elizabeth is color-

ful, with vendors selling t-shirts, model boats and handicrafts. Here you may see Baillar, a French Canadian artist, who now lives in Bequia and often sits in the square doing instant portraits or seascapes, and Maryanne whose Whyknot rope work is displayed in the back of an old landrover.

Bequia has a large range of small, pleasant boutiques. The new market has its own dinghy dock. Many shops here sell t-shirts, souvenirs and gifts and there is an ice cream shop and a bar.

The building of model boats is a Bequia specialty and you can find them at Mauvin's near the market or Sergeant's, toward Bequia Marina. They will build any design to order, but my favorites are the model whaling boats. You will find attractive local handmade clothing in Daphne's Restaurant, where she does her own hand screening.

Solana's has a large collection of hand painted t-shirts, shorts and batik work, also handicrafts, film, jewelry, books, videos, flags, phone cards and maps. Solana's is also the Federal Express agent.

Nearby, the Bequia Bookshop has an ex-cellent range of nautical books and charts, local books, videos and novels. They also sell film, postcards, local art and scrimshaw locally handcrafted by Sam McDowell. Sam's wife Donna creates intricate and elegant designs on boxes and mirrors from shells. (Donna mainly buys her shells from the old collections.) You will see some of her work in the shops or you can arrange to take a ride out to their Banana patch Studios in Paget Farm.

Art lovers should visit the Bequia gallery which shows the work of local artists, including some good paintings by Pinky who lives over in Friendship Bay.

Walk a few steps back behind the church and you will find quite a few businesses. One of these hidden jewels is Lulley's Tackle Shop, the oldest fishing shop in Bequia, with a really wide range, not only of fishing gear, but also of ropes, snorkeling gear and knives. Island Things has a wide range of clothing and souvenirs, all locally made. The Lighthouse Laundry is here as is the Patriot hair dressing shop for men and Caribbean Diesel.

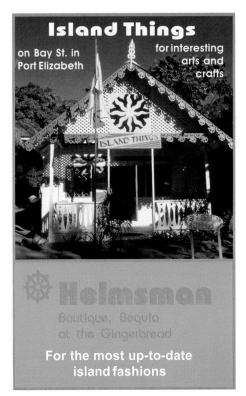
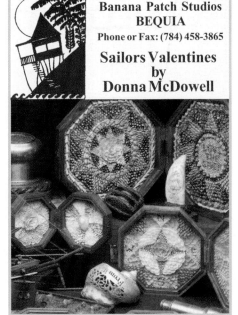
Creative Universe has jewelry, t-shirts and film. The Almond Tree Boutique sells clothing and souvenir items. In the new Shoreline Plaza there is a bakery, bank, stationery store, Baby Things, a video rental shop, a drug store (nonprescription), The Wine Rack, for wine and liquors, and the Potpourri shop which sells the New York Times. The boutique 96 Degrees in the Shade sells elegant hand painted and batik wear.

In a spacious upstairs location, Joan's Local Color has a wonderful selection of products from all over the Caribbean. There are many handicrafts and an even bigger range of clothing.

Melinda is an artist and was the first in Bequia to hand paint t-shirts. She used to row around the harbor, accompanied by her pet Labrador, selling them to the yachts. Now Melinda has a boutique, where you will find Bequia's most elegantly hand painted t-shirts, shorts, caps and visors. Melinda also crafts stained glass. Her major work is memorial windows in the Anglican Church. Smaller works sell in her bou-

tique, and they can be safely packed for travel. Next door, Sprotties specializes in silk screen clothing. The Garden has some pareos, batiks and long dresses.

As you wander toward the Frangipani on the waterfront track, you pass Noah's Arkade which has a wide range of Caribbean crafts, spices, handicrafts and local books, as well as some casual wear.

Along the waterfront, the Whaleboner Boutique offers hand made clothing from screened and batik fabrics and they also sell shorts and local model boats. Down at the Gingerbread you will find the Helmsman selling elegant swim wear and casual wear, including a range of brightly screened t-shirts from Trinidad.

By the time you've seen all these shops and walked to the Green Boley you will probably need a break. Stop at Maranne's and try some of her famous gourmet ice cream, frozen yogurt or sorbet. Everything is home made from fresh ingredients with local fruit flavors, unobtainable elsewhere in the world. While there ask Bob (he often minds the store) where his rock 'n roll group SOS will be playing. They are first rate entertainment. Right next door the Green Boley Boutique has colorful applique pictures, locally made clothes and souvenirs.

No shopping trip would be complete without a visit to the Crab Hole where they operate their own silk screen factory. You are welcome to visit the factory and see the process at work. In the shop you can choose from their fabrics and elegant casual wear with accessories to match.

Fancy an elegant French haircut or styling? Joelle, a French hair stylist works out of her home up the hill from Mac's Pizzeria. Contact her through her husband Richard at Turbulence sails by GYE.

Bequia has lovely walks. You can follow the path from the Sunny Caribbee over to Tony Gibbons Beach and on down to Lower Bay. If you laze on the beach and swim, keep an eye on your handbags and cameras. Don't set them down and wander away, as they too have been known to walk.

Watch a sunset from Mount Pleasant, or walk to Friendship Bay, Spring or Industry for lunch or dinner and enjoy the great variety of views along the way.

Spring makes an especially good destination on a Sunday when they have their famous curry lunch. One can hike to Hope, a lovely remote beach where the shallow water sets up long lines of breakers often suitable for body surfing (watch the undertow). Those on limited time or who don't like hiking should take a taxi tour. The Old Hegg Turtle sanctuary out at Industry is a great destination. Brother King takes turtle eggs and rears turtles till they are old enough to have a higher chance of survival. The establishment of the sanctuary has done much to raise environmental consciousness in Bequia. There is a small charge to visit which goes towards the cost of feeding and housing the turtles.

You can see the best and most scenic spots in a leisurely 3-hour tour. Each place you visit seems so different that sometimes Bequia feels like several islands in one. Highlights include an old fort looking over the harbor; Bequia's summit, Mount Pleasant, with a stop at The Old Fort bar and restaurant; the beautiful windward beach of Spring and a visit to the home of Athneal Olliviere, the island's head whale harpooner, who has a small whaling museum. The taxi drivers are proud of their island, and are

knowledgeable guides.

If you just want to visit Spring, Friendship or Lower Bay, hop on a taxi; the island is small so the fares are reasonable.

Tennis courts are available at Spring, Friendship Bay, the Plantation House and Sunsports. If you come at Easter you can get involved in the Bequia Regatta, a four-day extravaganza of local boat races, yacht races and lots of partying. Christmas is also a popular time in Bequia, but "9 Mornings" which starts some two weeks before Christmas, can make the town anchorage throb with disco music through the night.

The waterfront offers a wonderful mixture of bars and restaurants. The Frangipani Hotel [VHF:68, $B, closed September] is owned by Son Mitchell, the prime minister of St. Vincent and the Grenadines, and has been in his family since the turn of the century. The upper floor of the main building used to be the family home and downstairs was the storehouse for the Glorea Colita, which, at 131 feet long, was the largest schooner ever to be built in Bequia. In 1940 she disappeared and was found

drifting empty in the Bermuda triangle. Today the Frangipani is ably managed by Marie. By day it is a good place to meet people and enjoy a great fresh tuna sandwich for lunch. By night they offer romantic candlelight dinners of Caribbean specialties. Everyone comes by on a Thursday night when they have a barbecue and jump up to a steel band. They also have a string band on Mondays in season.

The most sociable and entertaining evening rendezvous is at Pat Mitchell's Gingerbread [VHF:68, $B-C]. The impressive Caribbean style building features highly intricate gingerbread trim and an immensely high wooden roof supported by mast-like poles. The spacious upstairs dining room has a grand harbor view and comfortable seats. The atmosphere is enlivened by Elvis and Knight Riders, a good unamplified group who play on Wednesdays and Sundays. The food is delicious, with curries a speciality. Reservations are advisable in season, or stop in for a drink. The Gingerbread is also open for breakfast. At lunchtime you can get soups, salads and sandwiches upstairs

or barbecue items outside under the trees downstairs. The coffee shop sells coffee and baked goodies.

Another place for those who enjoy entertainment is the Harpoon Saloon [VHF:68, $B-C] under the new management of Sonia. They offer Afro-Caribbean specialties. Below Harpoon Saloon Max's Maracuja is a lovely little bar built amid the rock foundations and out onto the Bequia Marina dock. Find your nook at the hanging seat bar on the south side or in the waterfront alcove on the north. They open from 0730 to 1900 with a happy hour from 1630-1800. They serve fresh juices, a variety of coffees and light fare from tasty tacos or a baked potato to hamburgers.

Mac's Pizzeria [$C-D] is a favorite haunt. Their tasty pizzas are legendary among yachtspeople, but you can also get quiches, salads, soups and goodies from their bakeshop, along with daily specials. The atmosphere is congenial, and it is inexpensive enough that you can gravitate here any time you do not feel like cooking. In season it is advisable to make a reservation to avoid a long wait.

There are plenty of first rate places to get inexpensive local food. The Hinkson's Whaleboner [$C-D] is conveniently situated next to the Frangipani and has its own dinghy dock. Much of the food comes from their farm so you know it is fresh. True to its name, the bar, stools and entrance have all

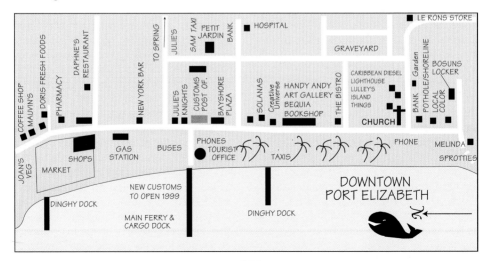

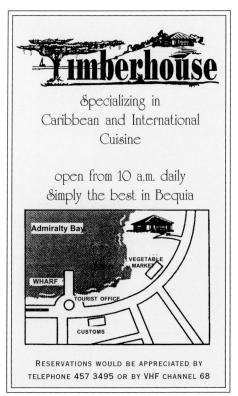

been built of whalebone from the old whaling days. Angela will cook good snacks, pizzas, chicken and fish. They also do full evening meals at a reasonable price, including curried and roast pork. In both cases the meat comes from their own hand raised animals. Chicken and fish are always available, as is lobster in season. The Old Fig Tree is right on the water overlooking the harbor. In times of northerly swells this part of the harbor seems to attract the biggest waves. During a hurricane the building nearly went into the sea, but was saved by the huge "Old Fig Tree" that gives it its name. Their local food is good value.

The Bistro in town is the new hot spot. The location is perfect and the open atmosphere gives it the feeling of an open air cafe on the Riviera but at local Bequia prices. They offer hearty local meals, pizzas and excellent hamburgers. It is also the perfect place to enjoy a few drinks or a cup of coffee and watch the world pass by outside.

If you have time to plan ahead, call Daphne's [VHF:68, $C] and discuss a special local meal with Daphne Grant, one of Bequia's really good local cooks whose meals have an individual flair. Daphne's is a great place to go in a small group. You can also drop in for a lunchtime roti. Noeline Taylor's Porthole [VHF:68, $C-D] is a popular meeting place for a lunch roti. She also cooks dinner. Walk in for her famous fish and chips. Other local restaurants include Lyston Williams' Green Boley [$D], good for rotis and snacks and Isola McIntosh's Julie's Guest House [VHF:68, $C] where advance booking is necessary. Yachties on a budget will appreciate the low prices for fried chicken and fish at the S & W snack bar [$D], upstairs over their supermarket. The Kingfisher Cafe near the town dinghy dock offers pastry, snacks and local fruit juices, and the Soda Fountain Coffee Shop offers good coffee, tasty pastries and baked goodies as well as lunchtime snacks.

For upscale gourmet cooking visit Le Petit Jardin [VHF:16,68, $A-B], owned by Owen Belmar from Bequia. Owen has returned to his native Bequia after years as a chef on huge corporate charter yachts. He studied at the Culinary Institute in the U.S.,

LE PETIT JARDIN

Restaurant, Bequia

VHF:16, 68
Phone:
(784) 458-3318
Fax:457-3134
Back Street
Port Elizabeth

major credit cards welcome

For Gourmet French Cuisine
Seafoods a specialty

Open: 1130-1400, 1830-2130

but his ability to produce wonderful melt-in-the-mouth delicacies to rival any French chef is unquestionably a gift. The food is served in an appropriately quiet, simple and slightly formal setting in a house of natural stone and varnished wood, which has a garden of herbs and fruit trees. Le Petit Jardin is open for both lunch and dinner. Reservations are advisable. Owen creates the recipes for the cooking section of Caribbean Compass.

Over on the north side of the harbor, Timberhouse [VHF:68, $B-C closed Sundays] is a good restaurant which serves consistently fine seafood and meat dishes. They also serve sandwiches and snacks at lunch. Michael at the bar will make you feel welcome and there is a view over the harbor. The nearest dinghy dock is the one by the local market. Walk out, turn left and it is on your left up a small hill.

Schooners [VHF:68, $C] is the local hangout for those anchored on the north side of the harbor. It has a big balcony offering a commanding view of the harbor. Locals and yachting folk gather for happy hour from 1730-1830. They specialize in Chinese food, which you can eat there or take out. Several nights a week they have after-dinner live musical entertainment featuring local groups including their home band Elvis and the Knight Riders.

The new Sailor's restaurant and bar run by Brinn is opposite S&W. Built on a deck it is completely open with shelters over the tables. Brinn does take out frozen meals for yachts and inside you can surf the net.

On the south side of the harbor, The Sunny Caribbee Plantation House [VHF:68, $A] started as a gracious hotel in traditional Caribbean style. The Italian banker owners have now adorned it with a concrete fence and lots of statues. It is open for breakfast, lunch and elegant evening meals. They sometimes bring in top chefs for the season. There is also a beach bar and a branch of their bank.

These are just the restaurants in Admiralty Bay. There are also good restaurants in other places, and taxi fares are reasonable ($12-20 EC).

Spring on Bequia [VHF:68, $B] is both a

206

hotel and a working estate and they grow most of their own produce. They are open from about November till June and are famous as a peaceful hideaway resort. Candy, the owner, works on the menus and they have a reputation for delicious food, but you must call them up and book in advance. (If you cannot get them on VHF:68, ask a Bequia taxi to relay for you.) It is a pleasant walk, about a mile, in the cool of the evening to work up your appetite for dinner. Spring on Bequia is also famous for Sunday curry lunches, and during the season they run a beach bar on Spring Beach.

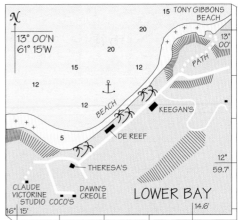

The Old Fort [VHF:68,73, $A] is built on the ruins of an ancient fortified estate house up in the cool hills of Mt. Pleasant. Run by Otmar Schaedle from Germany, its wonderful views make it a favored destination for hikers by day. At night atmosphere is their strong point with a fire in the dining room hearth where they serve a five-course set dinner. Reservations are essential.

Lower Bay has one of Bequia's best beaches, set in a low key, rural atmosphere of fishing boats and strung out nets. Great for swimming by day and romantic on a full moon night, it is a popular place to hang out, especially on Sunday. Recently people have begun to gravitate there of an evening for inexpensive seafood dinners. Lower Bay makes an acceptable anchorage in settled conditions and is within dinghy reach of Admiralty Bay. However, there is usually enough swell to make landing on the beach a damp affair, so it is better to take a cab over ($12-15 EC). By day it is interesting to follow the track from the Sunny Caribbee over the bluff to Tony Gibbon's Beach, then over the next bluff to Lower Bay. Once you arrive there are several local restaurants to choose from. Keegan's [VHF:68, $C-D], opposite the beach, offers inexpensive three course dinners, featuring chicken, shrimp, fish or conch. By day they do fish or chicken 'n chips and snacks. De Reef [VHF:68, $C-

D], right on the beach, is popular for lunch, and a major gathering place for locals on Sundays. You can get chicken, fish, conch or sandwiches any day of the week. By night they serve three course dinners by reservation, and from time to time they bring in a band and throw a great fete.

Theresa's [VHF:68, $C], just back from the beach, is a cutely converted little rum shop and a favorite watering hole for many expatriates and holiday returnees. Theresa and Englishman John Bennett are good hosts and offer excellent West Indian food. They also open at lunchtime for sandwiches and first rate hamburgers. On Sunday afternoons the Honky Tonics play jazz and visiting musicians are sometimes welcomed.

Coco's Place [VHF:68, $B-D] is a special find, way up a steep hill. You can perch up here like a bird with a panoramic view of the bay below. Coco works wonders with seafood and does excellent lambi. There are also many local meat dishes. The atmosphere is informal and friendly, with jump ups on Tuesdays and Fridays. For groups of 6-8 they have one delightful table set in a little gothic corner tower to the side of the building.

Dawn's Creole [VHF:68, $C], next to Coco's, has a quiet enchantment and they serve snacks or full meals to order. They

also have a few hideaway rooms and the views from some are unbeatable.

Fernando's Hideaway [$C] is simple, low key and serves good meals from local fish and meat. Advance reservations are pretty much essential. It is down a back road: take a taxi so you can find it easily.

While you are in Lower Bay, visit the home of French artist Claude Victorine [VHF:16 "Pigeon"], whose work is displayed along with that of her daughter, Louloune. Both are exceptionally talented. Louloune does both realistic paintings and intricate weavings of imagination and dreams. Claude's main medium is painting on silk and she creates superb cushion covers, wall hangings and fabrics which are guaranteed to add a touch of class to any boat or home. Claude accepts visitors during the day, and the sight of her pretty little house perched up in the hills is well worth the walk. She sometimes closes on Fridays.

Water sports

Sailboarding enthusiasts should check with Paradise Windsurfing at Friendship Bay and Lower Bay. Basil, an accredited instructor, will teach you how to windsurf, or if you already know, you can rent a board for the afternoon, or take one along with you for your cruise. Basil is also an artist who hand paints t-shirts.

Diving in Bequia is superb and not to be missed by scuba fans. For the uninitiated it is an ideal place for a resort course. There are two shops to choose from and to make sure you don't know which is which, both are near the Gingerbread and both are owned by a Bob. Since they are so close together you can chat with both and go with the one that suits you. Sunsports is right in the main Gingerbread building. For Dive Bequia, turn right at the head of the dock and walk about 60 feet. It is on your left.

Sunsports [VHF:68] is run by Bob Monnens from Minnesota. Bob is friendly, keen and experienced and likes to work with small groups and never takes more than eight divers on a trip. He enjoys night diving and will go to the more distant dive sites even for one person. The Sunsports retail shop has a good selection of fins, masks, dive books and accessories. Call Bob to arrange to be collected from your yacht.

Bob Sachs is one of scuba's greatest enthusiasts and Bequia's most experienced diver. He and his team of assistants have a flair for running groups that are always friendly and sociable. Call Dive Bequia [VHF:68,16] and Bob or his one of his staff will arrange to collect you from your yacht. Return to the bar later to socialize with them and other divers. Their seaworthy new dive boats allow for occasional diving and exploring trips up to the Falls of Baleine in St. Vincent or down to the Grenadines.

Dive Bequia also works with Dive St. Vincent and Grenadine Divers, so you can set up dive packages valid in all their locations or start a full certification course in one place and continue it as you sail through the islands.

For those diving on their own, the most accessible good dives are around Devil's Table. There is a pretty reef extending from the black and yellow beacon to the shore. There are moorings so you can tie up your

dinghy. From the shallow inshore end you can dive out along one side of the rocky shoal, and back on the other. The depth at the outer end of the reef is about 65 feet. There are plenty of different corals and reef fish. Sergeant majors may often be seen guarding their eggs. An even prettier dive is along the stretch of coast from inside this reef northwards to Northwest Point. There is a sloping reef all along this shore. The maximum depth is about 60 feet at Northwest Point. Coral formations include lots of pillar coral, and there are usually large schools of blue chromis. Over the sand garden eels undulate. On both dives you must mind the current.

Even more exciting dives are a long way from the anchorage. There is usually a lot of current, so they are best done as drift dives and are most easily accessible by dive boat. Flat Rock Drift Dive is on Bequia's northwest coast, starting at the western end of Anse Chemin. This is a gentle easy dive where you hardly have to use your fins and there is time to examine all the little creatures on the way. You swim along a captivat-

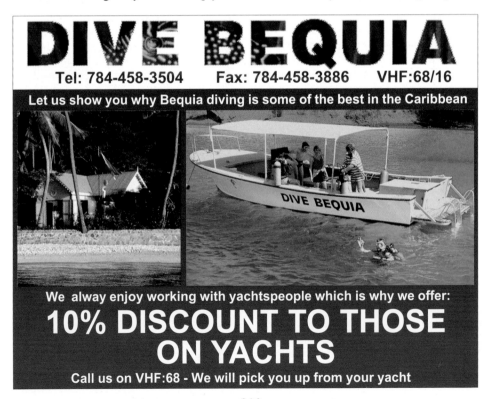

Friendship Bay

ing reef which slopes gently into sand at 60 feet. It offers an excellent selection of soft and hard corals, lots of fish, arrow crabs, lobsters, tube worms and anemones. A couple of spotted snake eels hang out here and one often sees a ray.

The Boulders is a pleasant drift dive about two-thirds of the way between Admiralty Bay and Moonhole. A gentle descent 60 feet down a coral slope takes you into an area where hundreds of fish, including huge schools of blue chromis and sennets, make ever-changing patterns as you drift with the current. Barracudas patrol up and down; moray eels, lobsters, crabs and shrimps can be found. The reef gets deeper till you come to the boulders, which are tall rock formations, each about 20 feet high, starting from a bottom depth of 93 feet. There are tunnels to pass through and holes and caverns which provide hiding places for nurse sharks, groupers, angelfish and jacks. As you return to the dive boat, you may see a frogfish or seahorse.

Pigeon Island is an outstanding dive area. The island slopes off steeply to around 100 feet. There are walls, overhangs, rifts and hollows decorated by deepwater lace coral. The visibility is generally excellent and you will see huge schools of blue and brown chromis, big groupers, passing pelagic fish and sometimes rays and turtles.

The Wall (West Cay, northern side) is an adventure dive to 114 feet, with dramatic vistas and the odd large pelagic. Moonhole (outside the Moonhole complex) offers temporary anchorage, though I would leave a crew member on board. Make sure you are anchored in sand and do not tie to the dive moorings. The easiest dive is to start right in the bay and follow the reef round the point to the east, watching for currents. This is a gentle dive to 60 feet with hard and soft corals and a variety of smaller fish.

The snorkeling is good around Devil's Table and along the coast to Northwest Point. Both dive shops also provide snorkeling trips.

MOONHOLE TO FRIENDSHIP BAY

If you are sailing from Admiralty Bay to West Cay, you will undoubtedly catch sight of Moonhole. This rather isolated community, where American architect Tom Johnson is king, is not easily accessible by either land or sea, there being no road or good anchorage. Moonhole houses are certainly different; the original was built under a natural arch known as "Moonhole." It was abandoned when a huge boulder fell from the ceiling and threatened to crush the bed. The other houses grow out of the rocks without straight lines or right angles. They have huge arches, fantastic views and lovely patios. There is seldom glass in the windows and the breeze is constant; there is no electricity. Moonhole is a special kind of vacation home for the right people. The architecture is worth marveling at as you sail by. Although Moonhole (VHF:06) is a very private place, Jim and Sheena Johnson do now offer tours (about $40 EC) on Tuesday afternoons. They will arrange tours on other days for groups of six or so. (All tours are by prior arrangement only.) A tour lasts an hour or two and takes you through several houses. (They select ones which are empty at the time.) You get to visit the original Moonhole and finish at their bar overlooking the sea, where there is time for a drink before going back. It is probably easiest to get to Moonhole by taxi, but the intrepid can dinghy down if there are no northerly swells. Landing takes considerable agility.

Bequia's new airport is built along the south coast. There is a dock about a third of a mile to its east off Paget Farm where you can get ashore from a tenable, if rolly, anchorage.

FRIENDSHIP BAY AND PETIT NEVIS

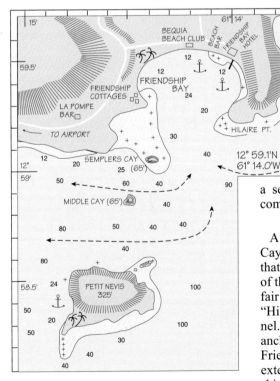

On the south side of Bequia, Friendship Bay is gorgeous, with a lovely white beach. The anchorage is secure with good holding and in times of northerly swells it offers better protection than Admiralty Bay. A swell often creeps in from the southeast so a second anchor from the stern to keep comfortable is advised.

Navigation

A reef extends from the shore to Semplers Cay and beyond. Don't try to sail in or out that way as some have. On the opposite side of the harbor there is a reef extending out a fair way from Hilaire Point (locally called "Hillary"). Keep in the center of the channel. Once inside, pick up a mooring or anchor to the east of the bay or off the Friendship Bay Beach Bar. Note that a reef extends from the west side of the Friendship Bay Hotel dock to a small breakwater near the beach bar.

Ashore

The Friendship Bay Resort [VHF:68, $A-B] has the air of a rather grand hotel, with lovely gardens and a cute "swing seat" beach

Friendship Bay

bar called Herby 'n Spicy. Cocktails, lunch and informal dinners are served here and as an alternative there is a panoramic glass-lined dining room. The view of Petit Nevis and Isle de Quatre is spectacular. It is run by Swedes Lars and Margit Abrahamson. The dock is being renovated and soon you should be able to come stern-to to take water when it is available along with outboard gas. They offer telephone and fax communications and they sell cube ice and bread. In addition full provisioning can be arranged through their associated company Gourmet Food Wholesale. If you have picked up a mooring, the fee is refunded if you visit for dinner (bring the receipt). The food is excellent; a blend of Swedish, French and local flavors with plenty of seafood and lobster in season. Wednesday night is Lobster barbecue night and on Saturday night they have the Real Ting Band. Friday is gourmet night and on Mondays is Asian night. Sandwiches and light lunches are available in the bar. Their lobster salad is great.

You can work off the calories on their tennis court or underwater with their dive shop. A tiny boutique is next to the beach bar. Special rates for yachtspeople are available when there are vacancies.

Just down the beach, the Bequia Beach Club [$B-C] offers beach-side dining with local and continental food. Lunch time snacks are available and there is a scuba shop.

Over near Friendship Cottages, La Pompe International Bar has a good selection of basic groceries, a pool table, Sunday evening videos and the world's hottest domino tournament. This is the place to meet the local fishermen and whalers.

Water sports

The snorkeling is worth a go in Friendship Bay, both along the shore between the Friendship Bay Resort dock and Herby 'n Spicy beach bar, also between Semplers Cay and the shore. Friendship Bay Hotel is a full SSI dive resort, they can take you diving, fill tanks and rent gear. Bequia Beach Club also has a dive shop.

Petit Nevis

Petit Nevis makes an interesting daytime anchorage. The snorkeling along the shore is good (out of the lee the current gets strong) and the whale rendering facilities make interesting exploring. If passing southwards, note the long southerly reef.

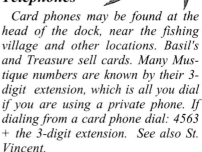

Regulations

Mustique has moorings and fees for staying overnight. See general text for details.

Yachts do not often clear in or out of Mustique, but it can be done. Customs and immigration will be found at the airport.

Jet skis and the like are strictly forbidden, as is spearfishing and anchoring on coral.

Water-skiing is not permitted in the yacht anchorage area.

Vessels carrying more than 25 passengers are not allowed in Mustique.

Daycharter yachts visiting Mustique pay an extra fee; for details see Ken Will at Mustique Co.

Shopping Hours

Corea's food store; Mon-Sat: 0800-1200, 1500-1800. Boutiques; 0900-1200 and 1400-1800. Treasure boutique, Alis & Corea's open Sunday mornings.

Holidays

See St. Vincent.

Telephones

Card phones may be found at the head of the dock, near the fishing village and other locations. Basil's and Treasure sell cards. Many Mustique numbers are known by their 3-digit extension, which is all you dial if you are using a private phone. If dialing from a card phone dial: 4563 + the 3-digit extension. See also St. Vincent.

Transport

Rental mules (heavy duty golf carts) and motor bikes are available from Mustique Mechanical Services. You can arrange this by calling extentions 316 or 378. Or call Mustique Moorings on VHF:68/16 and arrange it through them. You need a local license which costs $40 EC. Drive on the left.

Mustique is unique among the Grenadines. It is a privately owned island that has been developed as an area of holiday homes for the wealthy. Mansions with tennis courts and swimming pools sit on rolling grassy hills and long lawns stretch to sandy beaches. Each house lies in spacious grounds; there are only about 80 on the whole island, plus one hotel, a guest house, one beach bar, a few boutiques, a small local village and a fishing camp. A roll call of those who have owned property reveals some glamorous names, including Princess Margaret, Mick Jagger, David Bowie, and Raquel Welch. Parts of the island are wild; other areas are well tended. About half the houses are available for rent when the owners are not in residence. Many older homes were designed by Oliver Messel and are delightful to look at, with a showy but dignified appeal. As you would expect for an island of this type, prices are rather high as everything has to come in from the outside.

Navigation

Montezuma Shoal is about half to three quarters of a mile west of Britannia Bay. It presents a real hazard and has ground pieces off the hulls of a cruise ship, a large charter yacht and many a bareboat. A red and black striped beacon is placed on the reef. Stay at least a quarter of a mile away. (If you can see the colors you are probably too close.) If you come from the south, do not follow the coast too closely as there is also quite a reef extending seaward from the southern point of Britannia Bay.

The only acceptable anchorage is in Britannia Bay. The water is sparkling clear and this is a lovely area for swimming and snorkeling. The anchorage is generally rather rolly.

Regulations

The Mustique Company controls the anchorages in Mustique. There is a mandatory mooring system here with 33 moorings. Charges are $40 EC for the first night and $20 EC for each subsequent night. The moorings are operated by the Mustique Watersports. (Call Mustique Moorings on VHF:16/68). Attach your own line to the top of the buoy and leave as much scope as possible so you do not overstrain the moor-ing. Snorkel to check the condition of the chain. Note that some of the southern moorings are placed in sand in the reef area. Take care how you approach these and note that there may be depth limitations (we found the swinging room around one mooring to include a patch of coral about 7.5 feet deep). The outer moorings over sand have plenty of depth. If all the moorings are taken, you can

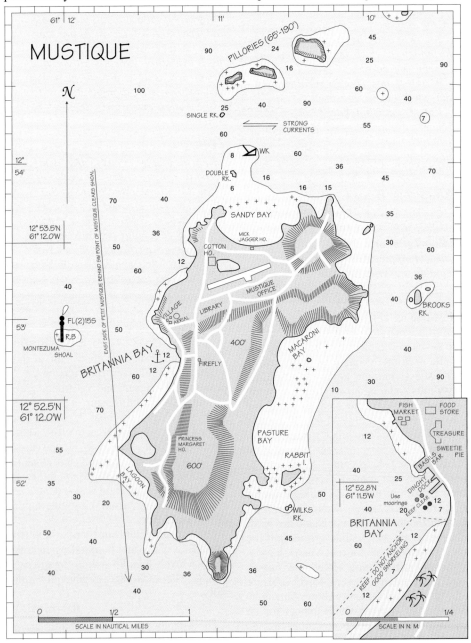

MUSTIQUE

N

PILLORIES (65'-190')

STRONG CURRENTS

SINGLE RK.

DOUBLE RK.

SANDY BAY

MICK JAGGER HO.

COTTON HO.

MUSTIQUE OFFICE

VILLAGE

AERIAL

LIBRARY

FL(2)15S R.B

MONTEZUMA SHOAL

BRITANNIA BAY

FIREFLY

MACARONI BAY

BROOKS RK.

PRINCESS MARGARET HO.

PASTURE BAY

RABBIT I.

LAGOON BAY

WILKS RK.

12° 54'
12° 53.5'N 61° 12.0'W
53'
12° 52.5'N 61° 12.0'W
52'

61° 12'
11'
10'

EAST SIDE OF PETIT MUSTIQUE BEHIND SW POINT OF MUSTIQUE CLEARS SHOAL

400'
600'

0   1/2   1
SCALE IN NAUTICAL MILES

FISH MARKET
FOOD STORE
TREASURE
SWEETIE PIE
BASIL'S BAR
DINGHY DOCK
KEEP CLEAR
Use moorings
12° 52.8'N 61° 11.5'W

BRITANNIA BAY

REEF - DO NOT ANCHOR
GOOD SNORKELING

0   1/4
SCALE IN N. M.

MAGICAL MUSTIQUE
St. Vincent Grenadines, The West Indies

Mustique Villas

An island of regal retreats and privileged privacy. Mustique is the jewel of the Grenadines. Pristine tropical surroundings with swaying palm groves, private white sand beaches and panoramas of azure seas and majestic sailing vessels.

Villa Rentals 784-458-4621

Cotton House
MUSTIQUE

The Cotton House, totally renovated, offers impeccable service, culinary creativity and idyllic escape to pleasure. The superbly refurbished deluxe suites and rooms are redecorated in truly luxury defined - Plantation style.

Reservations: 800-826-2809
Fax: 784-456-5887
Hotel tel: 784-456-4777, VHF:68

---

try to find a spot between them, or anchor to their west. Do not anchor around the southern moorings; they are close to the reef which it is protected by law. Leave a clear channel to the main dock.

Services

Card phones are dotted around the island. Cards are available at Treasure or Basil's. You can buy ice at Johanna's Banana. There is garbage disposal. Please separate your bottles and cans from the rest of the garbage and place them in the appropriate marked containers.

When you realize the roll is so bad you will never be able to sleep a wink, contact Firefly House or The Cotton House to see if they have available rooms. (Basil's Bar can put you in touch)

Ashore

You will find a small supermarket ashore and a fish market in the fishing village where you can buy fresh fish and lobster in season. Basil has a gourmet shop selling wines, cheeses and a few specialty foods. Mathew sets up his vegetable store near Basils on

Tuesday afternoon and is there all Wednesday. He returns Friday afternoon and is there all day Saturday.

Come morning, many Mustique residents put on the coffee pot and head down to the new Sweetie Pie Bakery [VHF:68] to stock up on fresh croissants, pain au chocolat and Danish along with many other pastries. French owner Ali, bakes these plus many excellent kinds of bread. This is a great place for charter yachts to stock up and Ali will be happy to discuss your requirements. Give him a little notice for large orders.

One good reason to step ashore is to visit Johanna Morris's little group of shops: Treasure, Johanna's Banana and Treasure Fashion. Treasure Fashion specializes in elegant and exotic clothing for both men and women. It has everything from bathing suits by Gottex and La Perla to long evening dresses. Men's clothing includes an excellent selection of shorts in many styles and smart casual wear by Tommy Hilfiger; for the women the wide range includes La Perla Italian linen clothing.

Treasure has a delightful collection of

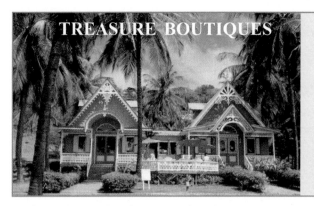

clothes and toys, including casual wear and swim suits, featuring makes like Jams. Plenty of hats, shoes, snorkeling gear, sunblocks and cosmetics are here, as are local books, film, maps, games and gifts of every description. Buy your postcards here, write them in Johanna Banana and bring them back and they will mail them for you. No one to write to? Then you can buy the latest magazines to read over your coffee.

Johanna Banana (closed for lunch) is a coffee shop where you sit outside under big sunshades and watch the boats come and go. They serve cocktails, fresh Italian espresso coffee, fresh fruit juices, ice cream, and home-baked treats, including coconut tarts, pain au chocolat and croissants.

Basil also has two shops. Basil's Boutique is over in Basil's Bar, and Across Forever, on the other side of the road, is an antique and collectibles shop. Basil travels to far eastern ports and brings back his favorite items for the shops.

Mustique is well worth a tour on foot, by taxi, mechanical mule, motor bike or horse. Horse riding is done in the cool of the day either at 0800, 0900 or 1500 and 1600. Vanessa Green keeps her horses well trained and you can book through the Mustique Company [VHF: 68,16]. Rental mules (heavy duty golf carts) and motor bikes are available, call Mustique Moorings (VHF:68, 16) or Mustique Mechanical Services (ext:316/378) for details.

Mustique has an excellent library run by Michelle. You can come here to read the latest magazines and peruse their books. They have some computers with color and black and white printers. You can get to work on these and send e-mails (some restrictions apply). You can also send faxes or do photocopies.

Stan and Elizabeth from England own a guest house and bar/restaurant called Firefly. [$B, VHF:10]. The dramatic view down over the floodlit swimming pool to Britannia Bay is beautiful. The atmosphere is elegant yet informal and friendly, making it popular with those who spend time on the island. Their food is an inventive blend of Caribbean cuisine using fresh ingredients and desserts you will love. For a taste of Mustique by day go for lunch by the pool and enjoy a swim in water that seems to blend seamlessly into the anchorage beyond and below. Piano music accompanies dinner on Tuesdays and Wednesdays. The short walk up will whet your appetite, but for those that prefer to ride, they will come and collect dinner guests from the dock.

For superb cuisine in lavish elegance, don your best evening pants or a dress (it is somewhat formal) and call the Cotton House [VHF:68, $A]. It is about a 15-minute walk away, but if you make dinner reservations they are happy to come and get you. Now run by Mustique Company, Cotton House is one of the fanciest hotels in the Caribbean. They always have top chefs and produce the best cuisine on the island. You can also enjoy lunch up at the pool area, artistically surrounded by fake ruins. In either case, reservations are essential. The Cotton House also has its own Mill Boutique with elegant casual and beachwear and a few gifts.

Basil's Bar [VHF:68, $A-B], built of thatch and bamboo, is perched on stilts over

MUSTIQUE: SHOWING MONTEZUMA SHOAL (FOREGROUND) IN FRONT OF BRITANNIA BAY

Firefly

Phone: (784)-456-3414
Fax: (784)-456-3514
VHF: CH 10

Enjoy Mustique like the residents - whether you lunch by the pool, drink in the bar, or sample our delicious dinners, **Vogue** (1995) called us *One of the Caribbean's loveliest guest houses*, The **Daily Mail** said *Stan's bar is legendary for attracting Mustiques hipper drinking crowd* (1998). **Frommers Guide** called us *One of the top four Caribbean hideaways*. Firefly is authentic Mustique. Walk up (it's steep, but only a few minutes) or we will collect dinner guests from the dock if they prefer. Reservations required. Dress code.

Mustique

the water with waves lapping underneath. Galvanizing seems to have replaced some of the older thatch, a measure designed, no doubt, to keep the glitterati dry as they eat dinner. This is the place to meet people, try to contact other establishments on the island by the modernized phone system, relax and look at the sunset, or get off your rolling boat for dinner. Many come just for the popular Wednesday night barbecue buffet followed by a jump up. Basil also has entertainment on other nights from Reggae to steel band, and he organizes an excellent blues festival towards the end of January to early February.

Mustique has wonderful walks and hikes with miles of unspoiled beaches and countryside. Nature trails have been placed towards the south of the island. Descriptions are given in "Exploring the Flora and Fauna of Mustique" (available at Treasure).

Water sports

You can arrange to go sailboarding or diving at Mustique Watersports [VHF: 68, 16]. They will pick divers up from their yachts. The water is generally very clear and diving is pleasant.

Walk in Reef is just off the dive shop dock and ideal for beginners. For South Britannia Drift Dive you let the current carry you through a delightful garden of soft corals as you watch large schools of Bermuda chubs and creole wrasses. The occasional sight of an eagle ray makes it perfect. The Wreck of the Jonas, a 90-foot dredge, lies in 40 feet on the east side of Montezuma Shoal. Beautiful coral formations are home to barracudas and nurse sharks. At South East Pillory Drift Dive the current sweeps you along a steep slope which drops from 20 feet to 90 feet. The scenery is always changing as you go along, with lots of reef fish and large soft corals. Dry Rock (on the south side of Petit Mustique) is the place for the big fish: schools of barracudas, nurse sharks, turtles and rays.

CANOUAN

(For customs, holidays and general information, see St. Vincent.)

Canouan is an island of bumpy hills, spectacular views and exquisite water colors. Hikers will find hidden beaches. There are a few hundred inhabitants, two major hotels and the interesting new Canouan Resort Development in the northern part of Canouan.

Rameau Bay is a pleasant spot far from the village. You may have to try a couple of times to get the anchor well dug in, and the wind shifts around, so two anchors are advisable. Corbay is a small anchorage but one of the most protected on the island. It is currently used for bringing materials and equipment in for the development, so will probably not be the most desirable spot to be for at least the first part of the life of this guide. However, a marina, houses, restaurants and facilities are eventually planned for this area.

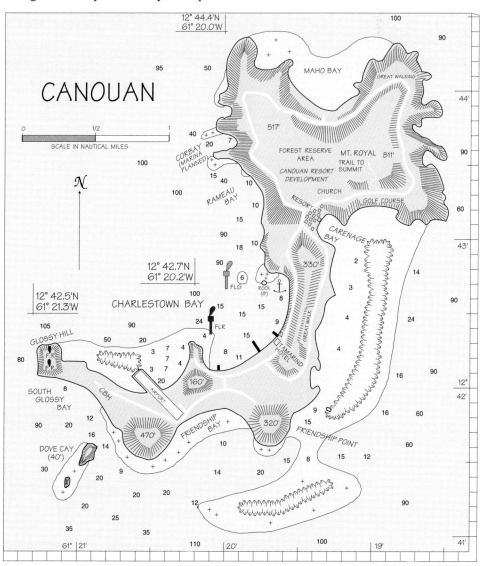

221

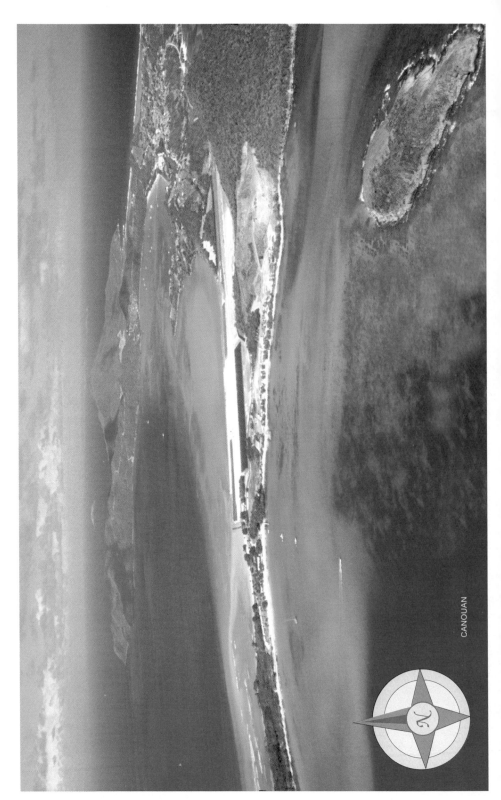

CANOUAN

Charlestown Bay is the main anchorage and the entrance is marked by red and green beacons on either side. Pass between them. Tamarind Bay Resort offers free moorings; make sure it is a Tamarind Beach Resort mooring as there are also a few local moorings for which you have to pay. You can anchor anywhere in the bay except for the area close to the Tamarind Bay Resort Beach. This anchorage is pleasant but northeasterly winds with northerly swells can make it uncomfortable. The wind tends to get held up in the hills and then shoots down from the north in intense gusts. There is a new large ferry dock off the beach, a good new dinghy dock off the Tamarind Beach Hotel and a small wooden dock in the southern part of the bay. Strange currents in the bay tend to deposit anything thrown overboard on the beach, so please do not even throw banana skins or food scraps over in this bay. (If necessary, take them out in the dinghy to well beyond the navigation markers).

Services

Tamarind Beach Hotel [VHF:16] sells water and ice. They have a laundry service, moorings for yachts and showers. Bread is available and a small food shop featuring wines, cheeses and lobster is planned. They can help you dispose of well-wrapped garbage. Mountain bikes are available for rent at the boutique and this is an excellent way to see the island. Taxis are also available.

You can get gasoline on Canouan. A new station was being built near the main dock. If this is not open ask where to get it.

Ashore

The Tamarind Bay Resort [VHF:16, $A-D] is part of the Canouan Resort Development. Yachts are welcome and a large new dock has been built which you can use for your dinghy or to come alongside to take on water. Great caution is needed in times of northerly swells when alongside docking would be dangerous and you will need an anchor to hold your dinghy off the dock. This elegant hotel has two waterfront restaurants under picturesque thatched roofs which have been built in the traditional South American method. The Pirate Cove Bar and Restaurant is informal and inexpensive. You will be welcome here barefoot and in shorts. (Take the walkway along the beach.) Comfortable seats in a garden setting overlooking the bay make this an ideal daytime hangout. Buy your postcards from the boutique and write them here. Sandwiches and hamburgers are available anytime from 1100 to 2200; pizzas and more elaborate dishes at lunch time and after 1930. It is worth sailing in here if only for their wonderful Italian pizzas and pastas. The bar has musical entertainment on Thursday and Sunday nights. La Palapa is the main hotel restaurant. You will want to wear at least long trousers, sports shirt and flip flops as it is somewhat more formal, and try to make reservations in advance as space is limited. On Thursdays and Saturdays their vast buffet sets a new standard for this kind of meal. On other days they have an a la carte menu and the cooking is excellent. Other features of this elegant hotel include the Petit Bazaar boutique and a beach bar.

The Canouan Resort Development owns the whole northern end of the island. The area surrounding Mount Royal is being left as a nature reserve and they have already marked a hiking trail to the top (ask at the hotel for details). The Frangipani golf course is near the Carenage and open for a fee. There is no problem walking along the main roadways in this part of the island and they make for wonderful hiking. You can make a circular tour, stopping at the gorgeous beach in Maho Bay at the northern end of the island. The new Canouan Resort has over a hundred houses and a beachside restaurant and bar overlooking a vast and fancy swimming pool. This completes the first stage of the development. Walk over for lunch, dinner or a drink (reservations can be arranged through the Tamarind Beach Hotel).

In the village you will find several general stores selling basics. There is also a bank. For a local meal out there are several possibilities; all welcome yachtspeople. Roland and Catherine have opened the R&C Bar [$D] high on a hill with a commanding view. (Turn left out of the Tamarind, walk uphill and look to your right). When I vis-

Carriacou   Mayreau   Union I.   Catholic Island   Glossy hill

Looking south in Canouan

ited it was just a pleasant bar, but they had started on the kitchen, which should be in action by the time this book comes out. Hyacinth Alexander's Honey Crome restaurant [$D] behind the police station serves fish and chicken for lunch. She opens for dinner by request. Pass by and discuss what you would like to eat. Her little store sometimes has local frozen fish for sale. Annie's Rooftop Bar [$D] is very local. Stop by for a drink. Just behind the church is Yvonne and George's Anchor Guest House and Restaurant [VHF:16, $C]. They will cook you a local meal if you give them a couple of hours notice.

Other anchorages

There is a really rolly anchorage by the Canouan Beach Hotel in South Glossy Bay. The water here is gorgeous and so is the beach. I would recommend it for a lunch stop. There is a dinghy dock, which is perilous in swells, and currents make swimming ashore inadvisable.

Ashore

Canouan Beach Hotel (CBH) [VHF:16, $A-B] is a classy French resort. They serve a great buffet lunch. This is also a good place for dinner, but you may want to anchor in Charlestown Bay and visit by cab. Yachtspeople are welcome but you must make a reservation and dress reasonably smartly. CBH can also occasionally help with ice and they sometimes sell delicious bread.

Keen snorkelers might be interested in a daytime stop at Friendship Bay on Canouan's south coast. Approach past Glossy Bay, pass between Dove Cay and Canouan, and follow the coast, keeping a good look out for coral heads. In settled conditions you can dinghy up the windward side of Canouan inside the reefs where the snorkeling is excellent.

Water sports

There are about ten good dives in Canouan and the staff at the Blueway Diving Center [VHF:16] at Tamarind Beach Resort (a five star Padi facility) are still discovering new ones. There are walls with giant boulders, sloping reefs and sharks, turtles and rays are often spotted. The Blueway staff are pleasant and put themselves out for yachting customers. They will pick you up from your yacht and all dives are within five minutes of the Tamarind Beach Hotel. They fill tanks and teach in English, Italian, French and Spanish.

For those diving on their own, the easiest spot to anchor for a dive is in Corbay. Dive to seaward of the rocky headland on the northern side of the bay. You can also dinghy north up the coast and look for your own spot. Another good dive if you are anchored in South Glossy Bay is right around Glossy Hill. Watch out for currents. Snorkeling is good around the rocks in Rameau Bay.

SOUTHERN GRENADINES PASSAGES

From Canouan to Carriacou the Grenadines huddle together, each just a short hop from the next. The islands are generally small and very quiet.

Any island with a few inhabitants will also have a rum shop where you can meet people and learn to drink Jack Iron – a powerful, rough white rum, sometimes distilled far from government inspectors. A small shot is poured into a glass and the idea is to down it all in one gulp, preferably without tasting. Then you reach for a large glass of water to put out the fire.

Navigation

The current sets to the west most of the time, so head east of your destination until you have got the feel of its strength. The southern Grenadines are strewn with keel-hungry reefs. This is the area where people make the most mistakes and several yachts have been lost. Usually this is because people misidentify islands. If you approach this area with just a shade of apprehension and self-questioning, you should be okay.

Several navigational beacons help. Most of them are on the edge of shoals so keep well clear.

Sailing south

When you round Glossy (Glass) Hill at Canouan, you must be sure you know which island is which. Mayreau lies in front of Union, and some people see the two as one island and then mistake the Tobago Cays for Mayreau. If you are heading for the lee of Mayreau your compass heading should be around 225-230° magnetic. If you find yourself sailing between south and 200° you are probably heading for the Tobago Cays . . . and trouble.

Tobago Cays. If you approach the Tobago Cays from the north, the easiest and best route is as follows: after you round Glossy Hill, head for the middle of Mayreau (about 228° magnetic). As you approach Mayreau you can see Baline Rocks. Leave these to port, giving them reasonable clearance, and sail on until you are about half way between them and Mayreau before heading up into the Tobago Cays. Line up the day markers in the Cays if you can see them. (Note: Petit Rameau and Petit Bateau look like one island for much of the approach.)

An alternative and much trickier approach is to head a bit to the east of Mayreau from Glossy Hill, then sail a hundred yards to the east of Baline rocks, between the rocks and the northwest end of Horseshoe Reef. This entrance channel is about a quarter of a mile wide, and Horseshoe Reef is often not visible, so caution is advised. The current can be strong, so make sure you are not being set down on the rocks. Once past the rocks, hold course until the day markers line up (see Tobago Cays sketch chart), then head up into the islands.

Mayreau. When approaching Mayreau, pass well to the east of the black and yellow beacon marking Dry Shingle. When sailing round the lee of Mayreau, watch out for the reef off Grand Col Point which is marked by a yellow and black beacon. Pass well

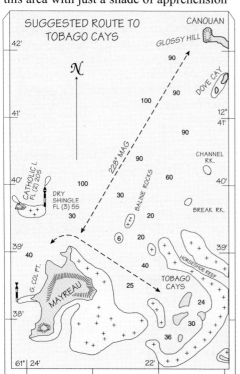

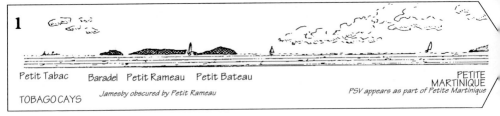

Petit Tabac   Baradel Petit Rameau   Petit Bateau   PETITE

                                        MARTINIQUE

Jamesby obscured by Petit Rameau   *PSV appears as part of Petite Martinique*

TOBAGO CAYS

outside this beacon which is in quite shallow water. When heading over to Palm or Union, you need to head well up, at least to the middle of Palm Island, until you figure out how much you are being set down, as the current can be very strong. Watching Union airport against Carriacou gives an idea of current set. Union's deadly windward reef (Newlands Reef) extends half way to Palm Island, so you have to sail almost to Palm before heading west into Clifton Harbor. Note that there are three red beacons on Newlands Reef. You leave these to starboard as you head into Clifton. Swing in a curve well outside them.

Grand de Coi, between Union and Palm, is a dangerous reef, almost never seen till it is too late. Numerous yachts have gone aground here and one or two have been destroyed. Now there is a yellow and black beacon on its western side. You must always pass to the west (Union Island side) of this beacon, keeping well clear. The following pointers may also be helpful in gauging your position.

All Directions: When there is a gap between PSV and Petite Martinique, you are too far south to hit Grand de Coi. When this gap is closed, keep clear of Grand de Coi by watching the western side of Mayreau against the new Union Island airport. If you keep the west of Mayreau behind the airport you will be west of Grand de Coi. A gap between the two stands you in danger.

For all directions south: sail right down to the entrance of Clifton Harbor then pass west of the Grand de Coi beacon.

To Carriacou: Head toward the northwest coast. When you approach Hillsborough it is safest to pass to the west of Jack a Dan before rounding up into town.

To PSV: When you have passed Grand de Coi, steer for the east side of Carriacou till PSV bears due east, then head on in, passing well to the south of Mopion, Pinese and all their surrounding reefs. Keep an eye on current set and compensate if necessary.

A much trickier and more dangerous way is to pass between the two little sand cays Mopion and Pinese. The course from the lee side of Grand de Coi is around 165-170° magnetic, though with current you may have to head considerably more to the east. A bearing of 160° magnetic on the highest peak of Petit Martinique takes you close enough to eyeball your way in. Mopion usually has a small thatch shelter on it. Always sail through the center of the passage, and do not round up too soon as the reef extends about a quarter of a mile southwest of Mopion (see our PSV and Petit Martinique chart). Treat this passage with caution.

Sailing north

From Carriacou to Clifton and Palm: The safest route is to pass to the west of Jack a Dan, then follow the coast up to Rapid Point. From Rapid Point aim for the east side of Union, checking on the current set by watching Frigate Island against Union. As you near Union you should be able to see the reefs between Frigate and

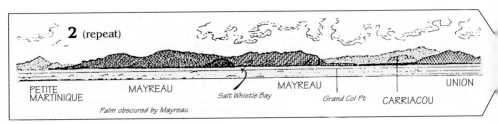

2 (repeat)

PETITE   MAYREAU   MAYREAU   UNION

MARTINIQUE   *Salt Whistle Bay*   *Grand Col Pt*   CARRIACOU

Palm obscured by Mayreau

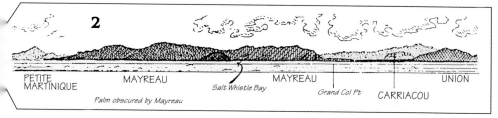

PETITE MARTINIQUE | MAYREAU | Salt Whistle Bay | MAYREAU | Grand Col Pt | CARRIACOU | UNION

Palm obscured by Mayreau

Clifton. Do not get too close to these as the current and wind are setting you down on them. On the other hand keep a good eye out for the Grand de Coi reef to the east. Stay to

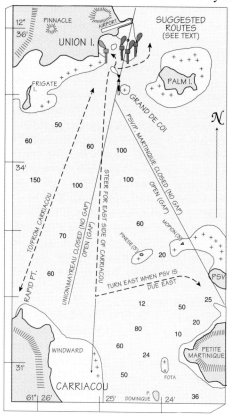

the west of the beacon that marks the reef (see also Grand de Coi notes above).

From PSV to Union: Sail due west till you are on a line between the east coasts of

Carriacou and Union before changing course to Clifton. Before the gap closes between PSV and Petite Martinique, edge westward till the finger of land on the western side of Mayreau disappears behind the new Union Island airport. Pass to the west of the Grand de Coi beacon. Experienced sailors could head out between Mopion and Pinese and then head for the Pinnacle until the finger of land on the western side of Mayreau disappears behind the new Union Island airport, or until the Grand de Coi beacon is identified. Always pass well to the west of the Grand de Coi beacon.

From Palm northwards: Always sail round the lee of Mayreau. Pass to the west of Grand Col Point staying well clear of the beacon. Then, as you get to the north of Mayreau, stay well east of Dry Shingle (marked by a black and yellow beacon) which extends eastward from Catholic Island.

Approaching the Tobago Cays from the south: Sail round the lee of Mayreau, then head straight up toward the middle of the Cays. If you are tacking under sail, favor the Mayreau side of the channel when passing Baline Rocks to avoid the shoal to their south. There is a southern entrance to the Cays, but it is tricky and should not be attempted without local knowledge. Many charter yachts have run aground here. However, if you are in the Cays on a quiet day with good reef visibility, you could try leaving by this route.

When leaving the Cays to go north: the

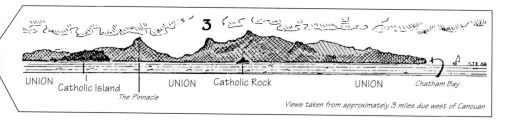

UNION | Catholic Island | UNION | Catholic Rock | UNION | Chatham Bay

The Pinnacle

Views taken from approximately 3 miles due west of Canouan

safest route is to sail from the anchorage to the north end of Mayreau, then head northward after you have passed Baline Rocks. There is also a channel to the east of Baline Rocks about a quarter of a mile wide. From the Cays you have to head just south of the rocks until you reach the channel and then turn north, or you are in danger of hitting the western edge of Horseshoe Reef.

DIVING IN THE SOUTHERN GRENADINES

When the water is clear the diving in the southern Grenadines is wonderful, though currents can be strong and many dives have to be done as drift dives. There is a good dive shop and you do not have to go there – one call and the dive boat will come by and pick you up from your yacht in the Tobago Cays, Mayreau or Union.

Grenadine Divers [VHF:16,68] is a pleasant, relaxed dive operation run by Glenroy Adams from Bequia. Based in Union, it is linked to Dive St. Vincent and Dive Bequia, and certification courses or dive packages can be arranged which work for all these dive shops. Glenroy or one of his instructors will collect you from your yacht in Union, Mayreau, PSV or the Tobago Cays. If you are short of ice or have run out of bread, they will happily bring some along on their way out.

One of the easiest dives to find for yourself is just west of Mayreau – the wreck of the first world war gunboat, Purina. It is marked on our chart. Tie your dinghy (not yacht) to the buoy.

While you can certainly get some elegant views of large schools of fish framed by pieces of wreckage, this dive does not compare in scenic beauty with the reef dives. As it is only 140 feet long neither is it a dive where you keep moving along looking at the view. The beauty of this dive is that you don't move – you are already there. This is a dive where you stop rushing around and instead get on more intimate terms with the fish and sea creatures of which there are a great abundance. Since the fish are very tame it is ideal for underwater photography. There is often a lot of current on the surface, but on the wreck it is not usually a problem. I like to start with a slow exploration to see the layout and also get a feel for the kinds of fish that are around. Then I examine each part of the wreck, concentrating on the invertebrates and letting the fish come to me as they will.

There is a spectacular area for diving in some cuts among the reefs between Mayreau and the Cays. Discovered by Glenroy, this area is called Mayreau Gardens. If you manage to dive one of these in clear visibility, it could turn out to be the dive of your holiday. There is usually lots of current here, so we are talking drift dives, sometimes so rapid that you surface over a mile from where you went down. You hardly need to fin. The current does all the work while you get wafted through a delightful garden of hard and soft corals, sponges and fish. My favorite part is on the southern side of the gardens coming out along the southern edge of the reefs. A sloping reef drops to a sand bottom in 40-60 feet. The reef has a wonderful texture made up of all kinds of corals. Boulder, pillar and plate corals rise in a variety of intricate shapes. There are areas of huge sea fans, so large you can play hide and seek behind them. The special luminous quality of the light typical in the Grenadines seems to extend below the waves. Massive schools of brown and blue chromis engulf you from time to time, swimming inches from your mask. A few yards away schools of snapper and jack swim by purposefully, creating a flurry of nervousness in the chromis. Angelfish, trumpetfish, large boxfish and brightly colored parrotfish are all there as well.

Diving is pretty outside Horseshoe Reef on either side of the small boat passage. This is best done as a drift dive as the currents can be very strong.

Always Wanted To Have A Place In The Islands?

Welcome Home.

When you buy a beautiful new yacht with SUN, you're not just buying a boat.

You're buying a home in the islands — your private corner of paradise with a spectacular 360° water view.

You're joining a family — a tight-knit group of sailors who know you and your boat by name, and who take excellent care of both of you.

You're becoming part of one of the industry's most respected ownership programs, the result of over two decades of experience in sensible, worry-free yacht ownership.

And it literally pays for itself.

All your expenses — boat payment, management costs, advertising, dockage, maintenance, insurance — are fully covered by monthly charter revenue. *Guaranteed.*

You're investing in a lifestyle you thought you could only dream of.

Welcome home.

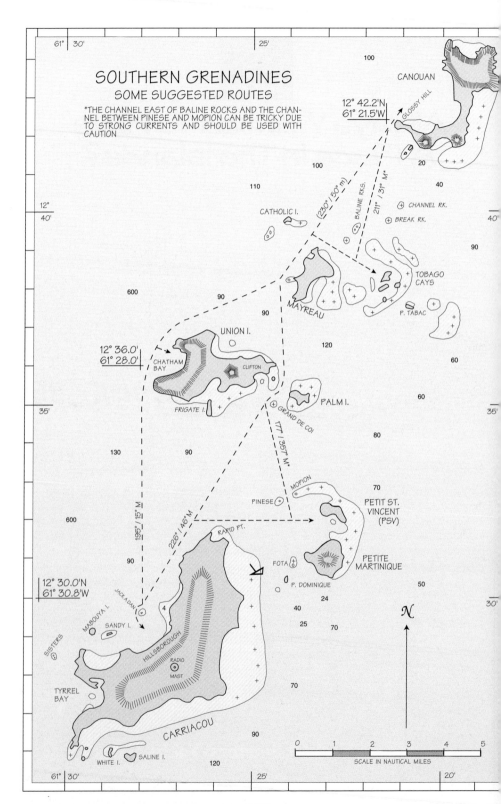

SOUTHERN GRENADINES
SOME SUGGESTED ROUTES

*THE CHANNEL EAST OF BALINE ROCKS AND THE CHAN-
NEL BETWEEN PINESE AND MOPION CAN BE TRICKY DUE
TO STRONG CURRENTS AND SHOULD BE USED WITH
CAUTION

CANOUAN

GLOSSY HILL

12° 42.2'N
61° 21.5'W

100

20

40

100

110

BALINE RKS.

211° / 31° M*

(230° / 50° M)

CHANNEL RK.

BREAK RK.

CATHOLIC I.

90

600

90

90

MAYREAU

TOBAGO
CAYS

P. TABAC

90

UNION I.

12° 36.0'
61° 28.0'

CHATHAM
BAY

CLIFTON

120

60

60

FRIGATE I.

PALM I.

GRAND DE COI

177° / 357° M*

80

130

90

600

90

195° / 15° M

226° / 46° M

MOPION

PINESE

PETIT ST.
VINCENT
(PSV)

70

RAPID PT.

PETITE
MARTINIQUE

12° 30.0'N
61° 30.8'W

JACKADAN

FOTA

P. DOMINIQUE

50

MABOUYA I.

SANDY I.

4

40

24

25

70

SISTERS

HILLSBOROUGH

RADIO
MAST

N

TYRREL
BAY

70

CARRIACOU

90

WHITE I.

SALINE I.

120

0   1   2   3   4   5

SCALE IN NAUTICAL MILES

230

MAYREAU

Mayreau is a one-road, two car island, rimmed with pristine beaches and affording spectacular views from up on the hill. Most islanders are happy to see you and it is well worth exploring on foot. Visit both the village and the windward beaches.

SALT WHISTLE BAY

SALT WHISTLE BAY

This beautiful bay has a sweeping half moon beach, and Salt Whistle Bay Club is tucked away behind it. The resort is so well hidden in the trees that people who sail in the bay often question whether it is really there.

Enter right in the middle of the bay as there are reefs to the north and south. The northern reef is about six feet deep, and not usually much of a problem. The southern reef is dangerous; both wind and swells will help drive the inattentive navigator hard onto the coral. Boats often come to grief here, so take care. The holding in the bay is good in sand if you avoid the weed patches. If there is a northerly swell, anchor bow and stern to cut the roll.

Ashore

Salt Whistle Bay Club [VHF:16, 68, $B] has a whimsical woodland atmosphere where the appearance of the Mad Hatter at tea would not be out of place. The unique dining area is set in the open among the trees and each table is built of stone with its own thatched roof. You can be sure of a top

SALT WHISTLE BAY
12° 39.0'N
61° 23.7'W

quality meal here with a set three-course dinner and a choice of fish or meat dishes. Lunch is a la carte, with soups, sandwiches, salads and local dishes. For a change from the boat, start the day ashore with one of their full breakfasts.

There is also a little boutique and beach bar. Manager Undine Potter speaks German and English and is nearly always on hand and very helpful.

Just across the low land there is another beach on the windward side where shells and driftwood wash ashore. Snorkeling on the reefs and rocks in the bay is fair but sometimes murky. A pretty trail leads up to the village from near the hotel dock.

SALINE BAY

Ashore

As you approach Saline Bay from the north keep to seaward of the black and yellow beacon that marks the long reef off Grand Col Point. It is placed right on the edge of the reef, so do not cut it too fine. The large Saline Bay anchorage offers good holding in sand if you avoid the weedy areas. A stern anchor may be advisable to cut the roll in northerly swells.

When cruise ships anchor, Saline Bay does a quick imitation of Coney Island. Luckily, they are always gone before nightfall.

Basic supplies (and sometimes fish) are available in several small groceries. A few handicrafts are available in small shops tucked in people's houses. Occasionally a roadside vendor sets up by the road.

A few years ago the only businesses ashore were a couple of very basic stores. Now yachting visitors support several Mayreau-owned restaurants and a few handicraft and t-shirt outlets. All good for the local economy.

It all began when an enterprising young man called Dennis was working as a charter

skipper and realized the potential of the island for yachts. You can see the arches of Dennis's Hideaway [VHF:68, $B-C] as well as his guest house from the anchorage. It is just a few minutes up the only road and is a grand spot to stop to take in the view and a beer or two. Late afternoon is the best time to meet other yachtsmen. Dennis offers tasty local cooking, using fish and lambi from the surrounding reefs, or livestock from the hillside. On Wednesdays and Saturdays he does a large seafood buffet with live music. Dennis's Hideaway also has a modern guest house and a traditional pizza oven for cooking lunch is planned.

J & C Bar and Restaurant [VHF: 68, 16] is just beyond Dennis's hideaway on your left. It has the best view of the harbor. It is owned by Jean and Claude. Their music is soft, so it is good for those who want to chat, and it is large enough to take a huge group. Jean and Claude are very friendly, they make a big effort and their large portions of lobster, fish and lambi are excellent value. The skipper gets his meal free with parties of four or more. Their lambi is especially

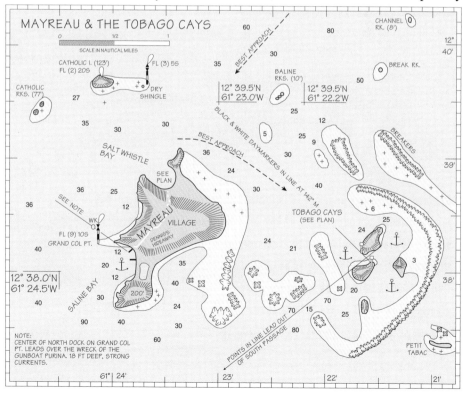

MAYREAU & THE TOBAGO CAYS

SCALE IN NAUTICAL MILES

NOTE:
CENTER OF NORTH DOCK ON GRAND COL
PT. LEADS OVER THE WRECK OF THE
GUNBOAT PURINA. 18 FT DEEP, STRONG
CURRENTS.

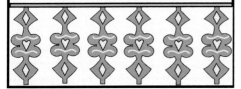

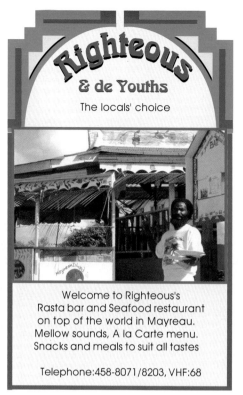
delicious and they often have whelks and curried goat. They also have a small supermarket and a boutique, and they run a water taxi. During the day, Jean and Claude often run a t-shirt stall over in Salt Whistle Bay.

It is hard to meet a more engaging and friendly restaurateur than James Alexander who has opened Island Paradise Restaurant [VHF: 68, $C]. It is well up the hill with a bird's eye view. This is not a place to come if you are in a hurry as everything is cooked from scratch, but their Creole fish and curried conch are well worth the wait. Best of all, if four or more come up to eat, the captain's meal is free. They have the biggest sound system on the island and for those who want to groove to some sounds, they can turn it up after dinner. They have a nightly happy hour from 1800-1900 with half-priced cocktails, and on Fridays, or whenever the demand is great enough, they offer a barbecue with a local string band. They offer free rides up the hill for anyone who does not want to walk.

Robert Lewis "Righteous" is a well known Rastafarian and you can groove to Bob Marley and other good sounds and have some good talks with Robert at Righteous & de Youths [VHF:68, $C-D]. This is the cool hang-out for a mixture of locals and visitors. Robert is welcoming and friendly and where most other restaurants serve full meals, Robert offers a less expensive a la carte seafood menu as well as snacks including pizzas, lobster sandwiches and burgers. He also has a small boutique.

For an after-dinner game of pool check out Victor Hazel's Pleasure Cave Bar or Michael Ollivierre's bar.

A walk eastward from Saline Bay along the salt pond will bring you to some long pristine beaches on the windward side.

Water sports
Snorkeling on the reef coming out from Grand Col Point is good. Dennis has a 39-foot charter yacht and takes yachtsmen fishing the local way and for large groups will organize a traditional Caribbean beach party.

THE TOBAGO CAYS

The Tobago Cays are a group of small deserted islands protected from the sea by Horseshoe Reef. The water and reef colors are a kaleidoscope of gold, brown, blue, turquoise and green. There are small sand beaches and clear water. On cloudless nights the stars are cast across the sky like wedding confetti thrown in an excessive gesture of bonhomie. Even squalls can be dramatically beautiful as they approach from afar. The anchorage is, however, open to the full force of the ocean winds which are occasionally strong.

The approach to the islands is helped by black and white day markers. Petit Rameau and Petit Bateau look like one island for most of the approach. It is important to avoid cutting corners lest you land on a coral head.

You can anchor just west of Petit Rameau, in the cut between Petit Rameau and Petit Bateau, or to the south of Baradel. There are strong currents in the cut anchorage, so bow and stern anchoring is necessary.

When heading south out of the Cays it is safest to pass round the lee of Mayreau, though the Cays do have a southern channel which is okay as an exit for the experienced when the light is good. Avoid using this southern route as an entrance as it is hard to find and many charter yachts have gone aground in the attempt.

Regulations

Tobago Cays is a national park. Park war-

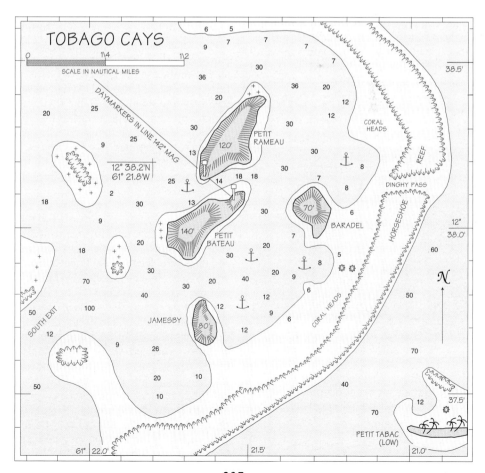

TOBAGO CAYS

dens will soon be patrolling and yachts will be charged, all fees going to the park. This is badly needed to protect this beautiful spot. Please help keep it wonderful. Fishing is not allowed, nor are jet skis. Use the dinghy moorings, do not anchor your dinghy near the coral. Do not give your garbage to youths for a fee — despite protestations to the contrary, they have been dumping it on the windward side of Baradel. If you have a beach barbecue make sure you remove all

your debris, including the charcoal. If you use a local to do a barbecue for you, return the next morning to make sure it has been cleaned up properly. The record of these barbecue vendors to date has been terrible, with big stacks of garbage left all around and so much charcoal getting mixed with the sand it is turning grey.

Ashore

The water here is so beautiful you will almost certainly want to jump right in and maybe snorkel to the nearest reef. Be careful! Speeding dinghies and local boats are a real danger to swimmers. Some fly through the crowded anchorage as fast as 20 knots. We hope this will be regulated when park wardens get appointed.

Local boats hang out in the Cays during the season selling everything from ice, bread and lobsters to jewelry.

Water sports

The snorkeling on Horseshoe Reef is superb, though it can be choppy out there, and in some places you will meet current. If you have beginner snorkelers on board, the east beach on Petit Bateau (facing Baradel) has good snorkeling that starts in calm shallow water. The Tobago Cays is also an excellent place for sailboarding, with miles of fairly protected water and a constant wind. Experts can sail out through the small dinghy passage into the ocean. Keep an eye out for swimmers and snorkelers.

To go scuba diving, contact Grenadines Dive who will come and collect you from your yacht. Currents can be very strong and most dives are done as drift dives.

TOBAGO CAYS

PALM ISLAND

Casuarina Beach, Palm I.

Palm Island [VHF:68, $A] is a lovely little resort that was created on an uninhabited island by John and Mary Caldwell and their local friends. After the Second World War John decided to sail from the U.S.A. to Australia so he could get back with Mary, despite the fact he had never sailed in his life before. His journey was a total disaster. He ran out of food and had to eat the slime off the bottom of his boat, he lost his mast and was finally wrecked on a Pacific island. This is all described in his book "Desperate Voyage." (I recommend it to everyone – especially those learning to sail.) He did better on his trip from Australia to the Caribbean, where he became known for planting palm trees wherever he went. He finally dropped anchor in Palm Island.

The anchorage is off the docks and holding is fair in 15 to 20 feet with a sand bottom. The anchorage can be rolly, so check it out for lunch and if you feel comfortable there, stay overnight.

Services

This is a good place to buy water. Call "Sunset" on VHF:16 for directions. The old stern-to dock was being removed and is to be replaced either by a water barge which would come alongside or a water buoy with hose attached. There is a small general store which sells ice and a variety of food and household items. There is a dock you can use for your dinghy, but you must use a stern anchor to keep it from riding underneath where it could be damaged.

Ashore

You step ashore on Casuarina Beach, a gorgeous expanse of golden sand lapped by translucent turquoise water: the ultimate picture-perfect Grenadine beach. The Sandy Feet Boutique is one of the largest boutiques in the Grenadines with casual clothing, gifts, books and handicrafts. A few steps away is the Sunset Bar and Restaurant [VHF:68, $B-D]. The Sunset Bar was designed for the yachting trade after it was found that the main hotel facilities were getting overcrowded. The atmosphere is casual and friendly, the prices reasonable and the sunset view perfect. Hamburgers, fishburgers, sandwiches and salads are always available and if you want to have a more elaborate dinner, make a reservation a little while in advance. They offer fish, steak and chicken and sometimes have Saturday night barbecues with a steel band. Sunset Bar sometimes closes for dinner during the summer months.

It is fun to walk over to the windward side and explore some of the other five beaches and perhaps find one to yourself. You can run or walk John's mile and a quarter long "Highway 90," a jogging or walking trail marked by hand painted signs. Snorkeling on the surrounding reefs is good. The hotel part of Palm is kept private, but those interested in seeing a room should ask in the main office.

UNION ISLAND

CLIFTON HARBOR

With its dramatically mountainous outline Union stands out from afar. Clifton, the main harbor, is protected by a reef which shows off its brilliant kaleidoscopic colors and patterns as you sail in.

Clifton

Clifton is a bustling small port with a cosmopolitan atmosphere and is the center of yachting in the southern Grenadines. It has a thriving day charter industry, with tourists flying into the small airport daily to tour the Grenadines. Do not anchor close to any of the innocent looking empty mooring buoys. Come 1600, the large day charter boats will return and pick them up regardless.

You may see Red Island on older charts. This is no longer. It has been bulldozed and connected by a causeway to Union which now forms the new airport runway.

When approaching Clifton from the north it is necessary to sail half way over to Palm Island to avoid Newlands Reef (keep well outside the three red beacons on its outer edge). When approaching from the south, give Grand de Coi a wide berth.

Clifton Harbor is protected by Newlands Reef and has a small reef in the center. The main entrance is just south of this center reef and marked by red and green beacons. It is also possible to sail to the east of the center reef and up behind Newlands Reef toward Green Island.

A pleasant anchorage is just behind Newlands Reef, but if you prefer to be nearer the action, anchor anywhere off the town.

Regulations

Clifton is St. Vincent's southern port of entry for customs clearance. Check with customs in the Bougainvilla building and immigration at the airport. Office hours are weekdays 0900-1500. Officers are also on hand on weekends.

Services

The Anchorage Yacht Club [VHF: 68, 16] has a 12-berth marina where you can tie stern to a floating dock, and they offer water, laundry, ice, mechanical help, card telephone, fax, mail pickup and showers. The marina office is right on the dock and

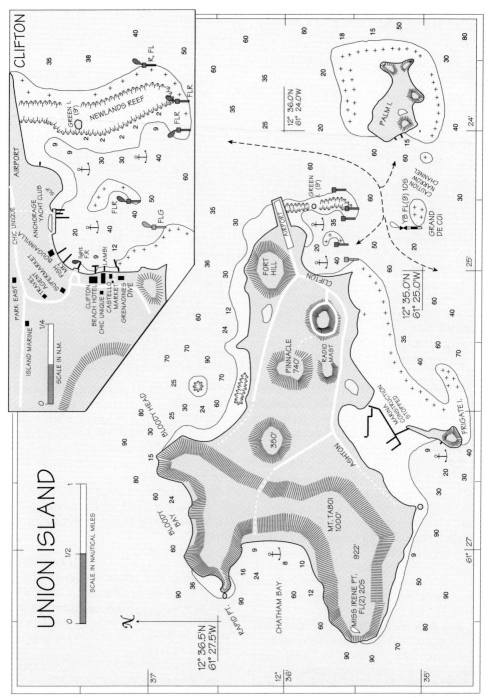

opens daily from 0700 to 1800 in season, 0800 to 1800 off season. The Anchorage is an agent for Mustique Airways as well as private charter companies. They offer inexpensive electric carriage transport to the airport and for shopping trips to the village. Mountain bikes can be rented from their office.

The Anchorage has a complete sail loft run by Gilles Griot who sailed to the Carib-

242

bean 12 years ago in a 24-foot yacht. Gilles worked as a sailmaker in France, runs a complete loft and can repair your old sails or awnings or build you new ones. You will find Stardust Charters at the Anchorage. Gilles Griot manages Stardust and whenever possible they will help passing yachtsmen.

Jean-Marc's Bougainvilla [VHF:16] is a marine mall, with stern-to berthing for 15 boats. They sell fuel, water and ice. Sub-bases are here for Star Voyage, Dufour Antilles, Wind and Sea and the Moorings. Air and sea charters are available. Bougainvilla includes shops and restaurants which we will mention later. If you need something fixed, talk to Laurent and Alex at Unitech Marine Service [VHF:16] in the Mall. They repair all kinds of gasoline and diesel motors including outboards, they weld iron and stainless and they do fiberglass and electrical repairs. They get new parts from Martinique. Unitech also sells cooking gas and can fill most boat cylinders.

Another first rate mechanical shop, Island Marine Special [VHF:16], is run by Earl Allen. If you walk though Bougainvilla to the back street and turn right, it is the workshop just a few hundred feet down the road on your left. Earl has worked on boats, generating plants and other machinery for several big hotels over the last 25 years and he can repair all makes of diesel engine, outboard, gear box or generator. If he doesn't have parts on hand, he can arrange to get them through his agent in Miami and, if the gods are smiling, they take about three days to arrive.

Lionel Fox at Castello Steel Work hails from Australia and is the local welder (ss and steel) and also fiberglass repair man. He makes and sells a range of fiberglass dinghies.

You can ask someone the way to Grenadines Engineering. They do a lot of construction, but Murphy, one of the owners, is an electrical and electronic engineer who originally came here with the VSO to teach. He is happy to work on yachts.

Clifton Beach Hotel [VHF:68, $B-C] is the base for Captain Yannis's fleet of char-

Anchorage Yacht Club

Telephone:
784-458-8221
Fax: 784-458-8365

VHF Ch 68 or 16
telex: St.Vincent
7595 AYC VQ

The Anchorage Yacht Club is the true center of the Grenadines

***12-BERTH MARINA *WATER *ICE
*MECHANIC *SAILMAKER *LAUNDRY
*BREAD *TELEPHONE, TELEX AND FAX.**

Best French/Creole restaurant and bar in the Grenadines
Jump up and dinner every Monday, Thursday, Friday and Saturday in season

Air conditioned beach bungalows and rooms
Nearby airport with daily flights to the rest of the Caribbean
Inexpensive bus service to and from the airport
Free ferry service for our customers to and from their yachts in season

BAKERY
Open from 0700, with croissants and
fresh coffee. Fresh bread, sandwiches,
baked goodies and ice cream.

ter boats and there is about nine feet at the end of their dock. You can come in here alongside or stern-to to buy ice and get your laundry done. Water is sometimes also available. You can also come stern-to at Lambi for water. Gasoline is available at Nollie Alexander's Eillon gas station.

If you need to fly out, Eagle Travel [VHF:68] can help book tickets. Ice is available at The Anchorage Yacht Club, Park East, Grand Union, Lambi, and many rum shops.

Ashore

Provisioning has vastly improved in Union recently. Not only is there a good selection of fresh fruits and vegetables in the market, but streetside vendors add to the choice. Small supermarkets cater to most of your shopping needs. Grand Union often has fresh local chicken, check out also Lambi's which grows every year. Buy your bread from Cash 'n Carry just by the turn to Castello's. It is freshly baked on the premises, inexpensive and good. For more specialty items Robert and Annie-France's Captain Gourmet has frozen shrimps, steak and prepared meals along with cheeses, yogurt and whipping cream for the charter cook. Philippe Vatier owns the Grenadine Wine Shop [VHF:16] in Bougainvilla, specializing in wines, liquors, and a few specialty food items.

Union is becoming quite the place for boutiques. The Anchorage Boutique has an impressive selection of casual wear, toiletries, books, and they even stock current overseas newspapers in season. In Bougainvilla, Susie's Okaou Boutique has artistic souvenirs, t-shirts, fashionable swimwear, local books and more. Chic Unique, with two branches, has good buys in elegant casual wear, t-shirts, books, artistic handicrafts, paintings and the best art postcards. Chic Unique is the local agent for Federal Express.

Castello is the art gallery and studio of Jutta Hartmann. It is in a pleasant Caribbean style building just beyond the market. You can watch Jutta at work and buy paintings or hand-painted garments. Jutta has a quaint little bar at the end of her shop with outside seating facing the bay with a multilingual book swap. Jutta is also building Castello Paradise, a gallery of local art on the street south of the main entrance to the Sunny Grenadines.

The Clifton Beach Hotel has the Art Shop with a wide range of both batik and silk screened casual wear. There are several other small stalls and shops for local handicrafts.

If you are planning to go snorkeling, you can frighten yourself by counting the sharks in the pool in front of the Anchorage Yacht Club. (If it is any comfort, they are only nurse sharks.) After that you may need a stiff drink and a bite to eat. In recent years Union Island has become the jump-up center of the Grenadines and you will find plenty of entertainment. Young men in boats often approach anchored yachts to tout the virtues of shoreside establishments. They are generally fine, but one or two have occasionally gone overboard, running down the competition and even telling people they are closed or out of business. If anyone annoys you, avoid the business they are representing.

The Anchorage Yacht Club [VHF:68, $A-B] is the smartest and prettiest of the Union Island hotels with a delightful view of the harbor and is the place to go if you want to dress up (but you don't have to). They have a good dock for tying up the dinghy and a pleasant bar for relaxing. Their bakery counter opens at seven a.m. with fresh coffee and croissants. They also sell sandwiches, snacks, excellent bread to take away and delicious ice cream.

The hotel is ably managed by Charlotte Honnart who is French and you will find good French and Creole cuisine with a nightly barbecue. Many nights in season are brightened by entertainment including steel and reggae bands. Monday, Friday and Saturday are often lively. They are well known for their large parties at Christmas and New Year's Eve.

The West Indies [$A-B] in the Bougainvilla is attractive and open to the breeze. Under the ownership of Joelle, the ambience and food is French and Italian with everything from smoked salmon and pizza to lobster and confit de canard. If you can save enough room for dessert chocolate mousse and cafe liegeois are among the choices. They make their own French bread which you can also buy to take away.

The Clifton Beach Hotel [VHF:68, $B-C], run by Marie Adams-Hazell, has a perfect open waterfront location and its own dinghy dock, which is most convenient for visiting town during the day. The bar is a popular meeting place. After you have finished shopping, try one of their first rate sandwiches. You can also visit for dinner and they have jump-ups three times a week.

Lambert is smiling these days and why not? His Lambi emporium [VHF:68, $B-C], consisting of a supermarket and two-story, two-dining room restaurant, is going well. Each time I come his building seems to have crept farther out to sea and rental rooms have been added. The conch shell walls give a rough and ready atmosphere. The food is local as is the entertainment with lively steel bands most nights of the week.

The Boll Head Restaurant and Bar [$B-D] is owned by Anthony "Boll Head" Frederick. His hair fell out at an early age,

earning him a nickname which has stayed with him. His bar is opposite the Clifton Beach Hotel with outside seats where you can watch the activity in the street outside. It is informal with local food and is a convenient place to get chicken, mutton, beef or lambi rotis for lunch.

T&N [$B-D] is cute, intimate and up-stairs, for tasty rotis and local food. Jennifer's Restaurant and Bar [$C-D] is on Clifton's main road beyond the turn-off to the Sunny Grenadines. Jennifer offers West Indian food at a reasonable price. Near the airport, Sydney's Bar is always worth checking out, and at the airport, Lorna serves very inexpensive local dishes and snacks.

Any walk in Union away from Clifton will be rewarded with peace, quiet and panoramic views. The view from the hill behind town shows up the reefs and water colors.

Water sports

You will find information on the dive shops and some dive sites under the southern Grenadine diving section. Clifton is the base of Grenadines Dive [VHF:16, 68].

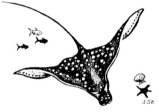

OTHER UNION ANCHORAGES

Frigate Island

Frigate Island, although just over a mile from Clifton, is generally deserted and reasonably well protected. You can anchor in the lee of the island but enter carefully as the bottom shelves quickly. Construction started on a large development, including a 300-berth marina. The company went bankrupt and the project stopped. Some walls were built and a few deep spots were dredged, but there are no new deep channels. There is good snorkeling on the reef to the windward of Frigate. Be careful of the current.

Chatham Bay

Chatham Bay, on the lee side of Union, is a large protected anchorage. The best spot to anchor is in the northeast corner. (You may have to move if the fishermen are seine netting.) The wind tends to come over the hills in shrieking gusts. There is a long beach to explore and some good snorkeling around the rocks off Rapid Point. The fish life here is particularly rich and attracts all kinds of birds, including pelicans. Paths lead over to Ashton. A development is planned.

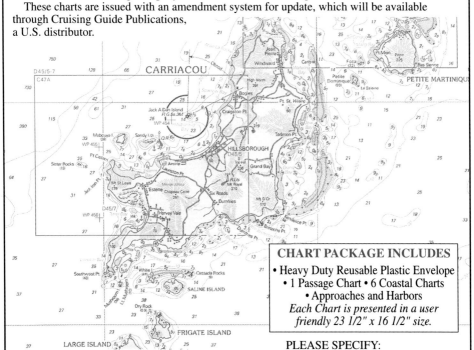
247

PSV AND PETITE MARTINIQUE

PSV (Petit St. Vincent) and Petite Martinique lie just a short sail southeast from Union. PSV is part of St. Vincent and Petite Martinique is part of Grenada.

PSV

The main anchorage is shown on the chart. There is current in the anchorage and if the wind drops yachts will swing about. The reef off the dinghy dock extends farther than some think.

Ashore

PSV [VHF:16 $A] is one of the Grenadines' great success stories. Back in the late 50's Haze Richardson and Doug Terman quit flying for the US Air Force and with what little money they could beg, borrow and scrape, they bought an old wooden

yacht called Jacinta and set sail for the Caribbean. They chartered and one of their clients was Willis Nichols who thought it would be fun to buy a Caribbean island and build a hotel. Haze and Doug were asked to build it, and started together, though eventually Doug went his own way and is now the highly successful author of spy novels. Haze got the hotel finished and tried to find a manager. This proved harder than he thought and he is still there holding the fort, though now as owner. PSV is a very quiet

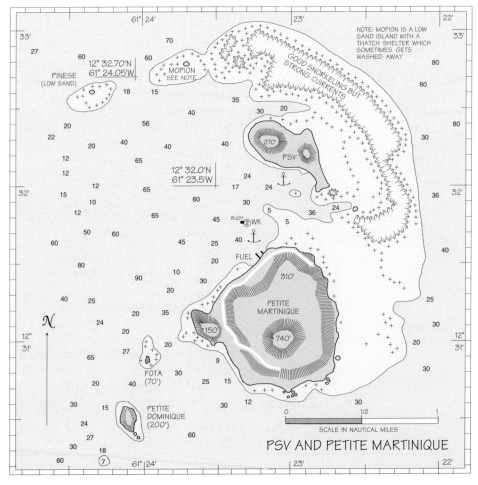

PSV AND PETITE MARTINIQUE

Petit St. Vincent Resort
The Grenadines, St. Vincent, West Indies

We welcome yachtsmen to visit our private island hideaway for special people. We pride ourselves on seclusion. No crowds, cruise ships, or calypso fire-eaters. Just superb food and fine wines in a secluded romantic atmosphere. We reserve just a few tables for visiting yachtsmen, so please book as early as possible.

Our bar has a perfect sunset view, and our boutique abounds in exotic clothes and gifts from all over the world. We can help out with ice, bread, and phone calls during office hours.

Many of our customers made their first visit by yacht and fell in love with our secluded cottages on the slopes and by the sea. Outdoor patios with glorious views provide a perfect setting for breakfast delivered by our "mini-moke" service. If you would like to see a cottage while visiting our island, please ask at the office.

Tel: 784-458-8801, VHF:16
in USA: P.O.Box 12506, Cincinnati, Ohio 45212
Tel: 800-654-9326/513-242-1333

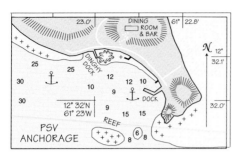

times available by arrangement from the main dock if you call in advance. Cube ice is normally available from the bar, as is homemade bread. The hotel has an excellent boutique, right next to the bar. They are happy to accept yachtspeople as dinner guests, but limited space means they can only take three or four groups each day, so book well in advance. They occasionally have live background music.

and exclusive resort where the guests get pampered in secluded stone cottages. Each cottage has a flagpole, used to summon room service, which soon appears in a mini moke. The hotel usually keeps full with rates at over $500 a night for a double cottage in season. Water and fuel are some-

Water sports

The snorkeling on the surrounding reefs is good. Mopion makes an exciting destination for a picnic by dinghy. The northern side of the reef surrounding Pinese makes a fair dive.

PETITE MARTINIQUE

The last outpost of Grenada, Petite Martinique (PM) is small and enchanting for those who like something off the usual tourist path. It is a great place to take on water and fuel and have a stroll and a meal. The inhabitants live by boatbuilding, seafaring and fishing, and in days of old, by smuggling. There are usually several cargo ves-

PSV ANCHORAGE, SHOWING PETITE MARTINIQUE ON RIGHT

sels at anchor. The wooden, pitched roof houses are photogenic, especially at the eastern end of the island. PM is a lot larger than it looks. If you turn right off the dock, the road winds right round to the south side of the island.

If you are coming north from Carriacou you can clear out and visit PM on your way to Union. Most yachts come over directly from PSV or the Grenadines, and indeed it is these yachts that keep the fuel dock and restaurant alive. While PM is part of Grenada, it is generally accepted that no one is going to sail from PSV to Carriacou to clear in then sail back to visit PM, so, to date the authorities have not worried about yachts overnighting as part of their Grenadines cruise. I expect this will continue. Anchor anywhere off the fuel dock among the other boats. If you are planning to eat at the Palm Beach, call them on the radio and pick up one of their moorings. PM can also be visited by dinghy from PSV. You can leave your dinghy on the fuel dock.

In 1998 a freighter sank at anchor about a quarter of a mile off the dock (see our sketch chart). The wreck is pretty deep, but the steel mast sits upright and within 2 feet of the surface. Probably by the time this guide comes out, someone will have sawn off the mast so it is no longer a danger to navigation. In the meantime it has been marked by an old oil drum. Watch out also for the shoals close to shore west of the docks.

Services

Glenn Clement and Reynold own B & C Fuels [VHF:16 Golf Sierra], a convenient fuel dock where Dexter will be ready to serve you. Easy approach and good prices have made this the main refueling station for large power yachts and bareboats in the Grenadines. You can approach the dock into the wind and it has about 16-18 feet of water alongside. They sell diesel, gasoline, water and cube ice. If you ask around you can also get good buys on cases of beer or liquor. A beach bar is planned.

A high speed ferry runs from the fuel dock calling at Carriacou and Grenada. It leaves PM twice a day at 0530 and 1530, stopping

Palm Beach Restaurant and Bar

VHF:16
Tel: (473) 443-9103

VISA MasterCard
cards welcome

We offer fresh seafood, including lobster, served daily in a delightful setting in the garden on the beach in Petite Martinique

FREE TAXI SERVICE FOR OUR GUESTS BETWEEN OUR RESTAURANT AND YACHTS IN PSV

You can also anchor off our restaurant or pick up a complimentary mooring. Call us on VHF: 16.

Petite Martinique Anchorage, looking towards P.S.V

in Carriacou and then going to Grenada. It returns from Grenada at about 0800 and 1730, calling in Carriacou before finishing in PM. It does not run on Wednesdays and only does one trip on Saturdays. However, schedules can change so ask before you pack your bags. If you are visiting Grenada or Carriacou make sure you have cleared in properly.

Ashore

Petite Martinique has a very pleasant restaurant, The Palm Beach [VHF: 16, $C-D]. It is family owned by Peterson, Augustina and Immanuel Clement. Immanuel is the manager. The setting is perfect – a pretty garden shaded by palms right on the beach. They serve fresh seafood from the local fishing fleet, with chicken for those who don't like fish, lambi or lobster. The food is delicious. If you are anchored in PSV, they offer a free ferry service to and from your yacht, which may be an advantage over using your own dinghy after dark.

There are several small supermarkets, rum shops and snack shops dotted around the island. These include Petronilla Caesar's Miracle Mart [$D], a local super-

market, rum shop and restaurant. Snack foods from rotis to chicken and chips are always available and Petronilla will cook more elaborate local seafood meals with a little bit of notice. This is the place to buy fresh bread.

Sunset View is another supermarket on the beach just below Miracle Mart. Both shops have rooms to rent.

Water Sports

The Seaside View Supermarket has a very professional looking setup for filling tanks and renting scuba gear which is mainly for local fishermen. This is not a sports establishment and has none of the safeguards which goes with a dive shop. They are happy to rent to yachts, and if your dinghy is small, ask owner Francis Logan if he can arrange for a local boat to take your group to the dive sites. This is very much less expensive than going with a dive shop but satisfy yourself the gear is in good condition and within its scheduled test period.

CARRIACOU

OPEN BOAT, HILLSBOROUGH

Regulations

Carriacou is part of Grenada and if you are coming from another country you must anchor in Hillsborough and clear with the customs facilities at the foot of the jetty before visiting any other port. If you arrive on a holiday, ask a taxi driver to take you to the nearest customs officer. Bring your own crew lists (four copies) or pay for photocopies. Those clearing outside normal office hours (0800-1145, 1300-1545 on weekdays) will pay a reasonable overtime fee. There are modest entry charges. For rates, see Hillsborough.

Spear fishing is not allowed around Sandy Island or on the reefs around White and Saline Islands, which are all underwater parks.

Holidays

See Grenada.

Shopping Hours

Shops and offices normally open from 0800-1200 and 1300-1600. Saturday is half day and most places are closed by noon. Banks open weekdays 0800-1200, 1300-1500 and on Fridays 0800-1200, 1500-1700.

Telephones

Card and coin phones may be found all over the island. You buy cards for the phone in post offices and selected shops. For the US dial 1 + number; other overseas calls dial 011 + country code + number. For collect and credit card calls, dial 0 + country code + number. For ATT dial 1-800-872-2881. When dialing from overseas, the area code is 473 followed by a 7-digit number.

Transport

There are inexpensive ($1.50-$6 EC) buses running to most villages. Taxis are plentiful. Sample taxi rates are:

	$EC
Hillsborough to Tyrrel Bay	20
Tyrrel Bay to Airport	15
Half day tour	150
By the hour	60

Rental cars are available (check our directory). You will need to buy a local license which costs $30 EC. Drive on the left.

CARRIACOU

"This is an island with over a hundred rum shops and only one gasoline station." Frances Kay, Carriacou.

Carriacou is the only place where I have frequently seen a pelican sitting on a buoy, with a seagull sitting on the pelican's head, both appearing content in the afternoon sun. Somehow this symbolizes the relaxed, easygoing nature of the island. As a Carriacou man said to me: "People does like it here, we move nice wid dem as we does wid each other – no corruptions or hatreds, all is like one."

Carriacou is enchanting, as anyone who takes a taxi ride or hike inland will find. The inhabitants live by farming, fishing and seafaring and must number among the friendliest in the Caribbean. The last few years have seen the emergence of many new restaurants and Carriacou now has the widest and best choice in the lower Grenadines for those wishing to eat out. Just about everywhere in Carriacou is of interest, but Windward should definitely be part of your tour, as should the road running from Windward to the north end of the island. Windward is

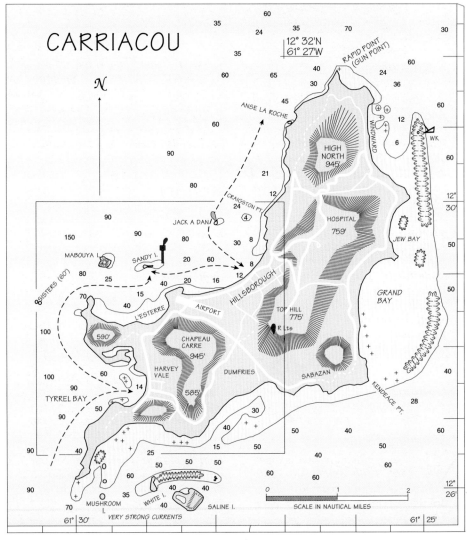

the traditional center of boat building and it is here you can see the fishing fleet arrive under sail. If you cannot afford a taxi, then take a bus over to Windward and hike. Another destination for a spectacular view is the hospital which sits high on the mountain overlooking the harbor.

Navigation

Carriacou is a Carib word meaning "island surrounded by reefs," but do not worry: the approach down the western coast is simple enough. When sailing from the north it is safest to pass to the west of Jack a Dan before heading up into Hillsborough. If you take the trickier route east of Jack a Dan, watch out for the shoal patch about one third of the way between Craigston Point and Jack a Dan. Favor the Jack a Dan side of the channel (but not too close). You can anchor almost anywhere off the town. Silver Beach Resort [VHF: 16] may get their moorings operational again. You are welcome to use their dinghy dock. Hillsborough is a good anchorage except in bad northerly swells, when you would be better off in Tyrrel Bay.

HILLSBOROUGH

There is a flashing green light on Jack a Dan and a flashing red light on the beacon east of Sandy Island.

Regulations

See "Regulations" at the beginning of the Carriacou section. Hillsborough is a port of clearance. Port entry fees are $45 EC up to 50 feet, $60 EC 50-100 feet and $70 over 100. In addition, vessels carrying passengers will pay $5 US per passenger. Less expensive yearly fees are available to Grenada-based charter boats.

Services

At the Silver Beach Resort [VHF:16] telephone, fax, laundry, complimentary showers, block and cube ice are available. They don't even mind getting rid of well wrapped garbage for restaurant customers.

A secret hideaway
with an unusually artistic
atmosphere amid splendid
views

Evening meals by reservation only
Skippers meal free when bringing a
party of four or more
Check out our beautiful self-
contained cottages just 60 feet
from the beach
tel: (473) 443-7841

Ashore

Supermarkets have proliferated, though you will have to visit the local market for fresh produce. Liquor prices are excellent throughout. Check Ade's Dream and Bullens which also has hardware. Do not miss The Unity Supermarket on Church Street. Owner Frankie and his sister Phyllis also own Millie's Guest House and the shop called M&M underneath, which is one of the better general hardware and appliance stores in town. Opposite Franky's is the new Kim's Plaza. Gramma's Bakery sells bread, baked goods, ice cream and lunch time rotis and specials. You can also find banks, travel agents and many quaint small variety stores each crammed with its owner's ideas of what sells in Carriacou.

The museum is worth the short walk and is open Monday through Friday 0900-1545, with an eclectic collection, from Arawak pottery to the first telephone exchange.

Silver Beach Resort [VHF:16, $C] is making a big effort to encourage tourism in Carriacou and they will try to help you in any way they can. They arrange island tours and rent cars. They have a charming open restaurant on the beach, specializing in freshly caught seafood. They will arrange a complimentary car to bring parties of four or more over from Tyrrel Bay for dinner. Happy hour is 1700-1900.

Eddie, Carriacou born but raised in England, was an electrical contractor in Birmingham. A holiday to his homeland made

Callaloo by the Sea

Restaurant and Bar
Phone: 443-8004

Opening hours:
10:00 AM - 10:00 PM
Mondays - Saturdays
and Sundays in season

Welcome to the finest restaurant in the Grenadines, serving delicious food. Our view is open to the beach and the sea. We are open for lunch and dinner, but please reserve for dinner.

him realize life could be better, so he created his own little heavenly corner, The Hillsborough Bar [VHF:16, $C-D], a high tech English pub style establishment with a built in disco. Nearly always open for dinner and open all day when Eddie is around.

Sandisland's [$C-D] dining room is light, airy, open to the sea and the gentle sound of waves brushing the shore. Easy chairs tempt one to a relaxing coffee break. The restaurant is open for breakfast and lunch, but I suspect once you have visited you will soon return for one of Esther Henry-Fleary's excellent dinners, which are by reservation only. While here, check out their little shop with a collection of both essentials and handicrafts.

The Callaloo by the sea [$C, closed Sunday and all September] is one of Carriacou's most popular restaurants. The setting is perfect, right on the beach with seagrape trees to frame the turquoise sea. Glenna Bullen makes sure that everything – from the local soups, seafood and meat to the homemade bread – is cooked to perfection. Drop by for lunch – make reservations for dinner.

Other inexpensive local bars include the Roof Gardens (rotis, local dishes), the Kyak Restaurant (paella, salads and rotis) and Exelcia's Bar (pizzas and rotis).

Should you happen to arrive on the first weekend in August, you will witness the famous Carriacou Regatta. It is no secret that the best trading and sailing sloops in the islands are built right here in Carriacou. Once a year they get together to race on this festive weekend. What amazes me is not just their tradition of boatbuilding, which is all done by eye on the beach, but the way they have managed to refine and speed up their designs so that now they can keep up with modern yachts to windward. The boats they build today are unbelievably fast and sweet, and if you are lucky enough to see one sailing into harbor, it is a joy to behold.

Needing some shore time in this area? Rooms are available at Ade's Dream, Silver Beach and Millie's Apartments.

Water sports

Diving is very good with excellent visibility most of the time. For those going on their own, the dive off the reef at the eastern end of Sandy Island is easy and quite delightful with a healthy coral slope full of angelfish, spadefish and many other reef creatures. Those with a large dinghy can try the Sisters off Tyrrel Bay but keep an eye on the current. For other dives go with one of the two dive shops, who know all the best sites. There are also superb dives down off Round Island and Kick em Jenny. Here the fish life is outstanding, with sharks, rays and big pelagic fish. There are 200-foot walls, caves and many reefs. Since it is a long trip, it is done as a two-tank dive only in fair weather.

Silver Diving [VHF:16] is efficiently run by Max and Claudia from Germany who are CMAS and PADI instructors. Apart from their station in Hillsborough, they are planning a second shop in Tyrrel Bay. They will be happy to arrange to collect you from your yacht just about anywhere in Carriacou.

Tanki's Watersports Paradise Dive Shop [VHF:16] is located on the beach opposite Sandy Island. If you contact him he will be happy to come by and pick you up from your yacht to go diving, fill your tanks, or bring a group over to Ali's restaurant for lunch. Cuthbert Snagg does boat tours, rents bikes (a great way to see Carriacou) and takes people water-skiing.

SANDY ISLAND AND L'ESTERRE BAY

Sandy Island is nothing but a flawless strip of sand, decorated by a few palms and surrounded by perfect snorkeling and diving reefs. Pelicans and seagulls will be your neighbors in this wonderful day time anchorage, which is okay for overnighting in settled conditions. There has been talk of putting in moorings and charging yachts, but it has not happened yet.

Long and thin for over a 100 years, Sandy Island is slowly changing and no one knows why. The middle of the island is now awash, making two islands, while the western end grows larger. Recent deterioration has everyone worried. It was thought that overuse might have been stopping stabilizing plants from growing. The Grenada Tourist Department has managed to get cruise ships to voluntarily use another area and would like yachts to limit themselves to under six in the anchorage at any one time. This is to cut down on the number of people ashore.

You can carry seven feet quite close to the middle of the island, but watch out for

SANDY ISLAND, UNION VISIBLE BEHIND

the reefs north and south. There is also one dark spot toward the western end of the anchorage that is made up of dead coral. It is a little under six feet deep and seems to be getting shallower. There is not much room to drag in Sandy Island, so make sure you are well anchored, preferably with two anchors.

L'Esterre Bay has a long flawless beach and is right opposite Sandy Island, well within dinghy reach. Here you will find Tanki's dive shop and his wife Ali's restaurant [VHF:16, $C-D]. Ali is the daughter of the famous local "naive" artist Canute

Caliste. The restaurant is right on the beach, a relaxing place to hang out and drink beers or eat Creole cooking. For a break you can wander up the hill and visit Canute Caliste, whose paintings catch the local spirit.

Water sports

A pleasant dive starts right at the red beacon to the east of Sandy. Descend down the slope and follow it to the left. The sloping reef is covered in hard and soft corals with plenty of reef fish. Snorkeling is excellent around Sandy Island. See also Hillsborough.

TYRREL BAY

Tyrrel Bay is deep and well protected, wide and easy to enter. Despite this a surprising number of people manage to run aground. The buoys are rather confusing. Whatever the original color, they end up Pelican guano white on top and rusty underneath. Buoys could be added or removed at any time without notice. There is a reef in the northern part of the bay towards the center. A channel to the north of this reef is marked by three buoys. However, the reef most people hit is along the southern shore. There is a small cul-de-sac in this reef and people manage to go right up in here and run hard aground. Right in the middle of the southern channel are two large unlit mooring buoys. One or both sink from time to

time. The easiest way to enter is in the southern half of the bay about one third of the way across. You are not in danger of hitting the center reef until you are over halfway across the bay. Be sure to give the southern shore good clearance: this is where most people come to grief. You can pass closely on either side of the big mooring buoys safely, though keep in mind buoys should not be relied upon. It should be noted there is a wreck in the bay at 12° 27.47'N, 61° 29.27'W which is just south of the southern part of the center reef. This wreck is 7.5 feet deep and so not a hazard to navigation for most yachts. However, you would not want to anchor on it. Holding is good in sand.

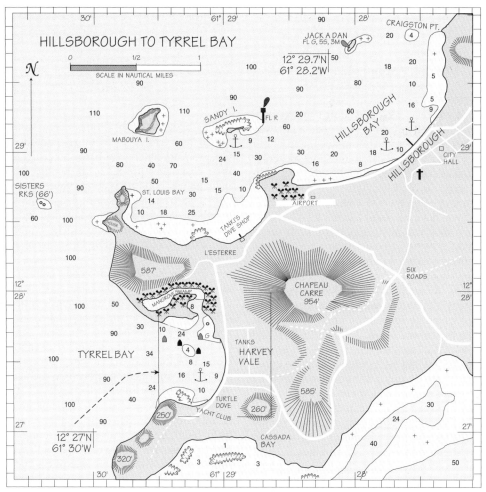

It is very peaceful here. Occasional sounds drift out; a bleating goat, a far away shout, the thump of dominoes, and closer by: "Hey, Skip, how about some oysters?" These salespeople refer to the local delicately flavored "mangrove oyster." Make sure opening them is included in the price. If you have run out of limes for your oysters they can also supply you with these. You may be offered jewelry and calypso music as well. John Bedeau has been at it the longest. He has long harbored ambitions to make adventurous cruises. He owns a hundred-year-old Carriacou sloop on which he sets out on great voyages for adventure and profit. John has a slow and thoughtful manner which does not always keep him out of trouble. He has single-handed to Bequia, and he once cornered the banana market and spent days frantically trying to sell a huge heap of bananas before they went ripe. John can sometimes supply lobsters. Another vendor of long standing is Simon who usually offers wines and beer at a good price. Simon also likes to work on yachts.

Services

The Carriacou Yacht Club is a great addition to the Tyrrel Bay yachting community. Owners Earl and Trevor Stanislas listen to their customers and keep improving. The main lounge building is comfortable with a book swap, bar and restaurant. They have telephone and fax service, a laundry, and a showers. Their mini mart stocks wines, liquors and foods, including those that have been requested by yachts. They sell ice and water by the jug. The tennis court is free to all customers, though the close fence will put a damper on your opponent's killer serve. They have a card phone that works and rooms are available at excellent rates for a night ashore. Their Sunday evening barbecue with inexpensive food and drinks out of the mini-mart has become a fixed item on many a cruisers itinerary.

Dominique [VHF:16] at Carriacou Aluminum Boats does wonders in aluminum, from building a new dinghy to fixing a broken mast. He also welds and polishes stainless steel. Biminis are one of his specialties. His wife Genevieve sews sails and

offers therapeutic massage for bad backs and sore necks. You will find him on his trimaraft-workshop not far from the boatyard.

Uwe at Tool Meister runs an excellent machine and mechanics shop, people come here from all over the Grenadines to get their problems solved, and much of his work is with cargo ships. He will completely rebuild your old engine or help you buy a new one and install it properly. He can fix just about anything that is broken and machine new parts if they are unavailable. For current parts he can order what you need and get it in short order through Fedex. He will also come onto your boat to fix minor problems. You will find him in his shop just above the Turtle Dove bar.

Cleandro is down the road leading back from the Old Rum Shop where he lives with his wife Mavis. Cleandro is a good welder, general and marine mechanic. He welds all types of metal and fixes any kind of engine including outboards. You will recognize his house by the engines outside.

Carriacou Boat Builders closed to the public in 1996.

You can arrange diesel fuel (duty free if you have cleared out) by the big storage tanks at the head of the schooner dock. It is piped down the dock. Enquire at Bullen's supermarket in town.

Lee and Leslie at the Studio run a yacht services office. The first thing to know is part of this office is a pleasant coffee shop/bar where you can relax and make new friends, get advice and general help. Take advantage of their full communications including e-mail and surfing the net and check the latest weather maps. Lee and Leslie also act as charter brokers.

Linky Taxi [VHF:16] is helpful, friendly and has a good sized minibus for island tours, shopping trips or anything else you need. Bubbles at the Turtle Dove [VHF:16] has a smaller 5-seat pickup truck for smaller groups. Both Barba and Alexis have fleets of fine self-drive rental cars and are happy to rent to yachtspeople.

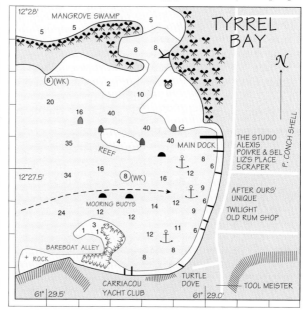

Ashore

There are several little supermarkets that stock a supply of liquor and beer, along with bread, canned and packaged food, eggs and chicken. Some also have electronic goods and household supplies. If you don't see what you want, it is worth asking. The Twilight Supermarket [VHF:16] is run by La Qua and Diana Augustin. They sometimes have block ice on hand, and if not you can get them to order you a block for the next morning. Alexis Supermarket is run by the Alexis family who own a fleet of boats, including some of the ferries that run to Grenada.

The newest supermarket is After Ours', which has not only a good range of general foods but also some delicacies like blue cheese, cream and grapes. Esther Fleary's Unique Boutique in the same building has a good range of clothing and souvenirs.

Leslie's Studio, next to Alexis Supermarket, has t-shirts and many other items all hand-painted or hand-printed right on the premises. Barba's Daughter's Boutique at Barba's, has a wide selection of clothing.

You can dinghy right up to The Twilight Restaurant and Bar [VHF:16] and use their dock. Twilight has a pleasant intimate atmosphere; the walls are brightly decorated with paintings, many from local artist Canute Caliste. Owner and chef Diana Augustin cooks excellent spicy West Indian Creole dishes and her customers often come back year after year. Fresh fish, lobster and lambi, local chicken and pork serve as ingredients. Local oysters are included on the menu as starters. If you feel like something special, drop by and talk with Diana who will be happy to create a meal to order. The Twilight has its own dinghy dock.

Next door, The Old Rum Shop, run by Alcina and Tibo, is a great hang out where you can meet locals and play dominos.

Poivre and Sel [VHF:16, $B-D] introduces a little Gallic flair to the Carriacou restaurant scene. It is run by Patrick and his ebullient chef/wife Magaly, both from the

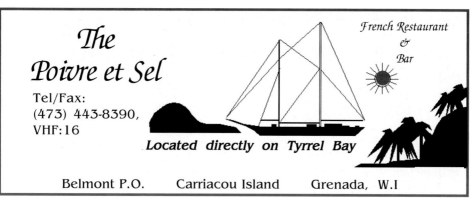

south of France. The imaginative menu makes good use of wine and creme-fraiche and will probably raise your spirits and make you loosen your belt. Specialities include lobster crepe, and a dish from Lyon called quenelle of fish. Consider also the fish in aurore sauce (onions, mushrooms, white wine and cream). Poivre et Sel is open for lunch and dinner. Breakfast can be arranged by request.

The Conch Shell [$C-D] is just down the street that leads back from Scrapers. This is a great place to bring a group to enjoy chef Leanora Pia's original Carriacou family recipes. Seafood predominates on the menu which includes fish, shrimp, lobster, lambi and chicken. All are beautifully prepared with light and delicious flavors. Prices are very reasonable.

After Ours' have built a handsome new restaurant/night club/conference center/stage. The upstairs restaurant has a magnificent view of the bay. They offer first rate Carriacou cooking and a place to hang

out after dinner. They have music, discos, occasional live bands and other entertainment. Every Friday they have a live group in the open air which everyone comes to enjoy. Also on their complex, the Bardoni Brothers from Genoa make wonderful Italian ice-cream and sorbets using local fruits. At breakfast you can get good coffee and croissants and their lunchtime specials include tosto Bardoni (pizza bread stuffed with ham and cheese) and cheese rolls.

Bubbles Turtle Dove [VHF:16, $C] is on the waterfront with a dinghy dock, though you will need a stern anchor or an extra line to tie onto Bubbles' workboat. This is a real "down home" Carriacou bar and restaurant. Bubbles the owner catches lobster, so ask about their menu.

The Mighty Scraper, one time calypso king of Carriacou, is one of Tyrrel Bay's most ambitious businessmen with his big new Scraper's Restaurant, boutique, Rum Punch Bar and apartments [VHF: 16, $C].

They have put a dinghy dock right outside the restaurant and they sell both cube and block ice. Yachtsmen may only use the dock as long as they patronize the bar.

There are several other inexpensive local hangouts. Liz's Place [$D] is friendly and you can get good local food at bargain basement prices. Al's Place [$D] is owned by the Alexis family. You can get a very inexpensive lobster and chips along with other local specialties. They have a table across the road right on the beach. The Mighty Runaway, a jovial Calypsonian and policeman has opened a local bar just above Tool Meister called Runaway's Hideaway.

Just a pleasant twenty-minute walk away lies the Cassada Bay Hotel [VHF:16, $B-C], whose bar and restaurant surely has one of the island's most impressive views. The view south over a carpet of blue-green sea is decorated by swirls of turquoise and brown reef from which several knobby islands rise. On a clear day Grenada looms in the distance. The view makes it one of the more enchanting places to eat out. Under manager Anne Matheson the food is both good and reasonably priced. Go for a drink while it still light, stay for dinner, or drop by for lunch. For large groups dinner reservations are helpful.

There are other restaurants for which you will have to take a cab. Bogles Round House [$B] is well worth the effort as the ambience is so different it is almost like moving into another world and is suitable for a special night out. You enter down a long driveway to where a few cottages are clustered overlooking the sea. The Round House is artistically built out of large river stones, with old wheels and parts from machines framing windows. The roof is supported by an old gum tree complete with branches and the ceiling beams are logs of blue maho. The cosy atmosphere inside is aided by the open fireplace (rarely used) and just five tables. Katie Stroebel, who runs it for owners Sue and Kim, offers a creative fixed menu which is excellent value. Evenings only and reservations are essential because of the small dining room.

The mangrove swamp in Tyrrel Bay is protected by fisheries and well worth a visit by dinghy. Switch off the engine and listen to the peace (take insect repellent). Yachts are not allowed in except during times of a hurricane warning. Dinghies must go at less than four knots and taking oysters is forbidden without a license.

There are plenty of hiking possibilities, including a walk up Chapeau Carre. For anyone wanting some shore time in this area, rooms are available at Constant Spring Guest House, Alexis apartments, Scraper's apartments or Cassada Bay Resort.

Water sports

Snorkelers can check out the two reefs in the bay and the new wreck. There is plenty of good diving. Right off The Sisters is another excellent dive where you find a sloping reef of soft and hard corals decorated with many sponges. Lots of fish gather here. You are bound to see angelfish, and stingrays and turtles are likely. Call Silver Beach Diving [VHF:16] or Tanki's Paradise Diving [VHF:16].

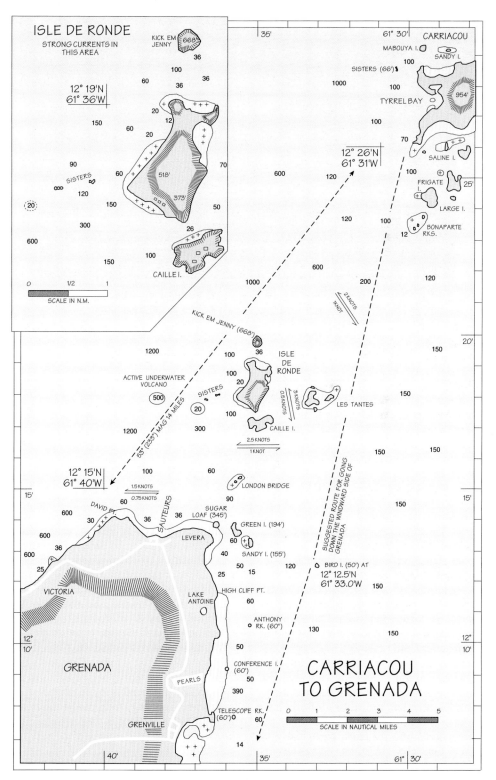

ISLE DE RONDE

STRONG CURRENTS IN
THIS AREA

12° 19'N
61° 36'W

KICK EM
JENNY   668

SISTERS

518'

373'

26

CAILLE I.

0   1/2   1
SCALE IN N.M.

CARRIACOU

MABOUYA I.
SANDY I.
SISTERS (66')
TYRREL BAY   954'

12° 26'N
61° 31'W

SALINE I.

FRIGATE
I.
LARGE I.

BONAPARTE
RKS.

KICK EM JENNY (668')

ISLE
DE
RONDE

ACTIVE UNDERWATER
VOLCANO
500
SISTERS
20

LES TANTES

2 KNOTS
1 KNOT

3 KNOTS
0.5 KNOTS

CAILLE I.

2.5 KNOTS
1 KNOT

53° (235°) MAG 14 MILES

12° 15'N
61° 40'W

1.5 KNOTS
0.75 KNOTS

LONDON BRIDGE

DAVID PT.
SAUTEURS
SUGAR
LOAF (345')
LEVERA
GREEN I. (194')
SANDY I. (155')

SUGGESTED ROUTE FOR GOING
DOWN THE WINDWARD SIDE OF
GRENADA

BIRD I. (50') AT
12° 12.5'N
61° 33.0'W

VICTORIA

LAKE
ANTOINE
HIGH CLIFF PT.

ANTHONY
RK. (60")

GRENADA

PEARLS

CONFERENCE I.
(60')

CARRIACOU
TO GRENADA

GRENVILLE

TELESCOPE RK.
(60')

0   1   2   3   4   5
SCALE IN NAUTICAL MILES

PASSAGES BETWEEN CARRIACOU & GRENADA

Unfortunately, none of the islands between Carriacou and Grenada affords good shelter. Isle de Ronde can be used in a pinch. The anchorage is in the bay on the northern side of the west coast, but it is likely to be rolly, even for lunch. This is a shame as the snorkeling is excellent and the island has some good walks. Only about 20 inhabitants live on the south coast and on the smaller Caille Island.

It is impossible to anchor at either Kick 'em Jenny or the Sisters, but both are interesting and may be approached reasonably closely, weather permitting. Both have large nesting bird populations and you can see boobies and pelicans, particularly on The Sisters. Beware of the strong currents, eddies and rip tides in this area.

An active volcano which lies about two miles west of Isle de Ronde, erupted in both 1988 and 1989. In times of eruption it is advisable to steer a course several miles clear of the volcano. Most of us take a chance for the rest of the time.

Kick 'em Jenny has the reputation of kicking up a nasty sea as you go north and this is particularly true if the tide is running east.

When sailing from Grenada to Carriacou, the fastest way to go is to hug Grenada's lee coast right to the north before heading to Carriacou. If the wind is in the northeast, it is even worth putting a tack into Sauteurs, as the west going current is weakest close to the Grenada coast.

Regulations

Grenada, Carriacou and Petite Martinique are one country with ports of clearance in Hillsborough, St. George's, Prickly Bay and Mt. Hartman Bay. Port charges are $45 EC up to 50 feet; $60 EC between 50 & 100 feet and $70 over 100 feet. Vessels carrying passengers also pay $5 US per passenger. Less expensive yearly fees are available to Grenada-based charter boats. If you do not come with your own crew lists, you may be charged a small fee for their photocopied ones. Normal office hours for customs are 0800-1145, 1300-1545 on weekdays. At other times you will be charged overtime fees which always seem higher in Grenada than Carriacou. If you have any questions about yachting, contact Liz Gorman in tourism, 440-2872.

Collecting or damaging coral or buying lobster out of season are strictly forbidden. (Lobstering season is 31 October to 31 April.) Spearfishing in Grenada, Carriacou and their surrounding islands may be banned by the time this book comes out. Those wanting to take dogs ashore will need a valid rabies certificate.

Holidays

January 1st - New Year's Day
January 2nd - Recovery Day
February 7th - Independence Day
Easter Friday through Monday.
  2nd-5th April 1999 and 21st-24th April 2000
First Monday in May - Labor Day
Whit Monday (24th May, 1999, & 12th June, 2000)
Corpus Christi (3rd June 1999, 22nd June 2000
Carriacou regatta & Carnival = First Monday and Tuesday in August

December 25th - Christmas
December 26th - Boxing Day

Shopping Hours

Shops and offices normally open 0800-1200 and 1300-1600. Saturday is half day and most places are closed by noon. Banks normally open weekdays till 1500, and on Fridays to 1700.

Telephones

Card and coin phones may be found all over the islands. You buy cards for the phone in post offices and selected shops. For overseas calls dial 1 for the USA, 011 plus the country code for other countries. For collect and credit card calls, dial 0 then the whole number. From some public phones you can get a USA direct line by dialing 1-800-872-2881. When dialing from overseas, the area code is 473 followed by a 7-digit number.

Transport

In Grenada there are inexpensive ($1.50 - $6 EC) buses running to most towns and villages. If you are going a long way check on the time of the last returning bus. Taxis are plentiful. Sample taxi rates are:

	$EC
Prickly Bay - St. George's	30
Airport - St. George's	40
Airport - Prickly Bay	25
Prickly Bay - Grand Anse	20
By the hour	52
Short Ride	10

Rental cars are available (check our directory). You will need to buy a local license which costs $30 EC. Drive on the left.

GRENADA

Prickly Bay

Grenada, a spectacularly beautiful island, has lush green mountains, crystal waterfalls, golden beaches and the fragrant spice trees that give the island its epithet "Isle of Spice." Come from late January to early March to get the added bonus of seeing the hills ablaze with hundreds of bright orange flowering immortelle trees: pure magic. Grenada's recent history has been lively. Much of it started with the transition to full independence in 1974. Most Grenadians felt this was premature and instead of jubilant celebrations, the island was on strike and in protest. Nonetheless, independence was thrust upon her and Grenada came of age under the rule of Sir Eric Gairy, a flamboyant and controversial figure who had a very divisive effect on the population, resulting in the 1979 left wing coup by Maurice Bishop, who greatly admired Fidel Castro. Bishop attempted to turn Grenada into a socialist state, improving medical care and education, but he did so at the cost of freedom: anyone who opposed him was thrown in jail, and all independent newspapers were banned.

However, this didn't insulate him from opposition within his own ranks. Second in command, Bernard Coard, his wife Phyllis Coard, and members of the army took Bishop prisoner. After a massive crowd freed him, an army group executed him along with half his cabinet. At this point the USA, along with Grenada's eastern Caribbean neighbors (the Organization of Eastern Caribbean States), launched a "rescue mission" and were welcomed with open arms. Grenada is now again a full democracy. Grenadians are a warm and hospitable people, exceptionally so once you get off the main tourist route.

The interior

Grenada is picturesque with beautiful waterfalls where a swim will leave you feeling wonderfully refreshed, your hair and skin seemingly extra soft. Annandale is the most accessible waterfall. You can drive almost all the way, but then so can all the tour buses, so it is sometimes crowded. Concord Falls are in beautiful countryside and anyone with a spark of adventure should hike the extra half hour to the upper falls. Seven Falls are the best, most secluded and difficult to get to (a one-hour muddy hike) and you need a guide.

The most spectacular road in Grenada is the road which runs from Gouyave over to St. Andrew. It splits in two at Rose Mount – the Clozier road is prettier, the Belvedere road is better maintained. Both run right across the middle of Grenada through verdant agricultural land with spectacular mountain views.

Grand Etang is a crater lake and the Forest Center is close by. Trails are laid out so you can wander into the forest. There are wonderful hikes, including one half way across the island (four hours). There are several places for a great country meal though for most of them you should book in advance. Helvellyn [$C] has a gorgeous location at

274

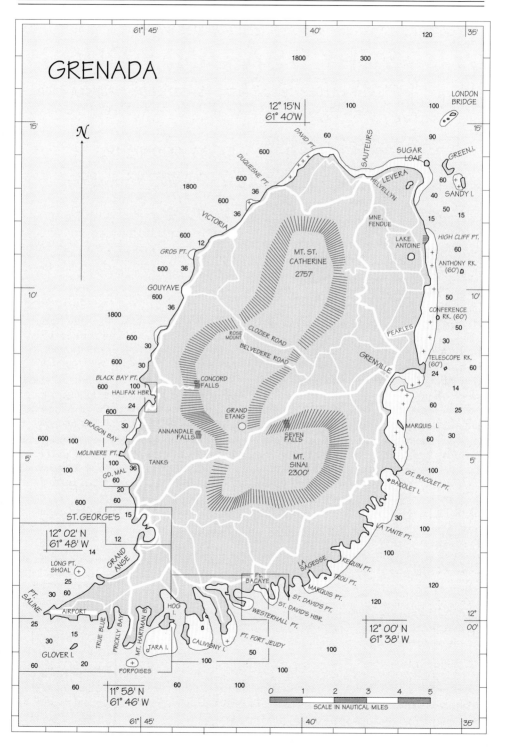

GRENADA

12° 15'N
61° 40'W

12° 02' N
61° 48' W

12° 00' N
61° 38' W

11° 58' N
61° 46' W

SCALE IN NAUTICAL MILES
0   1   2   3   4   5

Labels on map:

LONDON BRIDGE

SUGAR LOAF
GREEN.I.
LEVERA
HELVELLYN
SANDY I.
MNE. FENDUE
SAUTEURS
DAVID PT.
DUQUESNE PT.
VICTORIA
GROS PT.
GOUYAVE
LAKE ANTOINE
HIGH CLIFF PT.
ANTHONY RK. (60')
CONFERENCE RK. (60')
MT. ST. CATHERINE 2757'
CLOZIER ROAD
ROSE MOUNT
BELVEDERE ROAD
PEARLES
GRENVILLE
TELESCOPE RK. (60')
BLACK BAY PT.
HALIFAX HBR.
CONCORD FALLS
DRAGON BAY
MOLINIERE PT.
ANNANDALE FALLS
GRAND ETANG
SEVEN FALLS
MARQUIS I.
TANKS
GD. MAL
MT. SINAI 2300'
GT. BACOLET PT.
BACOLET I.
ST. GEORGE'S
LA TANTE PT.
GRAND ANSE
LONG PT. SHOAL
PT. SALINE
AIRPORT
TRUE BLUE
PRICKLY BAY
MT. HARTMAN B.
HOG I.
JARA I.
CALIVIGNY I.
GLOVER I.
PORPOISES
Pt. BACAYE
WESTERHALL PT.
PT. FORT JEUDY
ST. DAVID'S PT.
ST. DAVID'S HBR.
MARQUIS PT.
TROU PT.
RERUIN PT.
LA SAGESSE

275

the northern tip of the island close by Sauteurs, perched on a cliff overlooking the Grenadines to the north. Hang out and enjoy the picturesque garden, or follow the tortuous path down to a lovely secluded beach below. It is run by Sharon from Grenada and Bhad from the middle east, a young and enthusiastic couple. They serve an excellent West Indian lunch and the bar stays open till sunset.

Rose Mount on the Belvedere road is a working estate — nothing fancy but great local food at excellent prices and a warm welcome from owners Jane and Llewelyn Duncan [$C-D]. Fresh juice is available but no alcohol. You can buy cut flowers and spices here at an excellent price. Betty Mascoll's old estate house at Morne Fendu near Sauteurs [$B] is an experience in great food and crumbling splendor. The meal is a pleasant and leisurely experience. Lin and Norris Nelson turn out a good meal in their impeccable Mt. Rodney Estate House [$B] which has expansive gardens and a great sea view. The Victoria Hotel [$D] in Victoria on the west coast does excellent local food at very reasonable prices, the service is good and there is no need to book.

For hiking, Henry of Henry Safari Tours [VHF:68] is the best man to contact. He runs a taxi service, specializes in hikes and knows the trails well, including Seven Falls. Most other taxi drivers are reluctant to get their feet muddy, but there are a few exceptions including Selwyn Taxi, Rock Taxi, K&J Tours, Leroy and Funseeker Tours (see also our section on Prickly Bay).

A great day tour for those planning to rent a car is to drive up the west coast to Concord Falls for a swim, include a hike to the upper falls. Drive to Victoria or Rose Mount for lunch, and take the Clozier road across the island. Take your time; this is a great drive. You eventually join the main road that passes over Grand Etang. Stop at the crater lake and follow the short circular hike which takes you into the rain forest and then back down to Grand Etang Lake. This should leave you time for a leisurely drive back down the mountain.

In reading about Grenada, keep in mind that Prickly Bay, Grand Anse, True Blue and St. George's are all within an easy taxi ride, so wherever you anchor, read about all three.

Navigation

There is a major light on Point Saline, visible for 18 miles both to the north and south, flashing (2 + 1) every 20 seconds. There is a lower elevation quick-flashing light on Glovers Island, and another at the western end of the airport runway. The lights have not always proved reliable.

Grenada uses the IALA B (red right returning) rule. Unless you draw more than 10 feet you will not have to pay attention to the two big ship channel buoys outside St. George's or use the leading marks.

The west coast of Grenada is steep-to; a quarter of a mile offshore clears all dangers except Long Point Shoal.

Some people like to sail down Grenada's east coast to Prickly Bay. It can be rough, but trolling for fish is usually rewarded. It is only advisable in settled weather. Stay well off Grenada's east coast. Pass close inside Bird Island, but outside all other islands. Keep well away from The Porpoises as you

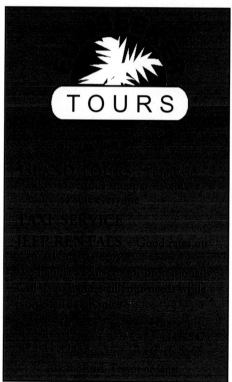

come along the south coast. They can be difficult to see, especially in the afternoon with the sun in your eyes. There are not many landmarks along the south coast, but you can look out for the development at Westerhall. Prickly Point has a distinctive saddle shape, and a conspicuous house that looks like a lighthouse.

GRENADA'S WEST COAST

Grenada's west coast has several anchorages useful as a last stop for northbound yachts. They are all susceptible to northerly swells. Halifax and Grand Mal are acceptable in most conditions; Dragon Bay and Happy Hill will get very uncomfortable in moderate swells and can be dangerous in large ones.

Halifax Harbour is a quiet spot enclosed by hills. It is a small bay without a village and easily missed unless you follow closely along the coast. A few landmarks help. Dragon Bay is about two miles up the coast from St. George's and Halifax Harbour is about two miles beyond that. Between them, but much closer to Dragon Bay, is a tall red and white striped aerial, and closer to Halifax is a village. A white house stands on the hill to the north overlooking the harbor. You have to tuck well in the harbor as the water in the middle is very deep. High tension cables have been strung across the southern part of the bay. The lowest wire is about 10 feet below the others. To estimate the height I anchored Helos, whose mast is 50 feet above sea level, right underneath and went ashore with a measuring stick . My best estimate is that the lowest wire is about 70 feet above sea level. But the method of measurement was rough so I would not recommend going under with masts over 60 feet high. Halifax is a really lovely bay, unfortunately spoiled in recent years by a nearby refuse depot which creates flies and bad smells. However, the dump will eventually be moved and if you arrive an hour or so before sunset the

flies will have already gone to bed on someone else's boat. Note the spectacular large silk cotton tree at the water's edge in the southern bay.

Happy Hill, just north of Dragon Bay, is more open but can be very peaceful. There is a narrow beach backed by a hill, and on the hill is another large old silk cotton tree. Avoid the southern part of the bay which is strewn with coral heads and anchor in the middle or closer to the northern headland.

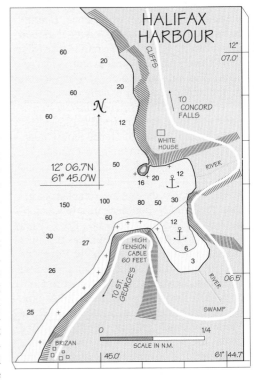

View from 1.5 miles west of Halifax Hbr.

BLACK BAY PT.   Low cliffs   HALIFAX HARBOUR   Conspicuous cluster of houses   Moliniere Pt. ST. GEORGE'S, 2 miles further down the coast, is hidden   Pt.. Saline just visible

We've Taken Time To Make Sure Your Vacation Is Perfect

About 30 Years

For three decades, The Moorings has been working to ensure your next vacation is as easy, enjoyable and fulfilling as it possibly can be. We established full-service bases in the world's best sailing areas of the Caribbean, the Mediterranean and the South Pacific. We built a superb fleet of immaculately maintained and fully-equipped yachts to suit every preference and level of sailing experience. And we created a worldwide system of communications and support to ensure a worry-free sailing vacation. When you're ready to get away, give us a call. With our 30 years of experience behind you, you've got one great vacation ahead of you.

The Moorings®
The Best Sailing Vacations In The World!

Call 1-800-535-7289
www.moorings.com

If jacks are running the fishermen may ask you to clear out at the crack of dawn, which will give you a good early start for Carriacou. There is good snorkeling in the southern part of the bay around the rocks.

Dragon Bay is a delightful anchorage with a palm-lined beach, but too small to allow more than two or three boats. Avoid anchoring in the south part of the bay as it is full of coral heads which make for good snorkeling. You can find a good sand bottom for anchoring in the middle of the bay. Both the snorkeling and the diving are first rate around Moliniere Point just south of Dragon Bay. Do not be tempted to anchor your yacht off Moliniere Point as you will damage the coral. If you dinghy round, you can anchor your dinghy in the odd patch of sand in shallow water.

Grand Mal is a well protected anchorage most of the time. The water is usually clean and the long beach attractive. There are gas storage tanks in Grand Mal, and two buoys offshore which are used for unloading tankers. Pipes run out from the small dock to the buoys, so avoid anchoring in this area. Anchor just north of these buoys, between them and the headland, or south of them just outside the fishing fleet.

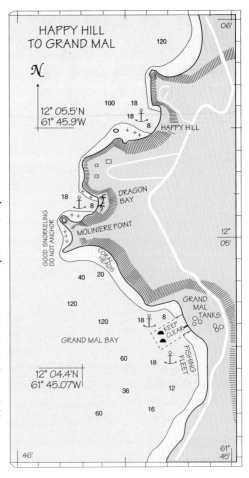

ST. GEORGE'S

St. George's is built on a ridge, with the sea on one side and the protected Carenage on the other. The houses mingle with shrubs and trees, giving splashes of bright color against a background of dark green. From afar it is as neat and pretty as a picture book illustration. The old brick buildings are capped with antique "fish scale" tile roofs, a reminder of long ago when the profitable journeys were outward bound, laden with rum, spices and fruit, and returning sailing ships would arrive "in ballast" of bricks and tiles.

When approaching from the north, the harbor entrance remains hidden until you reach it. On your left, as you enter, you will see Fort George. This fort spent a few socialist years as "Fort Rupert" in memory of Prime Minister Bishop's father. When Bishop was imprisoned by members of his own party and later freed by thousands of his followers, they came here in a euphoric mood. The army sent in armored cars, shot some civilians (several more hurt themselves jumping off the walls of the fort), and executed Prime Minister Bishop and half the cabinet. The ruins you see on your right-hand side are those of a building that started life as a hotel and was used by the socialist government as a main office building, Butler House. The damage is due not so much to the American assault forces as it is to a desperate attempt by the communists to destroy documents. Although the damage looks impressive, over three tons of paper were recovered. This building may soon be rebuilt as a hotel. Straight ahead on the hills above the lagoon you can see Fort Frederick, from which the attack on Bishop was launched, and the prison, where all the culprits, including the Coards, now sit.

The main anchorage is in the lagoon between Grenada Yacht Services (GYS) and the Grenada Yacht Club. A major reworking of the entrance has just about been completed. The channel will be marked and follows the main dock into the lagoon. Once inside it may be necessary to turn and follow the dock eastward towards the yacht club before heading out into the lagoon. The area outside the main dock is being dredged to 30 feet and the area as you turn to the east along is being dredged to 18 feet. The lagoon is about 15 to 20 feet deep, but there may be spots as shallow as 12 feet deep. When entering the harbor, head straight for the northern half of the big ship dock, then follow it south into the lagoon.

The harbor master has been discouraging anchoring or tying up in the Carenage. However, if you wish to do so, call the Grenada Port Authority on VHF:16. No town in the Windwards is completely free of theft and St. George's is no exception. Always lock up the boat and dinghy and if possible leave someone on board. Every few years, St. George's has outbreaks of petty boat theft that go beyond the normal. You can find out the current situation by calling Liz Gorman, the tourism officer in charge of yachts and cruise ships, at 440-2872.

Regulations
The customs office is located in the GYS complex. Normal office hours are weekdays 0800-1145, 1300-1545. When you clear in, tell the customs officers which ports you plan to visit.

Services
The Grenada Yacht Club [VHF:6,16 "GYC"] has a modern 28-berth marina with a fuel dock which offers both diesel and gas. You can buy this duty free when you have cleared out. The docks have electricity (110/220 volt, 50 cycle) and water, and the

rates are reasonable. Your warm welcome starts with a free rum drink courtesy of Westerhall. There is 24-hour security, making it the safest place to leave your yacht in the lagoon. The Yacht Club is informal. The office is open 0730-1700 when Judith will help you send a fax or get your mail (address mail to Grenada Yacht Club, P.O. Box 117, St. George's, Grenada). Courtesy flags and t-shirts are for sale in the office and you can swap your old books. Laundry, taxis and other services can be arranged. The yacht club bar opens at 0900 and stays open till 2200. Food is available from a mobile canteen which opens 0900-1430 and 1630-1900 except Saturday and Monday when they close. Friday night is barbecue night starting at 1700. If you are anchored out, you can still visit by using their dinghy dock.

The Grenada Yacht Club organizes the Grenada Sailing Festival, a week of racing and social events which is held in January. All entrants are welcome, from serious racing boats to live-aboards. The festival is usually lively and entertaining and often features match racing between Buddy Melges and Terry Neilson.

GYS [VHF:16] has been dreadfully dilapidated for many years. A change of hands and a multimillion dollar rebuild has been promised every other year for about a decade. Expect it "just now." Meanwhile, there are security guards (though there have still been a few break-ins) and a telephone. Fuel and water are available, and for those moments when rain destroys your still-wet varnish, there is a bar.

Henry's Safari Tours [VHF:68] offers a collect-and-deliver laundry service from

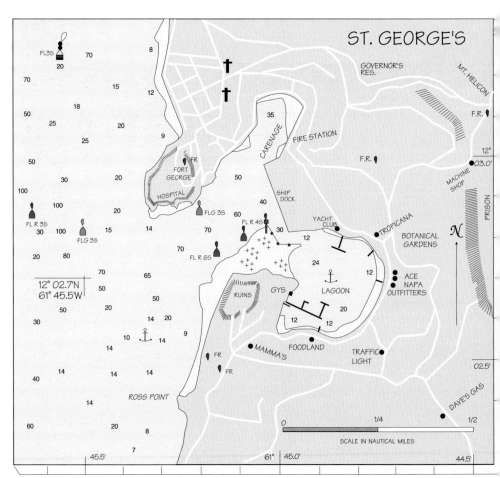

give him a call and he will come to your boat. He guarantees a 24-hour turnaround. If necessary he will collect your stove, repair it and deliver it back. He will service yachts in any of the major yacht anchorages.

Outfitters International [VHF:16] has an office and dinghy dock on the opposite side of the lagoon from GYS. It is owned by Alstin from Grenada and his wife Margaret from Ireland. Their famous Priority Parts Service is well known throughout the Caribbean. They will find whatever part or piece of equipment you need and deliver it to your yacht and they handle all the customs work. The price you pay depends on how quickly you need the part and what it is. You can get many chandlery items at around the USA list price. Margaret and Alstin will lend a helping hand — take laundry, organize engine or refrigeration repairs and arrange for rental cars or anything you might need. They also act as a mail drop (c/o Outfitters International, Box 581, St. George's, Grenada, W.I.). Alstin runs a few charter yachts.

Albert Lucas runs an excellent machine shop and is usually there every day including Sunday. He will often do small jobs while you wait. Finding him is more of a

any of Grenada's main anchorages. Henry passes on dinner reservations at no charge collects garbage, and fills cooking gas tanks. Otherwise, to fill cooking gas bottles you have to take a taxi to the filling depot in Mt. Gay, which is a fair way outside town. Henry will also find you cut flowers or organize anything else you might need.

Basil St. John at Lagoon Marine Refrigeration Services is a first class refrigeration repair man. You can call him up and he will pay a boat visit either in St. George's or in Prickly Bay.

Is your cooking stove playing up? David Benoit can fix it. His workshop is in Springs, but you don't have to go there. Just

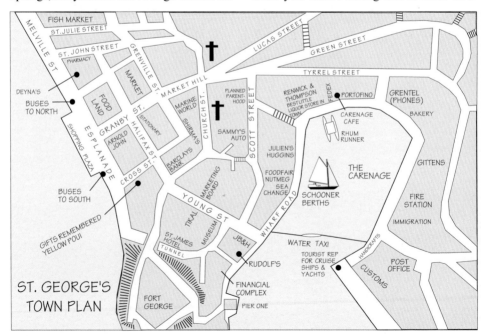

ST. GEORGE'S
TOWN PLAN

Rose Mount Waterfall

problem as he has no sign. At the Tropicana roundabout, turn right away from the sea. At the main road turn left and you will see a roundabout in front of you. Turn right up the hill at the roundabout. Eventually you will come to the Blue Danube bakery/supermarket, easily seen as lots of cars park outside. Albert is on the right-hand side of the road on the corner, just before you reach the Blue Danube. You will see steps going up forever, but you only have to take a few to reach Lucas and his workshop on the left.

Tech Metal Works is out on River Road and run by Theron Herbert. He can weld anything – aluminum, stainless, cast iron or bronze using Arc, Tig, or Mig welding. Ross's workshop, just down the road from GYS, will have a go at welding or fabricating anything.

Water taxis used to be readily available in town, but these days they generally only show up when the cruise ships are in. If you find one you can negotiate a fee to your yacht. There are plenty of hopeful laborers looking for a job, but it is best to get a local recommendation.

If you need a survey contact Mike Forshaw or Alan Hooper through GYS or Sea Breeze Yachts.

Ashore

You can take your dinghy from the lagoon over to town. If you take this guide with you, our town map will help. Tie up outside Food Fair or Pier One which is less dusty. An alternative is to walk to town from the Yacht Club, and return by water taxi.

St. George's is a busy place with plenty of traffic, including large colorful buses laden with people and goods, smaller mini buses with loud music, cars, trucks weighed down with building material, and sometimes it seems like they are all honking at once. People will shout "taxi" at you and vendors may offer fruits from baskets.

Most shops open from 0800 to 1200 and then from 1300 to 1600 on weekdays. Banks are open only till 1500, except Friday when they open to 1700. The post office moved near customs after the old post office building on the Carenage burned down in 1990. It is open over lunch, but closed all day Saturday. Most shops are closed Saturday afternoon and everything is closed on Sunday. The lovely old financial complex which used to house the post office is now restored creating some of the fanciest government offices in the Windwards. Nothing for the visitor to do here but it is worth wandering by for a look. The Library is open to the public and interesting to visit.

St. George's is a first-rate place to provision, with comfortable air-conditioned supermarkets. The newest is Foodland in the lagoon. It has its own dinghy dock and is often open quite late at night. Foodland has an excellent selection of regular items and a pleasing delicatessen section. It offers a five percent discount to charter yachts. In town, Food Fair is conveniently close to the water and you can tie up nearby. They are open weekdays till 1730, except Friday when they are open till 2045. On Saturdays they close at 2000. They too, offer a five percent discount to charter yachts.

Those wishing to buy wine or liquor should visit the Best Little Liquor Store in Town [VHF:16 "Rhum Runner Base"]. You can tie your dinghy close to the shop. Their selection includes over 125 different wines. If you are buying by the case, duty free prices are available. It is best to allow 48 hours for processing. On large orders

delivery to Prickly Bay is a possibility. You
can also buy block and cube ice here, send
your DHL packets, organize money
through Western Union, and ask them about
bringing you spares via Rush Order.

Visit the local market, preferably on a
Saturday morning. It is a riot of color where
determined ladies under big umbrellas sit
amid huge heaps of vegetables. You can get
fresh produce, spices and handicrafts. If
you feel peckish, try a freshly cooked fish
cake. The Marketing Board on Young Street
(opposite Tikal) has the best prices on fresh
produce, although the range is limited.

When GYS is restored it may feature a
chandlery. Meanwhile, there are several
good hardware stores. Arnold John is on the
Esplanade/Granby St. corner and Jonas
Browne and Hubbards Hardware is on the
Carenage. Marine World on Grenville
Street has a good selection of fishing gear,
snorkeling gear and charts as well as safety
gear and some hardware. Julien's on the
Carenage is the place to visit for chain and
big galvanized shackles.

In the lagoon, on the opposite side from
GYS, you will find a well stocked Ace
Hardware and NAPA agent. They have a
wide range of car parts as well as tools,
sealants, glues and a small marine hardware
selection that includes chain and stainless
shackles. Check out also the big Huggins
hardware store next door. Other auto parts
shops include Sammy's and Hubbards.

Some things are not where you expect
them. For some types of watch battery you
have to go to the Anglo American Funeral
Parlor and for locally made drums and mu-
sical instruments visit Arnold John's hardware store.

Souvenir items range from baskets of
spices to large woven mats, batik, art, perfumes and pottery. The Rolls Royce of the
boutiques in town is Jeanne Fisher's Tikal
on Young Street. It is stacked with quality
arts and crafts, including the local Art-
Fabrik batiks. You will find paintings, maps,
hammocks, ornaments, casual shirts, nautical charts and books and more.

When cruise ships visit, the craft stalls by
the cruise ship docks come alive – all
twenty of them selling apparently identical

souvenirs. Many small tourist shops now line the Carenage, many are local but they include Columbian Emeralds. Ganzee has the largest variety of t-shirts.

On the other side of town, visit Gifts Remembered on Cross Street. They have a large range of handicrafts from the Caribbean. If you like art, visit Jim Rudin's Yellow Poui Art Gallery above Gifts Remembered. He has wonderful local paintings, but his selection goes beyond this to antique maps, objets d'art and artistic postcards.

Just up the hill from GYS in a handsome traditional house surrounded by flowers, you will find the Arawak Islands packing plant and shop. Here they make soaps, perfumes and herbal teas, and as you walk in the door you are greeted with a pleasant spicy smell. You can walk round the plant and there are plenty of good gift ideas, including nutmeg kits, and gift packages of local products such as hot sauces and rums.

St. George's is best explored when you have plenty of time and nothing you have to do. There are wonderful views wherever you go; the more panoramic are around the fort, and by the cemetery (go up Church Street and keep going). There are plenty of steps and narrow alleys to explore and the museum is well worth a visit for the $1 US entrance fee. If the heat gets to you, pull up for a cold drink.

The Nutmeg [$C-D] is inexpensive with a bird's eye view from their perch above Food Fair. They serve first rate local food. It is a good place to stop for a snack or drink while shopping and it is very popular at lunch. Return for dinner when you can see St. George's lit up at night and take a leisurely meal in an uncrowded atmosphere. Groups of four wanting to come for dinner can give them a call and they will arrange free transportation from L'Anse aux Epines or Grand Anse.

Rudolf's [$B-D] is an excellent pub style restaurant with a cozy atmosphere and draft beer. They serve delectable seafood and steaks. They also offer a large range of tasty snacks. It is popular among the local business community for lunch, and as a dinner restaurant it is wonderful value and usually

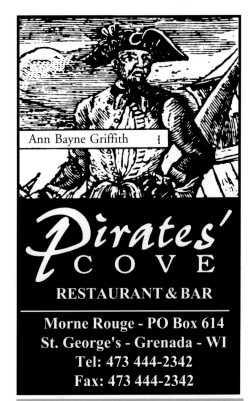

ST. GEORGE'S

uncrowded.

Pier One [$B-D], has a prime location right over the water with a superb harbor view and a dinghy dock. It is open from breakfast to dinner every day. Owner Shereen specializes in seafood with a wide variety of fish, shrimp and lobster dinners, though she also offers steak, chicken and vegetarian dishes. Happy hour is 1700-1800 nightly with musical entertainment most Fridays in season.

Grenada is the land of the unexpected, so it should come as no surprise to find Patrick, a friendly Irishman, running an Italian restaurant he took over from Goh, a Malayan, and running it very well. It is called Portofino [$B-D] and is upstairs on the Carenage with a view over the Carenage to Grand Anse. The service is good and you can get crisp salads and appetizing pizzas and pastas. For fancier tastes, there is lobster and steak. Patrick is active in environmental and cultural activities, and he brings in a jazz group on Friday nights and on special occasions. From time to time Patrick puts on a supper club, a late night event (2300-0300) with champagne cocktails, good food, cabaret style entertainment, and a band to keep you dancing into the wee hours.

This end of the Carenage has almost become a minor Italian quarter with the addition of The Carenage Cafe [$B-D]. You can sit outside and watch life go by, drink fresh squeezed fruit juice, a sophisticated cocktail or excellent espresso or cappucino coffee. Pizzas, pastries, lasagne, sandwiches and sorbets will take care of most appetites. They make their own bread and you can buy a loaf to take with you.

On the Esplanade side of town, adventurous eaters should try to find the Ye Olde Farmhouse Kitchen [$D] behind Gifts Remembered, where you can eat a hearty local lunch. On the same side of town, Deyna's Tasty Food [$D] is a local restaurant. If it is too hot upstairs, try the air-conditioned cellar-room. They do great local food at very reasonable prices and are open seven days a week. Walk up to the bar and order what you want.

There are also good restaurants in the lagoon. Horatio Brizan's Tropicana [$C-D] is Grenada's best inexpensive restaurant; cheap enough to eat at any time cooking seems too much of a chore. The food is Chinese and local with good rotis, fish and lambi dishes. You can tie your dinghy on their dinghy dock opposite the restaurant. It is excellent value for lunch or dinner, with a separate and speedy takeout section. Horatio has completely renovated the building and put in some clean modern and inexpensive rooms upstairs.

The Traffic Light [$C-D], run by the Andrews family is about a 10 minute walk from either the yacht club or GYS. Follow the lagoon road to Hi Tech Printery and take the road up the hill. The Traffic Light is to your right with a view right across the bay. Their restaurant is local, cheerful and very inexpensive. The best seat are out on the balcony or in one of the little balcony alcoves. They often have special nights in addition to their Wednesday night jazz (in season). Modern, inexpensive rooms available if you need some time ashore.

Mamma's [$B], run by Cleopatra, serves a very wide variety of local dishes all at the same time. You get served about 16 dishes including chicken, fish, beef, rabbit, conch, octopus, lambi and lots of different veg-

etables are all prepared in local style, making a fine feast. If you have special requirements or are a vegetarian you should discuss your tastes when you book. Cleo will certainly accommodate you. Mamma's is just up the road from GYS and in recent times Cleo tells me the police have done a good job of keeping it safe. Reservations are essential.

Mt. Helicon [$B-C] is a fancy restaurant with a spectacular view over St. George's. It is at the top of the hill that passes the Blue Danube and right opposite the Venezuelan embassy. It is a great place for a special night out. They also do inexpensive lunches [$D]- take a friend you want to impress and you won't have to spend your last dollar.

Grand Anse is what most people have in mind when they think about the Caribbean: a generous two-mile sweep of white-gold sand, backed by shady palms and almond trees. Although it forms the center of the Grenada hotel industry, there are strict protection laws and no hotel can be higher than the tallest coconut tree.

Anchoring is currently forbidden at Grand Anse, though this restriction may be lifted. Meanwhile, you can anchor just south of St. George's and dinghy down. There is currently no dock here which means dragging your dinghy up on the sand. The beach closest to the Coconut Beach French Restaurant is calmest. Grand Anse contains a wealth of shops and restaurants, and is easily visited by bus or taxi from St. George's or Prickly Bay.

Ashore

The shopping in Grand Anse is spread along a half-mile stretch of main road from the Food Fair Mall to Le Marquis Mall. Cars and buses hurtle down this piece of road with little thought for pedestrians. Luckily there is pavement or verge for the most part. However, take care, especially when crossing the road.

Food Fair at Grand Anse is air conditioned and spacious, making it a comfortable place to provision, and charter yachts are offered a five percent discount. It is part of a pleasant shopping center where you will also find Imagine, a terrific handicraft store with batiks, woodcraft, hand painted t-shirts, Spice Island cosmetics, books and much more. Other shops include Hubbard's Home Center, Rick's Cafe [$D], Chantilly for lingerie, Mitchell's Pharmacy [open till 2100] Sandra's hairdressing salon and Magic Photo Studio, where you can get your films developed. In the same center is Dr. Mike Radix who is the best man for

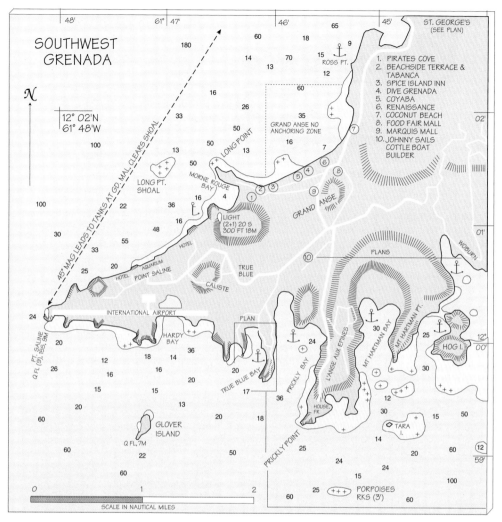

SOUTHWEST GRENADA

12° 02'N
61° 48'W

1. PIRATES COVE
2. BEACHSIDE TERRACE & TABANCA
3. SPICE ISLAND INN
4. DIVE GRENADA
5. COYABA
6. RENAISSANCE
7. COCONUT BEACH
8. FOOD FAIR MALL
9. MARQUIS MALL
10. JOHNNY SAILS COTTLE BOAT BUILDER

ST. GEORGE'S (SEE PLAN)

GRAND ANSE NO ANCHORING ZONE

SCALE IN NAUTICAL MILES

medical problems and used to dealing with people from yachts.

Just down the road, the handsome new Grenada Bank of Commerce will happily change money or give you cash from your Visa or Master Card. Close by, Gittens Drugmart is a full pharmacy, with everything from prescriptions to newspapers. A travel agent is in the same block.

On the other side of the road is the Marquis Mall. You have to walk right round the two buildings to find all the little shops which sell everything from donuts and clothing to shoes. Of importance to crewed charter yachts is Gourmet Food owned by L.J. Reese and Jan Edwards. They stock a variety of specialty foods you won't find in the supermarkets. These include special oils and mustards, good coffee, elegant pastas, designer chocolates and much more. Marcelle and Peter Toussaints lived for many years in the UK. Their gift shop, Presents, includes a wide range of local and other gifts as well as games and toys for children. You can buy books and overseas papers here. Of interest to sailors are the stainless steel thermos flasks. Cybernuts will find disks, print heads and ribbons at Onsite Software Support.

United Artists, run by Sue, is devoted to original art and craft such as hand-painted calabashes. You will find a good selection of paintings from Grenada, Carriacou and Petite Martinique.

La Boulangerie is a great bakery, run by Italians, with croissants, baguettes, pain au chocolat, Italian ice cream and more. Stock up for your next charter or just drop by for a lunchtime pizza or sandwich and the best cup of coffee in Grenada. Can't be bothered to cook? La Boulangerie delivers pizzas between 1800-2000 to Prickly Bay.

Toothache? Sunsmile Dental Clinic run by Dr. Roxanne Nedd is highly recommended. She is very pleasant and can handle anything from an emergency to a new cap.

Many cruising folk have been helped out here. Her clinic is on the right hand side of the main road going from the Sugar Mill to Le Marquis mall.

All the major hotels have boutiques. There is a good bus service to town.

The problem in Grenada is not to find a good restaurant — it is to choose which good restaurant. There are so many, each one different from the next. Many have lovely settings by the sea or in the hills with a view. Grand Anse has one of the widest

selections.

Coconut Beach, a French restaurant [$A-B], has a superb location right on the water's edge on Grand Anse Beach. A perfect beach hangout by day and very romantic at night especially on the rising moon. You can drive up to it in your dinghy or come by car. Good French cuisine has been adapted to local foods, under the diligent management of Grenadian "Scratch," nicknamed for his golfing abilities.

Lawrence Lambert is a Grenadian who spent some years in Canada and then returned to buy The Flamboyant Hotel and the Beachside Restaurant [$B-D]. It is at the western end of Grand Anse beach with a sweeping view to St. George's. The restaurant has good West Indian and continental food, with a big buffet and steel band on Wednesday nights in season. There is also crab racing Monday nights and a calypsonian Friday nights. They have a good, very cheap Sunday barbecue brunch which is geared toward families who come to enjoy the beach and the pool — so bring your kids.

Joe's Steak House [$B], run by Ellen and Mike Radix, has a prime location at Le Marquis mall within easy walking distance of all the Grand Anse hotels. A touch of Grenadian Americana, Joe's most popular dish is grilled lobster and their specialties include many seafoods as well as steak. Seating is intimate among potted plants and the service excellent.

Determined gourmets should make time to visit Eric's Canboulay [$A-B], one of the Windward's finest restaurants. It is on a hill behind Grand Anse with a panoramic view to St. George's. The food here is excellent; an imaginative contemporary cuisine based on local fresh fruits, vegetables, herbs and spices. Come with a large appetite because the price includes several courses and a delightful sorbet between the starter and main course.

Before you go to Pirates Cove [$B], call up and make sure you can reserve one of the seven tables on their traditional wooden balcony. Perched up here you are treated with a delightful view across the bay to the

night lights of St. George's. The emphasis is on seafood and the local chefs spent some time working with a French chef. As a result the sauces are a superb combination of local and French culinary art. The service, overseen by owner Anne Bayne Griffith, is gracious and pleasant, at a gentle island pace.

The most romantic and personal restaurant is Tabanca [$B, closed Tuesday], next door to Beachside Terrace. You sit under the stars in a garden setting with the sound of gentle surf on beach right below and the lights of St. George's across the bay. It is pure magic on a moonlit night. Austrian owner Kirsten has lived in Grenada many years and creates the menu, which features a good variety of seafood, including several varieties of fresh fish, local crab, lobster and shrimp. Reservations are essential.

Galaxy 1 is an internet cafe run by Eddie and Andrea Frederick. For the cybernuts there are six computers set up for e-mail and surfing the net, for everyone there are delightful seats with a gorgeous view over the St. George's approaches and a bar and restaurant which is inexpensive and friendly. They offer snacks, burgers and grilled food (fish chicken, pork, steak) served with local vegetables. Galaxy opens at 11 am but Eddie is open to special breakfast requests.

Atmosphere is everything at Casablanca [$C-D], an elegant hangout open from 5 pm right through to 3 am. The tastefully sophisticated atmosphere is reminiscent of an exclusive club, with pool tables, card tables, darts and other games set amid potted plants and cooled by ceiling fans. An antique piano which came to Grenada with the first high commissioner in Grenada's distant past and a snooker table reputed to have been on the island for 145 years enhance the decor. People drift in and out all through the night. Owner Fritz is from Germany and runs the place with easy elegance. The bar is stocked with a good supply of fresh local juices and fruity cocktails blended with ice are always available. Casablanca is more a bar than a restaurant, but they serve both snacks and daily specials at very reasonable prices. There is occasional entertainment in season (usually jazz) when there may be a cover charge.

Taffy is a Welshman and Taffy's Tavern [$D] is a casual hangout: the local pub with its gathering of faithful adherents. A good place to meet people, have good conversations, listen to music and relax. They have a pool table and darts and when you can't bear to leave the fun for dinner you can eat pub grub here at reasonable prices. Taffy came to Grenada on holiday and fell in love with the place — he is the perfect mine host, making sure everyone is happy.

While in Grenada, try to listen to a good steel band. You may have listened to one or two farther north and come to the mistaken conclusion that, while steelband is fun, it is repetitive and best listened to from a distance. Good "pan" sound is fantastic and there are very good groups in Grenada. There is entertainment at both Spice Island Inn and Renaissance Grenada Resort most nights. Steel bands play at the Renaissance on Saturday nights 2000-2200, at Beachside on Wednesday nights in season, and at Spice Island Inn on Friday nights with their barbecue. (See also Prickly Bay).

A short ride or healthy walk from Grand Anse is the beautiful but shallow Morne Rouge Bay. There is a complex here called the Gem Holiday Beach Resort. They run the Fantazia 2001 disco which is open on Wednesdays for Oldie Goldie night, and on Fridays and Saturdays with live music.

Water sports

There are several dive shops in Grenada, all keenly competitive and happy to take yachtspeople. If you call one they will collect you from your anchorage. All dive shops are Padi or Naui establishments offering all kinds of courses, including introductory resort courses.

David Coe at Ecodive [VHF:16] is based at the Coyaba Hotel. David runs an ecologi-

cally conscious dive shop and has put considerable effort into supporting the turtle population mainly through education. He plans to start land based turtle trips to watch nesting turtles. His instructors are knowledgeable about the undersea life and environment. David runs dives at 1000 and 1400 and for a real adventure he does two tank dives at Isle de Ronde. Ecodive also runs land based ecotreks off the beaten track with knowledgeable local guides.

Stephen Kaser at Dive Grenada [VHF:16] has a shop at the Alamanda Hotel in the middle of Grand Anse Beach. Dive Grenada has been in operation longer than most of the other shops. Stephen likes working with yachts and specializes in Bianca C dives, so this a good shop if that is your priority. Stephen is happy to fill tanks, but he does not normally rent gear. He usually dives at 1000 and 1400.

Victor Thompson is a Grenadian who spent most of his life in the UK. He and his English wife Sandra run Sanvic's, a full dive and watersports shop at the Renaissance Resort. They have their own bus and offer free transport from Prickly Bay, Mount Hartman or St. George's.

Grenada has a variety of good and interesting dives. For sheer drama you cannot beat the Bianca C, a 600-foot cruise ship that is sunk in 100-165 feet. The wreck is vast, though mainly broken, but there are splendid views up at the bow and the swimming pool is still intact on the deck. Large schools of small snappers, some midnight parrotfish and a few barracudas get framed by the wreckage. This is an advanced dive and most local dive shops will insist you do one other dive first so they are happy with your level of confidence.

Flamingo Reef starts just outside the north end of Happy Hill Bay and continues along the coast towards Dragon Bay. This colorful and lively reef offers a changing seascape as you swim along. There is a good balance of healthy hard and soft corals with a dense tall forest of waving sea whips, sea rods and sea fans at the top on the seaward end. This is the place to look for the flamingo tongue which gives the dive its name. Along the sloping reef are many grunts, squirrelfish, wrasses,

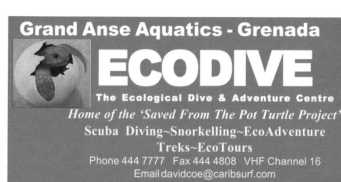

parrotfish and trumpetfish. Large schools of brown chromis pass by. Deeper on the reef you have a chance of seeing large groupers. In the sand are mixed schools of spotted and yellow goatfish probing the bottom with their barbels.

Dragon Bay and Moliniere Point join together and are the easiest dive to do from your dinghy. Make sure you anchor it in a patch of sand. You can start on the south side of Dragon Bay or go out from the little bay in Moliniere Point. These dives offer a mixture of large sand and coral patches going from shallow water down to about 60 feet. Much of the reef in this shallow area is densely covered in a wide variety of corals and sponges. When you get to about 30 to 40 feet you meet a drop off which goes down another 25-30 feet. Sometimes it is a steep slope, at other times a sheer wall. There are also a few rock outcroppings which make for dramatic valleys and deep sand filled gullies are cut into the drop off.

Boss Reef starts outside St. George's Harbour and continues to Point Saline, a distance of at least two and half miles. It varies in width from 200-500 yards. It would be possible to do many dives on this reef without covering the same territory. There can be strong currents here and it is best done as a drift dive with a dive shop. A popular dive is the middle section, swimming wherever the current takes you. The depth here varies from about 30-60 feet. The reef rises from the sand to a somewhat level top, which is broken by deep gullies and holes that drop down to sand. This is an exceptionally good dive for coral variety. The top is completely covered in a wonder-

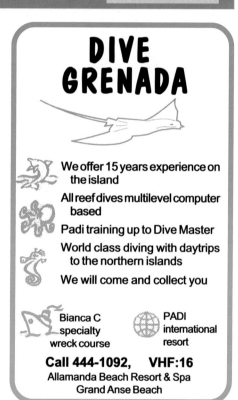
ful array of corals all packed close to each other. In places you can see corals competing, with one coral encroaching on another, killing it around the area of contact. There are lots of brightly colored fish, with large schools of blue and yellow Creole wrasse accompanied by blue and brown chromis. Grazing parrotfish and big schools of doctorfish will pass you by on the reef, and you will see schools of smaller grunts and perhaps a large Spanish grunt. Look under corals and in holes for spotted drums.

PT. SALINE TO PRICKLY BAY

When sailing between St. George's and Point Saline, keep well clear of Long Point Shoal. This may be done by heading west from St. George's and continuing till you are on the line between Point Saline and the tanks at Grand Mal before heading for Point Saline. Reverse this procedure when you return.

Coast hoppers may prefer to explore this shore which has several pretty beaches. You must, however, be very careful of Long Point Shoal and only approach when there is good light and you can see the reefs. It is possible to eyeball your way inside Long Point Shoal, but don't cut too close to Long Point as there are some shoals that come out about 150 feet from shore. As you round Long Point heading west, you will see the beautiful Morne Rouge Bay, which, unfortunately, is only about four feet deep. You can sometimes find lunchtime anchorage just outside Morne Rouge Bay.

As you sail round Point Saline and head toward Glovers Island, Prickly Point will be the farthest headland that you see. As you get closer, Prickly Bay is easily identified by all the yachts inside and the handsome houses on the hill. There is plenty of water for most yachts to sail inside Glovers Island. There is one good anchorage just before Prickly Bay called True Blue.

Uli and Rebecca's Aquarium Beach Club [$B-D] is of interest in this area but it is hard to approach by boat, so think about visiting by taxi or rent-a-car. The setting is spectacular under some giant rocks that form the headland at the end of an idyllic deserted beach. The architecture has made the most of these features and the dining room is open to the view. The fresh barbecued seafood is excellent and this is a great place to come for a quiet romantic seafood lunch or dinner, or bring a group and make it what you will. The Aquarium Beach Club is popular on Sundays when people come to swim, and snorkel. Rebecca is an artist and if you ask she will show you some of her work. You get to it by driving past the

TRUE BLUE INN

P.O.Box 308, St. George's, Grenada, W.I
Phone:(473) 444-2000, Fax:(473) 444-1247, VHF:68

Major credit cards welcome

Life just gets better.

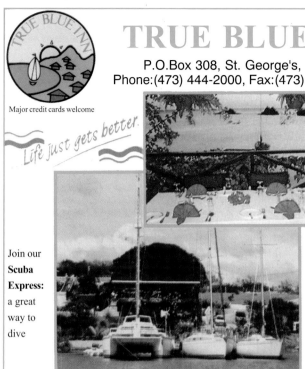

Join our **Scuba Express:** a great way to dive

Our **Indigo's Restaurant and Bar** offers first rate seafood lunches and dinners with a perfect sunset and view of the bay. The **Landing**, our dockside bar with lighter fare, is built on a deck over the water. Tie up to our dock and step ashore. True Blue Inn is ideal for a night ashore for yachtsmen. Calm anchorage, fresh water, 220/110-volt electricity, telephone and fax service. Close to shopping centers and the airport.

airport terminal, following the road towards Point Saline and looking for the sign on your right.

On a calm day you can anchor off The Beach House [$A-B] in the bay west of Morne Rouge Bay, and get a dinghy ashore to enjoy this restaurant which is managed by Stanley Minors. Specialties are seafood and steaks and they open 1100-1530 and 1800 till closing – last orders about 2200. Closed Mondays.

TRUE BLUE

True Blue is the bay just west of Prickly Bay. It is pretty, peaceful and conveniently placed as an overnight spot for charterers who want somewhere near their base for a first or last night.

There is a distinctive small island at the entrance. Enter in the middle of the bay between this island and True Blue Point. Go straight up into the bay and anchor inside or take one of Indigo's moorings. The water is about 25 feet deep at the entrance to the bay and there is 13 feet all the way up almost to the end of the bay. As with Prickly Bay, a surge can enter from time to time. If you find it rolly, use a stern anchor.

Ashore

Indigo's Restaurant [$B] and The landing [$C-D] are run by Trinidadians Tony and Gillian Potter. True to their nationality, they are excellent hosts and run a fine kitchen. This combined with the open waterfront location makes this establishment Grenada's best hideaway restaurant. They have a dock with 10 feet of water at the end and can provide water. Telephone and fax services are available. You are welcome to use one of the moorings they have put opposite their restaurant. Indigo's Restaurant is both intimate and airy and overlooks their unspoiled bay. The food is a delightful blend of West Indian and international dishes with offerings from the sea, including dolphin fish, lambi and lobster. The Landing Beach Bar and Grill is perched on a platform out over the water with a view along the shoreline to a tree which is usually full of roosting egrets. The Landing offers lighter meals and grilled foods. For those anchored elsewhere, a complimentary shuttle may be arranged by request. True Blue Inn behind the restaurant is under the same management and rooms are available.

Water sports

Indigo's is home to Scuba Express [VHF:16], a small, friendly shop run by Peter Lowe. It is the only dive shop in Grenada to run from a dock rather than a beach which makes for easy loading. They are happy to pick up yachtspeople in Prickly Bay by car or boat and from time to time they do all-day trips to Isle de Ronde. They generally dive twice a day, and can often modify times to suit your needs. They are one of the few dive shops to explore and use new dives on the south coast.

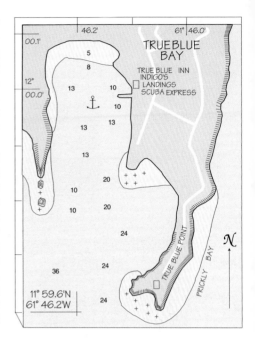

PRICKLY BAY

(Also known as L'Anse Aux Epines, pronounced "Lans O Peen")

Prickly Bay is delightful. The land is a tapestry of attractive gardens which form a background of green, speckled with bright flowers. Lovely homes and all kinds of roofs peek out over the vegetation. At the head of the bay is a palm fringed beach. You feel very much in the country here, with the sound of birds by day and tree frogs by night. Yet St. George's is only 15 minutes away by car and the airport and Grand Anse are even closer. The facilities of Spice Island Boatyard are close by, as are several hotels, restaurants and even a disco. It is an ideal place for those who want to have truck with civilization, yet feel apart from it.

Thomas, publisher, yacht restorer and currently realtor and builder, has built a prominent house at the end of L'Anse aux Epines Point, part of which looks just like a lighthouse. He shows a fixed red light as long as there is electricity. This makes Prickly Point very easy to recognize.

While Prickly Bay is easy to enter, don't get too careless. There is a reef marked by a nondescript buoy in the middle opposite the boatyard which is just deep enough to be hard to see. Reefs also extend nearly all the way up the eastern shore and one should give the True Blue headland reasonable clearance. Occasional southerly swells can make the bay uncomfortable, though a stern anchor will do much to restore a sense of calm.

Regulation

Prickly Bay is a port of entry with the customs at the boatyard. Anchoring is forbidden within 300 feet of the beach as it is reserved for swimmers.

Services

Spice Island Marine Boatyard [VHF:16] is a charming small marina where fresh green lawns are dotted with palms and almond trees. It has an informal atmosphere

PRICKLY BAY

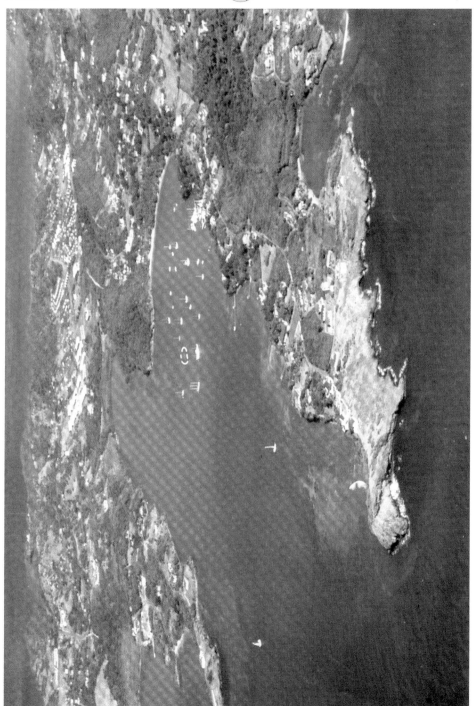

and docks for about 25 yachts. It is managed by Cyrus with the help of Annabelle. Showers, electricity (110/220, 50 cycle), fuel, water, ice, and cooking gas can be found here. There is a 35-ton travel lift and you can do your own work or hire their labor. Mechanical and electronic repairs can be arranged. There is a chandlery which offers many items duty free. Michael runs an efficient sail loft, and Spice Island are agents for Doyle Offshore Sails. Snagg will sell you fuel and help in any way he can. You can have your mail sent here and post outgoing letters. Buy telephone cards at the chandlery for the card phone. You will also find a fax and an uncertain bus service to town which leaves about 0930 in the morning. Confirm the time with the boatyard before you pack your shopping bag. Within the boatyard Shirley's Essentials [VHF:16] is a convenient mini-market and boutique. What Essentials lacks in size it makes up for in service (they are open every day including holidays) and Shirley will bring in anything you want that is not on the shelves. Or you can call on the radio for special orders or a full provisioning service. Spice Island Boatyard is the home of Seabreeze Yacht Charters, Tradewind Yachts and the Boatyard Restaurant (see below).

Henry Safari Tours [VHF: 68] has a sub-base in the boatyard with giant washing machines for on-the-spot laundry. Should it be closed, call him on the radio [VHF:68].

Jeff Fisher is an agent for Neil Pryde sails, made in Hong Kong. These sails are of good quality and reasonably priced. Jeff says he can arrange for new sails to reach Grenada within six weeks. He is often at the boatyard, so if you cannot get him on the telephone, ask around for him.

For mechanical problems talk to Ben. He is a good general mechanic who is reliable and reasonable.

Alternatively, contact McIntyre Bros. on the airport road. They have qualified diesel mechanics, and can fix most engines. They are also the sales and service agents for Yamaha outboards and can arrange sales to yachts at duty free prices. McIntyre also rents cars and will deliver to the boatyard.

Johnny Sails and Canvas [VHF: 16,66] is

a good sail loft down the Dusty Highway between the L'Anse Aux Epines stretch and True Blue. Johnny, a Grenadian, trained in Canada at Boston Sails for four years and for a time was charter manager at The Moorings. Johnny can repair old sails and make new ones. He carries and can bend stainless tubing so biminis are a breeze, as are awnings, covers, interior and exterior cushions. Johnny is also the man to see for rigging problems, he is agent for Profurl and stocks stainless rigging and Staylock fittings. Anything he does not have on hand he can quickly import.

In the same building you will currently find Cottle Boat Works, a full marine joinery and carpentry shop. Owner Jim Cottle has over 20 years experience in the business. He sailed to Grenada on his yacht J. Jeffrey. Jim can sometimes be found at The Moorings Rum Squall Bar after the sun has gone over the yard arm. Teak decks are one of Jim's specialties, along with wooden repairs and joinery work. He keeps a good supply of wood on hand. Many of his customers come from the large charter yachts. If business gets slack he builds handy cruising dinghies. Jim plans to move his shop to a new site near the Red Crab.

Anyone wishing to leave their yacht here and have someone reliable keep an eye on it should contact Selwyn Maxwell [VHF:68] or ask for Errol at Sea-Breeze Yacht Charters.

Tangey's Laundry and Dry Cleaning Service is reasonably priced. It is about a mile down the road, but if you call they will collect and deliver to Prickly Bay or St. George's.

Panabread at AJS Enterprises does an excellent job of sign painting, vinyl name transfers and number carving for registration for a very reasonable price.

Winston Julian, normally known as Sam or Tan Tan, has been around yachts for years and spent quite some sea time as a private yacht skipper. He now offers a maintenance service and will do good varnish or paint work. He generally works at Spice Island Marine or the Moorings Marina.

There are some excellent taxi drivers around. Selwyn Maxwell [VHF:68] spent

some years as a charter skipper so he is well acquainted with the whole yachting scene. He is charming, reliable and has a mini-van. He is willing to hike and can do the Seven Falls trip. Funseeker Tours [VHF:16], operated by Russ, Trevor and Janet, is another good operation. They offer all kinds of tours geared at showing how things are done in Grenada. They do hiking tours, offer a taxi service and rent good, but not brand new, jeeps.

It is also easy to call Boatyard Taxi [VHF:16]. This is a taxi drivers' association with a small office in Spice Island Marine. There is nearly always a good driver available.

Ashore

People needing to stock up on their wines will be delighted by North South Trading, a short walk from the boatyard, close by the Calabash. They stock wines from all over the world, Europe, Australia, South America, even South Africa. Manager Charles Hossle is a Grenadian citizen who has worked in the island for many years. You can sit down in a comfortable atmosphere and discuss your needs. This is a wholesale outfit, so wines are sold by the case, but they are often willing to mix cases for yachts and they can arrange duty-free delivery to your boat.

The Boatyard Grill and Tiki Bar [$B-C] is right in Spice Island Marine. It is a favorite yachty haunt, much improved by the new ownership of Myrna and Roger Spronk whose services include sending and receiving e-mail. Everyone gathers at happy hour (1730-1900) for cut-price drinks. Stay for dinner and enjoy first rate seafood, New York steaks, Mexican and Creole fare as you look out over the yachts and the harbor. Their suchimi will delight seafood lovers. Make a point of visiting on Fridays during the season when they have an excellent Grenadian steel band (it is popular, so book early if you plan on dinner). In season there is also live music on Wednesdays and Sundays. A pool and games room add to the atmosphere and a satellite TV is dusted off and turned on for important ball games or yachting events.

Three restaurants lie together just five minutes down the road. The gourmet will favor the Red Crab [$A-B]. Owner/Chef George Mueller is a German who speaks English with a Scottish accent. However,

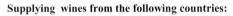

you will not be offered haggis. George is a professional chef with impressive credentials. He worked for many years with Hilton International as executive chef. At the Pan American Culinary Olympics he not only won gold, but was awarded honorary citizenship of New Orleans. In Trinidad he had his own TV program. The Red Crab offers such delights as "Crepe Voltare" – shrimp rolled in a thin French pancake capped with sauce chablis. Their rack of lamb and pepper steak will satisfy those who love good meat.

The Choo Light [$C-D] is a cruising yachty favorite run by the Choo family from Hong Kong. The prices are so reasonable you can eat here anytime you don't feel like cooking. The atmosphere is informal and the staff welcomes you warmly. They have a full range of dishes: seafood, vegetarian and meat which all come with plain rice. Their ginger shrimp and fish are excellent. They also offer a full takeout service.

Castaways [$B, closed Mondays] is the latest venture of Cleeve and Carol who have owned and run waterfront bars both in Grenada and Trinidad. The eating area is picturesque among flowers and the food

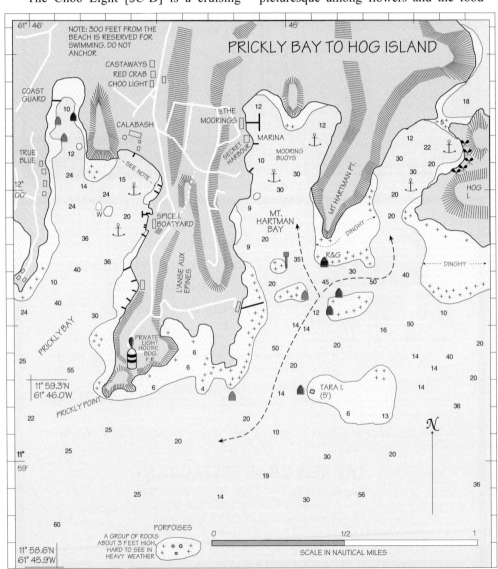

includes pub specials like steak and kidney pie. If you sit around the bar you will be joining and meeting a band of faithful adherents. There is a cavernous disco through a door at the back and this is put into action on Friday nights when they fire off with a live band at 2100. The disco is also open on Saturdays.

Other restaurants in the area include the Calabash [$A], where a pianist is frequently present, and there is a steel band on Friday nights and for Sunday barbecue lunch. A jazz band plays on Tuesday nights from 2000-2200.

If the tree frogs fail to lull you to sleep, you can hit the Sugar Mill Nightclub (Wednesday to Saturday) about a mile down the road by the roundabout. However, take care; it can be pretty rough.

You will find tennis courts at the hotels, a golf club in Golflands, ask directions.

THE SOUTH COAST BEYOND PRICKLY BAY

The south coast of Grenada offers beautiful, secluded and protected anchorages. A mass of reefs provides interesting if somewhat murky snorkeling. The area should be treated with caution and eyeball navigation is essential. On our charts we have marked as "too shallow" several areas of relatively shoal water (12-15 feet) which extend well offshore. In normal conditions you can sail over these, but when the going gets rough, seas start breaking on them and they are best avoided. The Porpoises, about half a mile off Prickly Point, awash and hard to spot, are as nasty a group of rocks as you could find to get wrecked on. Navigation into Mt. Hartman Bay has been greatly simplified by the new buoys put down and privately maintained by The Moorings. From Prickly Bay, pass about midway between Prickly Point and the Porpoises. Look out for Tara Island, a small coral island about five feet high. Leave Tara to starboard, passing half way between it and Prickly Point. From here follow the buoyage system into Mt. Hartman Bay.

MOUNT HARTMAN BAY

Mt. Hartman Bay is deep and well protected (see chart "Prickly Bay to Hog Island") with a modern marina, the luxury Secret Harbour Hotel and a charter base, all operated by The Moorings. This is a great area for dinghy sailing or sailboarding as there is protected water all the way to Calivigny Island. By land, it is a 20-minute walk from Prickly Bay.

Regulations

There is a customs officer stationed in Secret Harbour Marina and an immigration officer visits from time to time. You can clear in and out here, though in the absence of an immigration officer you may have to pop over to Prickly Bay to finish the paperwork.

Services

The Secret Harbour Marina [VHF:16/71] has 50 berths in the marina and 24 moorings off the hotel. Fuel, water, cube ice, showers, laundry, telephone, fax, and electricity (110/220V, 50 cycle) are included in the marina services. Duty free fuel is available in quantities of 300 gallons or more. There is a night watchman on the premises and long term storage can be arranged. Rock, also a taxi driver, is very reliable and willing

to look after yachts left in Secret Harbour Marina. If you need boat parts or equipment the Moorings are willing to sell you items from their spares stocks, and you can hire them to carry out any repair work you may need. The Moorings are happy to supply customers with a list of authorized casual laborers and varnishers who have been selected by their record. They ask that no other labor is brought into the marina without checking in the office first. Manager James Pascall will try to help in any way he can. You can use The Moorings as a mail drop: c/o The Moorings, Secret Harbour, P.O. Box 11, St. George's, Grenada, W.I.

Ashore

The Moorings Marina has managed to combine a low-key welcoming atmosphere for the cruising yachts alongside their up-market sophisticated charter fleet. Much of the activity revolves around the Rum Squall Bar, open daily from 1100-2200, with two happy hours – 1700-1800 and 2000-2100. You can fortify yourself for the next round with inexpensive bar snacks including baked potatoes. Wednesday night is steel band night, on Fridays a combo keeps things lively and on Sunday you can try the lunch barbecue. They have a mini-mart open from 0800-1600 daily, except Sundays and holidays, when it closes at 1500. A fresh vegetable van visits on Friday mornings. They have a book swap, and you can leave your laundry here for Henry Safari Tours' laundry service.

Secret Harbour [$A-B] is Grenada's most impressive hotel, with brick arches, carvings, heavy wooden ceilings and Italian tile floors. The rooms have four-poster beds and sunken tile bathtubs. The main building is up the hill, and you can take a drink in a secluded little alcove looking out across the bay. A visit will give rise to some "ohs" and "ahs" and impress your friends. It is a great setting for a special night out. An exotic menu caters to local and international taste. Lunch is served on the terrace with a wide choice which will satisfy the hungry or appeal to the weight conscious. They offer entertainment about twice a week. Call for details.

Buses run a couple days a week to town

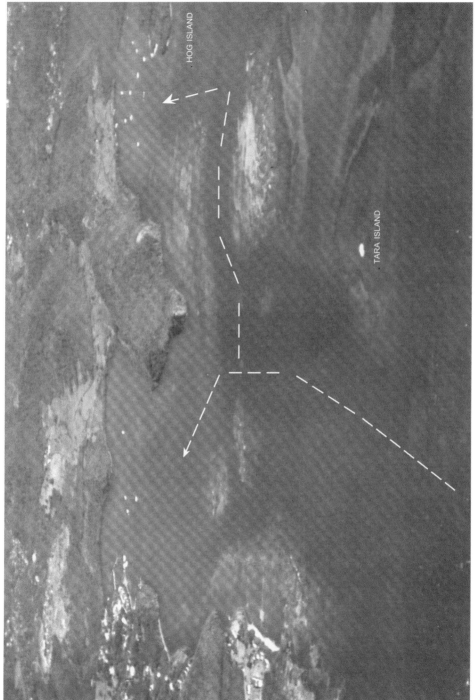

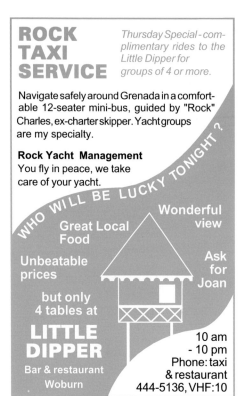
and there are some good reliable taxi drivers. Rochel (Rock) Charles [VHF:16] spent some years as a charter skipper so he is well acquainted with the whole yachting scene. He is charming, willing to hike and can do the Seven Falls trip. Keith Alexander of K&J is very pleasant and has a special interest in agriculture and herbs and their medicinal and other traditional uses. Leroy Taxi [VHF:16,68] also does driving and hiking tours, including Seven Falls, the Hot Springs and Fedon's Camp. Leroy has a particular interest in Grenada's history, so you can be sure of getting some good information.

Water sports

The Moorings have a very complete water sports section with rentals of kayaks, windsurfers and various small sailing boats ideal for exploring the south coast. Gerlinde and Peter Seupel run First Spice Divers, a new dive operation based at the Moorings. They are a Padi 5-star Golden Palm Resort and take people diving, do all kinds of courses and rent diving equipment to those going on charter.

HOG ISLAND

Behind Hog Island is a huge protected bay. When you anchor, there will be just a finger of horizon to remind you the sea is still there. Spiky mangrove roots stick upwards like bristles from a witches broom, their leaves bushing out in the form of a huge green Afro. A cow walks on the beach as though to say hello to the little blue heron who spends her day patrolling the shore, watching for little flurries of fish. The heron strides forward with huge but delicate steps, like a fastidious matron trying not to step on something unpleasant. Sometimes she grabs a wriggling silver catch, other times the fish churn the water into a frightening foaming hiss and she runs back to the safety of the sand.

Follow the buoys part way in from Tara Island and eyeball the rest. Anchor anywhere that takes your fancy. You can leave the same way or take the southern route into deep water. Pass close by the reef just south of Hog Island and head out on a bearing of 170° magnetic. Make sure the current is not setting you to the west. Hog's resident goats and cattle are owned and under no circumstances should they be hunted.

Ashore

You can buy vegetables from the farmers by the water tank on the mainland side or dinghy over to Woburn for ice or a bus to town. A large fancy resort is planned for this area – in the meantime, enjoy.

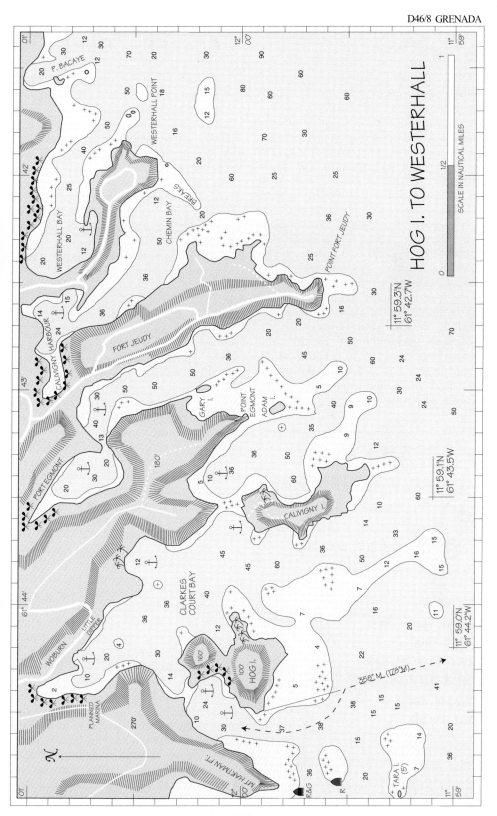

HOG I. TO WESTERHALL

SCALE IN NAUTICAL MILES

0   1/2   1

11° 59.3'N
61° 42.7'W

11° 59.1'N
61° 43.5'W

11° 59.0'N
61° 44.2'W

358° M. (178°M)

P. BACAYE

WESTERHALL POINT

WESTERHALL BAY

CHEMIN BAY

BREAKS

CALIVIGNY HARBOUR

POINT FORT JEUDY

FORT JEUDY

FORT EGMONT

GARY I.

POINT EGMONT

ADAM I.

KY

CALIVIGNY I.

WOBURN

LITTLE DIPPER

CLARKES COURT BAY

PLANNED MARINA

MT HARTMAN PT.

HOG I.

R&G   R

A TARA I. (5)

This large and sheltered bay offers enough anchoring possibilities to delight the confirmed gunkholer and you can explore and find your own spot. In the old days big sailing ships would anchor here to take on rum which was brought down the river to the head of the bay by small boat. Enter fairly close to Calivigny Island to avoid all the reefs and shoals that extend south of Hog Island. There are a few ruins on Calivigny Island. The most popular anchorage is just north of the island, off the beach. The bottom shelves steeply, so make sure you are well hooked.

Both Calivigny and Hog are dotted with hardy little frangipani trees. Their leaves fall in the dry season, leaving only sweet smelling, delicate white flowers.

There are tracks all over Calivigny and it is delightful to explore to the southern tip where rough waves try to pound down massive black rocks, and spume fills the air, forming little tide pools.

Ashore

You can anchor off Woburn or dinghy there and tie your dinghy to the village dock. Wander up to the road and turn left and you will find a little corner store called Nimrod and Sons Rum Shop. Nimrod is a part-time professional sign painter, but while there are plenty of other signs lying about, his own store is unposted. You can buy a little ice here along with bread, fresh chicken, lettuce, a few cans, beer and rum. This store is patronized by cruising people and there is a visitors' book to prove it – along with the Chin Up Tree Thinking Club. (Or should it be Drinking Club?) On the other side of the road a small bar serves fresh fish sandwiches and other goodies. The road here looks so rough and rural, with the odd chicken wandering over it, that it seems impossible to imagine a bus hurtling by, full of smiling faces and big shopping baskets, but it happens all the time. Whichever way it comes you can catch it to town. On the return run ask for a bus going to "Lower Woburn."

Woburn is also home to Little Dipper [$D], the cutest small restaurant in Grenada. Joan, who owns it with her husband Rock, the taxi driver, has cooked in several fancy restaurants and is now doing her own thing both well and very inexpensively. As you come onto the Woburn Road from the dinghy dock turn right and it is on your right-hand side just up the hill. Enjoy the sweeping view out over Hog Island as you taste fresh local seafood with a good variety of local vegetables. You won't find a better deal on lobster, fish or lambi. They open Monday to Saturday from 1000-2200. Rock will bring groups of four or more over from Prickly Bay or Secret Harbour on Thursdays at no charge.

Another good local restaurant here is called Island View. The upstairs balcony is open to the breeze and a view of the bay right out to Calivigny and Hog Islands. They specialize in seafood including lobster, lambi, shrimp and fish, which they cook in a variety of ways. Sometimes you can watch as the catch arrives on the dock outside.

Grencana are planning a 50-berth marina between Hog Island and Woburn. It is headed by Grenadian Bob Blanco. This will consist of floating docks, a restaurant and marina support services. Houses and

apartments are planned for a later stage. Progress so far has been minimal.

Boats left unattended have occasionally been robbed in the Calivigny/Woburn area.

EAST OF CALIVIGNY ISLAND

A little used anchorage offering good protection can be found to the east of Calivigny Island, between Calivigny Island and Point Egmont. It is easy to explore by dinghy from Clarkes Court Bay, but the entrance by yacht is somewhat tricky and should only be used by experienced reef navigators. You have to feel your way in

between the shoals that extend south from Adam Island and the shoals that extend east from Calivigny island. If you hit the channel right, there is at least 35 feet of water on your way in.

A palm backed beach heads the bay and the snorkeling off Adam Island and all the surrounding reefs is fair.

POINT FORT JEUDY. PORT EGMONT SHOWS, PARTLY HIDDEN.

PORT EGMONT

Port Egmont is a completely enclosed lagoon surrounded for the most part by mangroves. It is quite pretty and makes a first class hurricane hole. Enter the outer inlet fairly close to Fort Jeudy, keeping an eye out for the reefs which lie near the shore. Fort Jeudy is developed and there are several prosperous looking houses on the hill. Anchor anywhere in the inner harbor.

You can also anchor outside, off the little beach at the inner end of Fort Jeudy, but keep an eye out for the shoal off the northern end of the inlet.

The southwest shore of Port Egmont has recently been acquired for residential development. Anyone interested should contact Renwick and Thompson.

CALIVIGNY HARBOUR

Calivigny Harbour, sometimes called Old Harbour (not to be confused with Calivigny Island), is another enclosed harbor with a fine palm shaded beach. It makes an acceptable hurricane hole, though heavy rains can create currents which cause boats to lie sideways to the wind from time to time. The entrance to the outer harbor is between Fort Jeudy and Westerhall Point. You must have good enough visibility to see the reefs off Fort Jeudy. The shoals coming out from Westerhall Point are deeper and harder to see, though they often cause breaking seas. Stay with the devil you can see. Find the reef off Fort Jeudy and follow it into the outer harbor. This entrance can be hairy in heavy winds and large swells and I would only recommend it to sailors with a lot of experience in reef navigation in rough conditions. When passing into the inner harbor, favor the Fort Jeudy side as a shoal extends from the sand spit. Anchor anywhere in the inner harbor.

Aubrey's is a bar/restaurant shop right at the entrance to Westerhall Estate where you can also catch a bus to town. If you turn right at the main road and walk a while you come to a supermarket/bar. See also Petit Bacaye, which is a fair walk away.

WESTERHALL POINT

Westerhall Point is an attractive housing development with well tended grounds, easily seen by walking up from Calivigny Harbour. Westerhall Bay offers a protected anchorage if you tuck up in the southeast corner of the bay behind the mangroves. In rough conditions the entrance is tricky and the exit straight into wind and sea. I would suggest anchoring in Calivigny Harbour and walking over to take a look before you attempt this.

PETIT BACAYE

Petit Bacaye is an idyllic little bay full of flowers and palm trees with a little island you can swim out to. It has a micro hotel of the same name [$B] with a few thatch roofed rooms and small bar and restaurant. The hotel was built and is owned by Ivan Baker, a Grenadian builder who spends much time in the UK. His partner, Christine, is a professional musician who also writes books on Caribbean life, food and cooking. Take a book and swim things and laze away a day. Let them know you are coming as they will buy some fresh fish from the small boats that are based here. I do not recommend this bay as an overnight anchorage. Experienced navigators could feel their way in for lunch, otherwise visit by land from wherever you may be anchored along the south coast. It is on the main bus route heading eastward along the south coast.

ST. DAVID'S HARBOUR

St. David's Harbour lies 1.2 miles east of Westerhall point. Many years ago sailing ships would sail in here to load up on spices and produce bound for Europe. Although never the site of a town, it was an important harbor. It is deeply indented enough to be well protected and the reefs at the entrance seem to break up any swells when the trades turn south of east. St. David's Harbour is a lovely bay with a narrow sandy beach, palm

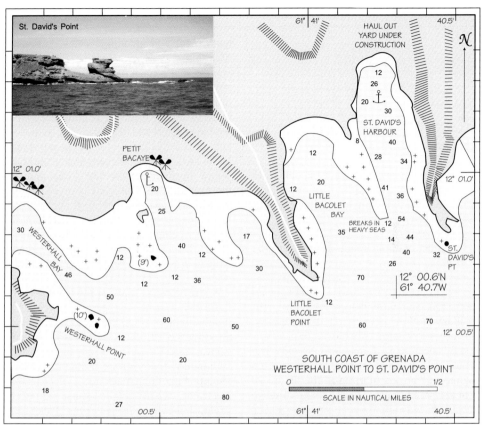

St. David's Point

HAUL OUT
YARD UNDER
CONSTRUCTION

61° 41'   40.5'

12

26

20

30

ST. DAVID'S
HARBOUR

8   40

PETIT
BACAYE

12° 01.0'

12   28   34

12° 01.0'

20

12   41   36

LITTLE
BACOLET
BAY

25   BREAKS IN 12   54

35 HEAVY SEAS   14   44

WESTERHALL BAY

30   17

40   12   40   32   ST. DAVID'S PT

12   (9')   30   26

46   12   36   70   12° 00.6'N 61° 40.7'W

50   LITTLE BACOLET POINT

(10')   60   12

WESTERHALL POINT   50   60   70

12   12° 00.5'

20   20

18   80

27   SOUTH COAST OF GRENADA
WESTERHALL POINT TO ST. DAVID'S POINT

00.5'   61° 41'   40.5'

0   1/2

SCALE IN NAUTICAL MILES

trees and jungly vegetation crowding down to the waterfront. At the moment it is completely deserted. Jason Fletcher has bought nine acres at the head of the bay and is planning to put in some docks and a haul-out and storage facility. The new company is called South Coast Holdings and they plan to order a 75-ton travel lift and alternative system for hauling catamarans. A restaurant/bar, chandlery and other support facilities will be included. This should be a very pleasant environment in which to haul, with good swimming and pleasant walks close

by. For a progress report talk to Jason at (473) 440-4961 or fax: (473) 440-8817.

A hotel is being built on the hill on the eastern side of the bay.

The entrance is easy if you approach in good light, provided you have correctly identified the bay. The middle reef is much harder to see than the one off St. David's Point, so favor the St. David's Point side of the channel, staying in the deep water. When the facility is completed, some navigational markers will probably be added.

319

Whether you want to go bareboat, fully crewed, one way, multihull or monohull, you can find something to suit in the Windwards. A list of charter companies is given in our directory.

For those without much experience, the easiest sail is from St. Vincent to Union or Grenada. Most charter companies will be happy to arrange one way charters for an extra fee, and most skippered yachts will pick up and drop off at ports of your choice for no extra charge.

The sail from St. Lucia to St. Vincent is a long hard day's sail. The return trip is often worse. If you are starting a charter in St. Lucia or Martinique, it makes a lot of sense to sail one way and finish in Union Island or Grenada. This is especially true if you only have a week or so.

Bareboating

I had the pleasure to run one of the first Caribbean bareboats — a little 31-footer called Rustler. When we said "bareboat," we meant it. Rustler came with a hand start diesel that would barely push her out of the anchorage, a small ice box full of ice and 40 gallons of water which were pumped up by

hand. Mechanical complexities consisted of a massive British marine toilet, with endless valves and pumps. This antiquity was almost impossible to clog, but at the same time, however much you worked on the packing gland, within a couple of days it tended to squirt you in the eye. The outboard was a close relative – all chrome and stainless with no cover. You had to wind the cord round the flywheel for every start and go through an elaborate system of switching valves and vents and bleeding for exactly the right number of seconds. The only thing to be said in its favor was that even the roughest of mechanics could do a major overhaul with a screwdriver, a big hammer and pair of pliers.

When I look at some of the bareboat ads these days it seems that people want to take it all with them when they get away from it all. Freezers, fridges, hair driers, microwave ovens, TV and video are all available.

One thing that years of sailing has taught me is that anything mechanical, electrical or electronic, when installed on a well-used yacht, will eventually go wrong. Bareboats are particularly susceptible because of all the different people using the gear. In practical terms this means that breakdowns are part and parcel of a modern sophisticated yacht, and not necessarily a reflection on the efficiency and ability of the charter company. The charter people realize this, they all help each other's yachts and do their best to have some kind of breakdown and back up service, despite the problems posed by the Windwards, which are well spread out. But It is important that bareboaters appreciate the essentially adventurous na-

ture of a bareboat holiday and not let it be ruined by a malfunctioning hair drier.

I still have the log book from Rustler and there is an entry I am specially fond of. At the beginning it is written in the hand of the group's self-appointed leader, Dr. Smith, who was not the least bit happy. Each day was another disaster. He couldn't make the outboard start, he couldn't find the boat hook, one of the navigation lights malfunctioned, he was "very disappointed" in the condition of the boat. Then the handwriting changed and the new entry said: "Dr. Smith had to return home for pressing personal reasons. Rustler is now a fine yacht, the weather is perfect, the sailing fantastic. We are having a marvelous time."

A good thing about chartering is that those occasions that are terrible at the time make great stories later. Not very long ago a bareboat was on a reef in the middle of nowhere and on the radio to the company's local representative who was trying to assess the situation.

"We are hard aground, the rudder is broken and we cannot steer," lamented the charterer.

"Ok. I've got that," said the rep. "Now tell me, are you taking on water?"

There was a pause of a few seconds, then back came a very definite answer, "Oh no, we did that yesterday in St. Vincent."

Crewed charters

Having spent years both running bareboats and skippering charters, I can attest without any question that skippered charters produce more glowing praise. A crewed charter is also a real holiday for everyone, with no galley and cleaning chores.

Many agents talk a lot about matching charterers to crew. In fact most charterers are happy, easy to please and good company, and good professional skippers can adapt themselves to all kinds of people. Cooks develop a sensitivity to produce the right kind of food.

It is worth keeping in mind that, although yacht crews really enjoy what they are doing and genuinely like their guests, there is some strain to always being on one's best behavior and there are a few things that can make life a lot easier. It is a huge help if all the charterers go ashore for a couple of hours each day, either to shop, walk, or go to the beach. At this point the crew can put on their favorite music full blast and clean the boat with much banging and gay abandon. The charterers will return to a clean boat and a much refreshed crew.

Cooks hate to be watched while they work. It makes them nervous and upsets their concentration. There is no way you would know this, because they are well trained to smile and answer a string of questions. Much better to leave them alone in the galley and give them the attention they deserve when they produce that final work of art.

The cook usually works much harder than the skipper so it is a great break if the guests decide to eat out, even if it is just a matter of having a sandwich ashore instead of returning for lunch. Unfairly, the best cooks get the fewest breaks, as no one can bear to miss a single meal.

It is a tradition that at some point the guests take their crew out for dinner. For the crew the break is more important than the dinner, and if you are on a budget, they don't mind if it is somewhere quite simple.

Tipping is a big item for most crews as this makes up a large part of their income. Unless otherwise stated, 10% of the total charter fee is the norm and an appropriate figure for good service. With the current costs of maintaining a yacht, owner-skippers are delighted to accept tips. However, if you feel embarrassed about tipping an owner, give it all to the cook, especially if the owner is a man and the cook is his wife or girl friend. If they have a good relationship she will split it with him and if they don't, she probably deserves all of it.

EXOTIC TROPICAL FOOD

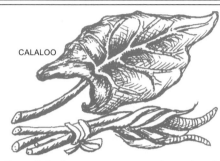

CALALOO

One of the best ways to experience local foods is to eat out. This way you don't have to slave over the stove and, best of all – no dishes to wash up. In this section we are going to introduce you to some wonderful local fruits and vegetables, as well as some ideas about sea food and locally obtainable meat. Those who cook for themselves will find recipes. For those who prefer to eat out, we will make some suggestions. But you cannot start without a drink in your hand, so why not make:

SKIPPER'S RUM PUNCH. Mix the juice from 3 limes, with ¼ cup of Grenadine syrup, 1 cup of brown rum and one liter of juice (orange, pineapple, or maybe local passion fruit). Serve with a lot of ice and liberally grate fresh nutmeg on top.

We are not going to be delving much into drinks, but for those who have a blender we should mention "smoothies." These are made by taking the flesh of any suitable local fruit (try mango, banana, guava, paw-paw, pineapple or soursop), adding a good slosh of rum, a good measure of ice, then blend. You can add lime or orange juice for flavor and you can try combinations. An evening of research should produce your favorite concoction and leave you so contented and full of fruit that you will probably be able to skip dinner.

We should also mention the Caribbean's very own natural soft drink: coconut water. If you are driving around the countryside, or even wandering around town, you will probably see a homemade barrow by the side of the road stocked high with green coconuts. These are "water-nuts" – young coconuts that have not yet developed a hard inner brown husk or firm white flesh, but are full of a delicious tasting liquid. The vendor will slice off the top of the nut for you. It is now ready for you to drink, straight from the shell. As with any other soft drink, coconut water works as a mixer and can be spiced with a squeeze of lime.

EATING OUT

Eating out, even in the most international of restaurants, will give you some idea of local food because they will almost certainly use the local vegetables, seafood and fruits. But it is also worth trying some of the inexpensive local restaurants. You can be offered amazing fare. My favorite is "Chair broiled SirLion steak." It would be a terrible mistake to eat steak in such a restaurant, though they often do excellent curries, creole style specialties and pepper pot. I usu-

ally go for lambi (conch). This is firm white flesh from a large sea shell and absolutely delicious. Soups are generally excellent in all restaurants, desserts better in the more expensive ones.

Those who go to the Windwards and eat hamburgers deserve what they get. Much better to eat as the locals do and have a "roti" which is the ideal lunch-time snack. A roti is curried meat or vegetables wrapped in a wheat flour tortilla-like shell. It usually comes in

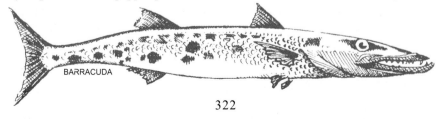

BARRACUDA

three flavors: beef, chicken and conch. The chicken roti is often made from "back and neck" and full of bones; locals love to chew on them, but others may not have acquired the taste. In the more expensive restaurants chicken rotis may be "boneless."

Mountain streams produce wonderful fresh water crayfish. These will occasionally appear in an inexpensive restaurant, but more often in a really good one. Nearly every menu lists lobster in season. Lobster is delicious, delicate and easy to ruin. Many restaurants parboil lobster, freeze it, then broil to serve. This all too often produces something dry, chewy and tasteless. To be on the safe side, only eat lobster at a restaurant where you can select your own alive and fresh from a pool.

Grenada is the world's second largest nutmeg producer. Buy some fresh nutmegs as soon as possible. You will find them in the market and in boutiques, not only in Grenada but also in the other Windwards. If possible buy them as a "kit" with a little grater. The outer hard dark brown husk must be removed before grating. Nutmeg is not only essential for rum punch but excellent for spicing up desserts, pancakes, french toast and some vegetables.

In the market and the supermarket you can buy something locally called saffron, which is in fact turmeric – a root which can be bought fresh or grated. It is good in curries and for coloring rice. True saffron (made from crocus) is expensive and only found in the bigger supermarkets.

If you are in St. Vincent and the Grenadines, look for their wonderful peanuts which are dry roasted and packed in recycled beer bottles. In Grenada you will find similarly packed local cashew nuts, also delicious.

Fabio's smoked fish, produced in Bequia, tastes wonderful and is available from Fabio in his house behind the Green Boley. You can also find it at Doris Freshfoods and some other foodstores.

Grenada's Spice Island Coffee is a superb, dark roast, freshly ground coffee.

TROPICAL VEGETABLES AND STAPLES

We do not mention the many vegetables, such as tomatoes, sweet pepper, cucumbers and beans familiar from home. Cooking suggestions and recipes assume basic cooking knowledge.

Coconuts are nutritious and cheap. Coconut milk (not to be confused with the water) is often used in Caribbean cooking, much as one would use cream where cows are more plentiful than palm trees.

To make coconut milk, you buy an older "flesh nut" – one of the brown ones you buy in the market. Grate the flesh, add any water from the nut, and add ordinary water till it is covered. Leave it for a few minutes, then squeeze the juices from the flesh into the water. Sieve, throw out the dry. The creamy liquid is coconut milk.

Breadfruit, plentiful and inexpensive year round, is a savior to the traveller on a budget. It is green, balloon sized, pocked

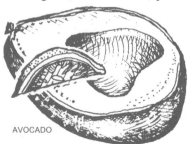

AVOCADO

and hard. Originally from the Pacific, it was imported here by Captain Bligh, but arrived late because of the mutiny. Watch it carefully or it will cause you grief, too. It remains nice and firm for a day or two, but when it decides to go soft and rotten, it can do so almost as quickly as Bligh could order a keel hauling. Best to cook it first and store after. Boil it (40 minutes in an ordinary pot or pressure cook for 10), or bake it in the oven (about 40 minutes). It will now store for some days in an ice box or fridge. Treat it like potato: mash it, cut slices off and fry it, use it in salad or stews. Mash it together with an egg and some cooked fish, season, then fry to make wonderful fish cakes. Buy one for a barbecue and cook it on the embers of a dying fire till you can slide a thin sliver of wood from opposite the stem up into the center. Cut it open and serve with salt, pepper and lashings of butter. Try making it like mashed potato, but mash with coconut milk instead of ordinary milk, cover with grated cheese and brown.

Calaloo, an elephant ear shaped green leaf, grows on wet ground such as the banks of small streams. Plentiful year round and inexpensive, available as bundles of leaves or in bags chopped and prepared for cooking. If you get the leaves with their stems it is necessary to remove the skin from the

stem and from the center vein. Always boil calaloo for 30 minutes. Eating it raw or undercooked has much the same effect on your mouth and throat as one imagines chewing on raw fiberglass would. The discomfort is temporary. Calaloo makes a wonderful soup and if you do not cook it for yourself, eat it in a restaurant at the first available opportunity. To use calaloo as a vegetable just boil it with a little salt for at least 30 minutes. Like spinach it boils down to very little.

Calaloo Soup, *½ lb chopped bacon, 1 pint of water, ¼ lb peeled shrimp, 2 bunches of prepared calaloo (about 1 lb.) 5 sliced okras, 1 sliced onion, ½ oz. butter, salt, pepper, garlic, thyme and hot sauce to taste.*

Fry the bacon and onion in butter, drain off excess fat. Add calaloo, okras, water and seasoning. Boil for 40 minutes, then add peeled shrimp. Cook a little longer and serve. For a thicker soup, blend, then serve.

Plantains. To the uninitiated these look just like bananas, but try putting one in a banana daiquairi and you will soon know the difference. Ask the market ladies to make sure you are getting what you want. Plantains have less sugar than bananas, and taste terrible raw, but when ripe, split down the middle and fried (a couple of minutes on each side) or baked whole (about half an hour), they are delicious. Plantains perfectly complement any kind of fish.

Pumpkin. The local pumpkin is green, streaked with white, and has an orange red pulp that is more akin to butternut squash than the Halloween pumpkin. It keeps a long time unopened and is both versatile and tasty. Remove the seeds before cooking. Boil or bake till soft and serve with butter, or boil and mash with seasoning (include a little nutmeg) and a little orange juice. If you want to make a meal out of a pumpkin, slice it longways down the middle and bake it. While it is cooking, fry onion, christophene, tomato and any left-overs you might have, melt in a quarter pound of cream cheese. and stuff the cooked pumpkin with this mixture. Pumpkin makes a delicious soup. Try it in a restaurant or make it yourself.

West Indian Pumpkin Soup. *1 small pumpkin, 1 chopped onion, 1 Tbs butter, 1 chicken stock cube, ½ pint fresh cream (or two cans of cream), ¼ glass of white wine, salt, pepper, grated nutmeg. Skin and seed the pumpkin and chop into small cubes. Lightly saute the onions in butter till cooked. Add pumpkin, stock cube and a minimum of water. Boil, using a lid. When soft, blend or sieve. Add the cream and wine, flavor with salt, pepper and nutmeg to taste. If too thick, thin with milk or water.*

Avocado. Local avocados are absolutely delicious, and reason enough to come down in the summer (available June to November, but peak season around August and September). Never store them with citrus. They can be eaten as they are, flavored with a little salt and lime juice, or stuffed with mayonnaise and shrimp. If they get a little over-ripe, mash them with lime, finely chopped onion,

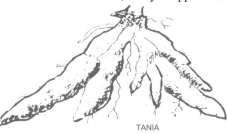

TANIA

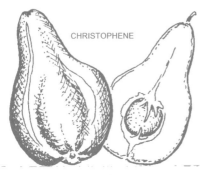

CHRISTOPHENE

garlic and seasoning. This makes an ideal dip to enjoy with your sunset drink.

Okra is a spear shaped green pod with slimy green seeds. Avoid the large ones which tend to be tough. They are somewhat slimy if boiled, much less so if sliced and fried. Good in soups.

Sweet potato and yam are sweet and tasty local root crops which take about 30 min-utes to cook. Nice with pork. Try mashing with a little orange juice.

Eddo, **tania & dasheen** are closely related brown hairy roots. They can be a bit dry, though mashing with oodles of butter and milk helps. Ask the ladies in the market for suggestions.

Christophene has ridges, is pear shaped, comes in either green or white and grows on a vine. Somewhat delicate in flavor, it makes an excellent vegetable dish or may be added to curries or stews. Peel it and remove the seed. This is best done under water, or with wet hands, otherwise it leaves a mess on your hands that gives the impression your skin is peeling off. It is excellent just boiled with salt, pepper and butter and is even better put in a white cheese sauce. It may also be used raw as a salad ingredient. The seed tastes good raw.

TROPICAL FRUITS

(These may be eaten raw or combined in a fruit salad)

Paw Paw (Papaya) is a lush tropical fruit that contains digestive enzymes, making it an ideal dessert. It starts green and is ready to eat when it turns yellow and becomes slightly soft. It is available year round but is delicate and hard to store. It must be eaten the same day it becomes ready. Slice like a melon and remove the seeds; add a squeeze of lime to flavor.

Citrus (oranges, grapefruit, tangerines, etc.) occur mainly in the winter. The quality varies from absolutely superb to dry and unusable. When you are shopping, buy one from the market lady to try. She will open it with a knife for you to taste. This is the only way to tell how good they are. Local oranges are usually green. Despite the outside color the inside is orange and ready to eat. Limes are generally available year round. They are essential for making rum punch and flavoring fish.

Guavas, available July to December, are green-yellow fruits a little bigger than golf balls. They may be eaten raw or are excellent stewed with sugar. They are used to make a sweet called "Guava cheese."

Cashew fruits (French Cashew, Plumrose), are pink fruits with white flesh, available June to August. Do not peel, but remove the stone. Delicious when chilled, good in fruit salad.

Pineapples. These are available most of

AUNT TiLLiE'S galley

ABOUT MANGOES...

IN GENERAL, THINK BIG ∞ THE TINY ONES TEND TO BE ALL STONE & STRINGS... THE LARGER "JULIE" OR "CEYLON" MANGOES, FOR EXAMPLE, ARE *LUSCIOUS*.

the year and very inexpensive in Martinique, but harder to come by and more costly elsewhere. Local pineapples can be absolutely delicious. Test for ripeness by pulling on a central leaf. If it pulls out easily it is ready.

Passion Fruit. Available May to November. A small yellow fruit with a slightly crinkly skin and very strong flavor. Makes an excellent drink and locally made passion fruit juice is usually available in the supermarkets.

Bananas Local bananas, which are naturally ripened, are delicious. As well as the "normal" banana, there are many other similar looking fruits, some of which are good eaten raw, and some of which need cooking. Consult your market lady. "Eating" bananas make excellent desserts; try the following:

Skipper's Banana Flambe (for 4). 4 bananas, ½ cup of dark rum, ½ cup fresh orange juice, 2 Tbs brown sugar, a slosh of white rum or vodka, seasoning of nutmeg, cinnamon and allspice.

Split the bananas in two and put in a frying pan, add the brown rum and orange juice, sprinkle on the sugar and spices, simmer for about 5 minutes. Pour on the white rum and ignite. (If vodka, you will have to warm gently in a pan first.)

Bananas Celeste, from Leyritz Plantation (for 4). 6 oz. cream cheese, ¼ cup brown sugar, ½ tsp cinnamon, 4 Tbs unsalted butter, ¼ cup of heavy cream (tinned OK), ¼ tsp cinnamon, 4 large bananas, peeled and split in half.

Mix the first 3 ingredients. Saute bananas in butter. Lay 4 halves in a buttered baking dish, spread with half of mix and repeat. Pour cream over and bake at 350° for 15 minutes. Sprinkle with remaining cinnamon and serve hot.

Soursop, available year round, is a knobbly green fruit which is ripe when it begins to go soft. It is messy to eat because of all the seeds. It can be blended with a little milk and ice to make an excellent drink.

Sapodilla is a small brown fruit, available in the winter. You need a very sweet tooth to enjoy these as they are, but they make an excellent addition to fruit salad.

Sorrel is a flower, available fresh around

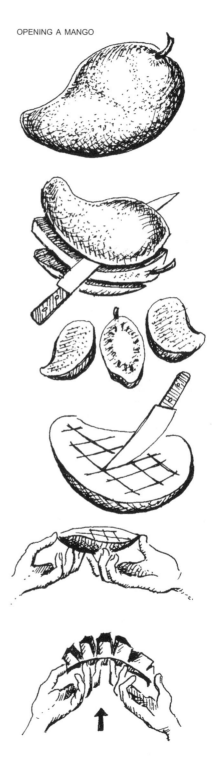

OPENING A MANGO

Christmas and dried the rest of the year. Pour boiling water on a couple of blossoms to make an excellent herb tea with a flavor not unlike "Red Zinger." Or boil a bunch of the flowers with water, adding a lot of sugar and spices. Serve as a delicious iced drink.

Mangos are delicious and available spring, summer and fall, but only rarely in the winter. They are harder to come by and more expensive in Martinique than the other Windwards. There are many different varieties. Grafted ones are bigger, better and have fewer strings.

FLYING FISH

SEAFOOD

Although seafood in the Windwards is excellent, it is not always in the local supermarket. The main towns of most islands have fish markets, and the one in St. George's, Grenada, is good, as is the fisherman's coop by Pointe Seraphine in St. Lucia. To get fish you often need to first catch your fisherman. In the Grenadines you can try asking fishermen in camps or those returning from fishing trips. Try asking any of the local people where, and at what time, the fishermen usually bring in their catch. On arrival they signal by blowing a conch horn. The fish is sold straight out of the boats when they arrive. Calliaqua in St. Vincent has a good little fish market, where the fish generally arrive at about 1600 hours. If you see fishermen untangling a bunch of

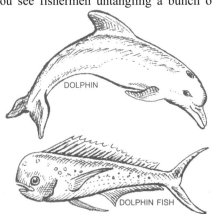

DOLPHIN

DOLPHIN FISH

large fish from a gill net, be cautious. Sometimes these nets have been left out for some days, and by the time the fish reach shore they are only good for salting. Among other fish you often find:

Barracuda — a delicious white-fleshed fish. It is probably best to find ones less than two feet long as ciguatera poisoning is possible, though very rare.

Dolphin – sometimes called "Dorado" or "Mahi Mahi." This pretty fish has white firm flesh, is excellent eating and is absolutely no relative of "Flipper."

Snapper – an excellent white-fleshed fish. The red snapper is most common.

Tuna – several varieties, dark fleshed, excellent flavor.

An easy way to cook most fish is to cut them into steaks or filets, season with salt, pepper and herbs and saute them in butter, or better still, barbecue them. When you get bored with that, try the following:

Baked Fish. One whole fish, scaled, finned and gutted, ½ lb butter, 1 onion, 1 tomato, juice of one lime, salt, pepper and garlic.

Make about 4 incisions, ¼ of an inch deep, across the fish on both sides. Take the butter and mash it with a fork into a bowl till soft, add the lime juice, salt, pepper and garlic to taste, rub this all over the fish and get plenty into the incisions and inside the fish. Place it on a sheet of tinfoil.

Thinly slice the tomatoes and onion. Stuff some inside the fish and the rest over the outside. Wrap in the tinfoil and bake in a medium oven for 20 to 40 minutes, depending on the size of fish.

Shirley's Fish Soup. *(Feeds 4, quantities very approximate). About a 4-lb fish, preferably a whole dolphin or barracuda, cut into pieces, 2 lbs potatoes, 1 lb tania, 2 green figs (cooking bananas) quartered, one big onion (chopped), 1/8 lb butter, juice of 3 limes, coconut milk made from 2 coconuts, salt, pepper, chives, thyme (ask for "Sive and thyme" in the market), 2/3 of a liter of water and up to a teaspoon of local hot sauce.*

Saute the onion and chives in the butter, along with the thyme and seasonings. Add the water and lime juice and simmer for about 20 minutes. Add the vegetables and coconut milk, boil till just cooked. Cut up the fish and add, cooking for a few minutes. Serve. To West Indians the head (eyes and all) goes in and this is the best part. But if you don't fancy it, leave it out. If making coconut milk is too much trouble, try adding cream at the last minute instead.

Seviche. *1 lb very fresh fish, 1 finely chopped onion, 1 chopped tomato, ¼ tsp of local hot sauce, lime juice, salt and pepper.*

Filet the fish and cut into small pieces. Put in a non-metallic container with the onion and tomato. Season with salt and pepper. Cover with lime juice into which the hot sauce has been mixed. Let stand in the fridge or ice box overnight, drain before serving.

Conch or Lambi. This mollusk lives in a huge spiral shell lined with a beautiful pink. The whole animal is called a conch, and "lambi" refers to the meat. If you are buying from a fisherman, get him to remove the shell. Then hold the conch up by the claw, remove all the thin skin and slime that hangs from the bottom, remove the eyes and mouth, cut open the gut and clean and remove the tough brown skin. Lastly, remove the claw. You should be left with a slab of white to slightly pink meat. Chop this up and tenderize by hammering. If you want to be sure your conch is going to be tender, cut it up and pressure cook it for an hour. One of the best ways to cook conch is in a curry. (With modifications this same recipe can be used for fish, chicken or peeled shrimp.)

Curry. Curries are very popular in the Windwards, due to the East Indian influence. Although simple, a curry can be made into a feast if you serve it with an array of garnishes in small bowls, to be sprinkled on top, or eaten beside the curry. Side dish suggestions are as follows: grated coconut, crushed peanuts, chutney, chopped onion, yoghurt, chopped mango, chopped tomato, raisins soaked in rum (drain before serving) and chopped cucumber soaked in vinegar mixed with pieces of fresh ginger (remove ginger and drain before serving). Curry should be served with a bowl of steaming hot rice.

Kristina's Curried Conch.

1 cleaned and chopped conch per person, 1 chopped onion, 2 crushed cloves of garlic, 1 tsp fresh grated ginger, 1 cup of coconut milk or coconut water, 1 can of drained tomatoes or 2 peeled fresh tomatoes, 1 plantain, 1 tsp thyme, 1 tsp turmeric, curry powder.

Saute the onions and garlic till tender and translucent. Add the herbs and spices. Start with 1 Tbs of curry powder and work up from there as strength can vary enormously. Blend them in. Add the rest of the ingredients and let them simmer for about 20 minutes.

This same recipe will work for meat, chicken, fish or shrimp. In the latter tow cases, cook the other ingredients first and only add the fish or shrimp at the last minute. If you wish to fill out the curry somewhat, add the chopped flesh from two christophenes. They will take about 20 minutes to cook.

Lobster (langouste). The local lobster is

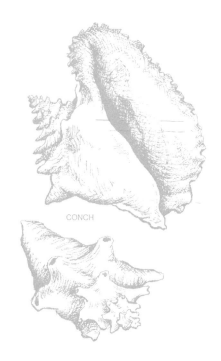

CONCH

lid, bring them up to pressure and cook for about 2 minutes.

Put the cooked lobster face up on a cutting board and, with a very sharp, tough knife, split it in two from head to tail. Serve with hot garlic-lime butter. Keep the shells and any odd bits; with these you can make an absolutely delicious bisque (you can also use shrimp heads and/or skins). This way you get twice the value for money out of your lobster (or shrimp).

Seafood Bisque. (Serves 4 as a first course or lunch)

Shells from 3 lbs of lobster (or the heads from 2 lbs shrimp), 9 Tbs of butter, 1 liter of water, ½ cup of white wine, 2 Tbs of tomato puree.

1 chopped onion, 2 cloves of garlic, 1 bay leaf, 2 Tbs of flour, 1 egg yolk, ½ cup of cream.

Saute the onions, garlic and lobster shells in 6 Tbs butter for about 15 minutes. Add water, wine, tomato puree and bay leaf. Bring to the boil and simmer for 20 minutes. Strain. Mix the rest of the butter with 3 Tbs flour, add to the stock and simmer for another 5 minutes, stirring constantly. Adjust seasoning (salt, pepper). Mix egg yolk with cream in a small bowl. Pour a small amount of soup in it and stir. Then pour it back into the soup very slowly, beating constantly. Taste again and serve immediately. Garnish with left over bits of lobster or shrimp (if any). Reheat very gently as boiling will ruin it. Serve with grated cheese if you wish.

a spiny variety without claws. It is illegal to buy lobsters with eggs (they sit in orange clusters under the tail), or during the summer when they are out of season, or those less than 9" long. Fines of $5000 are not unknown for first offenders.

Lobsters are best boiled alive. Submerge them rapidly in boiling water and they will quickly die. Tie up the legs and tail with string so you don't get splashed with boiling water. Boiling time is 10 to 20 minutes depending on size. We like to buy smaller ones (about 2 lbs) and put them with a pint of cold water in the pressure cooker. Close the

MEAT

The French are very particular about their meat, and you can get first class meats of all sorts in Martinique, both in the supermarkets and at the butcher's. They tend to sell it fresh rather than frozen, so it is easier to assess what you are getting. In the English-speaking Windwards the meat in supermarkets varies. The better supermarkets with delicatessen sections can have good meat. In St. Lucia there are several butchers who bring in top quality meat. For those on a

budget, kidney and liver are excellent buys, chicken livers are very reasonably priced. Pork tenderloins are less expensive than beef, just as delicious and very tender. In Grenada you can often find them in the supermarket. The big standby is chicken. Chicken is imported to all the islands in 5 lb boxes. You can get everything from breasts to backs and necks.

Barbecued Chicken (for 6). One 5-lb box of chicken parts (whichever kind you like or can afford), ½ lb peanut butter, ½ lb (local) marmalade, ¼ cup oil, ¼ cup orange juice, 3 oz. mustard, 1 tsp curry powder, salt and pepper.

Mix all the ingredients together well except the chicken, and put in a baking pan. Marinate the chicken in the mixture, then bake in the marinade for about 35 minutes in a medium oven. Remove and finish cooking the chicken on the barbecue, basting well with the marinade.

St. Lucian Pork Tenderloin (Ivan Howell). 4 lb pork loin, 1 oz chopped onion, 1 chopped sprig thyme, 3 crushed cloves garlic, ½ tsp salt, 1 oz chopped celery, lime juice, 2 whole cloves, dash of Worcestershire, 1½ lbs chicken, 1½ lb pork sausage, sprig of parsley.

Clean, butterfly and flatten pork. Season with next 8 ingredients. Chop sausage and boned chicken, spread over pork. Roll, wrap in foil, and bake for 45 minutes or until done. Remove roll and place pan over flame, add 1½ cups water, 1 oz more

chopped onion, salt and pepper. Cook 10 minutes. Mix 1 Tbs cornstarch in a little cold water, add to pan and allow to thicken slightly. Serve slices of pork roll in a pool of natural gravy.

PAW PAW

Your food notes

GENERAL INDEX

Acrylic Sheet 127
Admiralty Bay 188-206
Anse a L'Ane 81-82
Anse Chastanet 140
Anse Cochon 137
Anse Mitan 74-80
Anse Noir 82-83

Baggage (luggage) 18
Baie des Anglais 98-99
Bequia 184-214
Blue Lagoon 170, 179-180
Boat vendors 25-28, 138-140, 160-161, 162, 266
Britannia Bay 215-220
Bugs 20-22
Buoyage (beacons) 38

Calivigny Harbour 318
Calivigny Island 316, 317
Canouan 221-224
Caribs 12-14, 54, 71, 156, 163, 259
Carriacou 254-272
Case Pilote 58-59
Castries 126-131
Chartering 320-321
Charts 36-38
Chatham Bay 246
Chateaubelair 158-160
Clarkes Court Bay 316-318
Clifton 241-246
Cohe de Lamentin 72
Corbay 221, 224
Cul de Sac Marin see Marin
Cumberland Bay 160-161
Currency (change) 18
Currents 36
Customs see also regulations 40

Dangers 22-24
Diving & snorkeling 44-47
  - Bequia 209-211, 214
  - Canouan 224
  - Carriacou 262-263, 264, 270
  - Grenada 280, 297-299, 302, 314
  - Martinique 57, 80, 82, 83, 84, 85, 88, 97
  - Mustique 220
  - PSV 250
  - Petite Martinique 253
  - Southern Grenadines 228
  - St. Lucia 124-125, 136, 140-141, 142, 147
  - St. Vincent 159-160, 163, 165, 176-179
  - Tobago Cays 238
Dogs 40
Dragon's Bay 280
Drugs 19

Entertainment 30-31
Environment 40-44

Ferry 73, 74-75
Fish poisoning 29
Fishing 29
Flags 43
Food 322-331
Fort de France 59-71
Friendship Bay, Bequia 212-214
Friendship Bay, Canouan 224
Frigate Island 246

Garbage 42-43
Grand Anse 292-299
Grand Anse D'Arlet 83-84
Grand Mal 280
Green Flash 30
Greetings 19
Grenada 273-319
GPS 38-39

Halifax Harbour 278
Happy Hill 278-280
Hillsborough 259-263
Hog Island 314-316
Holidays 31
  - Martinique 51
  - Grenada & Carriacou 273
  - St. Lucia 103
  - St. Vincent & the Grenadines 155
Hummingbird Anchorage 141-142
Hurricanes 34-36

Immigration see also regulations 40

Jet ski 19, 155 185

Kick-em Jenny 272
Kingstown 166-170

L'Anse Aux Epines (see Prickly Bay)
L'Esterre Bay 263-264
Lobster
  -cooking 329-330
  -regulations 103, 155, 273
Lower Bay, Bequia 208-209

Mail drop see directory
Malgre Tout 145-146
Manchineel 22
Marigot Bay 132-136
Marin 88-97
Market (local) 19, 68-70, 126-127, 167, 198, 245, 260, 288

Martinique 48-99
Mayreau 231-236
Meat 330-331
Medical care 30
Mileage Table 41
Moonhole 211-212
Mount Hartman Bay 311-314
Museum 71, 158, 202, 260, 289
Mustique 215-220

Ottley Hall 166

Palm Island 240
Passages
 -Carriacou to Grenada 272
 -Martinique to St. lucia 99
 -Northern Grenadines 180-183
 -Southern Grenadines 225-227
 -St. Lucia to St. Vincent 151
Petit Anse D'Arlet 85
Petit Bacaye 318
Petit Byahaut 164-165
Petit Martinique 248, 250-253
Petit Nevis 212-214
Petit St. Vincent 248-250
Pigeon Island, Bequia 183, 211
Pigeon Island, St. Lucia 106
Photography 29
Pitons, The 138-147
Port Egmont 317
Prickly Bay 300, 302-311

Radio (AM, SSB FM) 35
Rameau Bay 221
Regatta 31, 71, 203, 262, 282
Regulations
 - Bequia 185
 - Carriacou 257
 - Grenada & Carriacou 273
 - Martinique 51
 - Mustique 215
 - St. Lucia 103
 - St. Vincent & the Grenadines 155
Rivière Salée 71-72
Rodney Bay 106-125

Saline Bay 232-236
Salt Whistle Bay 231-232
Sandy Island 263-264
Sisters, Carriacou 270
Sisters, Isle de Ronde 272
Snorkeling see diving & snorkeling
Soufriere 138-147
South Glossy Bay 224
Spearfishing (see also regulations) 42, 103, 155
 273
Special events (Entertainment) 30
St. Anne 85-88
St. David's Harbour 318-319

St. George's 280-291
St. Lucia 100-150
St. Pierre 54-57
St. Vincent 151-183
Star charts 10-11
Suntan 19

Telephones
 - Bequia 185
 - Carriacou 257
 - Grenada & Carriacou 273
 - Martinique 51
 - Mustique 215
 - St. Lucia 103
 - St. Vincent & the Grenadines 155
Thieves 28-29
Tides 36
Tobago Cays 237-239
Transport 19-20
 - Bequia 185
 - Carriacou 257
 - Grenada & Carriacou 273
 - Martinique 51
 - Mustique 215
 - St. Lucia 103
 - St. Vincent & the Grenadines 155
Trois Ilets 72-74
Trou au Diable 141
Trou Etienne 74
Troumaker Bay 160
True Blue 300, 301-302
Tyrrel Bay 265-271

Union Island 241-253

Vegetables 324-326
Vieux Fort 148-150
Vigie 126-131
Volcanos 54-55, 145, 156-158
 -underwater 272

Wallilabou 162-163
Weather 34-36
Westerhall Point 318
Windjammer Landings 125
Woburn 316

Young Island Cut 170-179

For information on all manner of
services and products available
in the islands, see our directory
Supplied with the initial printing of
this edition and some are distributed
free in the islands

ADVERTISERS INDEX

Ades Dream, 260
Admac, 109
Anchorage Yacht Club, 244
Antilles Marine Services, 95
Aquarium, 300
Aquarius Water Sports, 134

B&C Fuels, 250
Banana Patch Studio, 200
Bang, 146
Beach Front Bar, 158
Beachside Terrace, 295
Ben Taxi Service, 141
Bequia Bookshop, 193
Bequia Canvas, 195
Bequia Sweet, 203
Berend Botje Yachting, 235
Bluewater Books, 37
Bo'sun's Locker, 197
Boatphone, 23
Boatyard Grill and restaurant, 309
Boggles Round House, 260
Bougainvilla, 243
Bryden Liquor Store Supplies, 118
Budget Marine, 27

Callaloo by the Sea, 261
Camilla's Restaurant & Guest House, 145
Canboulay, 297
Capones, 120
Captain Gourmet,243
Caribbean Chateaux Ltd, 118
Carriacou Silver Diving, 264
Carriacou Yacht Club, 268
Casablanca, 294
Cassada Bay, 266
Cay Electronics, 111
CBS, 95
Centre de Carenage, 65
Chalmessin, 68
Charthouse, 123
Chateau Des Fleurs, 119
Chateau Mygo, 136
Chez Fanny, 80
Chez Gaby, 84
Chez Norris, 178
Choo Light, 309
Claude Victorine, 208
Coal Pot (The), 131
Coconut Beach, 295
Cocos Place, 207
Cool Breeze Car Rentals, 140
Coopemar, 67
Cottle Boat Works, 306
Cotton house, 217
Cox Marine, 112
Crab hole, 202
Cruising Guide Publications 247
CTL Rent a Car, 116

Daffocil Marine, 191
Dave's Gas Equipment Services, 289
Dennis's Hideaway, 234
Destination St. Lucia, 114
Diginav, 95
Dive Bequia, IFC-1, 210
Dive Grenada, 299
Dive St. Vincent,172
Doris fresh Foods, 198
Doyle Sails, OBC

Eagle Air Services, 125
Ed Hamilton, 31
ETPI, 71

Firefly, 220
Foodland, 283
Frangipani, 203
French Restaurant, 175

Friendship Bay Hotel, 213
Funseekers, 277

Gideon Taxi, 195
Gingerbread, 184
Gramma's Bakery, 261
Grand Anse Aquatics, 299
Grenada bank of Commerce, 298
Grenada Yacht Club, 272
Grenadines Dive, 238
GYE, 192

Handy Andy Rentals, 193
Hazeco Tours, 178
Helmsman, 200
Henry Safari Tours, 276
Home Services, 111
Hummingbird Resort, 143

Imagine, 305
Inboard Diesel Services, 58
Incidence Voiles, Marin, 75, 94
Indigo, 97
International Diesel and Marine, 129
Island Paradise, 234
Island View, 316

J&C Restaurant, 234
Jalousie Hilton Resort and Spa, 147
Joe's Steak House, 297
Johnny Sails and Canvas, 306
Johnsons Hardware, 112
Jonas Browne and Hubbard, 294
JQ's Supermarkets, 131

K & J Taxi Tours, 312
Key Largo, 119
KP Marine, 169

La Boulangerie, 292
La Creole, 120
Ladera Resort, 144
Le Marche de France, 117
Le Petit Conch Shell, 266
Le Ponton, 78
Le Poivre et Sel, 269
Le Ship, 94
Leroy Tropical Tours, 312
Lighthouse, 196
Linky Taxi Service, 263
Local Color, 201
Lully's Tackle Shop, 199

Mac's Pizzeria, 205
Madia Boat, 65
Maison Salaison, 131
Mango Bay, 96
Marigot Beach Club, 132
Marin Yacht Harbour, 90-91
Matheson Enterprises/After Hours, 263 & 268
Max Marine, 196
McIntyre Bros, 291
Mecanique Plaisance, 50
Melinda, 201
Mike's Frozen Foods, 150
Multicap Caraibes, 66

NationaL Commercial Bank of Grenada, 296
Nautical Publications, 38
Nichols Marine, 169
Noah's Arcade, 183
Non-Stop Services, 77
North South Trading (Grenada) Ltd, 308
Nutmeg, 288

Outfitters, 281

Palm Beach,252
Petit Byahaut, 165
Petit Jardin, 206
Pieces of Eight, 115
Pigeon Island Gift Shop, 109
Pirate's Cove Rest & Bar, 289
Plus Nautique, 63
Polymar, 65
Portofino, 288
Power Boats, 21
PSV Resort, 249

Razmataz, 123
Red Crab, 309
Renwick and Thompson, 287
Righteous & the Youths, 235
Rock Taxi, 314
Rodney Bay Marina, 102
Rondey Bay Ship Services, 109
Rosemond Trench Divers, 134
Royal Bank of Canada, 113
Rudolfs, 287

S & W, 190
Sail Loft at Rodney Bay Marina, 111
Saltwhistle Bay, 232
Sam Taxi Service, 170
Sandisland Cafe, 259
Sea Services, 62
Selwyn Maxwell, 284, 304
Servi Marine, 64
Silver Beach Resort, 259
Solana's, 188
Spice Island Marine, 307
Spinnakers Beach Bar, 123
Spring on Bequia, 207
St. Lucia Golf and Country Club, 125
St. Lucia Tourist board, 110
Subchandlers, 50
Sun Yacht Charters, 229
Sunshine Bookstore, 117
Sunsports, 209
Supermarche Annette, 96
Surfside,176
SVG General Services, 169
SVGair/Barefoot, 154

The Bistro, 121
The Bread Basket, 113
The Complete Dive Guide, 45
The Great House, 124
The Moorings, 279
The Studio, 269
Tikal, 283
Tim Wright, 181
Timberhouse, 205
Tool Meister, 267
Traffic Light Restaurant & Bar, 287
Travel World, 116
Treasure, 218
Tropical Shipping, 26
Tropicana, 291
True Blue Inn, 301
Turbulence Sails, 184
Twilight, 268

Valmont & Co., 130
Vena Bullen & Son, 262
Village Harbour Marina, 25
Voilerie Helenon, 61

Wallace & co, 196
Wallilabou, 162
Whaleboner, 204
Wilkie's Restaurant,172
WIND, 70

Yannis, 233

334

CRUISING GUIDE PUBLICATIONS

ORDER FORM

To order, please fill out coupon on back and send check or money order to:
Cruising Guide Publications, P.O. Box 1017, Dunedin, Florida 34697-1017.
For credit card orders only, call 1-800-330-9542 • 727-733-5322
E-mail: cgp@earthlink.net

❑ $19.95   CRUISING GUIDE TO THE VIRGIN ISLANDS
(9th Edition) by Simon and Nancy Scott. Expanded to include Spanish Virgin Islands.

❑ $24.95   VIRGIN ANCHORAGES (New color aerial photos and color graphics)

❑ $24.95   CRUISING GUIDE TO THE LEEWARD ISLANDS — *With GPS
Coordinates* (5th Edition) by Chris Doyle.

❑ $19.95   SAILOR'S GUIDE TO THE WINDWARD ISLANDS
(9th Edition) by Chris Doyle.

❑ $14.95   CRUISING GUIDE TO TRINIDAD AND TOBAGO (2nd Edition) by
Chris Doyle.

❑ $26.95   CRUISING GUIDE TO VENEZUELA & BONAIRE (2nd Edition) by Chris Doyle.
Provides Anchorage information GPS and full color charts.

❑ $24.95   CRUISING GUIDE TO CUBA — *With GPS Coordinates and Charts*
(2nd Edition) by Simon Charles.

❑ $24.95   GENTLEMAN'S GUIDE TO PASSAGES SOUTH — *6th Edition With GPS
Coordinates* — The "Thornless Path to Windward," by Bruce Van Sant.

❑ $15.95   CRUISING GUIDE TO THE SEA OF CORTEZ (From Mulege to La Paz)

❑ $19.95   CRUISING GUIDE TO THE FLORIDA KEYS by Capt. Frank Papy.

❑ $ 9.95   1999 CRUISING GUIDE TO ABACO BAHAMAS by Steve Dodge. (8½" x 11")
Containing charts from Walker's Cay south to Little Harbour. Includes GPS coordinates.

❑ $12.00   CRUISING MANUAL TO THE KINGDOM OF TONGA IN THE VAVA'U
GROUP (Chart included) The Moorings.

❑ $13.50   AT ANY COST: LOVE, LIFE & DEATH AT SEA (Hardcover)
By Peter Tangvald; thrilling autobiography of a cruising sailor whose primary home for 50 years was
a 49' handcrafted wooden sailboat.

❑ $12.50   SOAP OPERAS OF THE SKY by Jeannie Kuich. A whimisical look at the soap opera-like
tales surrounding the tropical constellations.

❑ $10.00   HOME IS WHERE THE BOAT IS by Emy Thomas. A glimpse into the
cruising way of life.

❑ $14.95   THE NATURE OF THE ISLANDS: PLANTS & ANIMALS OF THE
EASTERN CARIBBEAN by Chris Doyle and Virginia Barlow.

❑ $12.95   CARIBBEAN by Margaret Zellers with breathtaking photos by Bob Krist; —
perfect tropical souvenir or gift.

❑ $29.95   YACHTSMAN'S GUIDE TO JAMAICA by John Lethbridge. Only complete guide to
cruising Jamaica including 50 ports, harbours and anchorages of this island.

❑ $12.95   THE GUIDES TO DIVING AND SNORKELING IN THE BRITISH VIRGIN
ISLANDS or USVI. (Two separate books — $12.95 Each)

❑ $14.95   THE LEEWARDS, PUERTO RICO, VIRGIN ISLANDS, CHESAPEAKE
BAY, INTRACOASTAL WATERWAY, RESTAURANT GUIDES & RECIPE
BOOKS (Five separate books — $14.95 Each.)

❑ $35.00   SOUTHERN SHORES (2nd Edition, 9" x 12", 256 pp) by Roger Bansemer. Florida artist,
Bansemer has captured on canvas the rich texture of the south from the shoreline to the native
wildlife along Florida's coast, north to Savannah & Charleston with a stop in the Virgin Islands.

335

☐ $14.95 SHIP TO SHORE I (A collection of 680 recipes & cooking tips from Caribbean charter yacht chefs) compiled by Capt. Jan Robinson.

☐ $14.95 SLIM TO SHORE (more recipes from Capt. Jan Robinson).

☐ $14.95 SEA TO SHORE (280 seafood recipes and cooking hints.)

☐ $14.95 SWEET TO SHORE (Robinson's ultimate dessert collection).

☐ $10.95 SIP TO SHORE (Robinson's cocktails and hors d'oeuvres collection).

☐ $ 7.95 **MAVERICK SEA FARE: A CARIBBEAN COOK BOOK** by Dee Carstarphen (Simple shipboard recipes you can prepare at home).

☐ $12.00 **CALENDAR:** THE BRITISH VIRGIN ISLANDS. Photography by Dougal Thornton (New year available in October of preceding year).

☐ $29.95 **VIDEO** (VHS), or (PAL Add $10): SAILING THE WINDWARD ISLANDS by Chris Doyle & Jeff Fisher.

☐ $19.95 **VIDEO** (VHS): ISLAND PORTRAITS: ST. VINCENT & THE GRENADINES by Chris Doyle & Jeff Fisher.

☐ $19.95 **VIDEO** (VHS): CRUISING TRINIDAD & TOBAGO by Chris Doyle.

☐ $29.95 **VIDEO** (VHS), or (PAL Add $10): CRUISING THE NORTHERN LEEWARDS by Chris Doyle.

WATERPROOF CHARTS

☐ $18.95 U.S. & BRITISH VIRGIN ISLANDS

☐ $18.95 BRITISH VIRGIN ISLANDS

☐ $18.95 UPPER FLORIDA KEYS

☐ $18.95 LOWER FLORIDA KEYS

☐ $ 8.50 CLEAR, WATERPROOF, REUSABLE PLASTIC STORAGE TUBE

—— *CALL FOR A COMPLETE CATALOG* ——

ORDER FORM **VISA** DISCOVER MasterCard. *(For orders only, call 1-800-330-9542 or 727-733-5322).*

To order, check the appropriate box(es), fill out coupon and send check or money order to: Cruising Guide Publications, P.O. Box 1017, Dunedin, FL 34697-1017. Florida residents add 7% sales tax. See schedule for shipping charges. All books are shipped via UPS within 10 days of receipt of order.

SHIPPING & HANDLING:			
	U.S./Terr.	Canada	Other
Up to $15.00	$ 3.50	$ 5.50	$ 7.00
15.01-30.00	4.95	6.95	9.90
30.01-40.00	6.75	8.75	13.50
40.01-50.00	7.75	9.75	15.50
50.01-75.00	8.75	10.75	17.50
Over 75.00	9.75	11.75	19.50
Additional Address Add $3.25			

$ _____ Total Merchandise

$ _____ Sales Tax 7%
(Florida residents only)

$ _____ Shipping & Handling

$ _____ Total Enclosed

Name _____

Address _____

City _____ State _____ Zip _____

Daytime telephone (_____) _____